A HISTORY OF THE HORSE DRAWN CARRIAGE

A Collection of Historical Articles on Varieties of Coach and Their Evolution

BY

VARIOUS AUTHORS

British Library Cataloguing-in-Publication Data
A catalogue record for this book is available from
the British Library

Horses – Sports and Utility

The horse (*Equus ferus caballus*) is one of two extant subspecies of *Equus ferus*. It is an odd-toed ungulate mammal belonging to the taxonomic family 'Equidae'. The horse has evolved over the past 45 to 55 million years from a small multi-toed creature into the large, single-toed animal of today. Humans began to domesticate horses around 4000 BC, and their domestication is believed to have been widespread by 3000 BC. We, as humans have interacted with horses in a multitude of ways throughout history – from sport competitions and non-competitive recreational pursuits, to working activities such as police work, agriculture, entertainment and therapy. Horses have also been used in warfare, from which a wide variety of riding and driving techniques developed, using many different styles of equipment and methods of control. With this range of uses in mind, there is an equally extensive, specialized vocabulary used to describe equine-related concepts, covering everything from anatomy to life stages, size, colours, markings, breeds, locomotion, and behaviour.

Sporting events are some of the largest and best-known activities involving horses, and here – communication between human and horse is paramount. To aid this process, horses are usually ridden with a saddle on their backs to assist the rider with balance and positioning, and a bridle or related headgear to assist the rider in maintaining control. Historically, equestrians honed their craft through games and races; providing skills needed for battle, as well as entertainment for home crowds. Today, these competitions have evolved into racing, dressage, eventing and show jumping – many of which have their origins in military training, focused on control and balance of both the horse and rider. Other sports, such as rodeo, developed from practical skills such as those needed on working ranches and stations. Horse racing of all types evolved from impromptu competitions between riders or drivers, and has since become a multi-million pound industry. It is watched in almost every nation of the world, in its three main forms: 'flat racing' (long, even stretches), 'steeplechasing' (racing over jumps) and 'harness racing' (where horses trot or pace whilst pulling a driver in a small, light cart). A major part of horse racing's economic importance lies in the gambling associated with it.

All forms of competition, requiring demanding and specialized skills from both horse and rider, resulted in the systematic development of specialized breeds and equipment for each sport. Horse shows, which have their origins in medieval European fairs, are held around the world. They host a huge range of classes, covering all of the mounted and harness disciplines, as well as 'In-hand' classes where the horses are led, rather than ridden, to be evaluated on their conformation. The method of judging varies with the discipline, but winning usually depends on style and ability of both horse and rider. Sports such as polo do not judge the horse itself, but rather use the horse as a partner for human competitors as a necessary part of the game. Although the horse requires specialized training to participate, the details of its performance are not judged, only the result of the rider's actions—be it getting a ball through a goal or some other task. A similar, historical example of sports partnerships between human and horse is 'jousting', in which the main goal is for one rider to unseat the other. This pastime is still practiced by some sportsmen today.

There are certain jobs that horses do very well, and no technology has yet developed to fully replace them. For example, mounted police horses are still effective for certain types of patrol duties and crowd control. Cattle ranches still require riders on horseback to round up cattle that are scattered across remote, rugged terrain. In more urban areas, horses used to be the main form of transport, in the form of pulling carriages, and are still extensively used (especially in the UK) for ceremonial functions, i.e. horse-drawn carriages transporting dignitaries, military personnel or even the royal family. Horses can also be used in areas where it is necessary to avoid vehicular disruption to delicate soil, such as nature reserves. They may also be the only form of transport allowed in wilderness areas, often because of the fact that horses are quieter than motorised vehicles, therefore impacting less on their surroundings. Although machinery has replaced horses in many parts of the world, an estimated 100 million horses, donkeys and mules are still used for agriculture and transportation in less developed areas. This number includes around 27 million working animals in Africa alone.

As well as these labour intensive uses, horses can also be incredibly valuable for therapy. People of all ages with physical and mental disabilities obtain beneficial results from association with horses. Therapeutic riding is used to mentally and physically stimulate disabled persons and help them improve their lives through improved balance and coordination, increased self-confidence, and a greater feeling of freedom and independence. Horses also provide psychological benefits to people whether they actually ride or not. 'Equine-assisted' or 'equine-facilitated' therapy is a form of experiential psychotherapy that uses horses as companion animals to assist people with mental illness, including anxiety disorders, psychotic disorders, mood disorders, behavioural difficulties, and those who are going through major life changes. There are also experimental programs using horses in prison settings. Exposure to horses appears to improve the behaviour of inmates and help reduce recidivism when they leave.

As a concluding note, one of the most important aspects of equine care is farriery; a specialist in equine hoof care. Horses aid humans in so many ways, it is important to ensure that they are properly equipped and cared for. Farriers have largely replaced blacksmiths (after this specialism mostly became redundant after the industrial revolution), and are highly skilled in both metalwork and horse anatomy. Historically, the jobs of farrier and blacksmith were practically synonymous, shown by the etymology of the word: farrier comes from Middle French *ferrier* (blacksmith), and from the Latin word *ferrum* (iron). Modern day farriers usually specialize in horseshoeing though, focusing their time and effort on the care of the horse's hoof, including trimming and balancing of the hoof, as well as the placing of the shoes. Additional tasks for the farrier include dealing with injured or diseased hooves and application of special shoes for racing, training or 'cosmetic' purposes. In countries such as the United Kingdom, it is illegal for people other than registered farriers to call themselves a farrier or to carry out any farriery work, the primary aim being 'to prevent and avoid suffering by and cruelty to horses arising from the shoeing of horses by unskilled persons.' This is not the case in all countries however, where horse protection is severely lacking.

We hope the reader enjoys this book.

Contents

THE PRIMITIVE VEHICLE

> "This is a traveller, sir, knows men and
> Manners, and has plough'd up sea so far,
> Till both the poles have knock'd; has seen the sun
> Take coach, and can distinguish the colour
> Of his horses, and their kinds."
>
> *Beaumont and Fletcher.*

IT has been suggested that although in a generality of cases nature has forestalled the ingenious mechanician, man for his wheel has had to evolve an apparatus which has no counterpart in his primitive environment—in other words, that there is nothing in nature which corresponds to the *wheel.* Yet even the most superficial inquiry into the nature of the earliest vehicles must do much to refute such a suggestion. Primitive wheels were simply thick logs cut from a tree-trunk, probably for firewood. At some time or another these logs must have rolled of their own accord from a higher to a lower piece of ground, and from man's observation of this simple phenomenon must have come the first idea of a wheel. If a round object could roll of its own accord, it could also be made to roll.

Yet it is to be noticed that the earliest methods of locomotion, other than those purely muscular, such as walking and riding, knew nothing of wheels. Such methods depended primarily upon the enormously significant discovery that a man could drag a heavier weight than he could carry, and what applied to a man also applied to a beast. Possibly such discovery followed on the mere observation of objects being carried down the stream of some river, and perhaps a rudely constructed raft should be considered to be the earliest form of vehicle. From the raft proper to a raft to be used upon land was but a step, and the first land vehicle, whenever or wherever it was made, assuredly took a form which to this day is in common use in some countries. This was the sledge. On a sledge heavy loads could be dragged over the ground, and experience sooner or later must have shown what was the best form of apparatus for such work. As so often happens, moreover, in mechanical contrivances, the earliest sledge of which there is record—a sculptured representation in an Egyptian temple—bears a remarkable resemblance to those in use at the present time.[1] Then, as now, men used two long runners with upturned ends in front and cross-pieces to unite them and bear the load. Such sledges were largely used to convey the huge stones with which the Egyptians raised

1 "In Europe, sledge is the name applied to a low kind of cart, but in America the word has been abbreviated to sled or changed to sleigh, which in either case involves the idea that a *sliding* vehicle is meant. In the rural districts, the farmer employs a machine we call a stone-sledge. This is commonly made from a plank, the flat under surface of which is forced along the surface of the ground by ox-power." *The World on Wheels.* Ezra N. Stratton. New York, 1888.

their solemn masses of masonry and, incidentally, also as a hearse. In time, however, it was found that better results were obtained by the use of another and rather more complicated apparatus which had for its chief component—a wheel. This second discovery that to roll a burden proved an easier task than to drag it was fraught with such tremendous consequences as altered the entire history of the world.

It remained to find a better fulcrum than that afforded by the rough turf over which such logs, when burdened, were rolled. What probably followed is well described by Bridges Adams.[1] "The next process," he thinks, "would naturally be that of cutting a hole through the roller in which to insert the lever. The convenience of several holes in the circumference of the roller would then become apparent, and there would be formed an embryo wheel nave. It could not fail to be remarked also, that the larger the roller, the greater the facility for turning it, and consequently the greater the load that could be borne upon it." Owing to the difficulty of using such large logs, he goes on to suggest, a time would come when it was found that a roller need not bear upon the ground throughout its length, but only at its extremities. So from the single roller would be evolved two rough wheels joined by a beam, square at first though afterwards rounded, upon which could be fixed a frame for the load.

Such axle and wheels would revolve together and keep the required position by means of pieces of wood which may be compared with the thole-pins of a boat.

[1] *English Pleasure Carriages.* By William Bridges Adams. London, 1837.

And it is a remarkable fact that until last century such primitive carts were in use in Portugal and parts of South America. The chief drawback to a vehicle of this kind is its inability to turn in a small space, and the pioneers, whoever they were, finally discovered the principle of the fixed axle-tree, the wheels revolving upon their own centre. So, "instead of fixing the cross-beam or axle in a square hole," these pioneers "would contrive it to play easily in a round one of a conical form, that being the easiest form of adjustment." Such a car as this, with solid wheels and a rude frame, was used by the Romans, and is still to be seen in parts of Chili. The next process in the evolution of the wheel doubtless followed upon the necessity of economising with large sections of wood, and there was finally invented a wheel made of three portions—a central pierced part, the nave, an outside circular piece, the rim or felloe, and two or more cross-pieces, joining the two, the spokes. Of these the felloes would tend to wear soonest, and a double set would be applied to the spokes, as was the case until recently in the ox-carts of the Pampas, or *barcos de tierra*, as they were called by the natives.

And indeed, the first carriages of which we have particular information, the chariots of the Egyptians and their neighbours, differ essentially from such primitive carts only in the delicacy and ornamentation of the carriage body.

Various vehicles are mentioned in the Bible, though one must be chary of differentiating between them merely because the translators have given them different names. Both waggons and chariots are mentioned in

Types of Primitive Carts

Genesis. Jacob's family were sent to him in a waggon. Joseph rode in the second chariot of Pharaoh as a particular mark of favour. At the time of the Exodus, war-chariots formed an important part of the Egyptian army, and indeed, right through the various dynasties, there is an almost continuous mention of their use.[1] "The deft craftsmen of Egypt," says Breasted,[2] "soon mastered the art of chariot-making, and the stables of the Pharaoh contained thousands of the best horses to be had in Asia." About 1500 B.C. Thutmose III went forth to battle in "a glittering chariot of electrum." He slew the enemy's leader, and took captive their princes and "their chariots, wrought with gold, bound to their horses." These barbarians also had "chariots of silver," though this probably means that they were built of wood and strengthened or decorated with silver. At the dissolution of the Empire the Hittites had increased wonderfully in power, and it is told of them that they excelled all other nations in the art of chariotry. The Hittite chariot was larger and more heavily built than that of the Egyptians, as it bore three men, driver, bowman, and shield-bearer, while the Egyptian was satisfied with two. The enormous number of chariots used in warfare is shown by the fact that in the fourteenth century before Christ, when the Egyptians defeated the Syrians at Megiddo, nearly a thousand were captured, and against Ramses II the Hittites put no less than 2500 into the field.

1 "They also possessed baggage-carts shaped like the chariots. One of these appears to have had a very high, six-spoked wheel and a curved roof box. In front of the box is a low seat, from underneath which projects a crooked drag-pole." *Stratton.*

2 *A History of Egypt.* J. H. Breasted. New York. 1909.

"The Egyptian chariots," says H. A. White,[1] "were of light and simple construction, the material employed being wood, as is proved by sculptures representing the manufacture of chariots. The axle was set far back, and the bottom of the car, which rested on this and on the pole, was sometimes formed of a frame interlaced with a network of thongs or ropes. The chariot was entirely open behind and for the greater part of the sides, which were formed by a curved rail rising from each side of the back of the base, and resting on a wooden upright above the pole in front. From this rail, which was strengthened by leather thongs, a bow-case of leather, often richly ornamented, hung on the right-hand side, slanting forwards; while the quiver and spear cases inclined in the opposite direction. The wheels, which were fastened on the axle by a linch-pin secured with a short thong, had six spokes in the case of war chariots, but in private vehicles sometimes only four.[2] The pole sloped upwards, and to the end of it a curved yoke was attached. A small saddle at each end of the yoke rested on the withers of the horses, and was secured in its place by breast-band and girth. No traces are to be seen. The bridle was often ornamented; a bearing-rein was fastened to the saddle, and the other reins passed through a ring at the side of this. The number of horses to a chariot seems always to have been two; and in the car, which contained no seat, only rarely are more than two persons depicted, except in triumphal processions.

"Assyrian chariots did not differ in any essential points

[1] *Dictionary of the Bible.* 1906. Edited by J. Hastings. Art. *Chariot.*

[2] "We account for this difference by supposing that in battle, when success depended in a great measure upon the stability of the chariot, special care was taken to provide a strong wheel, while a weaker one was considered good enough for a more peaceful employment, a four-spoked wheel in those days being much cheaper and lighter." *Stratton.*

Assyrian Chariot

(From Smith's "Concise History of English Carriages")

from the Egyptian.[1] They were, however, completely panelled at the sides, and a shield was sometimes hung at the back. The wheels had six, or, at a later period, eight spokes; the felloes were broad, and seem to have been formed of three distinct circles of wood, sometimes surrounded by a metal tyre. While only two horses were attached to the yokes, in the older monuments a third horse is generally to be seen, which was probably used as a reserve. The later chariots are square in front, not rounded; the car itself is larger and higher; the cases for the weapons are placed in front, not at the side; and only two horses are used. The harness differs somewhat from the Egyptian. A broad collar passes round the neck, from which hangs a breast ornament, the whole being secured by a triple strap under the belly of the horse. As in Egypt there are no traces visible; two driving-reins are attached to each horse, but the bearing-rein seems to be unknown. In addition to the warrior and the charioteer, we often see a third man who bears a shield; and a fourth occupant of the chariot sometimes appears.

"The Hittite chariots, as represented on Egyptian monuments, regularly contain three warriors. In construction they are plainer and more solid than the Egyptian, and the sides are not open. The chariots on Persian sculptures closely resemble the Assyrian."

There is still preserved in the Archæological Museum at Florence an Egyptian chariot, a light, simple, two-wheeled affair with a single shaft and four spokes to the wheels. From the number of spokes it may be supposed that this particular chariot was not used in war. In New York, too, there is preserved the wheel

[1] The Assyrians also possessed curious litters. "Two eunuchs," says Stratton, "are shown carrying a sort of arm-chair on their shoulders, elegant in design, supplied with wheels, to be drawn by hand should the king have occasion to visit mountainous regions inaccessible for chariots."

of an Egyptian chariot found at Dashour. The particulars of this bear out Mr. White's description. The wheel itself is three feet high, with a long axle arm, six spokes, tapering towards the felloe, and a double rim. "The six inner felloes do not meet as in modern wheels," says Thrupp,[1] "but are spliced one over the other, with an overlap of three inches."

Artificial roads seem to have existed at an early period in Palestine, but the country was hardly suitable for vehicles, and one first hears of waggons in the flatter wastes of Egypt and the level plains of Philistia. Agricultural carts these were, though no doubt early used for passenger traffic. Some of these carts were most probably covered, though no coverings seem to have been fixed to the chariots. The Assyrians, however, occasionally took into their private chariots an attendant, who was provided with a covering shaped somewhat like a modern umbrella. This covering was held over the owner's head, and was sometimes provided with a curtain which hung down at the back.

Details of the private carriages in use during these Biblical times filter through the chronicles. In Syria the merchants despatched by Solomon to buy chariots had to pay 600 shekels each for them. Solomon in his quest for luxury seems to have been the first man to build a more elaborate car than satisfied his contemporaries. One to be used on state occasions was built of cedar wood and had "pillars of gold." Probably it was some form of litter. The number of private cars was increasing enormously in all these Eastern cities. The prophet Nahum in lamenting the future woes of Nineveh

[1] *The History of Coaches.* G. A. Thrupp. London, 1877.

speaks of "the noise of the whip, and the noise of the rattling of the wheels, and of the prancing horses, and of the jumping chariots," which will no longer bear witness to the city's prosperity. The absence of wide roads, however, militated against great changes of form in the carriages, which maintained their simple shape until many centuries later.

The war-chariot (*ἅρμα* or *δίφρος*) of the early Greeks was curved in front, and loftier than that of the Egyptians. The entrance was at the back. It was never covered, but frequently bore a curious basket-like arrangement, the *πείρινς*, upon or in which two people could sit. The *ἄντυξ*, or rim, in most cases ran round the three sides of the body, but occasionally there was only a curved barrier in front. The body itself was often strengthened by a trellis-work of strips of light wood or metal. The barrier was of varying height; in some chariots it did not reach above the driver's knee; in others it came up to his waist, but in war-chariots never higher than that. The axle was of oak, ash, elm, or even of iron, and precious metals, according to the legend, were used for the chariots of the gods. So of Juno's car we read:—

> "The whirling wheels are to the chariot hung.
> On the bright axle turns the bidden wheel
> Of sounding brass: the polish'd axle steel.
> Eight brazen spokes in radiant order flame;
> The circles gold, of uncorrupted frame,
> Such as the heavens produce; and round the gold
> Two brazen rings of work divine were roll'd.
> The bossy naves of solid silver shone;
> Braces of gold suspend the moving throne."

The last line suggests an innovation which was certainly not followed for some considerable time.

The chariot in general was about seven feet long, and could be lifted by a strong man like Diomed. Indeed, it could be driven over the bodies of dead warriors. The pole sloped sharply upwards, and sometimes ended in the head of a bird or animal. It emerged either from the floor of the car or from the axle. Towards its end the yoke for the horses was fastened about a pin fixed into it. Though the Lydians used chariots with two or even three poles, the Greeks never had more than one; and as with the Egyptians, there were no traces. If the pole broke, the horses must have dashed away with part of it, leaving the chariot at a standstill. Occasionally, too, a third horse was used, upon which sat a postilion.

At a later period several Grecian carriages were in common use, though not in warfare. Representations of such cars are to be found on the Elgin Marbles. And, as was the case a dozen or more centuries afterwards, the carriage became the outward sign of luxury. It invariably appeared in the state processions, and was made the receptacle for the most gorgeous ornamentation. Gold, ebony, copper, ivory, and white lead were all used for this purpose, while the interiors of the cars were made comfortable with soft cushions and fine tapestries. They appeared, too, in great numbers at the famous chariot races, at which four or more horses were driven abreast. Often the same man was rich enough to possess more than one carriage. So we read of Xerxes changing from his ἅρμα to his ἁρμάμαξα, or state-carriage, at the end of a march. Besides these, there were also the ἀπήνη, a kind of family sociable, the ἅμαξα, a waggon, the κάναθρον, and the φορεῖον, or litter.

The *ἁρμάμαξα* was a large four-wheeled waggon, enclosed by curtains and provided with a *καμάρα* or roof. Four or more horses were required to draw it. It was so large that a person could lie in it at full length, and, indeed, on many occasions it acted the part of a hearse. By far the most extraordinary hearse ever built was a *ἁρμάμαξα* used to convey the body of Alexander the Great—himself the possessor of numerous carriages—from Babylon to Alexandria.

"It was prepared," says Thrupp, "during two years, and was designed by the celebrated architect and engineer Hieronymus. It was 18 feet long and 12 feet wide, on four massive wheels, and drawn by sixty-four mules, eight abreast. The car was composed of a platform with a lofty roof supported by eighteen columns, and was profusely adorned with drapery and gold and jewels; round the edge of the roof was a row of golden bells; in the centre was a throne, and before it the coffin; around were placed the weapons of war and the arms that Alexander had used."

The *ἁρμάμαξα* was also largely used by the ladies of Greece, who when they drove forth were careful to see that the curtains completely enclosed them. The *ἅμαξα*, also a four-wheeled waggon, was probably similar to the *ἁρμάμαξα*, though built upon a less imposing scale. The *ἀπήνη* was a still lighter carriage. It is described by Herodotus, and seems to have been a covered vehicle surrounded by silken curtains which could be pulled back when required. Its interior was generally furnished with cushions of goat leather. Two wheels were more frequent, but four were sometimes found. It was said that Timoleon, an old blind man, drove upon one occasion into the senate house and delivered a speech from his ἀπήνη. In some cases a two-wheeled carriage of this kind was not furnished with curtains, but enclosed in an oval-shaped covering of basket-work. Hesiod objected to such a conveyance because of its inability to keep out the dust. Little is known of the κανάθρον, but it was a Laconian car made of wood, with an arched, plaited covering, used chiefly by women. Doubtless it was little different from the ἀπήνη.

Coming to the Romans, we find a far greater variety of vehicles, though the descriptions that have come down are meagre and not particularly distinctive. That the Romans early realised the enormous importance, both military and otherwise, of carriages, is shown by their amazing roads. Such roads had never before been constructed. They were, says Gibbon, "accurately divided by milestones, and ran in a direct line from one city to another, with very little respect for the obstacles, either of nature or private property. Mountains were perforated, and bold arches thrown over the broadest and most rapid streams. The middle part of the road was raised into a terrace, which commanded the adjacent country, consisted of several layers of sand, gravel, and cement, and was paved with large stones, or, in some places near the capital, with granite." Probably the most famous of these roads was the Appian Way, connecting Rome with Capua. It was wide enough, according to Procopius, who marched along it in the sixth century, for two chariots to pass one another without inconvenience or delay, a matter certainly not possible, for instance, in most of the Eastern cities at that time. And so, with the finest engineers the world had seen linking up various cities, cross-country travelling in a carriage, from being well-nigh impossible, became comparatively easy. Gibbon mentions in this connection the surprising feat of one Cæsarius, who journeyed from Antioch to Constantinople, a distance of 665 miles, in six days.

The Roman war-chariot, or *currus*, was practically the same as the Greek ἅρμα, though certain modifications were introduced. More than two horses were driven, and from their number came several words, such as *sejugis*, *octojugis*, and *decemjugis*, which sufficiently explain themselves. It appears, moreover, that the *currus* was occasionally driven by four horses without either pole or yoke, and it has been suggested that in such a case the driver probably stopped the car by bearing all his weight on to the back of the body, so that its floor would touch the ground, thus forming a primitive brake. Besides the *currus*, and even before their marvellous roads had been laid down, the Romans possessed other cars. The earliest of these seems to have been a long, covered, four-wheeled waggon, called *arcera*, which was mainly used to carry infirm or very old people. In this the driver sat on a seat in front of the body, and drove two horses abreast. Though the most ancient of the Roman carriages, the *arcera*, as seen on monuments, has a very modern appearance. In more luxurious times the *lectica*, a large litter, seems to have led to its gradual extinction.

The *essedum*, at one time very popular in Italy, was brought in the first place to Rome by Julius Cæsar. It was the war-chariot of the Britons, and was entirely unlike the Roman or Egyptian cars. The wheels were much larger, the entrance was in front and not at the back, there was a seat, and the pole, instead of running up to the horses' necks, remained horizontal, and was so wide that the driver could step along it. The British charioteers could drive their cars at a very great rate, and were exceedingly agile on the flat pole, from the extremity of which they threw their missiles. The cars were purposely made as noisy as possible to strike dismay into the enemy's lines. At times the wheels were furnished with scythes, which projected from the axle-tree ends, and helped to maim those unfortunate enough to be run down.[1] Cicero, hearing good opinions of it, besought a friend to bring him a good pattern from Britain, and took occasion to add that the chariot was the only pleasing thing which that benighted country produced. The *essedum* speedily became popular in Rome, though not as an engine of war. Decorated and constructed of fine materials, it was the fashionable pleasure carriage. Curiously enough, however, the seat which had been so conspicuous a feature of the chariot in its native place was not used in Rome. The owner drove the *essedum* himself, and yoked two horses to the pole. There was some opposition to its use on the grounds of undue luxury, and a tribune who rode abroad in one was on that account considered effeminate. Seneca put the *esseda deaurata* amongst things *quæ matronarum usibus necessaria sint.* Emperors and generals used them as travelling carriages, and they were to be hired at regular posting-stations. A somewhat similar carriage, the *covinus*, was also in use in various countries at this date. This was covered in except in front; like

Cisium
The Primitive Gig
(From a Roman Inscription)

Agrippina's Carpentum
(From a Roman Coin)

the *essedum*, it had no seat for the driver, and in times of war it seems to have had scythes attached to the axle in the British fashion. Little, however, is known of it, and it may be dismissed here with a mere mention of its existence.

The *essedum* is of particular importance insomuch as it may be considered to be the prototype of all the vehicles of the curricle or gig type. The first of these in use amongst the Romans was the *cisium*, whose form is well shown on a monumental column near Treves. It was surprisingly like the ordinary gig of modern times. The body at first was fixed to the frames, but afterwards seems to have been suspended by rough traces or straps. The entrance was in front, there was a seat for two, and underneath this a large box or case. Mules were generally used to draw it, one, a pair, or, according to Ausonius, three—in which case a postilion sat on the third horse. They were built primarily for speed, and were in common use throughout Italy and Gaul, though the ladies, unwilling to be seen in an uncovered carriage, drove in other conveyances. The *cisium* on the whole must have been comfortable and light. Seneca admits that you could write a letter easily while driving in one. And in due course the new carriage became so popular that it could be hired, and the *cisiarii*, or hackney coachmen, could be penalised for careless driving. Indeed, so very modern were the Roman ideas upon the question of travel, that there were certain places at which the *cisium* was always to be found—a kind of primitive cab-rank.

Coming to the larger waggons and carriages, there were the *sarracum*, the *plaustrum*, the *carpentum*, the *pilen-*

tum, the *benna*, the *reda*, the *carruca*, the *pegma*—a huge wheeled apparatus used for raising great weights, particularly in theatrical displays—and a mule-drawn litter, the *basterna*. Of these the *sarracum* was a common cart used by the country folk for conveying produce. It had either two or four wheels, and was occasionally used by passengers, though, as Cicero observed, as a conveyance the *sarracum* was very vulgar. It was not confined to Italy, but was common enough amongst those barbaric tribes against whom Rome was so often victorious. It was in *sarraca*, moreover, that the bodies were removed from Rome in times of plague. Rather lighter than this carriage, though heavy enough to our modern ideas, was the *plaustrum*,[1] an ancient two or four-wheeled waggon of rude construction. This was, in its primitive form, just a bare platform with a large pole projecting from the axle ; there were no supporting ribs at all, and the load was simply placed on the platform. Upright boards, or openwork rails, however, were used to make sides, and at a later period a large basket was fastened on to the platform by stout thongs. The wheels of the *plaustrum* were ordinarily solid, of a kind called *tympana*,

[1] Stratton treats of these Roman carriages and carts in considerable detail, and mentions in addition to the *plostellum*, or small *plaustrum*, the *carrus*, *monarchus*, and *birotum*. Of these the *carrus*, or cart, differed from the *plaustrum* in the following particulars : "The box or form could not be removed, as in the former case, but was fastened upon the axle-tree ; it lacked the broad flooring of planks or boards, which served as a receptacle for certain commodities when the sides were removed ; the wheels were higher [and] . . . spoked, not solid like the *tympana*." The *carrus clabularius*, or stave-waggon, could be lengthened or shortened as required. The *monarchus* was a very light two-wheeled vehicle something like the *cisium*. The *birotum* was also a small two-wheeled vehicle, with a leather-covered seat, used in the time of Constantine, an "early post-chaise," as Stratton puts it.

Pilentum
The State Carriage of the Romans

Benna

or drums, and were nearly a foot thick. Such a cart was but a slow vehicle, and could turn only with great difficulty. It was drawn by oxen or mules, and like the *sarracum* was also used to carry passengers.[1]

The *carpentum*, though two-wheeled, bore resemblance to the Greek *ἁρμάμαξα*. It had an arched covering. It was in use during very early times at Rome, though only distinguished citizens were privileged to ride in it. The *currus arcuatus*, given by Numa to the Flamines, was no doubt a form of *carpentum*, which was also the travelling carriage of the elder Tarquin. It seems to have been evolved from the *plaustrum*, being originally little more than a covered cart; but in the days of the Empire it became most luxurious, and was not only furnished with curtains of the richest silk, but seems to have had solid panellings and sculptures attached to the body. Agrippina's *carpentum*, for instance, had fine paintings on its panels, and its roof was supported by figures at the four corners. Like the *ἁρμάμαξα*, it was also used as a hearse. Two mules were required to

[1] The carts of north Italy in the eighteenth century had remained practically unchanged. Edward Wright, who visited Italy in 1719, thus describes them: "The carriages in Lombardy, and indeed throughout all Italy, are for the most part drawn with oxen; which are of a whitish colour: they have very low wheels. Some I saw without spokes, solid like mill-stones; such as I have seen describ'd in some antique basso-relievos and Mosaicks. The pole they draw by is sloped upwards towards the end; which is rais'd considerably above their heads; from whence a chain, or rope, is let down and fasten'd to their horns; which keeps up their heads, and serves to back the carriage. In some parts they use no yokes, but draw all by the horn, by a sort of a brace brought about the roots of them: the backs of the oxen are generally cover'd with a cloth. In the kingdom of Naples, and some other parts, they use buffaloes in their carriages, &c. These do somewhat resemble oxen: but are most sour, ill-looking animals, and very vicious; for the better management of them they generally put rings in their noses."

draw it. The *pilentum* was a carriage of a more official character. It may be called the state coach of the Romans—a four-wheeled becushioned car with a roof supported by pillars, but, unlike the *carpentum*, open at the sides. It was always considered to be the most comfortable of the Roman carriages, and may indeed have been hung upon "swing-poles" between the wheels. The social difference between the *pilentum* and the *carpentum* may be deduced from one of the many carriage laws passed by the Senate. The Roman matrons were allowed to drive in the *carpentum* on all occasions, but might use the *pilentum* only at the games or public festivals. Such "sumptuary laws" were constantly being passed, and a special vote was even required to enable the mother of Nero to drive in her carriage in the city itself. It was not until the fourth century A.D. that all such restrictions were banished.

Pliny mentions another carriage of imperial Rome—the *carruca*, which had four wheels and was used equally in the city and for long journeys. Nero travelled with great numbers of them—on one occasion with no less than three thousand. In Rome itself the fashionable citizen drove forth in a *carruca* that was covered with plates of bronze, silver, or even gold. Enormous sums were spent upon their decoration. Painters, sculptors, and embroiderers were employed. Martial speaks of an *aurea carruca* costing as much as a large farm. The *carruca*, indeed, may be said to correspond with the phaeton, which was so fashionable in England towards the end of the eighteenth century. As with the phaeton, so with the *carruca*—the higher it was built the better pleased was its owner. Various kinds of *carruca* existed.

The *carrucæ argentatæ* were those granted by Alexander Severus to the senators. There is also mention of a *carruca domestoria*. Unfortunately, however, no contemporary representation of a carriage can definitely be said to be a *carruca*. Little enough, moreover, is known of the two other waggons, the *reda* and the *benna*. The *reda* was a large four-wheeled waggon used mainly to convey agricultural produce. It seems to have been brought into Italy from Wallachia. The *benna* was a cart whose body was formed entirely of basket-work. There is a drawing of it on the column of Antoninus at Rome. A similar vehicle persists to this day in Italy, South Germany, and Belgium, and bears a similar name.

Under the Empire, then, carriage-building flourished, particularly after Alexander Severus had put an end to all the older restrictions. Various forms of carriages were to be seen on the roads, and there was, as I have hinted, even an attempt at a spring. One of the carriages of this period is definitely described as "borne on long poles, fixed to the axles." "Now a certain amount of spring," says Thrupp, "can be obtained from the centre of a long, light pole. The Neapolitan Calesse, the Norwegian Carriole, and the Yarmouth Cart were all made with a view to obtaining ease by suspension on poles between bearings placed far apart. In these the seat is placed midway between the two wheels and the horse, on very long shafts, which are there made into wooden springs." And in the old Roman carriages, he goes on to say, "the weight was carried between the front and hind axles, on long poles or wooden springs. The under-carriage of the later four-wheeled vehicles used by the Romans was, in all probability, the same as is in use at the present day, both in this country and on the Continent, and indeed in America, for the under-carriages of agricultural waggons." Even with such splendid roads as the Romans possessed, however, the streets of their towns do not seem to have been very wide, and this must be one of the reasons for the early appearance of another kind of conveyance, the litter, which, during the dark ages, was practically the only carriage to be used.

These litters came from the East. The Babylonians in particular preferred to be carried about in a chair or couch rather than to be jolted in a carriage. Ericthonius, a lame man, is supposed to have introduced them into Athens, where they were known as *φορεῖα* or *σκιμπόδια*. Speedily they became popular, especially with the women. Magnificently decorated, the *φορεῖον* was constantly carried along the narrow streets, and on being brought over to Rome proved no less agreeable to the Romans. The *lectica*, or, as it was called at a later period, the *sella*, may in the first instance have been used to carry the sick, but in a short time became a common form of conveyance. This palanquin had an arched roof of leather stretched over four posts. The sides were covered by curtains, though at a later period it would seem that crude windows of talc were used. The interior was furnished with pillows, and when standing the litter rested upon four feet. Two slaves bore it by means of long poles loosely attached. In Martial's time these *lecticarii* wore red liveries, and were sometimes preceded by a third slave to make way. Julius Cæsar restricted their numbers, and in the reign of Claudius permission to use them was granted only as a particular mark of the royal favour. Several varieties of litter appeared. The *sella portatoria* or *gestatoria* was a small sedan chair. Some, however, were constructed to hold two. The *cathedra*, which was probably identical with the *sella muliebris* mentioned by Suetonius, was mostly used by women. The *basterna* was a much larger litter, also used by women under the Empire, which was carried by two mules. In this carriage the sides might be opened or closed, and the whole body was frequently gilded.

A few other primitive carriages here call for mention. The Dacians, who inhabited parts of what is now Hungary, used square vehicles with four wheels, in which the six spokes widened towards the rims. The Scythians used a peculiar two-wheeled cart consisting of a platform on which was placed a conical covering, resembling in shape a beehive, and made of a basket-work of hazelwood, over which were stretched the skins of beasts or a thatching of reeds. When camping out these people would lift this covering bodily from the cart and use it as a tent. Much the same custom was followed by the wandering Tartars. "Their huts or tents," says Marco Polo, "are formed of rods covered with felt, and being exactly round and nicely put together, they can gather them into one bundle, and make them up as packages, which they carry along with them in their migrations, upon a sort of car with four wheels." "Besides these cars," he continues, "they have a superior kind of vehicle upon two wheels, covered likewise with black felt, and so effectually as to protect those within it from wet during a whole day of rain. These are drawn by oxen and camels, and serve to convey their wives and children, their utensils, and such provisions as they require." The same traveller described the carriages of Southern China. Speaking of Kin-sai, then the capital, he says, "The main street of the city . . . is paved with stone and brick to the width of ten paces on each side, the intermediate part being filled up with small gravel, and provided with arched drains for carrying off the rain-water that falls into the neighbouring canals, so that it remains always dry. On this gravel it is that the carriages are continually passing and re-passing. They are of a long shape, covered at top, having curtains and cushions of silk, and are capable of holding six persons. Both men and women who feel disposed to take their pleasure are in the daily practice of hiring them for that purpose, and accordingly at every hour you may see vast numbers of them driven along the middle part of the street." To this day such carriages as are here described can be had for hire in China, though in general they are of a smaller size. In some respects they resembled what is called in this country a tilted cart.

The Persians used large chariots in which was built a kind of turret from whose interior the warriors could at once throw their spears and obtain protection. One, taken from an ancient coin, is thus described by Sir Robert Ker Porter in his *Travels in Georgia, Persia, and Ancient Babylon* (1821) :—

" . . . a large chariot, which is drawn by a magnificent pair of horses; one of the men, in ampler garments than his compeers, and bareheaded, holds the bridle of the horses . . . [which] are without trappings, but the details of their bits and the manner of reining them are executed with the utmost care. The pole of the car is seen passing behind the horses, projecting from the centre of the carriage, which is in a cylindrical shape, elevated rather above the line of the animals' heads. The wheel of the car is extremely light and tastefully put together."

Here, too, it is to be noticed that the driver is shown with his arms over the backs of the animals. In another chariot, which most probably was Persian, the body seems to be made of a "light wood, as of interlaced canes. Similar chariots are seen in the Assyrian bas-reliefs and others, somewhat resembling this, on Etruscan and Grecian painted vases. A chariot thus constituted must have been of extreme rapidity and of scarcely any weight."[1]

The Persians also had an idol-car, which was a kind of moving platform, and their chariots were at one period armed with scythes. These scythes, generally considered to be the invention of Cyrus, do not seem to have hung from the axle-ends, as was the case in Britain, but from the body itself, "in order," thinks Ginzrot, who wrote on these early carriages, "to allow the wheels to turn unobstructed. In this way," he says, "the scythes had a firm hold, and could inflict more damage than if they had been applied to the wheels or felloes and revolved with them. Nearly all writers treating on this subject are of this opinion, and Curtius says: *Alias deinde falces summis rotarum orbibus hærebant* [thence curving downwards]. The scythes could

[1] *The World on Wheels.*

easily have been attached to the body . . . and, notwithstanding, it might be said they extended over the felloe, for Curtius said, not that the scythes revolved with the wheels, but *hærebant*."[1]

Early Indian carriages were probably not very different from some of those now in use amongst the natives. The common *gharry* is certainly built after a primitive model. In this there are two wheels, "a high axletree bed, and a long platform, frequently made of two bamboos, which join in front and form the pole, to which two oxen are yoked." In Arabia there was the *araba*, a primitive latticed carriage for women, which possessed "wing-guards"—pieces of wood shaped to the top of the wheels and projecting over them—a feature also to be found in the early Persian cars.

Taking these early carriages as a whole one may be inclined to feel surprise at the varieties displayed, yet there were not after all very great differences between them. They were two- or four-wheeled contrivances with a long pole in front, and it is only in mere size and decoration that discrimination can properly be made. "The Egyptians," says Thrupp, "with all their learning and skill, appear to have made no change during the centuries of experience; as at the beginning, so at the end, the kings stand by the side of their charioteers, or

[1] On the other hand, the scythes used by other nations may well have been on the wheels. Livy describes those used by Antiochus (*currus falcatus*): "Round the pole were sharp-pointed spears which extended from the yoke of the two outside horses about fifteen feet; with these they pierced everything in their way. On the end of the yoke were two scythes, one being placed horizontally, the other towards the ground. The first cut everything from the sides, the others catching those prostrate on the ground or trying to crawl under. The long spears (*cuspides*) were not on the yoke, as some say."

hold the reins themselves. The Persians and Hindoos introduced luxurious improvements, and in lofty vehicles elevated the nobles above the heads of the people, and secluded their women in curtained carriages. The Greeks introduced no new vehicles, but perfected so successfully the useful waggon, that their model is still seen throughout Europe, without change of principle or structure. The Romans, on the other hand, in their career of conquest, gathered from every nation what was good, and, wherever possible, improved upon it." After the fall of the Roman Empire, however, there was little further progress for several centuries. In the general retrogression, which, rightly or wrongly, one associates with those dark ages, the wheeled carriage, in common with a multitude of other adjuncts to civilisation, was to suffer.

THE AGE OF LITTERS

"There is a litter; lay him in 't and
drive toward Dover, friend!"
King Lear.

AS roadmakers, the Romans, if they can be said to have had successors at all, were succeeded by the monks. On the assumption that travellers were unfortunate people, as indeed they were, needing help, religious Orders were founded whose chief work was that of building bridges and repairing the roads. Other Orders likewise performed such tasks, though possibly for more selfish reasons, being as they were large owners of cattle, and immersed as much in agricultural as in theological occupations. So in many parts of Europe the *Pontife* Brothers, or bridge-makers, were to be found. There were also Gilds formed to repair the roads, such as the Gild of the Holy Cross in Birmingham, founded in the reign of Richard II, which "mainteigned . . . and kept in good reparaciouns the greate stone bridges, and divers foule and dangerous high wayes, the charge whereof the towne of hitsellfe ys not hable to mainteigne." In *Piers the Plowman*, too, the rich merchants are exhorted to repair the "wikked wayes" and see that the "brygges to-broke by the heye weyes" may be mended "in som manere wise." The maintenance of the roads in England, says M. Jusserand,[1] "greatly depended upon arbitrary chance, upon opportunity, or on the goodwill or the devotion of those to whom the adjoining land belonged. In the case of the roads, as of bridges, we find petitions of private persons who pray that a tax be levied upon those who pass along, towards the repair of the road." So in 1289, Walter Godelak of Walingford is praying for "the establishment of a custom to be collected from every cart of merchandize traversing the road between Jowemarsh and Newenham, on account of the depth, and for the repair, of the said way." Unfortunately for him—and doubtless he was no exception to the rule—the reply came: "The King will do nothing therein."

Indeed the roads were in a truly abominable condition. As often as not, deep ruts marred what surface there had ever been, and here and there brooks and pools rendered easy passage an impossibility. There is a patent of Edward III (Nov. 20, 1353) which ordered "the paving of the high road, *alta via*, running from Temple Bar"—then the western limit of London—"to Westminster." "This road," says M. Jusserand, "had been paved, but the King explains that it is 'so full of holes and bogs . . . and that the pavement is so damaged and broken' that the traffic has become very dangerous for men and carriages. In consequence, he orders each proprietor on both sides of the road to remake, at his own expense, a footway of seven feet up to the ditch, *usque canellum*," and see to it that the middle of the road is well paved. In France matters

[1] *English Wayfaring Life in the Middle Ages.* J. J. Jusserand. London, 1888.

were just as bad. "Outside the town of Paris," runs one fourteenth-century ordinance, "in several parts of the suburbs . . . there are many notable and ancient high-roads, bridges, lanes, and roads, which are much injured, damaged or decayed and otherwise hindered by ravines of water and great stones, by hedges, brambles, and many other trees which have grown there, and by many other hindrances which have happened there, because they have not been maintained and provided for in time past; and they are in such a bad state that they cannot be securely traversed on foot or horseback, nor by vehicles, without great perils and inconveniences; and some of them are abandoned at all parts because men cannot resort there." Wherefore it was proposed that the inhabitants should be compelled, by force if necessary, to attend to the matter.

While, however, the wretched state into which the roads were being allowed to fall had a great deal to do with the almost total, though indeed temporary, extinction of the wheeled pleasure carriage in western Europe, there is another fact which must be taken into consideration in any endeavour to account for it. As will appear in a little, the renaissance of carriage-building in the sixteenth century was for a time retarded in various places by a widespread feeling of distrust against anything that could be thought to lead to an accusation of effeminacy. Laws were passed—as was the case, for instance, in 1294, under Philip the Fair of France—forbidding people to ride in coaches, and sharp comparisons were drawn by the satirists between the hardy horsemen of old and the modern comfort-loving individuals who lolled, or were supposed to loll—though how they could have done so in those springless monstrosities is past comprehension—in their gaudily decorated carriages. I would not insist upon the point, but it may be that in the reaction against such undue luxuries as had helped to bring ruin to the Roman Empire, carriages for that reason became unpopular. From which, of course, it would follow that the disappearance of the carriage led, in part at any rate, to the neglect of the roads, and such new roads as were made would be laid down primarily for the convenience only of the horsemen. The same thing applied also to the litters, though their popularity naturally followed merely upon the state of the roads.

Before attempting to deal with these litters, it will be well to see what is known—it is not very much—of such wheeled carriages as there were at this time, and at the outset it is necessary to bear in mind that the old chroniclers used the word *carriage* in anything but its modern significance. To them a carriage was no more than an agricultural or baggage cart. Time and again you have accounts of this or that great man making his way, peaceably or otherwise, through some country, accompanied by numbers of carriages. These were simply his luggage carts, and although, as in earlier times, the cart, gaily ornamented, could very easily be converted into a pleasure carriage, it is important to remember the real meaning of the word. Such carts, in point of fact, were extremely common. In England they were generally square boxes made of planks borne on two wheels. Others, of a lighter pattern, were built of "slatts latticed with a willow trellis." Their chief peculiarity was to be found in their wheels, which were furnished with extraordinarily large nails with prominent heads. Contemporary manuscripts give rough pictures of such carts. One of these is shown drawn by three dogs. One man squats inside, a second helps to push it from behind. A most interesting illustration in the Louterell Psalter—a fourteenth-century manuscript—shows a reaper's cart going uphill. Here the two huge, six-spoked wheels with their projecting nails are clearly shown. The platform of the cart is strengthened by upright stakes with a cross-rail connecting them at the sides. The driver, standing over the wheels on the poles, is holding a long whip which is flicking the leader of three horses. Three other men are helping at the rear, and the stacks of wheat are held in position by ropes.

The earliest Anglo-Saxon carriage of which there is record belongs to the twelfth century. Strutt refers to a drawing in one of the Cottonian manuscripts, which represents a peculiar four-wheeled contrivance with two upright poles rising from the axle-trees, from which poles is slung a hammock. Such a chariot or *chaer* was apparently used by the more distinguished Anglo-Saxons when setting out upon long journeys. The drawing shows the figure of Joseph on his way to meet Jacob in Egypt, but is no doubt a correct representation of a travelling carriage in the artist's lifetime. This hammock is interesting as being a primitive form of suspension, which may or may not have led to the later experiments in that direction.

A most luxurious English carriage of the fourteenth century is shown in the Louterell Psalter. This was obviously evolved from a four-wheeled waggon. Five

Fourteenth Century English Carriage
(From the Louterell Psalter)

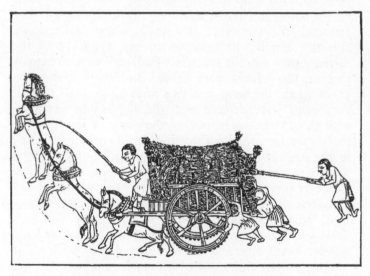

Fourteenth Century Reaper's Cart
(From the Louterell Psalter)

horses, harnessed at length, drew it, a postilion with a short whip riding on the second, and another with a long whip on the wheeler. The tunnel-like body was highly ornamented, and its front decorated with carved birds and men's heads. The frame of the body was continued in front as two poles, and underneath, hanging by a ring and looking rather ludicrous, is shown a small trunk. Women only appear in this carriage, the men riding behind it.

"Nothing," remarks M. Jusserand, "gives a better idea of the encumbering, awkward luxury which formed the splendour of civil life during this century than the structure of these heavy machines. The best had four wheels; three or four horses drew them, harnessed in a row, the postilion being mounted on one, armed with a short-handled whip of many thongs; solid beams rested on the axles, and above this framework rose an archway rounded like a tunnel; as a whole, ungraceful enough. But the details," he goes on to say, speaking of the carriage shown in the Louterell Psalter, "were extremely elegant, the wheels were carved and their spokes expanded near the hoop into ribs forming pointed arches; the beams were painted and gilt, the inside was hung with those dazzling tapestries, the glory of the age; the seats were furnished with embroidered cushions; a lady might stretch out there, half sitting, half lying; pillows were disposed in the corners as if to invite sleep, square windows pierced the sides and were hung with curtains. Thus travelled," he continues with a touch of picturesqueness, "the noble lady, slim in form, tightly clad in a dress which outlined every curve of the body, her long, slender hands caressing the favourite dog or bird. The knight, equally tightened in his *cote-hardie*, regarded her with a complacent eye, and, if he knew good manners, opened his heart to his dreamy companion in long phrases like those in the romances. The broad forehead of the lady, who has perhaps coquettishly plucked off her eyebrows and stray hairs, a process about which satirists were indignant, brightens up at moments, and her smile is like a ray of sunshine. Meanwhile the axles groan, the horse-shoes—also heavily nailed—crunch the ground, the machine advances by fits and starts, descends into the hollows, bounds altogether at the ditches, and falls violently back with a dull noise."

Other gaily decorated carriages, surprisingly like our modern vans, though on two wheels, are shown in *Le Roman du Roy Meliadus*, another fourteenth-century manuscript preserved in the British Museum, but only the richest and most powerful of the nobles could afford to keep them.

"They were bequeathed," says M. Jusserand, "by will from one another, and the gift was valuable. On September 25, 1355, Elizabeth de Burgh, Lady Clare, wrote her last will and endowed her eldest daughter with 'her great carriage with the coverture, carpets, and cushions.' In the twentieth year of Richard II, Roger Rouland received £400 sterling for a carriage destined for Queen Isabella; and John le Charer, in the sixth [year] of Edward III, received £1000 for the carriage of Lady Eleanor—the King's sister."

These were fabulous sums, when it is remembered that an ox cost about thirteen shillings and a sheep but one shilling and five pence.

Now it may be that such a "great carriage" as is shown in the Louterell Psalter was identical with the *whirlicote* in which, according to Stowe, Richard II and his mother took refuge on the occasion of Wat Tyler's rebellion.

"Of old time," says this honest tailor, who himself witnessed the introduction of coaches into England, "coaches were not known in this island, but chariots or whirlicotes, then so called, and they only used of princes or great estates, such as had their footmen about them; and for example to note, I read that Richard II, being threatened by the rebels of Kent, rode from the Tower of London to the Mile's End, and with him his mother, because she was sick and weak, in a whirlicote, the Earl of Buckingham . . . knights and Esquires attending on horseback. But in the next year [1381] the said King Richard took to wife Anne, daughter to the King of Bohemia, that first brought hither the riding upon side saddles; and so was the riding in whirlicotes and chariots forsaken, except at coronations and such like spectacles."

From this it would appear that the *whirlicote* (which may, as Bridges Adams suggests, have been derived from "whirling" or moving "cot" or house) was identical with the *chariot* or *chaer*. Unfortunately the translators of Froissart, who mentions the incident of Richard's ride from the Tower, cannot agree upon the correct word to render the original *charette*. *Charette*, *chariette*, *chare*, *chaer* (Wicliffe), and *char* (Chaucer) all occur in the early chronicles, and there seems no means, if, indeed, there is any need, of differentiating between them. All were probably waggons modified for the conveyance of such passengers as could afford to pay highly for the privilege. One fact, however, suggests that there were at any rate two different kinds of carriages in England at this time, for we read that the body of Richard II was borne to its last resting-place "upon a chariette or sort of litter on wheels, such as is used by citizens' wives who are not able or not allowed to keep

D

ordinary litters." With this in mind, it is difficult to agree with Sir Walter Gilbey when he says[1] that the *chare* was a horse litter, though it is fair to add that he acknowledges an opposite view.

The *charette* is obviously the French form of *caretta*, which was the carriage in which Beatrice, the wife of Charles of Anjou, entered Naples in 1267.[2] This vehicle is described as being covered both inside and without with sky-blue velvet powdered with golden lilies. Pope Gregory X entered Milan in 1273 in a similar carriage. The *caretta* was probably an open car "shaded simply by a canopy." In the next century, the *Anciennes Chroniques de Flandres*, a manuscript belonging to 1347, shows an illustration of Ermengarde, the wife of Salvard, Lord of Rousillon, travelling in a four-wheeled conveyance remarkably like the ordinary country waggon of to-day.

"The lady," says Sir Walter Gilbey, "is seated on the floor-boards of a springless four-wheeled cart or waggon, covered in with a tilt that could be raised or drawn aside; the body of the vehicle is of carved wood and the outer edges of the wheels are painted grey to represent iron tyres. The conveyance is drawn by two horses driven by a postilion who bestrides that on the near [left] side. The traces are apparently of rope, and the outer trace of the postilion's horse is represented as passing under the saddle-girth, a length of leather (?)

[1] *Early Carriages and Roads.* Sir Walter Gilbey, Bart. London, 1903.

[2] This appears to have been similar to the *carroccio*, described by Stratton as a very heavy four-wheeled car, surmounted by a tall staff, painted a bright red. Stratton also mentions the *cochio*, which he describes as a thirteenth-century carriage having a covering of red matting, under which, in the fore-part of the body, the ladies were seated, the gentlemen occupying the rear end. Both these *words*, however, seem to belong to a much later date and may be translations of an earlier original.

being let in for the purpose ; the traces are attached to swingle-bars carried on the end of a cross-piece secured to the base of the pole where it meets the body.

"Carriages of some kind," he continues, "appear also to have been used by men of rank when travelling on the Continent. *The Expeditions to Prussia and the Holy Land of Henry, Earl of Derby, in* 1390 *and* 1392–3 (Camden Society's Publications, 1894) indicate that the Earl, afterwards King Henry IV of England, travelled on wheels at least part of the way through Austria.

"The accounts kept by his Treasurer during the journey contain several entries relative to carriages; thus on November 14, 1392, payment is made for the expenses of two equerries named Hethcote and Mansel, who were left for one night at St. Michael, between Leoban and Kniltefeld, with thirteen carriage horses. On the following day the route lay over such rugged and mountainous country that the carriage wheels were broken despite the liberal use of grease ; and at last the narrowness of the way obliged the Earl to exchange his own carriage for two smaller ones better suited to the paths of the district.

"The Treasurer also records the sale of an old carriage at Friola for three florins. The exchange of the Earl's 'own carriage' is the significant entry : it seems very unlikely that a noble of his rank would have travelled so lightly that a single cart would contain his own luggage and that of his personal retinue ; and it is also unlikely that he used one luggage cart of his own. The record points directly to the conclusion that the carriages were passenger vehicles used by the Earl himself."

It is to be noted that the carriage of the Lady Ermengarde was a Flemish vehicle. Flanders, indeed, seems to have shared with Hungary the honour of playing pioneer in carriage-building throughout the ages, and long after the general adoption of coaches in Europe, Flemish models, and also Flemish mares, were freely imported into the various countries.

Another carriage of this time is described in a pre-Chaucerian poem called *The Squyr of Low Degree*, in which the father of a Hungarian princess is made to say:—

> "Tomorrow ye shall on hunting fare,
> And ride my daughter in a *chare*.
> It shall be covered with velvet red,
> And cloths of fine gold all about your head;
> With damask white, and azure blue,
> Well diapered with lilies new;
> Your pomelles shal be ended with gold,
> Your chains enammelled many a fold."

The pomelles no doubt were "the handles to the rods affixed to the roof, and were for the purpose of holding on by, when deep ruts or obstacles in the road caused an unusual jerk in the vehicle." One notices that lilies were apparently a common form of decoration on these early carriages, but it is to be regretted that the accounts in general are so scanty.

We come to the litters.

Of these the commonest, both in England and on the Continent, seem to have been modifications of the Roman *basterna*. Generally they were covered with a sort of vault with various openings. Two horses, one at either end, carried them. The great majority held only one person. Thrupp describes them in some detail.

"They were," he says, "long and narrow—long enough for a person to recline in—and no wider than could be carried between the poles which were placed on either side of the horses. They were about four to five feet long, and two feet six inches wide, with low sides and higher ends. The entrance was in the middle, on both sides, the doors being formed sometimes by a sliding panel and sometimes simply by a cross-bar. The steps were of leather or iron loops, the latter being hinged to turn up when the litter was placed on the ground. The upper part was formed by a few broad wooden hoops, united along the top by four or five slats, and over the whole a canopy was placed, which opened in the middle, at the sides, and ends, for air and light."

Isolated references to these horse-litters are scattered throughout the old chronicles, but afford meagre information. William of Malmesbury states that the body of William Rufus was placed on a *reda caballaria*, a horse-litter, the name of which suggests its origin. According to Matthew of Westminster, King John, during his illness in 1216, was removed from Swinstead Abbey to Newark in a similar vehicle, the *lectica equestre*. Generally, however, the horse-litter was reserved exclusively for women, men being unwilling to risk an accusation of effeminacy. So, in recording the death of Earl Ferrers in 1254, from injuries received in an accident to his conveyance, the historian is careful to explain that his Lordship suffered from the gout, which was why he happened to be in a litter at all.

As time passed, the litter rather than the wheeled carriage became the state vehicle. Froissart, writing of the second wife of Richard II, describes "la june Royne d'Angleterre" as travelling "en une litere moult riche qui etoit ordonée pour elle." Margaret, the daughter of Henry VII, journeyed to Scotland, it is true, on the back of a "faire palfrey," but she was followed by "one vary riche litere, borne by two faire coursers vary nobly drest; in wich litere the sayd queene was borne in the intryng of the good townes, or otherwise to her good playsher." But on the Continent new improvements were being made in wheeled carriages, and when in 1432 Henry VI wrote to the Archbishop of Canterbury and other high dignitaries of the Church, with regard to the widow of Henry of Navarre, he ordered them to place two *chares* at her disposal, rather than the litter to which one might have thought she would be entitled. Sir Walter Gilbey translates the word to mean a horse-litter, but Markland, in his paper on the *Early Use of Carriages in England* (*Archæologia*, Vol. XX), differentiates between the two, ascribing a more ceremonial use to the litter, and this seems to me to be nearer the truth. Both vehicles, for instance, are mentioned by Holinshed in his description of the coronation ceremony of Catherine of Aragon in 1509. The Queen herself rode in a litter of "white clothe of golde, not covered nor bailed, which was led by two palfreys clad in white damask doone to the ground, head and all, led by her footman. Over her was borne a canopie of cloth of gold, with four gilt staves, and four silver bells. For the bearing of which canopie were appointed sixteen knights, foure to beare it one space on foot, and other foure another space." But the Queen's ladies followed her in *chariots* decorated in red, and the same thing is true of Anne Boleyn, who in 1533 rode to her coronation in a litter, but was followed by four chariots, three decorated with red, and one with white. Such chariots probably resembled those to be described in the next chapter; the point to notice here is that they were being used now, and although the litters still continued until the time of Charles II—Mary de Medicis, the Queen-Mother of France, entered London in 1638 in a litter, though she had travelled from Harwich in a coach, and as late as 1680 "an accident happened to General Shippon, who came in a horse-litter wounded to London; when he paused by the brewhouse in St. John Street a mastiff attacked the horses, and he was tossed like a dog in a blanket"—the wheeled carriage once again became the vehicle of honour, and at the coronation of Mary in 1553 a chariot[1] and not a litter was used by the Queen. This had six horses, and was covered with a "cloth of tissue." Whatever its discomforts may have been, it cannot have been less dignified than the litter which it had, now for all time, supplanted.

[1] "The xxx day of September the Queen's Grace came from the Tower through London, riding in a charrett gorgeously beseen, unto Westminster." MS. Cotton. Vitellius, F.v.

INTRODUCTION OF THE COACH (1450-1600)

> "Go—call a Coach; and let a Coach be called:
> Let him that calls the Coach, be called the Caller!
> And in his calling, let him no thing call,
> But Coach! COACH!! COACH!!!"
>
> *Chrononhotonthologos.*

BOTH horse-litters and early wheeled carriages seem to have had some pretensions towards comfort. They afforded protection against the inclemency of the weather; there had been certain rude attempts at suspension, and the soft cushions helped to minimise the unpleasant joltings to which every carriage was liable. When, however, the renaissance of carriage-building occurred, people seem to have been but little more progressive than they had been centuries before. There were, as I have already hinted, still two factors which militated against a speedy adoption of such vehicles, more comfortable though they undoubtedly were, as now began to be made—the state of the roads, and the dislike of anything bordering upon the effeminate.

The roads had become no better. Even those most eager to welcome the new carriages must have been dismayed at the state of the country, not only in England, but in every European country. As one writer of the sixteenth century complains, the roads, "by reason of straitness and disrepair, breed a loathsome weariness to the passenger." Nor is this writer a solitary grumbler: there are numerous complaints. In 1537 Richard Bellasis, one of the monastery-wreckers, was unable to proceed with his work: "lead from the roofs," he reports, "cannot be conveyed away till next summer, for the ways in that countrie are so foule and deepe that no carriage [cart] can pass in winter." Indeed, no one seems to have looked after the roads with any care, either in the fifteenth or the sixteenth century. Yet there were, in this country, repeated bequests for their preservation. Henry Clifford, Earl of Cumberland, a sufferer himself, left one hundred marks to be bestowed on the highways in Craven, and the same sum on those of Westmorland. John Lyon, the founder of Harrow School, gave certain rents for the repair of the roads from Harrow and Edgware to London. This was in 1592, and Lyon's example was speedily followed by Sutton, the founder of the Charterhouse. There was, indeed, legislation of a kind, but in general the roads were in a terrible condition, and for a long time, so far as men were concerned, the saddle remained triumphant.

And for an even longer time continued that prejudice against carriages which led to the framing of actual prohibitive laws. Even women were occasionally forbidden the use of coaches, and there is the story of the luxurious duchess who in 1546 found great difficulty in obtaining from the Elector of Saxony permission to be driven in a covered carriage to the baths—such leave being granted only on the understanding that none of her attendants were to be allowed the same privilege.

So, too, in 1564, Pope Pius IV was exhorting his cardinals and bishops to leave the new-fangled machines to women, and twenty-four years later Julius, Duke of Brunswick, found it necessary to issue an edict—it makes quaint reading now—ordering his "vassals, servants, and kinsmen, without distinction, young and old," who "have dared to give themselves up to indolence and to riding in coaches . . . to take notice that when We order them to assemble, either altogether or in part, in Times of Turbulence, or to receive their Fiefs, or when on other occasions they visit Our Court, they shall not travel or appear in Coaches, but on their riding Horses." More stringent is the edict, preserved amongst the archives of the German county of Mark, in which the nobility was forbidden the use of coaches "under penalty of incurring the punishment of felony." So, also, we have the case of René de Laval, Lord of Bois-Dauphin, an extremely obese nobleman living in Paris, whose only excuse for possessing a coach was his inability to be set upon a horse, or to keep in that position if the horse chanced to move. This was in 1550. In England there was a similar feeling of opposition. In 1584 John Lyly, in his play *Alexander and Campaspe*, makes one of his characters complain of the new luxury. In the old days, he says, those who used to enter the battlefield on hard-trotting horses, now ride in coaches and think of nothing but the pleasures of the flesh. The once famous Bishop Hall speaks bitterly of the "sin-guilty" coach :—

"Is't not a shame to see each homely groome
Sit perched in an idle chariot roome
That were not meete some pannel to bestride
Sursingled to a galled hackney's hide ?

> Nor can it nought our gallant's praises reap,
> Unless it be done in staring cheap
> In a sin-guilty coach, not closely pent,
> Jogging along the harder pavement."

Possibly the same idea is to be found in the framing of a Parliamentary Bill of 1601 "to restrain the excessive use of coaches," which, however, was thrown out. So again in 1623, the delightful though sadly biased water-poet, John Taylor, is lamenting the decadence of England, due, according to him, to the growing custom of driving in coaches.

"For whereas," he says, "within our memories, our Nobility and Gentry would ride well mounted (and sometimes walke on foote) gallantly attended with three or four, score brave fellowes in blue coates, which was a glory to our Nation; and gave more content to the beholders, then [*sic*] forty of your Leather tumbrels: Then men preserv'd their bodies strong and able by walking, riding, and other manly exercises: Then saddlers was a good Trade, and the name of a Coach was Heathen Greek. Who ever saw (but upon extraordinary occasions)," he goes on to ask, "Sir *Philip Sidney*, Sir *Francis Drake*, Sir *John Norris*, Sir *William Winter*, Sir *Roger Williams*, or (whom I should have nam'd first) the famous Lord *Gray* and *Willoughby*, when the renowned *George* Earle of *Cumberland*, or *Robert* Earle of *Essex?* These sonnes of *Mars*, who in their time were the glorious Brooches of our Nation, and admirable terrour to our Enemies: these, I say, did make small use of Coaches, and there were two mayne reasons for it, the one was, that there were but few Coaches in most of their times: and the second is, they were deadly foes to all sloth and effeminacy."

To Taylor, indeed, and probably to every one of his fellow-watermen, a coach was always a "hell-cart" designed on purpose to put an end to his own most worthy calling. But less biased poets than outspoken Taylor gave tongue to an opposition which continued for nearly two centuries. Gay, for instance, looked on the vastly improved vehicle of his day as no more than an excuse for extravagant display:—

> "O happy streets, to rumbling wheels unknown,
> No carts, no coaches shake the floating town!
> Thus was of old *Britannia's* city bless'd,
> Ere pride and luxury her sons profess'd."

And again:—

> "Now gaudy pride corrupts the lavish age,
> And the streets flame with glaring equipage;
> The tricking gamester insolently rides,
> With *Loves* and *Graces* on his chariot's sides;
> In saucy state the griping broker sits,
> And laughs at honesty, and trudging wits."

Perhaps he is thinking of some personal inconvenience, rather than of mere unnecessary luxury, when he asks:—

> "What walker shall his mean ambition fix
> On the false lustre of a coach and six?"

And so late as 1770, the eccentric Lord Monboddo, who still maintained the superiority of a savage life, refused to "sit in a box drawn by brutes." It is, of course, easy to magnify such opposition to coaches as followed on the grounds of mere luxury and display, but in the earlier history of the coach, to which we are now come, it is a factor which must by no means be neglected. The coach, like every other novelty, had to fight its way, and if one is inclined to believe, after reading such accusations as there are of the earliest coaches with their magnificent adornments and numerous attendants, that the owners altogether deserved the reproaches of their more Spartan fellows, it may be well to recall Macaulay's words. In his sketch of the state of England in 1685, when coaches were still lavishly adorned, he says of them: "We attribute to magnificence what was really the effect of a very disagreeable necessity. People in the time of Charles the Second travelled with six horses, because with a smaller number there was great danger of sticking fast in the mire." And what is true of 1685 is certainly true of 1585.

Buckingham is supposed to have been the first man to use a coach and six in this country, though this is by no means certain. Of him a well-known story apropos of this question of undue luxury is told. "The stout old Earl of *Northumberland*," it runs, "when he got loose, hearing that the great Favourite *Buckingham* was drawn about with a Coach and six horses (which was wondered at then as a *novelty*, and imputed to him as a *mastring pride*) thought if *Buckingham* had six he might very well have eight in his Coach, with which he rode through the City of *London* to the *Bath*, to the vulgar talk and admiration. . . . Nor did this addition of two horses by *Buckingham* grow higher than a little *murmur*. For in the late Queen's time there were no coaches, and the first [had] but two Horses; the rest crept in by *Degrees* as men at first venture to *sea*."[1] Yet what may have been true of Buckingham, whose love of luxury was notorious, need not have been true of those other owners of coaches, who were constantly travelling about the country.

Finally there is the other side of the question to be remembered, and, as M. Ramée quaintly points out in

[1] *History of Great Britain.* Arthur Wilson. London, 1653.

his *History of Locomotion*, the very luxury which people so disliked had a beneficent effect; for "after the development of the use of carriages, and their frequent employment by the court and nobility, the liberty to throw everything out of the window became intolerable! Thus the carriage of luxury has been the cause of cleanliness in the streets."

Now it must be understood that the coach proper differs from all earlier vehicles in being not only a covered, but also a suspended carriage. The canopy has given place to the roof, a roof, that is to say, which forms part of the framing of the body; and the body itself is swung in some fashion, however primitive, from posts or other supports. Further, it seems reasonable to suppose, on the analogy of the *berlin* and the *landau*—two later carriages which took their names from the towns in which they were first made—that the first coaches were built in a small Hungarian town then called Kotzee. Yet it is to be observed that Spain, Italy, and France, in the persons of various enthusiasts, have claimed the invention—their claims being mainly based on such similarities as may be observed between the real coach and the earlier cars and charettes.[1] Bridges Adams, indeed, not to be outdone, hazards the suggestion that England might also be included in such a list by reason of her invention of the whirlicote,

[1] cf. Spenser, who uses three words which appear to be interchangeable.

"Tho', up him taking in their tender hands
They easily unto her charett beare;
Her teme at her commandement quiet stands,
Whiles they the corse unto her wagon reare.
And strowe with flowers the lamentable beare;
Then all the rest into their Coches climb."

though he is obliged to admit that nobody knows *exactly* what a whirlicote was like. It is probably due to these patriotic gentlemen that several rather ludicrous suggestions have been made to explain the derivation of the word *coach*, which has a similar sound in nearly all European languages. Menange rashly suggests a corruption of the Latin *vehiculum.* Another writer puts forward the Greek verb ὀχέω, to carry. Wachten, a German, finds in *kutten*, to cover, a suitable explanation, and Lye produces the Flemish *koetsen*, to lie along. This last, perhaps, is the most reasonable suggestion of those unwilling to give the palm to Hungary, for not only were the Flemish vehicles well known before the introduction of the new carriage, but there is also some confusion, at any rate, in this country, between the two words *coach* and *couch*, both being found in the old account books. Even in the sixteenth century the word seems to have bothered people. There is an amusing reference to this point in an early seventeenth-century tract called *Coach and Sedan Pleasantly Disputing*, of which I shall have more to say in the next chapter.

"Their first invention," says a character in this dialogue, "and use was in the Kingdome of *Hungarie*, about the time when *Frier George*, compelled the Queen and her young sonne the King, to seeke to *Soliman* the Turkish Emperour, for aid against the Frier, and some of the Nobilitie, to the utter ruine of that most rich and flourishing Kingdome, where they were first called *Kottcze*, and in the *Slavonian* tongue *Cottri*, not of *Coucher* the French to lie-downe, nor of *Cuchey*, the Cambridge Carrier, as some body made Master *Minshaw*, when hee (rather wee) perfected his Etymologicall dictionarie, whence we call them to this day *Coaches*."

It is also to be noted that the first English coaches, so called, were probably not suspended at all, but merely upholstered carts for reclining—in fact nothing more than the old chariots. In the second half of the sixteenth century, practically every pleasure carriage in England, though not on the Continent, was called a *coach* or a *carroche*. Consequently it is difficult to give a date for the importation of the first real coach into this country. Indeed, it is impossible to say with any degree of certainty precisely when carriages of the suspended type were first made. Such early accounts as exist are at once fragmentary and obscure, and the few illustrations little better than caricatures with a perspective reminiscent of that in Hogarth's famous example of false drawing. It can only be repeated that the hammock slung from the four posts of a waggon, such as we have seen existed amongst the Anglo-Saxons and possibly was also in use in parts of Europe, may have provided the idea of permanent suspension as a means to comfort, and that such scanty evidence as there is goes to prove that the carriages exported from Hungary towards the end of the fifteenth century seem to have been the first *coaches* to be built.

So early as 1457 there is mention of such a carriage, given by Ladislaus, King of Hungary, to the French King, Charles VII. The Parisians who saw it described it as "branlant et moulte riche." What this "trembling" carriage was like there is no means of discovering, but it certainly suggests an attempt at suspension, and may perhaps be taken for the earliest coach to be recorded by history. This obviously was Hungarian, and Hungary is again mentioned in the same connection by Stephanus Broderithus, who relates that in 1526, "when the archbishop received intelligence that the Turks had entered Hungary, not content with informing the King of this event, he speedily got into one of those light carriages which from the name of the place we call kotcze, and hastened to His Majesty." And apparently these light carriages were actually used for military purposes, Taylor avowing that "they carried soldiers on each side with cross-bowes," this being the best purpose to which he considered the coach had ever been put or was likely to be put in the future. All this is clear enough, but Beckmann, in his *History of Inventions*, mentions another circumstance which strengthens the evidence: "Siegmund, Baron de Herberstein, ambassador from Louis II, to the King of Hungary, says in his *Commentarie de rebus Moscoviticis*, where he occasionally mentions some travelling-stages in Hungary: 'The fourth stage for stopping to give the horses breath is six miles below Taurinum, in the village of Cotzi, from which both drivers and carriages take their name, and are generally called cotzi.'"[1]

Very probably these new Hungarian carriages were seen in most European countries before 1530. "At tournaments," says Bridges Adams, "they were made objects for display; they are spoken of as being gilded all over, and the hangings were of crimson satin. Electresses and duchesses were seldom without them;

[1] It is probable that the closed carriage in which the Emperor Frederick III paid a visit to Frankfort in 1474 was one of these cotzi. Here the interesting point is that the Emperor's attendants, apparently for the first time, were relieved of the necessity of holding a canopy over His Majesty's head, except when he went to and returned from the Council Chamber.

E

and there was as much rivalry in their days of public exhibition as there is now [1837] amongst the aspirants of fashion in their well-appointed equipages at a queen's drawing-room."

What did these early coaches look like? Shorn of their hangings, they must have resembled nothing so much as the hearse of to-day. The first illustrations show no signs of suspension, and portray what appear to be gaudily decorated waggons, and that in effect is what they were. The first coachmakers of Hungary, like their predecessors, were certainly content to take for their model the common agricultural waggon of Germany. Indeed, Hungary seems to have played pioneer in this respect at a very early date. Von Ginzrot, in his work on early vehicles, gives an illustration of a closed passenger carriage which bears more than a superficial resemblance to the later coaches. "The body," says Thrupp, "is a disguised waggon; the tilt-top has two leather flaps to fall over the doorway, and the panels are of wickerwork." It would have been quite easy, he continues, to use such waggons, as had been the case long before, for passenger traffic, "by placing the planks across the sides, or suspending seats by straps from the sides"; and he further mentions an oil painting at Nuremberg, of two waggons "with carved and gilt standard posts both in front and behind the body"—an interesting stage in the transformation from rude cart to private coach. There is a detailed and technical description of these waggons in Thrupp's own book, but it will be enough here to notice that they were generally narrower at the bottom than at the top, as were the first coaches, and that the four wheels were nearly of the same size. Working from such a model, the Hungarian artificers produced a comparatively light, though large, four-wheeled carriage with some pretensions to grace of line, a roofed body, broad seats, and a side entrance. The body, however, was not completely enclosed by solid panels, which only took the place of the curtains at a later date. Carvings and other ornamentation followed on the owner's rank and taste. And towards the end of the sixteenth century, if not before, the actual body was suspended on straps or braces. There are preserved at Coburg and Verona one or two coach-bodies which show signs of the iron hoops by which they were hung. The earliest of these was built for Duke Frederick of Saxony in 1527, and Count Gozzadini, in a slim folio which he privately printed some sixty years ago, describes a coach-body built in 1549 which still shows traces of its heraldic ornamentation on the framework.

"This coach," says Thrupp, acting as the Count's translator, "was built under the direction of an Italian at Brussels, for the ceremony of the marriage of Alexander, the son of Octavius Farnese, Duke of Parma, with a Portuguese princess. The wedding took place in 1565 at Brussels. There were four carriages Flanders fashion [? charettes] and four coaches after the Italian fashion, swinging on leather braces. The chief, or state, coach is described as being in the most beautiful manner, with four statues at the ends, the spokes of the wheels like fluted columns. There were seraphims' heads at the end of the roof and over the doorway, and festoons of fruit in relief over the framing of the body. The coachman was supported by two carved figures of lions, two similar lions were at the hind wheel, and the leather braces that supported the body and the harness were embossed with heads of animals. The ends of the steps were serpents' heads. The whole of the wood and ironwork was covered with gold relieved with white. The coach was drawn by four horses, with red and white plumes of feathers, and the covering of the body and of the horses was gold brocade with knotted red silk fringe. The cushions of gold-embroidered stuff were perfumed with amber and musk, that infused the soul of all who entered the coach with life, joy, and supreme pleasure."

Truly a Southern notion!

What is apparently the oldest coach to be preserved practically intact is to be seen at Coburg. This coach was built for a particular occasion—the marriage of John, Elector of Saxony, in 1584. The body is long and ornate, and is hung from four carved standard posts surmounted by crowned lions. The wheels are large—four feet eight inches and five feet—and the roof is at a slightly higher level than the lions' heads. Mounting steps must have existed, but have been lost.

Not unnaturally the advent of these coaches followed upon the commercial prosperity of each country. Germany seems to have imported a number of carriages from Hungary, and made others from Hungarian models, but even more prosperous than Germany at this time was Holland, which probably possessed more coaches than any other country in Europe. Here there would have been native designs to follow and improve upon, and, as I shall show in a moment, it was probably from the Netherlands that the first coach was imported into England. Antwerp, for instance, a superlatively rich city in the sixteenth century, is credited by Macpherson with having no less than five hundred coaches

—and so five hundred scandals, according to the local philosophers—in 1560, at which date London had but two, and Paris no more than three. Of the French trio of *carosses*, as they were called, one was the Queen's property, a second belonged to the fashionable Diana of Poitiers, and the third had been built for the use of that corpulent noble who has already been mentioned. Some Italian towns possessed many, others none. There is preserved at the Musée Cluny in Paris a Veronese *carriole* built in the sixteenth century by Giovanna Batta Maretto, with panels painted by a distinguished artist of the time. Verona, indeed, seems to have had many coaches. But it was easily surpassed by Ferrara, which so early as 1509 is credited with the possession of no less than sixty coaches, the whole of these forming the Duke's procession on the occasion of a state visit from the Pope. And, as Thrupp points out, these sixty carriages were not litters or cars, as might be supposed, but coaches, for it is particularly mentioned by the historian that "the Duchess of Ferrara rode in a *litter*, and her ladies followed her in twenty-two *cars*." Spain had apparently no coaches until 1546, and here again there was considerable opposition to their use. Yet although England, France, and Spain seem to have been behind other countries in taking to the new carriages, all three possessed a flourishing, if not very large, coach-building trade before 1600.

Here, perhaps, we may consider the introduction of the coach into England in rather greater detail. "It is a doubtful question," remarks Taylor in his ill-natured way, "whether the divell brought *Tobacco* into England in a *Coach*, or else brought a *Coach* in a fogge or mist of

Tobacco." Apparently he had an equal dislike for both coach and tobacco. But although we owe to the water-poet such contemporary satirical writings on the subject as there are, he is not to be trusted as an historian. Taylor, indeed, is a very bad historian, not so much on account of his inability to see two sides of a question, as because, like many another poet, he has made of exaggeration a fine art, and allowed his memory to play second fiddle to his inclinations. It is to the worthy Stowe that we must turn for the facts. Stowe liked the coaches little better than did Taylor, but his training had made him exact, and we may take it for granted that he is more or less correct when he says that the first coach to be seen upon British roads belonged to the year 1555. Curiously enough, this is the date of the first General Highways Act. The preamble of this Bill stated that certain roads were "now both very noisesome and tedious to travel in and dangerous to all passengers and carriages [carts]." The local authorities were empowered to compel parishioners to give four days' work every year to the repairing of the roads, though how far such orders were carried out it would be impossible to say. The merit of actually introducing the coach is given by Stowe to Henry Manners, second Earl of Rutland, who caused one Walter Rippon to build him a carriage from some foreign, most probably Dutch, pattern. This Earl of Rutland had borne the Spurs at the coronation of Edward VI, and in 1547 had been made Constable of Nottingham Castle. He had received the French hostages in 1550 at the time of the treaty which followed on the loss of Boulogne. It is to be regretted that neither in his correspondence nor in the family account-books preserved at Belvoir is there mention of either Rippon or his coach. There is, indeed, the "Book of John Leek of riding charges carriages [carts] and forrene paymentes" in 1550, and another book compiled by Leek's successor, George Pilkington, in the following year, but all travelling entries concern only horses and the cartage of goods. In 1555 "George Lassells, Esquyer" was "Comptroller to the householde" and paid "to Edward Hopkynson for ij ryding roddes of bone for my Ladye and other thinges, xxij*d*," but there is no mention of any carriage for his Lordship's own use. What is more unfortunate is that there are no account-books of the Manners family between 1559 and 1585, and it is not until 1587, when a fourth Earl of Rutland was head of his house, that this significant entry occurs :—

"Coach, a newe, bought in London, xxxviij*li*.xiij*s*.ij*d*."

To go back to Rippon, it is not known who he was. He is supposed to have built a coach for Queen Mary in 1556, and in 1564 the first "hollow turning coach" with pillars and arches, for Queen Elizabeth, though precisely what is meant by a "hollow turning" coach it is difficult to conjecture. This same Rippon twenty-four years later built another coach for the Queen, which is described as "a chariot throne with foure pillars behind, to beare a crowne imperiale on the toppe, and before two lower pillars, whereon stood a lion and a dragon, the supporters of the armes of England." It cannot have been very comfortable, and Elizabeth seems to have preferred another coach brought out of Holland by one William Boonen, who about 1560 was made her coachman, a position he was still occupying at the end of the century. This Boonen was a Dutchman, whose wife is said to have introduced the art of starching into England, whence followed those huge ruffs so conspicuous in all the Elizabethan portraits. Boonen's coach could be opened and closed at pleasure. On the occasion of the Queen's passing through the town of Warwick, she had "every part and side of her coach to be opened, that all her subjects present might behold her, which most gladly they desired." This coach is described as "on four wheels with seven spokes, which are apparently bound round with a thick wooden rim secured by pegs. It is precisely such a vehicle," adds the anonymous historian in the *Carriage Builder's and Harness Maker's Art Journal*, "as is now [1860] used by the brewers, with a tilt over it, which opens in the centre on one side, and would contain half a dozen persons." On the other hand, one may safely assert that no brewer's cart was ever decorated in the same way, for the framing of Elizabeth's carriage was of wood carved in a shell pattern and gilded. "The whole composition," runs another account, "contains many beautiful curves. The shell-work creeps up to the roof, which it supports, and which is dome-shaped. . . . The roof is capped by five waving ostrich feathers, one at each corner, and the fifth on the centre of the roof, and springing from a kind of crown." The driver's seat was apparently a kind of movable stool, and two horses were used. Even this coach, however, of which there is a print by Hoefnagle, dated 1582, cannot have been very comfortable, and in 1568, when the French ambassador obtained an audience, Elizabeth was complaining of "aching pains" from being knocked about in a coach driven too fast a few days before. "No wonder," comments one historian, "that the great queen used her coach only when occasions of state demanded." Whenever possible, indeed, she used her horse. "When Queen Elizabeth came to Norwich, 1578," wrote Sir Thomas Browne a hundred years later, "she came on horseback from Ipswich, by the high road to Norwich, in the summer time; but she had a coach or two," he added, "in her trayne."

In the print just mentioned there is shown a second coach, which is perhaps a better example of the carriage of the period. One sees again its hearse-like appearance, though the top is broader than the bottom, and the body is partially enclosed; but there is one peculiarity which deserves particular mention. This was a small seat which projected on either side, between the wheels. It was known as the boot. Here sat the pages or grooms or the ladies in attendance. Taylor, of course, has his fling against it. The booted coach, he says, is like a perpetual cheater, wears "two Bootes and no Spurs, sometimes having two paire of Legs and one boote; and oftentimes (against nature) most preposterously it makes faire Ladies weare the boote; and if you note, they are carrried backe to backe like people surpriz'd by Pyrats to be tyed in that miserable manner, and throwne overboard into the Sea. Moreover, it makes people imitate Sea-crabs, in being drawne Side-wayes, as they are when they sit in the boote of the Coach." The boot, however, was already tending to disappear in Taylor's day. How it originated is not clear. It was always uncovered, whence followed much hardship, particularly if the weather was unfavourable. Nor can one think that it was very capacious. There is an early seventeenth-century pamphlet entitled *My Journie*, in which a stout old lady is put into the boot of a coach, and cannot move. When going uphill all the passengers are supposed to get out and walk, but the old lady, once settled, refuses to budge, and, indeed, cannot be extricated until the end of the journey. There is further mention of the discomfort in a boot in 1663, when Edward Barker, writing to his father, a Lancashire squire, complains of his troubles in the side seat. "I got to London," he says, "on Saturday last, my journey was noe ways pleasant, being forced to ride in the boote all the waye, y[e] company y[t] came up wth mee were persons of greate quality as knightes and ladyes. My journeys expence was 30 *s*. This traval hath soe indisposed mee, y[t] I am resolved never to ride againe in y[e] coatch. I am extreamly hot and feverish." The monstrous width of these early coaches followed, of course, on their projecting side seats, which only entirely disappeared when the coach had come to be completely enclosed and provided with glass windows.

It may be that the boot in process of time was metamorphosed into the large, deep, four-sided basket which was strapped to the back of public coaches in the seventeenth and eighteenth centuries, and, indeed, this basket seems to have been called the boot in eighteenth-century stage coaches. It was probably in such a basket-boot as this that Mr. Pepys put his great barrel of oysters, "as big as sixteen others," which was given him in 1664.

An interesting point in this connection is that those who travelled on the seatless and presumably most uncomfortable roof of a coach plying for hire, paid more for the privilege than did those who rode in the boot.

However greatly the chroniclers may differ as to the date of the actual introduction, and others besides Taylor disagree with Stowe, there seems no doubt that by 1585 many of the nobility and some wealthy commoners owned private coaches, and, indeed, certain enterprising tradesmen, as will appear, let other coaches on hire at so much per day.

"After a while," says Stowe, "divers great ladies, with a great jealousy of the Queen's displeasure, made them coaches and rid them up and down the countries, to the great admiration of all the beholders, but then little by little they grew usual amongst the nobilitie and others of sort, and within twenty years became a great trade of coach-making."

Indeed, every one of any wealth was eager to possess them. A private coach settled any doubts as to your quality. It was a new fashion, a new excitement. "So a woman," says Quicksilver, the rake, in *Eastward Hoe*, "marry to ride in a coach, she cares not if she rides to her ruin. 'Tis the great end of many of their marriages." And again, in Ben Jonson's *Alchemist* it is said of the Countess that she

> ". . . has her pages, ushers
> Her six mares—
> Nay, eight!
> To hurry her through London, to the Exchange,
> Bethlem, the china-houses—
> Yes, and have
> The citizens gape at her, and praise her tires."

Even the plain country-folk seem to have been smitten with the new toy, for toy it was to them. "Has he ne'er a little odd cart," asks Waspe in *Bartholomew*

Fair, " for you to make a coach on, in the country, with four pied hobby-horses ? " Any shift for a coach, thought he, and no doubt voiced public opinion.

The first owners of coaches appear to have been those who had travelled abroad. So early as 1556, Sir Thomas Hoby, who had been our ambassador to France, possessed a coach and offered to lend it to the Lady Cecil. The account-book for 1573 of the Kytson family, of Hengrave, in Suffolk, mentions another early coach. "For my m^{res} [mistress's] coche, with all the furniture thereto belonging except horses—xxxiiij*li*.xiiij*s*. For the painting of my m^{r} and m^{res} armes upon the coche—ij*s*.vj*d*." In 1579 the Earl of Arundel is said to have brought a coach into England from Germany, and this coach is interesting from the fact that certain historians have credited it with being the first coach in England. How such a tradition arose is not clear, but it may be that this German coach had certain features which more nearly approached those of the later Stuart, fully-enclosed, coaches. Further details are to be found in the Manners notebooks, and these afford a glimpse of the methods adopted by the coach-makers, not yet a large body, of the day. In the notebooks of Thomas Screven, 1596–97, after an item for twenty-eight shillings for three-quarters of "scarlet sleves and labelles for his L[ordship's] parlyament robes" comes another of six shillings "to my Lady Adeline's coachman," and one, just below, of greater interest :—

"Item paid to Wm. Wright, coach-maker, in parte of xl*li*. for a coache now made, xx*li*."

After that, in the 1598–99 book comes an item to "the Countess of South[ampton's] coachman that wayted on my Lord to Dertford, *vs.*" This suggests the growing popularity of the coach, more especially as there is another disbursement in the same year to the Countess of Essex's coachman. Then follow from November 25th, 1598, details of the expenses of the new coach for my Lord's own use—which apparently took considerable time to furnish.

"Item for ij paire of new wheeles for the coache, tymber worke and iron work, and setting them on the axeltrees, iij*li.*xiij*s.*iiij*d.*; payntinge them in oyle colour, vj*s.*viij*d.*; a new pole for the horses to drawe by, ij*s.*vj*d.*; a paire of springe trees, iij*s.*iij*d.*"

The provender bill for six horses is given, also an item "for setting up the coach horses at dyvers times at Walsingham Howse, iiij*s.*; at Hatton Howse, xij*d.*; at Baynardes Castle, ij*s.*; dressing and oyling the coach, ij*s.*"; while the most necessary whip costs Mr. Screven twelve pence. Other payments are six shillings for two new bearing braces for the "double hanging" of the coach—here at any rate is definite mention of suspension, a fact which might suggest that, after all, either Rippon's or Lord Arundel's coach had been of the suspended type—four shillings for a long spring brace, two shillings and sixpence for a new "wynge," and sixteen pence for two "bearing raynes." The new coach, however, is not ready in time for his Lordship, who thereupon hires one with three horses to take him "to the Court at Nonesuch, 23, 24, and 25 of September, at xvj*s.* *per diem.*" Meanwhile payments for his own coach continue. For four "skynnes of orange colour leather goate" he pays various sums; for the timber work, for more painting, for a covering in "black lether," and for making the "curtaynes, and setting on the firinge, and making the blew cloth cover" a sum of twenty-six pounds, nineteen shillings, is expended. Nor is this all. My Lord was evidently determined to make his coach as gorgeous as possible. Nine yards of "marygold coulour velvet for the seat and bed in the coach" were required, and each yard cost twenty-three shillings. The quilting for the bed cost forty shillings. In addition, there was a lace of "crymosin silk" and no less than "v elles of crymosin taffaty for curtaynes," costing three pounds fifteen shillings; also "9 yardes of blew clothe for a cover." Then, of great interest, comes the final entry:—

"Item, paid to Ryly, embroderer, in full for embrodering iij sumpter clothes of crymosin with his L[ordship's] armes thereon at large, and vij otheres embrodered onely with great peacocks, with carsey for the garding and tasselles and frynge, 14 July, lxiiij*li.*"

Mr. Ryly was well paid for his work[1].

From such details it is possible to imagine what this and other coaches of the time were like. You figure a huge, gaudy, curtained apparatus with projecting sides and incomplete panels, large enough to contain a fair-sized bed, hung roughly from four posts, and capable of being dragged at little better than a snail's pace—"four-wheeled Tortoyses" Taylor calls them—along roads hardly worthy of the name. Twenty miles a day was

[1] Taylor mentions in one place that "for the mending of the Harnesse, a Knights Coachman brought in a bill to his master of 25 pounds." He also says that the owners of coaches liked to match their horses if possible.

considered good going. Says Portia, in the *Merchant of Venice* :—

> ". . . I'll tell thee all my whole device
> When I am in my coach, which stays for us
> At the park gate; and therefore haste away,
> For we must measure twenty miles to-day."

The coachman, as we learn from the water-poet, was "mounted (his fellow-horses and himselfe being all in a finery) with as many varieties of laces, facings, Clothes and Colours as are in the Rainebowe." Nor was he over-polite, particularly if the coach he drove was hired. In Jonson's *Staple of News* one of the pieces of mock-news to appear in the ideal paper concerns the fraternity :—

> "and coachmen
> To mount their boxes reverently, and drive
> Like lapwings with a shell upon their heads
> Through the streets."

They seem to have thought that their finery allowed them to treat the pedestrians with but scant respect. And no wonder these "way-stopping whirligigges," as Taylor calls the coaches, surprised the inhabitants. When one of them was seen for the first time, "some said it was a great Crab-shell brought out of *China*, and some imagin'd it to be one of the Pagan Temples in which the Cannibals adored the devill." For some time, indeed, the coaches must have given the common folk something to think about. A coach rumbling along brought them to their windows, just as the horseless carriage, centuries later, proved a similar attraction. There is a scene in *Eastward Hoe* which well illustrates this point.

Enter a Coachman in haste in 's frock, feeding.

Coach. Here's a stir when citizens ride out of town indeed, as if all the house were afire! 'Slight, they will not give a man leave to eat 's breakfast afore he rises.

Enter Hamlet, a footman, in haste.

Ham. What coachman? My lady's coach, for shame! her ladyship's ready to come down.

Enter Potkin, a tankard bearer.

Pot. 'Sfoot, Hamlet, are you mad? whither run you now? . . .

Enter Mrs. Fond and Mrs. Gazer.

Fond. Come, sweet mistress Gazer, let's watch here, and see my Lady Flash take coach.

Gazer. O' my word, here's a most fine place to stand in. Did you see the new ship launch'd last day, Mrs. Fond?

Fond. O God, and we citizens should lose such a sight!

Gazer. I warrant here will be double as many people to see her take coach, as there were to see it take water.

My lady's point of view is put forward by Lady Eitherside in *The Devil is an Ass.* Says she :—

> "If we once see it under the seals, wench, then,
> Have with them for the great caroch, six horses,
> And the two coachmen, with my Ambler bare,
> And my three women; we will live, i' faith,
> The example of the town, and govern it.
> I'll lead the fashion still."

Contemporary references to coaches, however, are but scarce. The most important of these is Taylor's own

The World runnes on Wheeles: or, Oddes betwixt Carts and Coaches, an amusing pamphlet written in prose and not in verse, because the author, as he says, was lame at the time of its composition, and because beyond the three words, broach, Roach, and encroach, he could find no suitable rhymes. Encroach, however, he thinks might have done, for that word, as he explains in his dedication to various companies likely to suffer from the importation of the coach, "best befits it, for I think never such an impudent, proud Intruder or Encroacher came into the world as a Coach is; for it hath driven many honest Families out of their Houses, many Knights to Beggers, Corporations to poverty, Almesdeedes to all misdeedes, Hospitality to extortion, Plenty to famine, Humility to pride, Compassion to oppression, and all Earthly goodnes to an utter confusion." To the cart he does not object, but for the "hyred Hackney-hell-carts" he cannot find sufficient abuse. His arguments in favour of carts as against coaches are certainly novel, if not entirely convincing as coming from a waterman well used to live passengers himself.

"And as necessities and things," he says, "whose commodious uses cannot be wanted, are to be respected before Toyes and trifles (whose beginning is Folly, continuance Pride, and whose End is Ruine) I say as necessity is to be preferred before superfluity, so is the *Cart* before the *Coach;* For Stones, Timber, Corne, Wine, Beere, or any thing that wants life, there is a necessity they should be carried, because they are dead things and cannot go on foot, which necessity the honest *Cart* doth supply: But the *Coach*, like a superfluous bable, or uncharitable Miser, doth seldom or never carry or help any dead or helplesse thing; but on the

F

contrary, it helps those that can helpe themselves . . . and carries men and women, who are able to goe or run; *Ergo*, the *Cart* is necessary, and the *Coach* superfluous."

In fact, the coach, according to poor Taylor, is directly responsible for every calamity from which the country has suffered since its introduction. Leather has become dearer, the horses in their traces are being prostituted, and there is a "universal decay of the best ash-trees."

"A Wheele-wright," he continues, "or a maker of Carts, is an ancient, a profitable and a Trade, which by no meanes can be wanted: yet so poore it is, that scarce the best amongst them can hardly ever attaine to better than a Calves skin fate, or a piece of beefe and Carret rootes to dinner on a Sunday; nor scarcely any of them is ever mounted to any Office above the degree of a Scavenger, or a Tything-man at the most. On the contrary, your Coachmakers trade is the most gainefullest about the Towne, they are apparelled in Sattens and Velvets, and Masters of their Parish, Vestry-men, who fare like the Emperors *Heliogabalus* or *Sardanapalus*, seldome without their Mackroones, Parmisants, Jellies and Kickshawes, with baked Swannes, Pasties hot, or cold red Deere Pyes, which they have frō their Debtor Worships in the Country: neither are these Coaches onely thus cumbersome by their Rumbling and Rutting, as they are by their standing still, and damming up the streetes and lanes, as the Blacke Friers, and divers other places can witnes, and against Coach-makers doores the streets are so pestered and clogg'd with them, that neither man, horse or cart can passe for them; in so much as my Lord Maior is highly to bee commended for his care in their restraint, sending in February last, many of them to the Courtes for their carelessnesse herein."

In another work of Taylor's, *The Thiefe*, there is a passage of equal interest :—

"Carroaches, Coaches, Jades and Flanders Mares
Do rob us of our shares, our wares, our Fares :
Against the ground we stand and knock our heeles,
Whilest all our profit runs away on wheeles ;
And whosoever but observes and notes,
The great increase of Coaches and of Boats,
Shall finde their number more than e'r they were
By halfe and more within these thirty yeeres.
Then water-men at Sea had service still,
And those that staid at home had worke at will :
Then upstart Helcart-Coaches were to seeke,
A man could scarce see twenty in a weeke,
But now I thinke a man may daily see,
More than the Whirries on the *Thames* can be.
When Queen *Elizabeth* came to the Crowne,
A Coach in *England* then was scarcely knowne,
Then 'twas as rare to see one, as to spy
A Tradesman that had never told a lye."

It will be seen from the first of these lines, that a difference is made between the coach and the caroche (carroch or carroache). On this point there is a definite statement in the Elizabethan play *Tu Quoque* :—

"Prepare yourself to like this gentleman,
Who can maintain thee in thy choice of gowns,
Of tires, of servants, and of costly jewels ;
Nay, for a need, out of his easy nature,
May'st draw him to the keeping of a coach
For country, and carroch for London."

This, too, is borne out by the speech of Lady Eitherside already quoted. Many servants were needed for the carroch. Massinger speaks of one being drawn by six Flanders mares, and having its coachman, groom, postilion, and footman, to look after it. "These carroaches," says Croal[1] "were larger and clumsier" than the coaches, "but were considered more stately." Taylor speaks of the town Vehicle as "a mere Engine of Pride," and gives a rather ludicrous account of some common women who had hired one of them to go to "the Greene-Goose faire at *Stratford* the *Bowe*." The occupants of this carroch "were so be-madam'd, be-mistrist, and Ladified by the beggers, that the foolish Women began to swell with a proud Supposition or Imaginary greatnes, and gave all their mony to the mendicanting Canters."

Poor Taylor! He felt very deeply on the question of these new coaches which were to put an end once and for all time to his trade. He must have felt that Henry of Navarre's assassination in 1610 would never have taken place but for that monarch's affection for his coach; yet in spite of his deep hatred, he was once prevailed upon to ride inside one of them. "It was but my chance" he records, "once to bee brought from Whitehall to the Tower in my Master Sir William Waades Coach, and before I had been drawn twenty yardes, such a Timpany of Pride puft me up, that I was ready to burst with the winde chollicke of vaine-glory. In what state I would leane over the boote, and looke, and pry if I saw any of my acquaintance, and then I would stand up vailing my Bonnet."

It almost looks as though he had enjoyed his ride!

[1] *A Book about Travelling, Past and Present.* Thomas Croal. London, 1877.

INTERLUDE OF THE CHAIR

> "I love sedans, cause they do plod
> And amble everywhere,
> Which prancers are with leather shod,
> And ne'er disturb the eare.
> Heigh doune, derry derry doune,
> With the hackney Coaches doune,
> Their jumping make
> The pavements shake,
> Their noise doth mad the toune."
>
> *Ancient Ballad.*

JUST as the horse-litter gave way before the coach, so the coach, not long after its appearance, found a serious rival in the man-drawn litter or Sedan chair. When or where this chair came from, or who brought it into use once again, is not known. That Sedan itself was the first place to adopt this chair may be true—the analogy already mentioned holding good—but beyond a few half-serious words in a curious seventeenth-century pamphlet to be quoted in a little, there is no positive evidence whatever. Several writers, indeed, assert that Sedan had nothing to do with the chair for ever associated with its name, but in that tantalising manner which is unfortunately characteristic of former times, omit to state their reason. It has been suggested that *sedan* was the name of the cloth with which the chair was lined, but if this were so, the cloth most probably took its name from the chair it adorned. But wherever it was first made it is reasonable to suppose that the narrowness of the streets made a smaller vehicle than either coach or horse-litter convenient.

The earliest chair, other than those ancient *lecticæ* and *φορεῖα* mentioned in the first chapter, appears to have belonged to the Emperor Charles V, in the first half of the sixteenth century. This, indeed, does bear some resemblance to the common conception of a *chair*, but the first Sedans of some fifty years later resembled nothing so much as a modern dog-kennel provided with two poles. A more unsociable apparatus was surely never built, and yet its almost immediate popularity is easily explained. With the urban streets not yet properly paved and the eternal jolting of the coach, to the accompaniment of such a clatter as must have made speech almost impossible, anything in the nature of a conveyance that made at once for physical comfort and comparative silence would have been favourably received.

There is mention of a chair being shown in England in 1581—just at the time when the country was beginning to show an interest in carriages—but it was not until after the death of Elizabeth that such a novelty was seen in the streets of London. You are not wholly surprised, moreover, to hear that the innovation was due to Buckingham, that apostle of luxury, who probably first saw the chair on his visit to Spain with Prince Charles. Indeed the Prince is supposed to have brought back three of them with him.

At first, of course, there was opposition.

"Every new thing the People disaffect," wrote Arthur Wilson, the historian, "They stumble sometimes, at the *action* for the *person*, which rises like a little *cloud* but soon after vanishes. So after, when *Buckingham* came to be carried upon Men's shoulders the *clamour* and the *noise* of it was so extravagant that the People would rail on him in the Streets, loathing that Men should be brought to as servile a condition as Horses. So irksome is every little new impression that breaks an old *Custom* and rubs and grates against the *public humour*. But when Time had made these Chairs common, every loose *Minion* used them, so that that which got at first so much scandal was the means to convey those privately to such places where they might give much more. Just like *long hair*, at one time described as abominable, at another time approved as beautiful. So various are the *fancies* of the *times!*"

It is to be noticed that Buckingham, according to this account, was carried upon men's shoulders. This was the case at first, but such a mode was speedily changed for that of hand-poles—at once safer and more comfortable for the occupant, and certainly more convenient for the men.[1]

John Evelyn disagrees with Wilson and ascribes the introduction of the chair into England to Sir Saunders Duncombe, a Gentleman-Pensioner knighted by James I in Scotland in 1617, who enjoyed Buckingham's patronage. In his Diary for 1645, he writes of the Neapolitans: "They greatly affect the Spanish gravity in their habit; delight in good horses; the streets are full of gallants on horse-back, in coaches and sedans, from hence brought first into England by Sir Saunders Duncombe." Undoubtedly Duncombe was responsible

[1] So Massinger in *The Bondman* says:—

"For their pomp and ease being borne
In triumph on men's shoulders."

for the great popularity of the chair in England, and for a time held a monopoly in such chairs as could be had for hire, but it may be that Buckingham suggested this monopoly in the first place, after the temporary opposition to their use had been overcome. Which rather suggests that Spain was actually the first country where they were used, though this is mere conjecture.

In the meantime much was happening to the coaches. They were increasing enormously in number, not only those privately owned, but also those hired out by the day. These latter soon became known as hackney-coaches.[1] They seem to have been put on the streets as early as 1605, but "remained in the owner's yards until sent for." In 1633 the Strand was chosen as the first regular stand for such coaches by a Captain Bailey, one of the pioneers of the movement.

"I cannot omit to mention," writes Lord Stafford, "any new thing that comes up amongst us though ever so trivial. Here is one Captain Bailey, he hath been a sea captain, but now lives on land about this city where he tries experiments. He hath erected, according to his ability, some four hackney coaches, put his men in livery and appointed them to stand at the Maypole in the Strand, giving them instructions at what rate to carry men into several parts of the town where all day they may be had. Other hackney men veering this way, they flocked to the same place and performed their journeys at the same rate, so that sometimes there is twenty of them together, which dispose up and down, that they and others are to be had everywhere, as watermen are to be had at the waterside. Everybody is

[1] The word hackney, possibly derived from the old French *Haquenée*, was the natural word to be used for a public coach, it being merely a synonym, used by Shakespeare and others, for *common*.

much pleased with it, for whereas before coaches could be had but at great rate"—one recalls the prices paid by Lord Rutland a few years before—"now a man may have one much cheaper."

Most of these coaches that were put on to the streets seem to have been old and disused carriages belonging to the quality. Many of them still bore noble arms, and, indeed, it would seem that when the hackneys were no longer disused noblemen's carriages, the proprietors found it advisable to pretend that they were. Nearly every hansom and four-wheeled cab at the end of the nineteenth century bore some sort of coronet on its panels.

The drivers of these first hackneys wore large coats with several capes, one over the other, for warmth. London, however, seems to have been the only town in which they were to be seen. "Coaches," wrote Fynes Morison in 1617, "are not to be hired anywhere but in London. For a day's journey a coach with two horses is let for about 10s. a day, or 15s. with three horses, the coachman finding the horses' feed." From the same author it would appear that most travellers still doggedly kept to their horses, and indeed, in some counties a horse could be hired for threepence a day, an incredibly small sum. "Carriers," he also records, "have long covered waggons in which they carry passengers too and fro; but this kind of journeying is very tedious; so that none but women and people of inferior condition travel in this sort." These were the stage-waggons which in due course gave rise to the stage-coaches, which in their turn were superseded by the mail-coaches.

A similar movement in France gave rise to the *fiacres*, so called from the sign of St. Fiacre, which adorned one of the principal inns in Paris, in front of which the public coaches stood. In Scotland, too, one Henry Andersen, a native of Pomerania, had in 1610 been granted a royal patent to provide public coaches in Scotland, and for some years ran a service between Edinburgh and Leith. England had yet to follow Andersen's example, but the hackneys were increasing so rapidly in London that in 1635 a proclamation was issued to suppress them. And it is to be noticed that Taylor's diatribes were directed more particularly against these public conveyances than against the privately owned carriages, which, after all, could hardly affect his trade. The proclamation was as follows :—

"That the great numbers of Hackney Coaches of late time seen and kept in London, Westminster, and their Suburbs, and the general and promiscuous use of Coaches there, were not only *a great disturbance to his Majesty, his dearest Consort the Queen, the Nobility, and others of place and degree, in their passage through the Streets;* but the Streets themselves were so pestered, and the pavements so broken up, that the common passage is thereby hindered and more dangerous ; and the prices of hay and provender and other provisions of stable, thereby made exceeding dear : Wherefore We expressly command and forbid, That, from the feast of St. John the Baptist next coming, no Hackney or Hired Coach, be used or suffered in London, Westminster, or the Suburbs or Liberties thereof, excepting they be to travel at least three miles out of London or Westminster, or the Suburbs thereof. And also, that no person shall go in a Coach in the said Streets, except the owner of the Coach shall constantly keep up Four able Horses for our Service, when required."

It is dated January 19th, 1635/6, and must have had a considerable, if temporary, effect, for as Samuel Pegge points out in his unfinished manuscript on the early use of coaches[1] it could not "operate much in the King's favour, as it would hardly be worth a Coach-master's while to be at so great a contingent charge as the keeping of four horses to be furnished at a moment's warning for His Majesty's occasional employment."

It was then that Sir Saunders Duncombe obtained his monopoly, and, of course, everything was in his favour. The actual patent granted to him belongs to the previous year, but the two are approximately contemporary. From a letter written in 1634 to Lord Stafford, it appears that Duncombe had in that year forty or fifty chairs "making ready for use." Possibly the whole thing was worked up by Buckingham and his satellites. Duncombe's patent gave the enterprising knight the right "to put forth and lett for hire" the new chairs for a term of fourteen years. In his petition he had explained that "in many parts beyond the seas, the people there are much carried in the Streets in Chairs that are covered; by which means very few Coaches are used amongst them." And so Duncombe was allowed to "reap some fruit and benefit of his industry," and might "recompense himself of the costs, charges, and expences" to which he had, or said he had, been put.

For two years these covered chairs held the advantage, and indeed seem to have been exceedingly popular. There is a most amusing pamphlet, which I have already

[1] *Curialia Miscellanea.* Samuel Pegge, F.S.A. London, 1818.

mentioned, "printed by Robert Raworth, for John Crooch," in 1636, entitled *Coach and Sedan pleasantly disputing for Place and Precedence, the Brewer's Cart being Moderator*. It is signed "Mis-amaxius," and is dedicated "to the Valorous, and worthy all title of Honor, Sr Elias Hicks." "Light stuffe," the author calls it, and tells us that he is "no ordinary Pamphleteer . . . onely in Mirth I tried what I could doe upon a running subject, at the request of a friend in the *Strand*: whose leggs, not so sound as his Judgement, enforce him to keepe his Chamber, where hee can neither sleepe or studie for the clattering of *Coaches*." It is an interesting little production, both for its own whimsicalities and for the sidelights it affords into the town's views on the subject of vehicles at the time. It starts with the cuckoo warning the milkmaids of Islington to get back to *Finsburie*. The writer, accompanied by a Frenchman and a tailor, walks back to the city, and in a narrow street comes across a coach and a sedan quarrelling about which of them is to "take the wall."

"Wee perceived two lustie fellowes to justle for the wall, and almost readie to fall together by the eares, the one (the lesser of the two) was in a suite of greene after a strange manner, windowed before and behind with *Isen-glasse*, having two handsome fellowes in greene coats attending him, the one went before, the other came behind; their coats were lac'd down the back with a greene-lace sutable, so were their halfe sleeves, which perswaded me at first they were some cast suites of their Masters; their backs were harnessed with leather cingles, cut out of a hide, as broad as *Dutch*-collops of *Bacon*.

"The other was a thick burly square sett fellow, in a doublet of Black-leather, Brasse-button'd down the brest,

Backe, Sleeves, and winges, with monstrous wide bootes, fringed at the top, with a net fringe, and a round breech (after the old fashion) guilded, and on his back-side an Atcheivement of sundry Coats in their propper colors, quarterd with Crest, Helme and Mantle, besides here and there, on the sides of a single Escutchion or crest, with some Emblematicall *Word* or other ; I supposed, they were made of some Pendants, or Banners, that had beene stollen, from over some Monument, where they had long hung in a Church.

"Hee had onely one man before him, wrapt in a red cloake, with wide sleeves, turned up at the hands, and cudgell'd thick on the backe and shoulders with broad shining lace (not much unlike that which Mummers make of strawe hatts) and of each side of him, went a Lacquay, the one a French boy, the other Irish, all sutable alike : The *French-man* (as I learned afterward) when his Master was in the Countrey, taught his lady and his daughter *French :* Ushers them abroad to publicke meetings, and assemblies, all saving the Church whither shee never came : The other went on errands, help'd the maide to beate Bucks, fetch in water, carried up meate, and waited at the Table."

The writer attempts mediation, and his offer is favourably received. The combatants explain who they are. The burly fellow speaks first :—

"My name Sir (quoth hee) is *Coach*, who am a Gentleman of an anciente house, as you may perceive by my so many quarter'd coates, of *Dukes*, *Marquises*, *Earles*, *Viscounts*, *Barons*, Knights, and Gentlemen, there is never a Lord or Lady in the land but is of my acquaintance ; my imployment is so great, that I am never at quiet, day or night ; I am a Benefactor to all Meetings, Play-houses, Mercers shops, Taverns, and some other houses of recreation. . . . This other that offers me the wrong, they call him Mounsier *Sedan*, some Mr. *Chair*, a Greene-goose hatch'd but the other day . . . and whereas hee is able with all the helpe and furtherance hee can make and devise, to goe not above a mile in an houre ; as grosse as I am, I can runne three or foure in halfe an houre ; yea, after dinner, when my belly is as full as it can hold (and I may say to you) of dainty bitts too."

Whereupon the sedan chimes in :—

"Sir, the occasion of our difference was this : Whether an emptie Coach, that has a Lords head painted Coate and Crest, as Lion, Bull, Elephant, &c. upon it without, might take the wall of a *Sedan* that had a knighte alive within it." I confess, he goes on to say, I am "a meere stranger, till of late in *England ;* therefore, if the Law of Hospitalitie be observed (as *England* hath beene accounted the most hospitable kingdome of the World,) I ought to be the better entertained, and used, (as I am sure I shall) and find as good friends, as Coach hath any,it is not his bigge lookes, nor his nimble tongue, that so runnes upon wheeles, shall scare mee ; hee shall know that I am above him both in esteeme, and dignitie, and hereafter will know my place better. . . . Neither, I hope, will any thinke the worse of mee, for that I am a Forreiner ; hath not your Countrey Coach of England been extreemly enriched by strangers ?"

Indeed, all your luxuries, he continues, are foreign, your perfumes are Italian, and your perukes made in France.

For some time it seems that Sedan is getting the best of it. Whereas the coach, he argues, has to wait out in the cold streets often for hours at a time, he is many times admitted into the privacy of my Lady's chamber, where he is rubbed clean both within and without. "And the plain troath is," he concludes, "I will no longer bee made a foole by you . . . the kenell is your naturall walke." At this moment a carman appears and supports the sedan. Coaches, he says, keep the town awake, endanger the lives of children, and, particularly in the suburbs, "be-dash gentlemen's gowns." There then follows a curious piece of dialogue between Sedan and Powel, a Welshman, one of his attendants:—

"*Sedan.* We have our name from *Sedanum*, or *Sedan*, that famous Citie and Universitie, belonging to the Dukes of *Bevillon*, and where hee keepes his Court."

"*Powel.* Nay, doe you heare mee Master, it is from *Sedanny*, which in our British language, is a brave, faire, daintie well-favoured Ladie, or prettie sweete wench, and wee carrie such some time Master. . . ."

Most of the morning is wasted by such desultory talk, and the street becomes blocked. There comes on the scene a waterman, who, of course, is equally antagonistic to both, and would throw coach and sedan into the Thames if he were not afraid of blocking the stream, and so bringing harm to himself. There follows him a country farmer, who thinks the sedan the honester and humbler of the two, but really knows very little about it. "I heare no great ill of you," he is good enough to say, but is bound to add, "I have had no acquaintance with your cowcumber-cullor'd men." Yet in the country he has in his way tried a sedan-chair, which is a "plaine wheele-barrow," just as his cart is his coach "wherein now and then for my pleasure I ride, my maides going along with me." But if they both come to Lincolnshire, the sedan, he thinks, will receive a warmer welcome than the coach.

After him comes a country vicar who has no hesitation in accusing the coach of all sorts of robberies.

Soon, he cries, you will be "turned off." You never cared for church, and indeed, during service, you disturb everybody rumbling your loudest outside. Also you are so set up that you will never give place "either to cart or carre." A surveyor is less personal than the vicar, but has little good to say of the coach, although he agrees with most of the others that for a nobleman of high rank, it is something of a necessity.

Finally the brewer appears and speedily puts an end to the wrangle.

"With that, comes up unto us a lustie tall fellow, sitting betweene two mōstrous great wheeles, drawne by a great old jade blinde of an eie, in a leather pilch, two emptie beere-barrels upon a brewer's slings besides him, and old blew-cap all bedaub'd, and stincking with yest. . . . My name is *Beere-cart*, quoth hee, I came into England in *Henry* the Seventh's time."

And the decision of the cart is, of course, that both coach and sedan shall give way to *him*. They are both to exercise great care, and the sedan is to have the wall. And he adds, turning to the smaller vehicle, a sentence which it is difficult to understand.

"You shall never," he says, "carrie Coachman againe, for the first you ever carried was a Coach-man, for which you had like to have sufferd, had not your Master beene more mercifull."

Such quarrels were very frequent, not only at this time, but right on through the eighteenth century. Swift in one of his letters to Stella mentions an accident due to the carelessness of a chairman. "The chairman that carried me," he says, "squeezed a great fellow against a wall, who wisely turned his back, and broke one of the side glasses in a thousand pieces. I fell a scolding, pretended I was like to be cut to pieces, and made them set down the chair in the Park, while they picked out the bits of glasses: and when I paid them, I quarrelled still, so they dared not grumble, and I came off for my fare: but I was plaguily afraid they would have said, God bless your honour, won't you give us something for our glass?"

Swift was the author of an amusing satire on the same subject, wherein coach and sedan were no better friends than of old.

A CONFERENCE BETWEEN SIR HARRY PIERCE'S CHARIOT AND MRS. D. STOPFORD'S CHAIR

Chariot

"My pretty dear Cuz, tho' I've roved the town o'er,
To dispatch in an hour some visits a score;
Though, since first on the wheels, I've been everyday
At the 'Change, at a raffling, at church, or a play;
And the fops of the town are pleased with the notion
Of calling your slave the perpetual motion;—
Though oft at your door I have whined [out] my love
As my knight does grin his at your Lady above;
Yet, ne'er before this though I used all my care,
I e'er was so happy to meet my dear Chair;
And since we're so near, like birds of a feather,
Let's e'en, as they say, set our horses together.

Chair

"By your awkward address, you're that thing which should carry,
With one footman behind, our lover Sir Harry.
By your language, I judge, you think me a wench;
He that makes love to me, must make it in French.
Thou that's drawn by two beasts, and carry'st a brute,
Canst thou vainly e'er hope, I'll answer thy suit?
Though sometimes you pretend to appear with your six,
No regard to their colour, their sexes you mix:

G

Then on the grand-paw you'd look very great,
With your new-fashion'd glasses, and nasty old seat.
Thus a beau I have seen strut with a cock'd hat,
And newly rigg'd out, with a dirty cravat.
You may think that you make a figure most shining,
But it's plain that you have an old cloak for a lining.
Are those double-gilt nails? Where's the lustre of Kerry,
To set off the Knight, and to finish the Jerry?
If you hope I'll be kind, you must tell me what's due
In George's-lane for you, ere I'll buckle to.

CHARIOT

"Why, how now, Doll Diamond, you're very alert;
Is it your French breeding has made you so pert?
Because I was civil, here's a stir with a pox:
Who is it that values your —— or your fox?
Sure 'tis to her honour, he ever should bed
His bloody red hand to her bloody red head.
You're proud of your gilding; but I tell you each nail
Is only just tinged with a rub at her tail;
And although it may pass for gold on a ninny,
Sure we know a Bath shilling soon from a guinea.
Nay, her foretop's a cheat; each morn she does black it,
Yet, ere it be night, it's the same with her placket.
I'll ne'er be run down any more with your cant;
Your velvet was wore before in a mant,
On the back of her mother; but now 'tis much duller,—
The fire she carries hath changed its colour.
Those creatures that draw me you never would mind,
If you'd but look on your own Pharaoh's lean kine;
They're taken for spectres, they're so meagre and spare,
Drawn damnably low by your sorrel mare.
We know how your lady was on you befriended;
You're not to be paid for 'till the lawsuit is ended:
But her bond it is good, he need not to doubt;
She is two or three years above being out.
Could my Knight be advised, he should ne'er spend his vigour
On one he can't hope of e'er making *bigger*."

Gay seems to have shared the watermen's disgust at both coach and sedan.

"Boxed within the chair, contemn the street
And trust their safety to another's feet,"

he says of those willing to use the chair. In another place he is comparing the two :—

> "The gilded chariots while they loll at ease
> And lazily insure a life's disease ;
> While softer chairs the tawdry load convey
> To court, to *White's*, assemblies or the play."

Elsewhere he exhorts the pedestrian to assert his rights :—

> "Let not the chairman, with assuming stride,
> Press near the wall, and rudely thrust thy side ;
> The laws have set him bounds ; his servile feet
> Should ne'er encroach where posts defend the street."

By this time, however, many changes in the chairs had taken place. They seem to have been introduced into Paris in 1617 by M. de Montbrun, though unfortunately from whence this gentleman brought them we are nowhere informed. They were called *chaises à porteurs*. Possibly English and French chairs were at first quite similar to each other in appearance—square boxes with a pent-house—but in the middle of the century—in Paris, at any rate, they became far more elegant in form, and began to be ornamented and richly upholstered. Some of them resembled, in shape, the body of the modern hansom-cab. This was particularly the case with a new carriage, introduced about 1668, called the *brouette* (wheelbarrow), *roulette*, or *vanaigrette*, which was merely a sedan upon two wheels. It was drawn in the usual way by a man, and was an early form of that vehicle which still survives in the East as the jin-rick-shaw. The brouette held but one person, its wheels were large, and its two poles projected some way in front. One Dupin was apparently the only person to manufacture them, and after his first experiments he applied "two elbow-springs beneath the front, and attached them to the axletree by long shackles, the axletree working up and down in a groove beneath the inside-seat." This improvement is of more than ordinary interest in so far as it is the first mention of steel springs to carriages. In the ordinary coaches these steel springs were first applied beneath the bottom of the body. They were probably formed out of a single piece of metal.

In the case of the brouette there was the usual opposition—this time from the proprietors of the ordinary sedans—but although a temporary prohibition was made, the brouette triumphed, and in 1671 was a common sight in the streets of Paris. It was not very suitable for decoration. As one French writer remarks, it was enough if the machine were solidly constructed. The brouette had windows at the sides and a small support in front of the wheels to allow the carriage to maintain its proper position when not held up by an attendant.

The brouette does not seem to have come immediately to England, though in the eighteenth century there was a *sedan cart*, similar in appearance to it, to be seen in London. On the other hand, the ordinary sedans were rapidly gaining in popularity, and maintained that popularity right through the reigns of the first three Georges.

In appearance they became rather more graceful towards the middle of the century, though less so in later days. The public chairs were generally made of black or dark green leather, ornamented with gold "beading," the frame and roof, which had a double slope, being of wood, as was also the small square window-frame. Private chairs, however, could be as gorgeous as the owner pleased, though in this respect continental chairs far surpassed our own. At Paris are shown two magnificent chairs which belonged to Louis XV.

"These," says Croal, "have glass windows in side and front, through which the sumptuous lining of crimson velvet is discernible. The outside is beautifully painted and gilt, and though now somewhat faded, the splendour of the vehicles can be imagined, even in their decay. The gorgeously attired king within, or it might be the queen or some reigning favourite, would be attended by a gay escort of gentlemen of the court, with a crowd of bearers and lacqueys, not to speak of armed guards, whose liveries probably equalled in grandeur the courtly habits of the greater men who surrounded the royal chair."

At South Kensington a private English chair of about 1760 is shown, "rather handsomely ornamented in ormolu, the sides being divided into four panels, but without windows. In form," continues Croal, "the chair may be described as 'carriage-bodied,' not being, as the later chairs, square at the bottom. At the two front corners heavy tassels are hung, and through the door in front it can be seen that the interior lining is of figured damask. The bearing rings through which the poles passed are of brass." This, however, cannot compare with an Italian nobleman's large conveyance of the early eighteenth century which shows a profusion of gold filigree work on the roof that calls to mind nothing so strongly as a Buszard wedding-cake. It belonged to a member of the Grand Ducal family of Tuscany, by whom it was used on baptismal occasions. Here, besides the gilt work on the roof, there is a medallion-painting of figures in antique costume over the door. The walls are painted a pale French grey "with elaborately carved mouldings round the panels, with groups of flowers painted in the middle. The interior is lined with satin corresponding to the painting outside, being in gold and colours upon a pale ground."

The chairmen do not seem to have been a particularly agreeable lot of fellows. In London they were generally Irish or Welsh. They were often drunk, often careless, and nearly always uncivil. Says Gay :—

> "The drunken chairman in the kennel spurns,
> The glasses shatter, and his charge o'erturns."

In Edinburgh, however, where there were ninety chairs in 1738, the chairmen were Highlanders and rather more civil. "An inhabitant of Edinburgh," says Hugh Arnot in his history of that city (1789), "who visits the metropolis can hardly suppress his laughter at seeing the awkward hobble of a street chair in the city of London." We learn from Markland that in 1740 a chair in Edinburgh could be hired for four shillings a day or twenty shillings a week.[1] In London, according to George Selwyn, you could be

[1] Which was about the same sum that Defoe had to pay in London earlier in the century. "We are carried to these places [the coffee-houses]," he wrote in 1702, "in chairs which are here very cheap—a guinea a week, or a shilling per hour; and your chairmen serve you for porters, to run on errands, as your gondoliers do at Venice."

carried three miles for a shilling.[1] In Edinburgh, again, where chairs were used at a later date than anywhere in England, rules were made for the public convenience in 1740, the most interesting of these being one which forbade a soldier in the service of the city guard to carry a chair at any time. By 1789 their numbers had increased to 238, including fifty privately owned.

Scattered mention of them occurs amongst British authors. Steele, in one of his *Tatler* papers, proposes to levy a tax upon them, and regrets that the sumptuary laws of the old Romans have never been revived. The chairmen, or "slaves of the rich," he says, "take up the whole street, while we Peripatetics are very glad to watch an opportunity to whisk across a passage, very thankful that we are not run over for interrupting the machine, that carries in it a person neither more handsome, wise, nor valiant, than the meanest of us."

Matthew Bramble in *Humphrey Clinker* is made to draw a wretched picture of the chairs which abounded in Bath at the middle of the century :—

"The valetudinarian," he writes, "is carried in a chair, betwixt the heels of a double row of horses, wincing under the curry-combs of grooms and postilions, over and above the hazard of being obstructed or overturned by the carriages which are continually making their exit or their entrance. I suppose, after some chairmen shall have been maimed, and a few lives lost

[1] cf. "With chest begirt by leathern bands,
The chairman at his corner stands ;
The poles stuck up against the wall
Are ready at a moment's call.
For customers they're always willing
And ready aye to earn a shilling."
Echoes of the Street.

by those accidents, the corporation will think in earnest about providing a more safe and commodious passage. . . . If, instead of the areas and iron rails, which seem to be of very little use, there had been a corridor with arcades all round, as in Covent Garden, the appearance of the whole would have been more magnificent and striking; those arcades would have afforded an agreeable covered walk, and sheltered the poor chairmen and their carriages from the rain, which is here almost perpetual. At present the chairs stand soaking in the open street from morning to night, till they become so many boxes of wet leather, for the benefit of the gouty and rheumatic, who are transported in them from place to place. Indeed, this is a shocking inconvenience, that extends over the whole city; and I am persuaded it produces infinite mischief to the delicate and infirm. Even the close chairs, contrived for the sick, by standing in the open air, have their fringe linings impregnated, like so many sponges, with the moisture of the atmosphere."

It was to Bath that Princess Amelia was carried in a sedan by eight chairmen from St. James's, in April, 1728. This must easily have been the longest, and, so far as the chairmen were concerned, the most wearisome journey ever performed by a chair.

John Wilkes mentions in one of his letters to his daughter that he ascended Mont Cenis in a chair "carried by two men and assisted by four more." "This," he says, "was not a sedan chair, but a small wicker chair with two long poles; there is no covering of any kind to it." Such open chairs seem to have been very uncommon, and were, I imagine, unknown in England. Some, however, had more glass than others, and their size fluctuated. Fashionable ladies must

"The Social Pinch"
By John Kay

Sedans in "The Present Age"
By L. P. Boitard (1767)

have found a difficulty in getting into a public chair of the ordinary size at the time of the large hoop petticoat, and there is a satiric print, dated 1733, which shows a lady thus attired, being hauled out through the opened roof of one with ropes and pulleys. Similarly, when forty or fifty years later the head-dress of the women became so enormous, a ludicrous print appeared showing a patent arrangement whereby the roof of a chair could be raised on rods to as great a height as was required.

In general the roof opened upwards, being hinged at the back. This is clearly shown in a print published in 1768, called *The Female Orators*, in which a clergyman is stepping out of his chair, and the chairmen very obviously demanding their fare. Another print published about 1786, called the *Social Pinch*, shows a very famous chairman, Donald Kennedy, offering his "mull" to Donald Balack, a native of Ross-shire, whom he had just set down. Here the structure of the public chair in use at this date is clearly shown.

At the beginning of the nineteenth century, however, the chair as a mode of conveyance was on the wane. Fenimore Cooper in his *Sketches of English Society* (1837) was able to write: "Sedan chairs appear to have finally disappeared from St. James' Street. Even in 1826 I saw a stand of them that has since vanished. The chairs may still be used on particular occasions, but were Cecilia now in existence, she would find it difficult to be set down in Mrs. Benfield's entry from a machine so lumbering." Which suggests that the chair had not only degenerated in numbers, but also in appearance. They had become larger and uncouth in Cooper's day. One is reminded of that chair in *Pickwick*, which "having been originally built for a gouty gentleman with funded property, would hold Mr. Pickwick and Mr. Tupman at least as comfortably as a modern post-chaise." Yet so late as 1775 the popularity of the chair had been at its highest. It was the old story. With the new century were coming new ideas. The chair slowly and quite naturally was dropping out of existence.

In Edinburgh, as I have said, it lingered on for rather a longer time. In 1806 stringent regulations were still required. Those chairs which maintained their stand at night had to have "a light fixed on the fore part of one of the poles." On the occasion of a fire or a mob the chairmen had to hurry to the scene of excitement, and there await the magistrate's orders. They were not allowed to charge more than ninepence a mile, seven-and-six a day, or a guinea and a half a week. Such rates, too, continued to be set out in the *Edinburgh Almanac* until 1830. After that comes an ominous silence. By that time only the private chair was in use.

"Lady Don," says Lord Cockburn in his *Memorials*, "was about the last person (so far as I recollect) in Edinburgh, who kept a private sedan chair. Hers stood in the lobby and was as handsome and comfortable as silk, velvet, and gilding could make it. And when she wished to use it two well-known respectable chairmen, enveloped in her livery cloaks, were the envy of her [superannuated] brethren. She and Mrs. Rochead both sat in Tron Church; and well do I remember how I used to form one of the cluster that always took its station to see these beautiful relics emerge from coach and chair."

The time, indeed, had come when the sight of a chair was as much a public entertainment as it had been when Buckingham had been borne through the streets "on men's shoulders."

Yet although they so rapidly disappeared off the face of Europe, in Asia they lost little of their popularity, and in many places to-day are the only methods of conveyance in common use. China, in particular, had long been a land of sedans. John Barrow in his *Collection of Authentic, Useful, and Entertaining Voyages and Discoveries*, 1765, mentions the fact that at an early date the Chinese "small covered carriages on two wheels, not unlike in appearance to our funeral hearses, but only about half their length," had been superseded by chairs. To a European, he relates, this was hardly surprising, as the carriage was anything but comfortable, and required you to sit on your haunches at the bottom—"the most uneasy vehicle that can be imagined."

"'The Chinese,' records another eighteenth-century traveller, 'occasionally travel on horseback, but their best land conveyance by far is the sedan, a vehicle which certainly exists among them in perfection. Whether viewed with regard to lightness, comfort, or any other quality associated with such mode of carriage, there is nothing so convenient elsewhere. Two bearers place upon their shoulders the poles, which are thin and elastic and in shape something like the shafts of a gig, connected near the ends, and in this manner they proceed forward with a measured step in an almost imperceptible motion, and sometimes with considerable speed. Instead of panels, the sides and back of the chair consist of woollen cloth for the sake of lightness with a covering of oilcloth against rain. The front is closed with a hanging blind of the same materials in lieu of a door, with a circular aperture of gauze to see through. . . . Private persons among the Chinese are restricted to two bearers, ordinary magistrates to four, and the viceroys to eight, while the Emperor alone is great enough to require sixteen.' "

There is further mention of these Chinese chairs in Oliphant's much later account of Lord Elgin's mission. Lord Elgin himself travelled in a chair of the kind usually reserved for mandarins of the highest rank, which was larger than those in ordinary use and had a fine brass knob on the top. Eight bearers carried it. In processions a *hwakeaou* or flowered chair was often used.

Japan, too, had early had sedans both for travelling and for more purely ceremonial purposes. Light bamboo chairs, they were, called *kangoes* or *norimons*, which were borne by two or more persons. On the introduction of the European coach, however, a kind of brouette, as I have said, was substituted, and in a few years there were hundreds of thousands of these *jin-rick-shaws* on the streets, not only in Japan, but throughout Asia. At first many of these were grotesquely adorned, but their appearance is too well-known at the present day for need of a lengthy description. Equipped with "every modern convenience" and very well built indeed, they afford a European a delightful sensation on his first ride, even though he may have visions of those earlier days of his youth when he was carried about in a similar way (though at a less speed) in the homely perambulator.

SEVENTEENTH-CENTURY INNOVATIONS

> " We took our coach, two coachmen and four horses,
> And merrily from London made our courses.
> We wheel'd the top of th' heavy hill called Holborne
> (Up which hath been full many a sinful soule borne,)
> And so along we jolted past St. Gileses,
> Which place from Brainford six (or neare) seven miles is."
>
> *Taylor.*

THE seventeenth century saw great changes in vehicular design. In 1660 the first *berlin* was made. Steel springs, as we have seen, appeared a few years later in the brouette. About this time, too, a hooded gig or *calèche* made its appearance in the streets of Paris, the first of many carriages to be built upon entirely new lines. Glass windows and complete doors were used in the coaches, both public and private, which became smaller, more compact, and certainly more graceful. Improvements were not confined to one country, but proceeded simultaneously not only in various European countries, but also in South America. Roads, too, were improved, and laws for the regulation of traffic framed with some regularity and effect.

John Evelyn in his Diary gives interesting glimpses of such carriages and other vehicles as he saw during his several European tours. In Brussels (1641) he was allowed the use of Sir Henry de Vic's coach and six, and travelled luxuriously in it as far as Ghent. "On the way," he notes, "I met with divers little waggons, prettily contrived, and full of peddling merchandize, drawn by mastiff dogs, harnessed completely like so many coach-horses; in some four, in others six, as in Brussels itself I had observed. In Antwerp I saw, as I remember, four dogs draw five lusty children in a chariot." When dogs were first used for the purpose of traction does not appear, but they are still to be seen in the Netherlands in a like capacity. A few days later, to continue with Evelyn's observations, he was going from Ostend to Dunkirk "by waggon . . . the journey being made all on the sea sands." On his return to England, however, it is to be noticed that he rode post to Canterbury. In 1643 he was again in Paris, mentioning "the multitude of coaches passing every moment over the bridge," this being, he says, to a new spectator, "an agreeable diversion." In the following year, while standing in the garden of the Tuileries, he saw "so many coaches as one would hardly think could be maintained in the whole city, going late as it was, towards the course"—the fashionable rendezvous of the day—"the circle being capable of containing a hundred coaches to turn commodiously, and the larger of the plantations for five or six coaches a-breast." The road from Paris to Orleans he describes as "excellent." Coming to Italy, he found Milan, in spite of the narrowness of its streets, abounding in rich coaches. In Paris again, two or three years afterwards, the design of a new coach so took his fancy that he determined, like his friend Mr. Pepys, to possess one for himself. And so on May 29th, 1652, "I went," he writes, "to give orders about a coach to be made against my wife's coming, being my first coach, the pattern whereof I brought out of Paris." This was probably "booted," but differed from the earlier coaches in having a curved roof.

The commonest French coach of this time seems to have been the *corbillard*, a flat-bottomed, half-open, half-close coach, furnished with curtains of cloth or leather in the front part. These were merely tied on to the supports, and would roll up when required. Doors there were none, but there was a "movable rail, over which a leather screen was hung" at the back portion of the carriage, which was about six feet long, and here were the seats. There were also projecting movable step-seats. Possibly Evelyn saw a newer model with a curved bottom and door half-way up, panelled in the lower part, but curtained above. Such a carriage was hung low, and would have swung from side to side, giving such passengers as were "bad sailors" a fit of nausea.

The English-designed coaches of this time, though without glass windows, were almost completely enclosed, and, compared with the new *chariots*, which were just upon making their appearance, of a huge size. In many of them three people could sit abreast, and seven or eight find room for themselves. In 1641 when Charles I passed through London on his return from Scotland, his was the only coach in the royal procession, but seven people, including His Majesty, were driving, apparently in comfort, within it.

The Commonwealth produced no new carriage, although isolated experiments were already being made. Cromwell himself was wont to drive his own coach and six "for recreation-sake" in Hyde Park, then as now a fashionable resort.

"When my Lord Protector's coach," wrote Misson, a Frenchman then on a visit to England, "came into the Park with Colonel Ingleby and my Lord's three daughters, the coaches and horses flocked about them like some miracle. But they galloped (after the mode court-pace now) round and round the Park, and all that great multitude hunted them and caught them still at the turn like a hare, and then made a lane with all reverent haste for them, and so after them again, and I never saw the like in my life."

Cromwell's desire to play coachman once led to an accident which might have been serious. The particulars are given in a letter from the Dutch Ambassador to the States-General, dated October 16th, 1654:—

"His Highness, only accompanied with secretary Thurloe and some few of his gentlemen and servants, went to take the air in Hyde Park, when he caused some dishes of meat to be brought, when he had his dinner; and afterwards had a mind to drive the coach himself. Having put only the secretary into it," he whipped up "those six grey horses, which the Count of Oldenburgh had presented unto His Highness, who drove pretty handsomely for some time. But at last, provoking these horses too much with the whip, they grew unruly and ran so fast that the postillion could not hold them in, whereby His Highness was flung out of the coach upon the pole. . . . The secretary's ankle was hurt leaping out, and he keeps his chamber."

Coach in the time of Charles I
(From "Coach and Sedan Pleasantly Disputing")

Coach in the time of Charles II
(From Thrupp's "History of Coaches")

"From this," comments Sir Walter Gilbey, who quotes the letter, "it is evident that when six horses were used a postillion rode one of the leaders and controlled them; while the driver managed the wheelers and middle pair. When four horses were driven," he continues, "it was the custom to have two outriders, one to ride at the leaders' heads, and one at the two wheelers'. In town this would be merely display, but on a journey the outriders' horses might replace those of the team in case of accident, or, more frequently, be added to them to help drag the coach over a stretch of bad road."

It is just possible that this coach which was overturned by Cromwell's faulty driving is at present in existence, repaired, of course, and redecorated, and, incidentally, painted by Cipriani, as Mr. Speaker's coach. This undoubtedly belongs to the period, and one writer actually commits himself to the statement that the two are identical. A commoner report assigns the Speaker's coach in the first place to Lenthall, Cromwell's Speaker. Whatever be its history, the coach is a fine example of Jacobean work. It is of carved oak, the body being hung upon leather braces. The workmanship, Mr. Oakley Williams thinks,[1] is Flemish. Cipriani's work, added late in the eighteenth century, is still in good preservation. Five people can comfortably sit inside. "The Speaker," says Mr. Williams, "presumably occupied the seat of honour alone. Opposite him sat his Chaplain and the Sergeant-at-Arms. For the accommodation of his other attendants . . . a low bench is arranged across the floor of the coach, with

[1] In an article in the *Pall Mall Magazine* for March, 1912.

H

a semicircular space for the legs of its occupants scooped out against either door"—relic, of course, of the boot. "The coach," he continues, after mentioning that the Speaker always has his own arms painted on the side of the body, and is allowed an escort of a single Lifeguardsman, "weighs two tons one hundredweight and several pounds, yet for all its size it so beautifully hung and balanced that an able-bodied man was able without undue effort to draw it out for my inspection. Its coach-house is one of the vaults in the inner courtyard of the House of Lords." Both origin and subsequent history of this coach, however, are wrapped in an impenetrable mystery.

Cromwell's mishap naturally gave the Royalist writers an opportunity for satire. Cleveland wrote the following lines :—

"The whip again; away! 'tis too absurd
That thou should lash with whipcord now, but sword.
I'm pleased to fancy how the glad compact
Of Hackney coachmen sneer at the last act.
Hark! how the scoffing concourse hence derives
The proverb, 'Needs must go when th' devil drives.'
Yonder a whisper cries, ''Tis a plain case
He turned us out to put himself in place;
But, God-a-mercy, horses once for aye
Stood to 't, and turned him out as well as we.'
Another, not behind him with his mocks,
Cries out, 'Sir, faith, you were in the wrong box.'
He did presume to rule because, forsooth,
He's been a horse-commander since his youth,
But he must know there's a difference in the reins
Of horses fed with oats and fed with grains.
I wonder at his frolic, for be sure
Four hamper'd coach-horses can fling a brewer;
But pride will have a fall; such the world's course is.
He [who] can rule three realms can't guide four horses;

> See him that trampell'd thousands in their gore;
> Dismounted by a party but of four.
> But we have done with 't, and we may call
> The driving Jehu, Phaeton in his fall.
> I wish to God, for these three kingdoms' sake,
> His neck, and not the whip, had giv'n the crack."

Evelyn met with a similar mishap, but fortunately escaped injury. He, too, was accustomed to ride in Hyde Park, and on one occasion is grumbling that "every coach" there "was made to pay a shilling, and a horse sixpence, by a sordid fellow who had purchased it of the State, as they called it."

Such experiments as were being made in this country were in the direction of a safer and swifter vehicle than those in general use. So early as 1625, one Edward Knapp had been granted a patent for "hanging the bodies of carriages on springs of steel." Apparently Knapp was wholly unsuccessful, but forty years later Colonel Blunt, working upon similar lines, produced several carriages which, if not entirely satisfactory in themselves, led the way towards a wider appreciation of the problems in question. If, as seems probable, he was identical with the Blunt or Blount of Wicklemarsh, near Blackheath (afterwards Sir Harry Blount), who had travelled extensively in Turkey and elsewhere, it may be that he had brought back with him several continental curiosities. We hear, indeed, of a French chariot in his possession. In 1657 the Colonel was making experiments with a "way-wiser" or "adometer" which exactly "measured the miles . . . showing these by an index as we went on. It had three circles, one pointing to the number of rods, another to the miles, by 10 to 1000, with all the subdivisions of quarters; very pretty," opines Evelyn, "and useful." This seems to have been the first instrument of the kind, and is overlooked by Beckmann in his account of such contrivances. The Colonel's work was brought to the notice of the newly formed Royal Society, and a committee was formed to investigate it. The first model shown to this committee was of "a chariot with four springs, esteemed by him very easy both to the rider and the horse, and at the same time cheap." The Committee also examined the designs of Dr. Robert Hooke, a distinguished member of the Society, and Professor of Geometry at Gresham College, who "produced the model of a chariot with two wheels and short double springs to be driven by one horse; the chair of it being so fixed upon two springs that the person sitting just over or rather a little behind the axletree was, when the experiment was made at Colonel Blunt's house, carried with as much ease as one could be in the French chariot without at all burthening the horse."[1] Dr. Hooke showed "two drafts of this model having this circumstantial difference—one of these was contrived so that the boy sitting on a seat made for him behind the chair and guiding the reins over the top of it, drives the horse. The other by placing the chair behind and the saddle on the horse's back being to be borne up by the shafts, that the boy riding on it and driving the horse should be little or no burden to the horse."

The Colonel continued experimenting both with the older coaches and a new light chariot. In 1665 Mr. Pepys was taken to see an improvement of his on a coach.

[1] Birch's *History of the Royal Society*.

"I met my Lord Brouncker, Sir Frederick Murrey, Dean Wilkins, and Mr. Hooke, going by coach to Colonel Blunt's to dinner. . . . No extraordinary dinner, nor any other entertainment good; but afterwards to the tryal of some experiments about making of coaches easy. And several we tried; but one did prove mighty easy, not here for me to describe, but the whole body of the coach lies upon one long spring, and we all, one after another, rid in it; and it is very fine and likely to take."

A few months later Pepys saw the new chariot itself.

"After dinner comes Colonel Blunt in his new chariot made with springs; as that was of wicker, where in a while since we rode at his house. And he hath rode, he says, now his journey, many miles in it with one horse, and out-drives any coach, and out-goes any horse, and so easy he says. So for curiosity, I went into it to try it, and up the hill [Shooter's Hill] to the heath [Blackheath], and over the cart ruts, and found it pretty well, but not so easy as he pretends."

The Colonel persevered. At the beginning of the next year the Royal Society's committee met again at his house to consider, says Pepys, "of the business of chariots, and to try their new invention, which I saw here my Lord Brouncker ride in: where the coachman sits astride upon a pole over the horse, but do not touch the horse, which is a pretty odde thing; but it seems it is most easy for the horse, and, as they say, for the man also."

Others were also at work upon carriage improvement, and in 1667 the Royal Society "generally approved" of a chariot invented by a Dr. Croune. "No particulars of the vehicle are given," says Sir Walter Gilbey, "we are only told that 'some fence was proposed to be made for the coachman against the kicking of the horse.'" In the same year, Sir William Pen possessed a light chariot in which Pepys drove out one day. This, he says, was "plain, but pretty and more fashionable in shape than any coaches he hath, and yet do not cost him, harness and all, above £32."

All such experiments were undoubtedly in the direction of a light, swift carriage, such as was built about 1660 in Germany by Philip de Chiesa, a Piedmontese, in the service of the Duke of Prussia. Indeed, it is quite possible that Colonel Blunt either possessed, or had seen, one of de Chiesa's carriages, which were none other than the famous and popular *berlins*.[1]

So far Germany had been taking the lead. Her State coaches were the most wonderful in the world, and her coachbuilders were designing lesser coaches for the ordinary folk. But the *berlin* was the first of these lesser carriages to catch the public fancy, and enjoy more than a local success. Now the *berlin* differed in the first place

[1] Some people have considered that the name was not derived from the city of Berlin, but from an Italian word *berlina*, "a name given by the Italians to a kind of stage on which criminals are exposed to public ignominy." This seems rather far-fetched. In England it was always thought to have been built first in Berlin, and was a common enough term for a coach early in the eighteenth century. Swift mentions it in his *Answer to a Scandalous Poem* (1733):—

"And jealous Juno, ever snarling,
Is drawn by peacocks in her berlin."

"It should be noted," says Croal, "that we find the word differently applied in the earlier years of the century, and in such a way as to cast doubts on the derivations quoted. In some of the last Acts passed by the Scottish Parliaments before the Union, there are references to a kind of *ship* or boat, called a berline. The royal burghs on the west coast of Scotland were in 1705 ordered to maintain two 'berlines' to prevent the importation of 'victual' from Ireland, this importation being forbidden at the time, and two years later an Act was passed to pay the expenses of the berlines."

from previous carriages in having two perches instead of the single pole, "and between these two perches, from the front transom to the hind axle-bed, two strong leather braces were placed, with jacks or small windlasses, to wind them up tighter if they stretched." The bottom of the coach was no longer flat, and these braces of leather allowed the body to play up and down instead of swinging from side to side as before. Here, then, you had an entirely new principle.

"In the Imperial mews at Vienna," says Thrupp, "are four coach berlins, which, I think, may belong to this period. They are said to have been built for the Emperor Leopold who reigned at Vienna from 1658 to 1700, and Kink describes this Emperor's carriage as covered with red cloth and as having glass panels; he also says they were called the Imperial glass coaches. It is possible that the coaches have been a little altered from the time of their construction, but I consider that in these four we have the oldest coaches with solid doors and glasses all round that exist in Europe. Whether they are identical with the Emperor Leopold's wedding-carriages matters much less than the influence the *berlin* undoubtedly had upon the coachbuilding of that period. It was the means of introducing the double perch, which, although it is not now in fashion, was adopted for very many carriages both in England and abroad, up to 1810. Crane-necks to perches were suggested by the form of the *berlin* perch; and as bodies swinging from standard posts suggested the position of the C spring, so bodies resting upon long leather braces suggested the horizontal and elbow springs to which we owe so much. The first *berlin* was made as a small *vis-à-vis* coach—small because it was to be used as a light travelling carriage, and narrow because it was to hang between the two perches, and was only needed to carry two persons inside. It was such an improvement in lightness and appearance upon the cumbersome coaches that carried eight persons, that it at once found favour, and was imitated in Paris and still more in London."

These early *berlins* were not nearly so gorgeous as the heavier coaches which they gradually supplanted. Red cloth and black nails had taken the place of the gilt ornamentation and crimson hangings of the previous generation.[1] Only on festivals, we learn, the black harness "was ornamented with silk fringe." The coaches used by the Emperor himself had leather traces, but the ladies of his suite had to be content with carriages the traces of which were made of rope.

The glass windows which were such a conspicuous feature of the *berlins*, were also used in the larger coaches, finally, as I have said, eliminating the boot. Mr. Charles Harper thinks that the first English coach to possess them belonged in 1661 to the Duke of York. At first these windows seem to have caused trouble, and there is the ludicrous incident mentioned by Pepys, of my Lady Peterborough who "being in her glass-coach with the glass up and seeing a lady pass by in a coach whom she would salute, the glass was so clear that she thought it had been open, and so ran her head through the glass!" Lady Ashly did not like the new invention, because, as she said, the windows were for ever flying open while the coach was running over a bad

[1] A point of minor interest may here be noticed. When leather was first used for the covering of the coach quarters, the heads of the nails showed. But about 1660, "these nail-heads were covered with a strip of metal made to imitate a row of beads; from this practice arose the name of 'beading' which has been retained, although beading is now made in a continuous, level piece, either rounded or angular." *Thrupp.*

piece of road. Lady Peterborough's misfortune was tribute indeed to the maker!

In this matter of the glass it would seem that Spain had taken the lead, and it is quite possible that Spain invented the first two-seated chariots. In 1631, thirty years before the first *berlin* was made, an Infanta of Spain is reported to have traversed Carinthia "in a glass-carriage in which no more than two persons could sit." What this was like we do not know. It may have had rude springs, and been built from the common coach models to a smaller measurement; it was certainly bootless, and framed glass or mica took the place of curtains. In France the first coaches to have glass windows, according to M. Roubo, created something of a Court scandal in the time of Louis XIII. The glass, he says, was first used in the upper panels of the doors, but was soon extended to the whole of the upper half of the sides and front of the body, so making of the carriage literally a glass-coach.

You may learn more of the English seventeenth-century carriages from Pepys than from any other writer; nor is this a matter for wonder. Pepys had a knack of knowing just exactly what posterity would desire to know. From his Diary, we learn incidentally that the watermen were still endeavouring to regain their lost prestige and custom, but by this time coaches had enormously increased in number—in 1662 there were nearly 2500 hackneys in London alone—and thenceforth they are hardly heard of. To be any one, moreover, you had to have your private coach. Doctors, for instance, found it very well worth their while to keep a coach, though, as Sir Thomas Browne told his son, they were certainly "more for state than for businesse." On the other hand those who were well able to keep a private carriage occasionally preferred the use of a hackney, and sometimes at times when they had no business to do so. Mr. Pepys, with clear ideas upon the dignity and responsibilities of rank, was indignant at any such foolery. He was told, he recalls in one place, "of the ridiculous humour of our King and Knights of the Garter the other day, who, whereas heretofore their robes were only to be worn during their ceremonies and service, these, as proud of their coats, did wear them all day till night, and then rode into the Park with them on. Nay, and he tells us he did see my Lord Oxford and Duke of Monmouth in a hackney-coach with two footmen in the Park, with their robes on; which is a most scandalous thing, so as all gravity may be said to be lost amongst us."

The private coach, too, was the last luxury to be given up after financial embarrassment. So we have Lady Flippant, in Wycherley's *Love in a Wood*, saying, "Ah, Mrs. Joyner, nothing grieves me like the putting down my coach! For the fine clothes, the fine lodgings,—let 'em go; for a lodging is as unnecessary a thing to a widow that has a coach, as a hat to a man that has a good peruke. For, as you see about town, she is most probably at home in her coach:—she eats, and drinks, and sleeps in her coach; and for her visits, she receives them in the playhouse." No lady's virtue, according to this cynical dramatist, was proof against a coach and six.

At the time of the introduction of the light, two-seated chariots, ordinary private coaches were also changing in shape. In Charles I's reign they had been both very long and very wide; in his son's time they became much slenderer and less unwieldy. Alterations in this direction were possibly suggested by the ubiquitous and most convenient sedans, and, indeed, there is an allusion to this change of shape in Sir William Davenant's *First Day's Entertainment at Rutland House*, in which, during a dialogue between a Russian and a Londoner, the foreigner says: "I have now left your houses, and am passing through your streets; but not in a coach, for they are uneasily hung, and so narrow that I took them for sedans upon wheels."

Stage-coaches, however, remained just as huge and just as gorgeous as ever. They were built, more particularly in Italy, in the old fashion—unenclosed and curtained. Count Gozzadini describes a State coach built in 1629 for the marriage of Duke Edward Farnese with the Lady Margaret of Tuscany, and as we shall see in a moment, this differed only in the details of its ornamentation from the State coach in which Lord Castlemaine made his public entry into Rome sixty years later.

The body of the Farnese coach, says Gozzadini, "was lined with crimson velvet and gold thread, and the woodwork covered with silver plates, chased and embossed and perforated, in half relief. It could carry eight persons, four on the seats attached to the doors, and four in the back and front. The roof was supported by eight silver columns, on the roof were eight silver vases, and unicorns' heads and lilies in full relief projected from the roof and ends of the body here and there. The roof was composed of twenty sticks, converging from the edge to the centre, which was crowned with a great rose with silver leaves on the outside, and inside by the armorial bearings of the Princes of Tuscany and Farnese held up by cupids. The curtains of the sides and back of the coach were of crimson velvet, embroidered with silver lilies with gold leaves. At the back and front of the coach-carriage were statues of unicorns, surrounded by cupids and wreathed with lilies, grouped round the standards from which the body was suspended; on the tops of the standards were silver vases, with festoons of fruit, and wraught in silver. In the front were also statues of Justice and Mercy, supporting the coachman's seat. The braces suspending the body were of leather, covered with crimson velvet; the wheels and pole were plated with polished silver. The whole was drawn by six horses, with harness and trappings covered with velvet, embroidered with gold and silver thread, and with silver buckles. It is said that twenty-five excellent silversmiths worked at this coach for two years, and used up 25,000 ounces of silver; and that the work was superintended by two master coachbuilders, one from Parma and the other from Piacenza." Lord Castlemaine's procession into Rome contained three hundred and thirty coaches, of which thirteen were his own property; and of these two were State coaches. These likewise were not properly enclosed, and had no glass.

"They were hung," says Thrupp, "inside and out, with beautifully embroidered cloths, the one coach with crimson, the other with azure-blue velvet, and gold and silver work. The roofs were adorned with scroll work and vases gilt; under the roof were curtains of silver fringes, and the ambassador's armorial bearings. The carriage of the principal coach was adorned in front with two large Tritons, of carved wood, gilt all over, that supported a cushion for the coachman between them, and from their shoulders the braces depended. The footboard was formed by a conch shell, between two dolphins. In the rear of the coach were two more Tritons, supporting not only the leather braces of the coach, but two other statues of Neptune and Cybele, who in turn held a royal crown. Below Neptune and Cybele, and projecting backwards, were a lion and a unicorn, and several cupids and wreaths of flowers. The wheels had moulded rims, and the spokes were hidden by curving foliage carving. The second coach had plainer wheels and fewer statues about it."

They may have been magnificent, but they were certainly not very beautiful. Much the same, too, might be said of those coaches in which foreign ambassadors made their public entry into London. In 1660 Evelyn saw the Prince de Ligne, Ambassador-Extraordinary from Spain, make a splendid entry with seventeen coaches, and a month later Pepys was watching "the Duke de Soissons go from his audience with a very great deal of state : his own coach all red velvet covered with gold lace, and drawn by six barbes, and attended by twenty pages very rich in cloths."

In this year, 1660, there was a proclamation against the excessive number of hackney-coaches, and two years later Commissioners were appointed "for reforming the buildings, ways, streets and incumbrances, and regulating the hackney-coaches in the city of London." Of this body Evelyn was sworn a member in May, 1662. Pepys, however, never found any difficulty in obtaining one when he desired, and, indeed, of late years, pressure of business had made a hackney-coach an almost daily necessity. Finally, he found it cheaper to possess one of his own, and the story of this coach is particularly interesting, and may be told in some detail.

Long ago, Mr. Pepys had dreamt of owning a private coach. "Talking long in bed with my wife," he writes on March 2nd, 1661–2, "about our frugal life for the time to come, proposing to her what I could and would do, if I were worth £2000, that is, be a knight, and keep my coach, which pleased her." Times were bad, however, and although Pepys enjoyed many a ride in a friend's coach and witnessed Colonel Blunt's experiments, the great idea did not mature. But one of his particular friends, Thomas Povey, M.P., who had been a colleague of his on the Tangier committee, himself the owner of at least one coach, seems to have kept Pepys's ambitions astir. This was more especially the case in 1665, at which time Mr. Povey had purchased one of the new and already fashionable chariots. This excited Pepys's admiration. "Comes Mr. Povey's coach," he records, "and so rode most nobly, in his most pretty and best-contrived chariot in the world, with many new contrivances, his never having till now, within a day or two, been yet finished." Povey was something of an inventor himself. Evelyn calls him a "nice contriver of all elegancies, and most formal." The necessary money was apparently not forthcoming for a year or two, but in April, 1667, Pepys had a mind "to buy enough ground to build a coach-house and stable; for," says he, "I have had it much in my thoughts lately that it is not too much for me now, in degree or cost, to keep a coach, but contrarily, that I am almost ashamed to be seen in a hackney." Accordingly, Mr. Commander, his lawyer, was bidden to look for a suitable piece of ground. The idea had now taken definite shape, and Pepys was committed. "I find it necessary," he says, "for me, both in respect of honour and the profit of it also, my expence in Hackney coaches being now so great, to keep a coach, and therefore will do it." The next entry shows the first of his disappointments :—

"Mr. Commander tells me, after all, that I cannot have a lease of the ground for my coach-house and stable, till a lawsuit be ended. I am a little sorry, because I am pretty full in my mind of keeping a coach ; but yet," he adds philosophically—the date was June 4th, 1667—"when I think of it again, the Dutch and French both at sea, and we poor, and still out of order, I know not yet what turns there may be."

So the summer passed, and "most of our discourse," he admits, "is about our keeping a coach the next year, which pleases my wife mightily ; and if I continue as able as now, it will save me money." At the beginning of the new year Will Griffin was ordered to make fresh inquiries about the most necessary coach-house, but nothing seems to have been done until the autumn. Then Pepys, more or less it would seem on the spur of the moment, chose a coach for himself, and immediately disliked it. No one seems to have given him the same advice. Some ladies, for instance, Mrs. Pepys amongst them, preferred the large old-fashioned coaches. Others wanted the latest thing from Paris. Says Mrs. Flirt in *The Gentleman Dancing-Master :* "But take notice, I will have no little, dirty, second-hand chariot, new furnished, but a large, sociable, well-painted coach ; nor will I keep it till it be as well-known as myself, and it comes to be called Flirt-coach." Her friend, Monsieur Paris, shrugs his shoulders. "'Tis very well," says he, "you must have your great, gilt, fine painted coach. I'm sure they are grown so common already amongst you that ladies of quality begin to take up with hackneys again." It was felt, no doubt, that fashion in carriages as in everything else would speedily change. Mr. Pepys must have found considerable difficulty in making up his mind. The new chariots were small, light and, so far as he knew, most fashionable ; but possibly they were not quite to his taste, and equally possibly they might not be fashionable in ten years' time. Also they perhaps lacked the solid dignity of the older carriages, and were less likely to attract public attention—two important considerations. In the end, however, he seems to have chosen a large coach of the old style. Mr. Povey saw it, and poor Pepys knew at once that a dreadful mistake had been made.

"He and I . . . talk of my coach," runs the Diary for 30th October, "and I got him to go and see it, where he finds most infinite fault with it, both as to being out of fashion and heavy, with so good reason, that I am mightily glad of his having corrected me in it ; and so I do resolve to have one of his build, and with his advice, both in coach and horses, he being the fittest man in the world for it."

Accordingly on the following Sunday, "Mr. Povey sent his coach for my wife and I to see, which we liked mightily, and will endeavour to have him get us just such another." Mr. Povey thought that his own coachmaker had a replica for sale. Pepys thereupon went down into the neighbourhood of Lincoln's Inn Fields, found the man, but learnt to his disgust that the coach had been sold that very morning. At the end of the week, however, in company with his friend, he "spent the afternoon going up and down the coachmakers in Cow Lane, and did see several, and last did pitch upon a little chariott, whose body was framed, but not covered, at the widow's, that made Mr. Lowther's fine coach; and we are mightily pleased with it, it being light, and will be very genteel and sober; to be covered with leather, but yet will hold four. Being much satisfied with this, I carried him to White Hall. Home, where I give my wife a good account of the day's work."

Having bought the coach, it was necessary to complete the arrangements about a coach-house, and in the same week Pepys fared forth again for the purpose.

"This afternoon I did go out towards Sir D. Gauden's, thinking to have bespoke a place for my coach and horses, when I have them, at the Victualling Office; but find the way so bad and long that I returned, and looked up and down for places elsewhere, in an inne, which I hope to get with more convenience than there."

This not proving satisfactory, Sir Richard Ford was persuaded to lend his own coach-yard. Then follow in quick succession the other entries:—

"*28th November*, 1668.—All the morning at the Office, where, while I was sitting, one comes and tells me that my coach is come. So I was forced to go out, and to Sir Richard Ford's, where I spoke to him, and he is very willing to have it brought

I

in, and stand there: and so I ordered it, to my great content, it being mighty pretty, only the horses do not please me, and, therefore, resolve to have better."

"*29th November.*—This morning my coachman's clothes come home and I like the livery mightily. . . . Sir W. Warren . . . tells me, as soon as he saw my coach yesterday, he wished that the owner might not contract envy by it; but I told him it was now manifestly for my profit to keep a coach, and that, after employments like mine for eight years, it were hard if I could not be thought to be justly able to do that."[1]

"*30th November.*—My wife after dinner, went abroad the first time in her coach, calling on Roger Pepys, and visiting Mrs. Creed, and my cozen Turner. Thus ended this month, with very good intent, but most expenseful to my purse on things of pleasure, having furnished my wife's closet and the best chamber, and a coach and horses, that ever I knew in the world; and I am put into the greatest condition of outward state that ever I was in, or hoped ever to be, or desired; and this at a time when we do daily expect great changes in this office; and by all reports we must, all of us, turn out."

"*2nd December.*—Abroad with my wife, the first time that ever I rode in my own coach, which do make my heart rejoice, and praise God, and pray him to bless it to me and continue it."

"*3rd December.*— . . . and so home, it being mighty pleasure to go alone with my poor wife, in a coach of our own, to a play, and makes us appear mighty great, I think, in the world; at least, greater than ever I could, or my friends for me, have once expected; or, I think, than ever any of my family ever yet lived, in my memory, but my cozen Pepys in Salisbury Court."

"*4th December*.—I carried my wife . . . to Smithfield, where they sit in the coach, while Mr. Pickering, who meets me at Smithfield and I, and W. Hewer and a friend of his, a jockey did go about to see several pairs of horses, for my coach; but it was late, and we agreed on none, but left it to another time: but here I do see instances of a piece of craft and cunning that I never dreamed of, concerning the buying and choosing of horses."

There were plenty of horses to be had, it seems, but either Mr. Pepys did not like them or he was afraid of being cheated. "Up and down," he is recording a week or so later, "all the afternoon about horses, and did see the knaveries and tricks of jockeys. At last, however, we concluded upon giving £50 for a fine pair of black horses we saw this day se'nnight; and so set Mr. Pickering down near his house, whom I am much beholden to, for his care herein, and he hath admired skill, I perceive, in this business, and so home." So the horses were changed, and for a while Mr. Pepys was obliged to revert to the despised hackney, his "coachman being this day about breaking of my horses to the coach, they having never yet drawn." Towards the end of the month the new horses were ready, and their master made his first ride behind them on a visit to the Temple, though later in the day he was again using the old pair, "not daring yet to use the others too much, but only to enter them." Then, before the new year, came the first mishap.

"Up, and vexed a little to be forced to pay 40s. for a glass of my coach, which was broke the other day, nobody knows how, within the door, while it was down; but I do doubt that I did break it myself with my knees."

At the beginning of February another misfortune is recorded :—

"Just at Holborn Circuit the bolt broke, that holds the fore-wheels to the perch, and so the horses went away with them, and left the coachman and us ; but being near our coachmaker's and we staying in a little ironmonger's shop, we were presently supplied with another."

Accidents of this kind were continually happening. Glasses smashed, bolts broke, and, what seems incredible, doors were lost! Even so late as 1710, a reward of 30s. was offered for a lost door. "Lost," runs this remarkable advertisement, "the side door of a Chariot, painted Coffee Colour, with a Round Cipher in the Pannel, Lin'd with White Cloath embos'd with Red, having a Glass in one Frame, and White Canvas in another, with Red Strings to the Frames."

To return to Pepys. In a month or two another matter connected with his coach was occupying his attention. There were some people who did not think that a man in the comparatively humble position of Secretary to the Admiralty had any right to possess a coach, even though, in its owner's estimation, it might be "genteel and sober."

"To the Park," he is recording in April, "my wife and I ; and here Sir W. Coventry did first see me and my wife in a coach of our own ; and so did also this night the Duke of York, who did eye my wife mightily. But I begin to doubt that my being so much seen in my own coach at this time, may be observed to my prejudice, but I must venture it now."

This was no idle fear, for in a while there was printed an ill-written and scurrilous pamphlet called *Plane Truth*, *or Closet Discorse betwixt Pepys and Hewer*, in which the following passage occurs :—

"There is one thing more you must be mightily sorry for with all speed. Your presumption in your coach in which you daily ride as if you had been son and heir to the great Emperor Neptune, or as if you had been infallibly to have succeeded him in his government of the Ocean, all which was presumption in the highest degree. First, you had upon the forepart of your chariot, tempestuous waves and wrecks of ships ; on your left hand, forts and great guns, and ships a fighting; on your right hand was a fair harbour and galleys riding, with their flags and pennants spread, kindly saluting each other, just like P[epys] and H[ewer—his chief clerk]."

How far Pepys's carriage was decorated is not known, though this description does not tally in the least with Pepys's own. In any case, he took no notice of such attacks, and so far from making his coach less conspicuous, arranged to have it newly painted and varnished.

"19*th April*, 1669.—After dinner out again, and, calling about my coach, which was at the coachmaker's, and hath been there for these two or three days, to be new painted, and the window-frames gilt against next May-day, went on with my hackney to White Hall."

A few days later he gave orders for some "new sort of varnish" to be used on the standards at a cost of forty shillings, this being in his view very cheap. Indeed, "the doing of the biggest coach all over," he learnt, "comes not above £6." On his next visit to the coachmaker, he was surprised to find several great ladies "sitting in the body of a coach that must be ended tomorrow . . . eating of bread and butter and drinking ale." His own coach had been silvered over, "but no varnish yet laid on, so I put it in a way of doing." A few hours later he called back again,

"and there vexed to see nothing yet done to my coach, at three in the afternoon; but I set it in doing, and stood by till eight at night, and saw the painter varnish it which is pretty to see how every doing it over do make it more and more yellow: and it dries as fast in the sun as it can be laid on almost; and most coaches are, now-a-days, done so, and it is very pretty when laid on well, and not too pale, as some are, even to show the silver. Here I did make the workmen drink, and saw my coach cleaned and oyled."

And so eager was he to have it without delay that his coachman and horses were sent to fetch it that very evening, and on the following gala day, May 1st,

"we went alone through the town with our new liveries of serge, and the horses' manes and tails tied with red ribbons, and the standards gilt with varnish, and all clean, and green reines, the people did mightily look upon us; and, the truth is, I did not see any coach more pretty, though more gay, than ours all the day. But we set out, out of humour—I because Betty, whom I expected, was not come to go with us; and my wife that I would sit on the same seat with her, which she likes not, being so fine: and she then expected me to meet Sheres, which we did in Pell Mell, and against my will, I was forced to take him into the coach, but was sullen all day almost, and little complaisant; the day being unpleasing, though the Park full of coaches, but dusty and windy, and cold, and now and then a little dribbling of rain; and what made it worse, there were so many hackney-coaches as spoiled the sight of the gentlemen's; and so we had little pleasure."

Henceforth Mr. Pepys, in spite of sundry warnings from his friend Mr. Povey and others, continued to use his coach, and although perhaps as he grew older, his coach was less brilliantly adorned, there seems no reason to suppose that he ever regretted its purchase.

Though it is not my intention to speak in any detail of public conveyances, a word must be said here of the stage-coaches,[1] which made their appearance on English roads in 1640. These were large coaches, leather-curtained at first—glass does not seem to have been used until 1680—and capable of seating six or eight passengers. Their chief feature was the huge basket strapped to the back.

"There is of late," says Chamberlayne in his well-known *Present State of Great Britain* (1649), "such an admirable commodiousness both for men and women, to travel from London to the principal towns in the country, that the like hath not been known in the world; and that is by stage-coaches, wherein one may be transported to any place sheltered from foul weather and foul ways, free from endangering of one's health and one's body by hard jogging or over-violent motion on horseback; and this not only at the low price of about a shilling for every five miles, but with such velocity and speed in an hour as the foreign post can make but in one day."

Of course, there was opposition to these public coaches. In 1662, when there was not a round dozen of them, one writer was already exhorting their extinction on the ground that simple country gentlemen and

[1] The reader is referred for the fullest information on the subject of these stage-coaches to Mr. Charles G. Harper's *Stage-Coach and Mail in Days of Yore*. 2 vols. London, 1903.

their simple country wives could now come to London without due occasion, and there learn all the vice and luxury that were rampant. So in 1673, in a singular production called *The Grand Concern of England*, amongst the many proposals set forth for the country's good, was one "that the Multitude of Stage Coaches and Caravans be suppressed." One or two pamphlets of no particular interest appeared, both for and against these coaches, but it may be sufficient here to observe that they steadily increased in numbers and maintained their existence until the mail-coaches finally superseded them.

One other public carriage of this time also deserves mention. This was the *carosse à cinq sous*, which appeared in the streets of Paris in 1662. The history of this primitive omnibus is well told by Mr. Henry Charles Moore.[1]

"The leading spirits in this enterprise were the Duc de Rouanès, Governor of Poitou, the Marquis de Sourches, Grand Prévôt, the Marquis de Crenan, Grand Cup-bearer, and Blaise Pascal, the author of *Lettres Provinciales*. The idea was Pascal's, but not being sufficiently wealthy to carry it out unaided, he laid the matter before his friend the Duc de Rouanès, who suggested that a company should be formed to start the vehicles. Pascal consented to this being done, and the Duc set to work at once to prevail upon members of the aristocracy to take shares in the venture." After obtaining a royal decree, "seven vehicles to carry eight passengers each, all inside, were built, and on March 18th, 1662, they began running. The first one was timed to start at seven o'clock in the morning, but an hour or two earlier a huge crowd had assembled to witness the

[1] *Omnibuses and Cabs.* London, 1902.

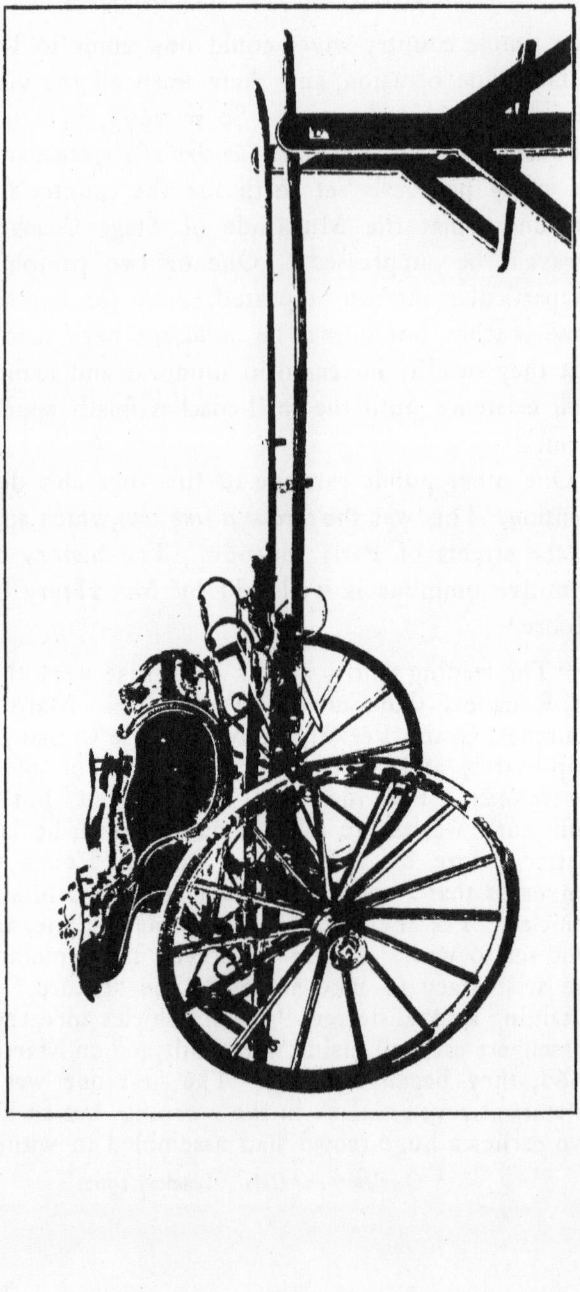

Early (?) French Gig at the South Kensington Museum

inauguration ceremony, which was performed by two Commissaires of the Châtelet, attired in their official robes. Accompanying them were four guards of the Grand Prévôt, twenty men of the City Archers, and a troop of cavalry. The procession, on arriving at the line of route, divided into two parts, one Commissaire and half of the attendants proceeded to the Luxembourg, and the others to the Porte St. Antoine. At the latter place three of the twopenny-halfpenny coaches were stationed, the other four being at the Luxembourg. Each Commissaire then made a speech, in which he pointed out the boon that *carosses à cinq sous* would be to the public, and laid great stress on the fact that they would start punctually at certain times whether full or empty. Moreover, he warned the people that the king was determined to punish severely any person who interfered with the coaches, their drivers, conductors, or passengers. The public was also warned that any person starting similar vehicles without permission would be fined 3000 francs, and his horses and coaches confiscated.

"At the conclusion of his address, the Commissaire commanded the coachmen to advance, and, after giving them a few words of advice and caution, presented each one with a long blue coat, with the City arms embroidered on the front in brilliant colours. Having donned their livery, the drivers returned to their vehicles and climbed up to their seats. Then the command to start was given, and the two vehicles drove off amidst a scene of tremendous enthusiasm. The first coach each way carried no passengers—a very unbusinesslike arrangement—the conductor sitting inside in solitary state. But the next two, which were sent off a quarter of an hour after the first, started work in earnest, and it need scarcely be said that there were no lack of passengers. The difficulty experienced was in preventing people from crowding in after the eight seats were occupied. At the beginning of every journey the struggle to get into the coach was repeated, and many charming costumes were ruined in the crush. Paris, in short, went mad over its *carosses à cinq sous*, and the excitement soon spread to the suburbs, sending their inhabitants flocking to the city to see the new vehicles. But very few of the visitors managed to obtain a ride, for day by day the rush for seats became greater. The king himself had a ride in one coach, and the aristocracy and wealthy classes hastened to follow his example, struggling with their poorer brethren to obtain a seat. Many persons who possessed private coaches daily drove to the starting-point, and yet failed to get a drive in one for a week or two.

"Four other routes were opened in less than four months, but at last the fashionable craze came to an end, and as soon as the upper classes ceased to patronise the new coaches the middle and lower classes found that it was cheaper to walk than to ride. The result was that Pascal, who died only five months after the coaches began running, lived long enough to see the vehicles travelling to and fro, half, and sometimes quite, empty.

"For many months after Pascal's death the coaches lingered on, but every week found them less patronised, and eventually they were discontinued. They had never been of any real utility, and were regarded by the public much in the same light as we regard a switchback railway."

And, indeed, it was a century and a half before the next omnibus was tried.

So then, at the middle of the century, when heavy and slow stage-coaches were making their appearance on the English country roads, and the unsuccessful *carosse à cinq sous* was being tried in the streets of Paris, the success of the *berlin*, the *brouette*, and other chariots, was in process of remodelling men's ideas upon the most feasible carriage for town use. The older coaches, as I have said, were still retained for particular occasions, and, indeed, continued to be built with more ornamentation than ever before. The very spokes of the wheels were decorated, paintings appeared on the panels, and every inch of the coach made as brilliant as possible. France in particular possessed carriages of the most gorgeous possible description. These were not only entirely gilded over, but in some cases actually bejewelled. The richest stuffs lined their interiors, and masters painted their panels. Immense sums were spent. There is preserved at Toulouse a carriage of this date which shows most of these features. The interior "is, or rather was, lined with white brocade embroidered with a diaper of pink roses, the roof being lined with the same, while its angles are hidden by little smiling cupids gilded from top to toe. The surface of the panels is, or rather was, a piece of opaque white, exceedingly well varnished, and edged with a thick moulding of pink roses ; the foliage, instead of being green, was highly gilded and burnished."

But the ever-increasing traffic rendered necessary a much smaller vehicle than these monstrosities for general use, and this led, somewhere about 1670, to the introduction of the *gig*. This was a French invention, which, while no doubt the logical outcome of the *brouette*, bore resemblance to the old Roman *cisium*, and led ultimately to the cabriolets, once so popular both in France and England. Certain experiments tending towards a gig had been made earlier in the century with a chair fixed to a small cart. The first successful gig was a slender, two-wheeled contrivance, "the body little more than a shell," says Thrupp, provided with a hood "composed of three iron hoop-sticks joined in the middle to fall upwards." It was the prototype of the *calèche* in France, the *carriole* of Norway, the *calesso* of Naples, and the *volante* of Cuba. Gozzadini describes one of them as "an affair with a curved seat fixed on two long bending shafts, placed in front on the back of the horse and behind upon the two wheels." They were introduced into Florence, he says, in 1672, and "so increased in numbers that in a few years there were nearly a thousand in the city." An early gig of this kind is preserved at South Kensington. It is a forlorn-looking vehicle. The body is curved, but there is no hood. The seat is absurdly small and "beneath the shafts are two long straps of leather and a windlass to tighten them—this apparatus was, no doubt, to regulate the spring of the vehicle to the road travelled over."

The gig speedily underwent several minor changes of form. In France it was known as *calèche*[1] or *chaise*, in England, as *calash*, *calesh*, or *chaise*, in America as *shay*. Unfortunately there is small mention of them in con-

[1] It was over a *calèche* presented by the Chevalier de Grammont to Charles II, that the famous quarrel took place between Lady Castlemaine and Miss Stewart, afterwards the Duchess of Richmond. The ladies had been complaining that coaches with glass windows, but lately introduced, did not allow a sufficiently free display of their charms, whence followed the gift of a French *calèche* which cost two thousand livres. When the queen drove out in it, both the ladies agreed with de Grammont that it afforded far better opportunities than a coach for showing off their figures, and both endeavoured to get the first loan of it. In the fierce quarrel that followed Miss Stewart came off the conqueror.

temporary writings, and one is left to suppose that for some time they did not, except in certain cities, prove serious rivals to the *berlins* and other four-wheeled chariots. It may be that the *berlin* itself was taken as a model from which these lighter carriages were evolved. You had first the big double *berlins* for four people, then you had a *vis-à-vis* for two or more persons facing each other. Later the front part of the carriage would be cut away for the sake of lightness. When not covered such a vehicle as this seems to have been known as a *berlingot*. Two could travel in these *berlingots* sitting side by side, "while a third person might travel uncomfortably in front on a kind of movable seat, which was not much patronised; for it was not only dangerous, but what was much worse in the eyes of the grand court gentlemen who used them—ridiculous." There was also evolved a smaller and narrower *berlin* with the front cut away and capable of holding only one passenger, called the *désobligeante*. The bodies of the ordinary chaises, which seated one or two people, seem to have differed from those of the older *berlins* in being placed partly below the frame. There were no side doors, but one at the back which opened horizontally. When and where all such changes were made, however, it is impossible to say. The accounts, such as they are, are often contradictory, and the same names used to describe what are obviously not identical carriages. But the two-wheeled gig having appeared there was nothing to prevent improvements of every conceivable sort or shape, and innumerable hybrid carriages appeared, some of which are only known by name.

There is mention of a truly remarkable calash which

was tried in Dublin in 1685. Exactly who the inventor was is not known, but Sir Richard Bulkeley interested himself in the experiments, and read a paper on his carriage before the Royal Society. Evelyn was one of those who were present on this occasion.

"Sir Richard Bulkeley," he says, "described to us a model of a chariot he had invented which it was not possible to overthrow in whatever uneven way it was drawn, giving us a wonderful relation of what it had performed in that kind, for ease, expedition, and safety; there were some inconveniences yet to be remedied—it would not contain more than one person; was ready to take fire every few miles; and being placed and playing on no fewer than ten rollers, it made a most prodigious noise, almost intolerable."

It is to be deeply regretted that there is no print of this remarkable carriage, but further details may be found in a letter, dated May 5th, 1685, from Sir Richard Bulkeley himself.

"Sir William Petty," he writes, "Mr. Molyneux, and I have spent this day in making experiments with a new invented calesh, along with the inventor thereof; 'tis he that was in London when I was there, but he never made any of these caleshes there, for his invention is much improv'd since he came from thence: it is in all points different from any machine I have ever seen: it goes on two wheels, carries one person, and is light enough. As for its performance, though it hangs not on braces, yet it is easier than the common coach, both in the highway, in ploughed fields, cross the ridges, directly and obliquely. A common coach will overturn, if one wheel go on a superficies a foot and a half higher than that of the other; but this will admit of the difference of three feet and a half in height of

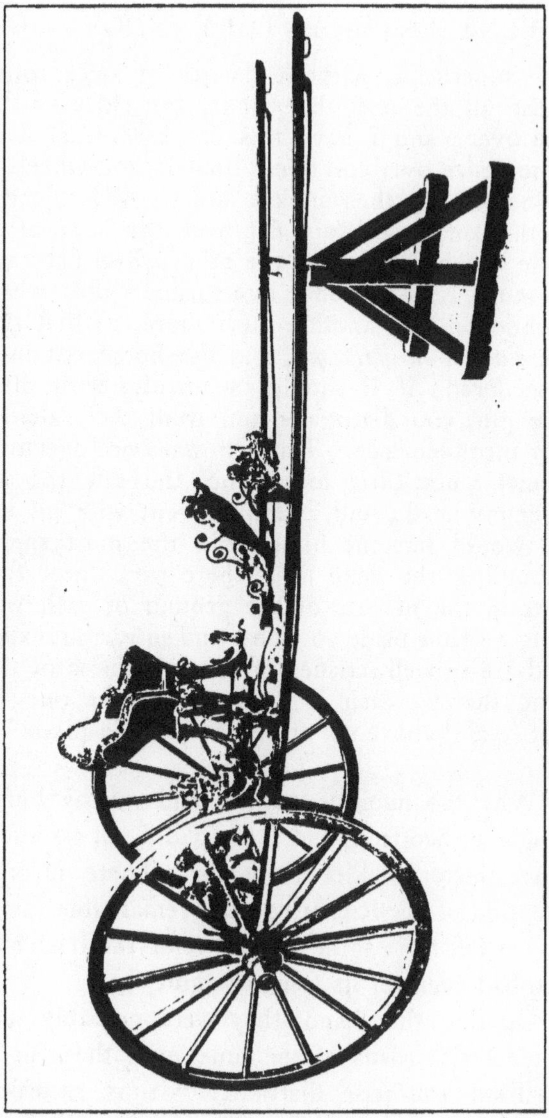

Early Italian Gig at the South Kensington Museum

the superficies, without danger of overturning. We chose all the irregular banks, the sides of ditches to run over; and I have this day seen it, at five several times, turn over and over; that is, the wheels so overturned as that their spokes laid parallel to the horizon, so that one wheel laid flat over the head of him that rode in the Calesh, and the other wheel flat under him; so much I all but once overturned. But what I have mentioned was another turn more, so that the wheels were again *in statu quo*, and the horse not in the least disordered: if it should be unruly, with the help of one pin, you disengage him from the Calesh without any inconvenience. I myself was once overturned, and knew it not, till I looked up, and saw the wheel flat over my head; and, if a man went with his eyes shut, he would imagine himself in the most smooth way, though, at the same time, there were three feet difference in the heights of the ground of each wheel. In fine, we have made so many, and so various experiments, and are so well satisfied of the usefulness of the invention, that we each of us have bespoke one; they are not (plain) above six or eight pounds a-piece."

Why the nobility, gentry, and worthy burgesses of England, Scotland, and Ireland did not go and do likewise, history hides from us. There is no further mention of Sir Richard's truly remarkable carriage, and one is left to imagine that some of the Irish roads were too bad even for its freakish agility.

On the other hand, they were probably superior to the Scottish roads of the time, even those in the more civilised southern districts. "It is recorded," says Croal, "that in 1678"—the year after the founding of the Coach and Coach-Harness Makers' Company in London—"the difficulties in the way of rapid communication were such that an agreement was made to run a coach between Edinburgh and Glasgow, a distance of forty-four miles, which was to be drawn by six horses, and to perform the journey to Glasgow and back in six days!"

Cross-country travelling, indeed, was very bad, and the rough tracks over which the heavy stage-coaches rumbled along would have proved too much for the lighter chariots and gigs which were so popular in town. I may conclude this chapter by quoting an amusing description of such cross-country travelling at the end of the century, taken from Sir John Vanbrugh's *Provoked Husband.* A family is going in its private coach from Yorkshire to London:—

Lord Townley. Mr. Moody, your servant; I am glad to see you in London. I hope all the family is well.

John Moody. Thanks be praised, your honour, they are all in pretty good heart, thof' we have had a power of crosses upo' the road.

Lady Grace. I hope my Lady has no hurt, Mr. Moody.

John. Noa, an't please your ladyship, she was never in better humour: There's money enough stirring now.

Manly. What has been the matter, John?

John. Why, we came up in such a hurry, you mun think that our tackle was not so tight as it should be.

Manly. Come, tell us all: pray how do they travel?

John. Why i' the auld coach, Measter; and cause my Lady loves to do things handsome, to be sure, she would have a couple of cart horses clapt to th' four old geldings, that neighbours might see she went up to London in her coach and six! And so Giles Joulter the ploughman rides postilion!

. . . . . .

Lord Townley. And when do you expect them here, John?

John. Why, we were in hopes to ha' come yesterday, an' it had no' been that th' owld wheaze-belly horse tired; and then we were so cruelly loaden, that the two forewheels came crash down at once in Waggon-Rut Lane; and there we lost four hours 'fore we could set things to rights again.

Manly. So they bring all their baggage with the coach then?

John. Ay, ay, and good store on't there is. Why, my Lady's gear alone were as much as filled four portmantel trunks, besides the great deal box that heavy Ralph and the monkey sit on behind.

Lady Grace. Well, Mr. Moody, and pray how many are there within the coach?

John. Why, there's my Lady and his Worship, and the young squoire, and Miss Jenny, and the fat lap-dog, and my lady's maid Mrs. Handy, and Doll Tripe the cook; that's all. Only Doll puked a little with riding backward, so they hoisted her into the coach-box, and then her stomach was easy.

Lady Grace. Oh! I see 'em go by me. Ah! ha!

John. Then, you mun think, Measter, there was some stowage for the belly, as well as th' back too; such cargoes of plum cake, and baskets of tongues, and biscuits and cheese, and cold boiled beef, and then in

K

case of sickness, bottles of cherry-brandy, plague-water, sack, tent, and strong beer, so plenty as made the owld coach crack again! Mercy upon 'em! and send 'em all well to town, I say.

Manly. Ay! and well on't again, John.

John. Ods bud! Measter, you're a wise mon; and for that matter, so am I. Whoam's whoam, I say; I'm sure we got but little good e'er we turned our backs on't. Nothing but mischief! Some devil's trick or other plagued us, aw th' day lung. Crack goes one thing: Bawnce goes another. Woa, says Roger. Then souse! we are all set fast in a sleugh. Whaw! cries Miss; scream go the maids; and bawl! just as thof' they were struck! And so, mercy on us! this was the trade from morning to night.

COMPILED BY
W. C. A. BLEW.

THE old stage-coaches, except in very far-away districts, had long been off the road, and Clark's Brighton coach, The Age, was the last link left between the old days, when coaching was in its zenith, and those to come, which were but little dreamed of then, when we were once more to witness its revival, and pretty nearly a dozen coaches rattling down Piccadilly every day. The Age, of which Mr. Eden, who afterwards put on the High Wycombe coach, was one of the supporters, after having stopped for a year or two, was started again and ran through 1862, on alternate days, driven by the Duke of Beaufort, Sir George Wombwell, or Clark, from the Globe, Baker Street, every Tuesday, Thursday and Saturday, at 10.30 A.M., calling at the Gloucester, in Oxford Street; Griffin's Green Man and Still, also in Oxford Street; the Universal Office at Regent's Circus, and Hatchett's White Horse Cellar,—the time at the latter place was 11 o'clock—both in Piccadilly; then on to Slark's office, Knightsbridge, after which stoppage they fairly began to go,. and travelled quickly along through Richmond, Kingston, Leatherhead, Dorking, Horsham, Cowfold, and Henfield, arriving at Brighton at 6 P.M., returning from Castle Square on the alternate days. The distance was sixty-two miles, which makes the time look slow; but it must be remembered that there were five stoppages before the London stones were left behind, and a good deal of time was lost in picking up parcels and passengers; while in older days heavily laden coaches, like the Royal Sovereign to Leamington, and many others, used to be allowed an hour from the City to the Marble Arch.

In the year 1854, Mr. Charles Lawrie, who at that time horsed the coach from Kingston to Dorking with bays and browns, had a picture of the Age painted, and it was engraved for Clark's benefit through the kindness of the same gentleman. The off-side leader had originally run in Kershaw's Baldock and Hitchin coach, but was bought when the concern was sold off, after the road had been for a century occupied by the Kershaw family. One of the wheelers had been employed in the duty of drawing an old lady's carriage, but having one day run away, and, it was said, caused the death of its owner, it came to coach-work. The team, as represented in the picture, was the property of Dick Carpenter, who used to drive the original Age with Sir St. Vincent Cotton, and who it is believed died in Hanwell Asylum. What next became of the picture is not known; but, soon after the Brighton road was revived, a picture of the new coach made its appearance, in which the grouping, &c., was identical with that of Mr. Lawrie's picture, only the colours were changed. In the November of the year 1888, however, the original painting turned up at Albert Gate, its price being, it is believed, 35*l*.

After the Duke, Sir George, and Clark had hung up their whips in 1862, coaching seemed to be, in the expressive language of the Ring, 'dead settled.' For four long years the sound of the bars and the echo of the horn were not heard in Piccadilly, and the ancient steps of Hatchett's were deserted by all save those who were lodging in the hotel. In 1866, however, a slight sign of the coming revival appeared on the coaching horizon. Captain Haworth led the way, and was joined by the Duke of Beaufort, Colonel Armitage, Mr. Lawrie, Mr. B. J. Angell, Lord H. Thynne, Mr. Chandos Pole, Mr. C. Lyley, with another or two. This little band instituted a subscription coach, which they called the Old Times, and ran it to Brighton, on alternate days, with William Pratt as their professional coachman. In the course of its brief season the coach carried a good many passengers; but the venture turned out a failure; coach, horses, harness, and all belongings being sold at Tattersall's in the autumn, when the confederacy was broken up.

The pecuniary failure of the opening year of the coaching revival, however, so far from tending to damp the enthusiasm for the road, appears to have stimulated it; as in 1867 we find Mr. Chandos Pole, Mr. Angell, and the Duke of Beaufort engaged in a much more ambitious venture than that of 1866. This took the form of running a coach up and down, between London and Brighton, every day. William Pratt, who had formerly driven a coach between Malvern and Cheltenham, retained his old berth, and, with George Dackombe as guard, drove on 'one side of the road,' while Alfred Tedder (who remained on the Brighton road till the time of his death, in December 1872), was on the other coach, with Phillips as his guard. The London terminus was the White Horse Cellar; the Albion Hotel was the corresponding point at London-super-Mare; and the coaches were two new ones, built by Holland & Holland. Mr. Chandos Pole worked out of Brighton; Mr. Chandos-Pole-Gell, a sleeping partner in the concern, for his name did not appear in the list of proprietors, horsed the coach from Cuckfield to Friars Oak; the Duke of Beaufort had the middle ground, and Mr. Angell found the horses for the two stages in and out of London, the two coaches meeting for lunch at Horley.

The Brighton road did not, however, have the revival all to itself in 1867, as another coaching disciple arose in the person of Mr. C. A. R. Hoare, lately Master of the Vale of White Horse hounds, who in the autumn started a coach called the Exquisite, between Beckenham and Sevenoaks, the horses for which were provided by E. Fownes. When the Brighton double-coach was taken off for the season, the horses belonging to Mr. Angell were sold; but Mr. Chandos Pole determined to run to Brighton on his own account all the winter. Mr. Chandos-Pole-Gell agreed to let his horses remain; some additional ones, several of which had been working during the summer in the Ilfracombe coach, were purchased, and the coach ran 'single' all the winter, with Tedder and Dackombe as coachman and guard.

Some years previously Mr. Chandos Pole bought, at Gloucester, what was probably the last of the old 'Patent Mails.' It had been newly done up, and was lettered for 'Gloucester and Carmarthen,' the continuation of the old London and Gloucester mail, which in pre-railroad days Alfred Tedder had driven between London and Oxford. This coach was used by Mr. Chandos Pole on the Brighton road during the winter season of 1867–68, because it was lighter than either of those by Messrs. Holland & Holland, and quite roomy enough for the passengers likely to patronise the undertaking; and so it came about that Tedder, at the outset of the revival, found himself on the box of the identical coach he had driven years before. It must have been terribly dreary work, however, and fortune made but a poor requital for the proprietor's pluck and perseverance. The professionals often had the coach to themselves, when, of course, no 'tips' accrued to relieve the monotony of their drive; and the coach barely earned its tolls.

The summer of 1868 saw coaching once more to the fore. Mr. Chandos-Pole-Gell (brother to the late Mr. Chandos Pole).

who assumed the name of Gell in 1863, now joined his brother; and the partners carried on the Brighton road upon the same lines as during the preceding season; that is to say, two coaches were put on. Tedder and Phillips still kept each other company; while, Pratt having left the service, E. Cracknell became the professional on the other side of the road (when Mr. Chandos Pole had to give up driving through illness), Dackombe remaining as guard. At the beginning of the season Mr. Chandos-Pole-Gell horsed the coach from London to Streatham, Mr. Chandos Pole being responsible for the horses thence to Stoat's Nest. At the latter place Mr. Chandos-Pole-Gell's horses were used to Merstham and thence to Lowfield Heath, from which point Mr. Chandos Pole ran to Brighton. In the course of the season, however, Mr. G. Meek was desirous of joining the confederacy, and horsed the coaches between Lowfield Heath and Staplefield Common, where he lived. Mr. Charles Hoare appeared for the second year in the *rôle* of coach proprietor; but this time ran from London to Sevenoaks instead of between Beckenham and Sevenoaks, with Comley as professional coachman, and Ike Simmons as guard. Mr. Hoare's coach was another link with the past. It was one of the mails built in the year 1831 by Wright, and when it was bought by Messrs. Holland & Holland (by whom it was let to Mr. Hoare on the usual mileage terms), it had V. R. and a crown on it, a proof that it had seen mail service during the reign of Her Majesty. It had, of course, a single seat only behind for the guard, whose blunderbuss case was opposite, and where the second seat would be. The hind boot opened at the top, beneath the guard's feet, so that he could easily drop his mail-bags into the depths below. In order to give as much room as possible for the letter-bags, the hind boot was deeper than usual; and, differing from the general plan, the boot was brought out flush with the body of the coach. In order to allow of the extra depth of boot, the hind axle was bent downwards. The 'old school' will perhaps smile at notice being drawn to these details; but they will pardon the digression on remembering that since coaches were driven off the road, a race has arisen to which the 'revival' is history, and the fashion of the Park drags a pattern. Such, at all events, was the Sevenoaks coach when it first came into the possession of Messrs. Holland & Holland; but, in order to adapt it to modern requirements, the guard's seat was lengthened to carry four, and a like number of passengers were accommodated where the guard's armoury had erstwhile been. This old mail eventually became 'Cooper's coach' on the Box Hill and Dorking road, and Mr. Cooper was driving it when, in 1875, the pole broke within 150 yards of the journey's end. Let into what is technically known as the 'boot tread' (that is to say, the step on the front boot), on each side was a lamp with the object of throwing a clear light on both roller bolts. A pleasing wind-up to the coaching season of 1868 was the presentation of a well-deserved testimonial, in the shape of a silver flagon, to Mr. Chandos Pole and a silver tankard to Tedder.

'The light of other days' shone brilliantly in 1869, an *annus mirabilis* in the history of the coaching revival. The Duke of Beaufort was, indeed, no longer a patron of the road; but Mr. Chandos Pole and Mr. Chandos-Pole-Gell were still faithful to the bench, and were now helped in their undertaking by Lord Londesborough, Colonel Stracey-Clitherow (who, as 'Tom' Stracey—his real name is Edward—had long been known as a first class coachman), and Mr. G. Meek. The coach was now but a single one, running each way on alternate days. The London terminus was the Ship, Charing Cross, the choice being made in order to avoid the clatter over the stones between that place and Hatchett's; for wood and asphalte were then unknown, unlaid. Tedder was still professional; and we find a note to the effect that in this year 'shouldering'—the time-honoured subject of a time-honoured toast—was abolished, in theory at least. Lord Londesborough was responsible for the horses to Croydon, Colonel Clitherow ran thence to Redhill, Mr. Chandos-Pole-Gell to Lowfield Heath; then came Mr. Meek to Staplefield Common, where

Mr. Chandos Pole came on, and went to Brighton. There was, however, one other circumstance which in a marked degree contributed to the success, not of the Brighton road only, but subsequently of other routes as well. It was this: in 1869 the proprietors were fortunate enough to secure as Honorary Secretary Mr. Arthur Guillum Scott, of the India Office, who freely advertised the coach, and brought to bear upon its welfare untiring energy, perseverance, and great judgment. Everybody knew about the Brighton coach now; handbills and posters were encountered everywhere; cards, setting forth the hours and places of its arrival and departure, found their way to the chief continental hotels, and to go to Brighton by road was soon the proper thing to do; so the speculation prospered, and the horses found their loads much heavier than did those which drew Mr. Chandos Pole's coach in the winter of 1867–68. In short, the season was said to be remunerative, and when the coach was taken off the road at the beginning of October, it was with the understanding that the succeeding spring would again find it running.

Meantime Mr. Charles Hoare had chosen Tunbridge Wells as his destination, though between that place and Sevenoaks the horsing was entrusted to Mr. W. Pawley, who used to run platers at the Bromley Steeplechases, and nephew to the Mr. Pawley who ran a coach from Sevenoaks, in Kent, to some place in the neighbourhood of Sloane Street down to the year 1851. The example of the three previous years tempted Lord Carrington to enrol himself in the list of coach proprietors. Preferring a partner to share the driving and the profits—or losses—he met with one in the person of Mr. Angell, who had now left the Brighton confederacy, and the two started a coach to Windsor, *viâ* Hounslow, with G. Dackombe, late of the Brighton, as coachman and guard. That it was capitally horsed and driven need not be said; but if proof be wanted it is forthcoming in the fact that the journey of 21 miles was sometimes performed in an hour and fifty-five minutes. The proprietors were unremitting in their attention to passengers; indeed one gallant colonel was so pleased with Mr. Angell's performance that he insisted on his accepting half a sovereign, which the recipient used to wear on his watch-chain. It was in 1869, too, that the memories of the Oxford road were revived; for Mr. John Eden, with Lord Aveland, and one or two more as subscribers, put on the Prince of Wales coach, which started from the Scotch Stores, Oxford Street, to High Wycombe, *viâ* Gerrard's Cross, following the course of the Wendover 'bus through Uxbridge; E. Elston was the first coachman and guard. Mr. Wm. Sheather, subsequently well known on the Dorking road, found the horses, and continued to do so, we believe, as long as the coach ran.

In 1870 Mr. Hoare still ran to Tunbridge Wells, but, instead of working single-handed, had for partners Lord Kenlis, Colonel Chaplin and Colonel Hathorn; while General Dickson and Captain Candy tried their luck with a coach to Virginia Water. This venture, however, was not a success, and, as it worked on Sundays, scandalised some of the weaker brethren. The Windsor coach, in the same hands as in the preceding year, had a rather merry season, and, during the Ascot week, did good business by running through to the racecourse, leaving Hatchett's at ten in the morning. On Tuesday, Wednesday and Friday the fare was 1*l.*, with 10*s.* extra for the box-seat, but on Thursday this tariff was doubled. This, however, was its last season for some time. The Brighton road still flourished, though Mr. Chandos-Pole-Gell's name was no longer found in the list of proprietors. As the horses were stabled in Farm Street Mews, through the kindness of Mr. Willis, a great friend to the undertaking, the Ship at Charing Cross was given up, and the coach once more started from Hatchett's. The usual arrangement was for Colonel Stracey-Clitherow to drive as far as Redhill, where he was relieved by Mr. Chandos Pole, who made way for Mr. G. Meek at Lowfield Heath, Mr. C. Pole again taking the reins at Friars Oak. When his services were required Tedder was still professional, and McIntyre guard.

In the autumn of 1870, it was announced that Sir Henry de Bathe and Colonel Withington would run a coach from Hatchett's to the Fleur-de-Lys Hotel at Canterbury. It was to be called the Old Stager, and its colours were to be those of the I Zingari—black, red and yellow—a very sporting programme indeed.

At this juncture, the Hon. Sec., the indefatigable Mr. A. G. Scott, had his say, and, having convinced Sir Henry and the Colonel that they were about to embark on an undertaking which would prove most unprofitable, succeeded in inducing them to run from London to Dorking instead. They took his advice, and were, in 1871, the first to open out this very favourite road, with F. Moon as coachman and Simmons as guard; while, taking a leaf out of the Windsor book, the coach ran to Epsom on all four days of the summer meeting there.

For some reason or other, the season was a very short one, the coach being taken off the road on August 22. Neither the Windsor nor Virginia Water road was taken this year; but the Tunbridge Wells and Brighton coaches showed no signs of stopping, both being in the same hands as before, except that Mr. Cooper joined the management of the latter, and Mr. C. Smith was said to 'have a wheel.' The Brighton season finished on October 21, and on the 23rd some of the regular patrons of the coach organised a party to meet at the Chequers, Horley (where, in 1867, the up and down coaches used to meet—as they did in 1888—for lunch), to wish well to Tedder, the professional, who had become landlord of that coaching inn. Colonel Tyrwhitt and Lord Norreys (the present Earl of Abingdon), it should be added, started a coach to Oatlands Park, with Timms as professional; but this turned out badly, while an attempt to carry coaching from London to Southend, *viâ* Rochford in Essex, proved a mighty fiasco. For a year or two previously Lord Bective had found the horses, and had sometimes driven; but he now withdrew, and hence the sudden collapse, the coach making but one journey, i.e. from London to Southend. When it returned it was on the train.

The spring of 1872 saw the Dorking coach make its first journey for the season on May 11. Mr. Godsell joined Sir Henry de Bathe and Colonel Withington in the proprietorship. The new comer, who never drove, found the horses for the Cheam and Epsom ground, and one extra change was made on the road. Notwithstanding that the weather was wretched during the early season, and a seat on a coach apparently the most uncomfortable of perches, the booking office was besieged, and on Whitsun Monday three coaches might have been sent off, so eager were the British public to drive to Dorking. The season lasted till September 26, and the venture had proved so successful that the proposal was mooted of running, when the next season came round, an afternoon 'Dorking,' leaving town after business hours, and setting forth from Dorking early on the following morning.

The Brighton coach, over which Mr. Chandos Pole, Colonel Stracey-Clitherow, Mr. G. Meek, and Mr. W. H. Cooper still reigned, began their season on May 27, the guard being now clad in scarlet. Colonel Clitherow horsed the coach for the first three stages, to Redhill that is to say; then came Mr. Cooper and Mr. Meek, while Mr. Chandos Pole looked after the Brighton end. Mr. Charles Hoare had now left the Tunbridge Wells road, and Lord Bective, who succeeded, carried on the affair with Colonel Hathorn, Colonel Chaplin retiring, the professional being James Selby—subsequently of the Old Times—who made his *début* as a four-in-hand coachman, and kept to the same road for half a dozen seasons. Simmons was guard, but, having the misfortune to break his leg, made way for Cracknell, son of the coachman of the Tantivy. The present Earl of Fife (then Lord Macduff) and Lord Muncaster put on a new coach to Sunbury, in conjunction with Captain Percival. The original intention was to go as far as Hampton Court only, but that home of holiday-makers being within the Metropolitan district, the coachman would have been obliged to wear a badge, like an omnibus-driver; hence the extension of the journey. Lord Norreys and Colonel Tyrwhitt gave up the Oatlands Park, and ran to Reigate instead, with Timms for professional as before. On December 11 the proprietors of the Brighton coach lost the services of Alfred Tedder, who died at the age of sixty; he began his career on the Oxford road, and at one time used to keep the Royal Hotel, Truro; so that in taking the Chequers, Horley, he was not, as some supposed at the time, embarking in a business of which he knew nothing.

The season of 1873 saw twelve coaches running in and out of London, with here and there a change in the proprietors of the old-established concerns. The number of previously existing coaches was increased by Sir Henry de Bathe (who quitted the Dorking confederacy) and Major Furnivall taking the Westerham road, with Moon coachman and E. Spencer guard. The inauguration, if we remember rightly, was scarcely a happy one, as some portion of the harness gave way, and a lady sustained an injury. Mr. Sedgwick bethought him of Watford, and, with Saunders as professional, and Brown as guard, started the Tantivy on a road which, at the outset, seemed scarcely likely to pay. After a short time, however, the coach made two journeys a day. It reached Piccadilly from Watford about 11 A.M.; a fresh team having been put to, it started again, returning in the afternoon. When the Tantivy made its first appearance it was seen that the harness-maker had become somewhat confused between the technical language of stag- and fox-hunting; for he had decorated the blinkers and pads with foxes which, had the coach been named the Tally-ho, would have been quite appropriate. The Tantivy required a stag. A third new speculation was the Guildford coach, which, though beginning late in the season, afforded an opportunity for Mr. Angell, then out of harness, to display his skill on the box. He was the sole proprietor, and when he was absent, Cracknell, the once famous Tantivy coachman, took his place. Captain Haworth, who had been instrumental in giving coaching a fresh start in 1866, put on the Rochester coach with Mr. Lawrie. Certainly one of the most arduous undertakings chronicled since the beginning of the revival was the establishment of the Aldershot coach, of which Lord Guilford and Mr. Reginald Herbert were proprietors. The last train for the military centre left London at about twelve at night, too early to allow the soldiers to attend a ball in London, yet it was not possible to travel by any other train, when it was necessary to attend early parade. It therefore occurred to the gentlemen above mentioned that to tide over the difficulty through the medium of wheels would be to supply a want. Accordingly it was arranged that the coach should leave London at 3 A.M.; but the starting-point was the puzzle, as at that unseasonable hour all hotels would have been long shut. Ultimately, however, Brandon's Cigar Stores were fixed upon, and, with all the old time surroundings of sleepy horse-keepers, &c. the new venture was launched. But it was scantily patronised, and did not last long.

Now we come to a most successful new departure, which was without doubt the feature of the season, the starting of the afternoon Dorking coach. This had been a pet project of Mr. Scott's for some time, and now that Mr. W. H. Cooper, who lived at Stoke D'Abernon, was willing to undertake the horsing and driving, the time was ripe for a start, which was made in due course, Edwin Fownes (who at the age of fourteen acted as guard of the Tunbridge Telegraph) being the professional, and thus began the successful career of 'Cooper's coach,' which now travelled *viâ* Mitcham. Two coaches were built by Ventham, of Leatherhead, from Mr. Cooper's own designs, assisted by a genuine old mail-coach model built either by Wright or Wand of the Old Kent Road; but, whichever was the builder, on the coach could be seen the peculiarity of the perch-bolt working perfectly loose.

Meantime the Brighton road fell from its high estate. All the old proprietors deserted it in a body; and when the afternoon Dorking became an accomplished fact, Mr. Scott resigned his post as honorary secretary, and devoted himself exclusively to the two Dorkings. The fate of the Brighton road hung for some time in the balance; but at last it was worked by Mr. Tiffany, an American gentleman, who obtained his horses, and likewise his instruction, from Charles Ward, of the Paxton stables. Mr. Tiffany did the thing very well: he had two coaches, one by Peters, and the other built for him by Messrs. Laurie & Marner; one of the two had pigskin cushions.

Colonel Tyrwhitt and Lord Norreys kept on to Reigate; Captain Waller Otway and Captain Williams, with H. Thorogood, professional, worked the Sunbury and Weybridge road; while Sir H. de Bathe, having quitted the Dorking coach for the Westerham, left the former in the hands of Lord Macduff and Colonel Withington, with whom was John Thorogood, nephew to the old coachman of the Norwich Times. The guard was Byford. Lord Bective and Colonel Hathorn looked after the Tunbridge Wells coach, and, when it finished the season, the proprietors, together with Selby and Cracknell, transferred their services to the St. Albans road for the winter. The High Wycombe coach, under Mr. John Eden's management, went on as usual. In two instances there was a little needless interference by one coach with the route of another; but in other respects the season passed off satisfactorily. On three days in the week, Mr. Tiffany ran through Reigate, and by so doing caused a certain amount of harm to the regular Reigate coach, which, by the way, left London at the same time as the Brighton coach. Then the morning Dorking travelled *viâ* Vauxhall Bridge, and for some distance accompanied the Westerham coach.

In 1874 the interest in road-coaching appears to have been well sustained, though there were several changes from the order of 1873. Lord Norreys and Colonel Tyrwhitt had given up the Reigate road; the Weybridge coach was a thing of the past; while Lord Guilford and Mr. Reginald Herbert had been so badly patronised by the soldiers at Aldershot that they brought their first season (1873) to a premature end, and never put their coach on the road again. On May 12 Mr. Angell —'Cherry' Angell as he was called, from the colour of his racing jacket—died. He had, as is well known, won the Grand National with Alcibiade in 1865.

The Tunbridge Wells made an early start on April 20 under the former proprietors, and, before starting on its first journey from Piccadilly, a whip was presented to Colonel Hathorn. James Selby was still professional, and Cracknell acted as guard. Mr. Sedgwick once more worked the Watford Tantivy; but the locals were sparing of their patronage; the fears entertained at the outset as to the chance of non-success were realised, and the proprietor had a very poor season. Lord Macduff having retired from the Dorking coach (which at one point in the journey used to be regularly raced by a team of four boys in hand, driven by a fifth), Colonel Withington had for partners the Marquis of Blandford (the present Duke of Marlborough) and Mr. W. M. Praed, whose coach, as surely as the Epsom Summer Meeting comes round, is seen in his private 'pew' opposite the stand. No change took place in connection with the High Wycombe coach, which had a circus-like team of skewbalds out of London, nor with the Westerham, except that the route was altered so as to include the Crystal Palace and Beckenham. Mr. Cooper remained faithful to the afternoon Dorking, which now stopped short at Box Hill, going *viâ* Sutton, and, in order to meet the convenience of his up-passengers, ran straight to the Royal Exchange in the morning, so as to land City men at the doors of the places wherein the golden calf had to be worshipped till the coach started in the afternoon. General Dickson took the Guildford, *vice* the late Mr. Angell; Mr. Tiffany was succeeded on the Brighton road by Captain Haworth, who, during the early part of the season ran to Rochester, as in 1873, but, becoming disgusted with the road, changed to Brighton; the Windsor route was revived under Mr. Williams (late of the Virginia Water), and Mr.

Hurman, with whom was Captain Waller Otway, and Mr. Bailey set up the St. Albans coach in succession to the confederacy by which it had been worked during the winter; so that the number of coaches working out of London in 1874 was eleven: one less than in 1873.

During the winter of 1874 London was not left coachless, as Mr. Cooper ran to Box Hill on alternate days, and there was also a winter coach to St. Albans. Then again coaching was kept alive by the Road Club, of which mention has already been made. Major Furnivall was the proprietor, and the Committee of the Club included the Duke of Beaufort, Sir Henry de Bathe, Mr. E. Godsell, Colonel Withington, Marquis of Blandford, Colonel Hathorn, Colonel Dickson, Lord Bective, Colonel Tyrwhitt, and Major Furnivall. The opening dinner, with Sir Henry de Bathe in the chair, took place on November 7 at the Club house, 4 Park Place, St. James's Street. In December, however, the coaching world had to mourn the loss of one of its most esteemed members. Mr. G. Meek—'handsome Meek' he was often called—contemplated driving a coach during the forthcoming season, but ere his intention could be carried out, he took a chill and died at the age of 48.

Hitherto the coaches had commenced running at such times as to the several proprietors seemed best, having regard to their convenience, and the amount of business likely to be done. Prior to the beginning of the season of 1875, however, a suggestion was made that a leaf be taken out of the book of the ancients, and that the season should be opened with a procession of coaches on April 28, in imitation of the mail procession of old on the King's birthday. This would naturally have been a novel and imposing sight to Londoners; but there were difficulties in the way, and the proposal was not acted upon. Another suggestion was that the Road Club should take a house at Twickenham, let part of it for the purposes of an hotel, and retain the remainder of the premises as a sort of country home for coaching men. This suggestion, however, like the former one, came to nothing, and the season began and ran its course in the ordinary way.

In 1875 Colonel Chaplin rejoined the Tunbridge Wells coach, from which Colonel Hathorn retired, so that Lord Bective was Colonel Chaplin's sole partner; with James Selby for professional, and A. Fownes, instead of H. Cracknell, as guard. At the beginning of the season the day Dorking started as in the previous year, but scarcely had a commencement been made ere Colonel Withington, the 'Peter' of many friends, died, to the honest grief of those who had been associated with him. This left the coach under the dual control of Lord Blandford and Mr. M. Praed, while Mr. Cooper—who at the end of the season was presented with a whip by the Clapham and Tooting omnibus men, at the dinner he gave to them every year—again made Box Hill his terminus, and had as professional B. Hubble, who succeeded E. Fownes. Hubble came upon the coaching world with great suddenness. He had been driving a four-horse omnibus, and while acting in that capacity was seen by Mr. Scott, who, when Fownes left, suggested the engagement of Hubble. Mr. Cooper, as an old coachman, was at first rather averse to appointing an unknown man; but, on the strong recommendation of Mr. Scott, saw for himself, and was satisfied. Colonel de Lancey Kane, an American gentleman, took the road to Virginia Water, and to him went E. Fownes on quitting the Box Hill. The Windsor road now passed into the hands of Colonel Greenall, Mr. Hurman, and Captain Chichester, the coach travelling by way of Richmond, Hampton Court, and Staines, with Harry Thorogood and Bob Rear as coachman and guard. On the Guildford road General Dickson was single-handed; but in the early part of the season he had John Thorogood to help him in the driving; but the latter was presently replaced by Timms; E. Spencer was guard. Mr. F. G. Hobson and Captain Ramsay put on the Criterion coach to Maidenhead, and Mr. Stewart Freeman ran to Brighton, *viâ* Sutton and Reigate, with McIntyre as guard and Pope as coachman; but in mid-season J. Thorogood left the Guildford and succeeded Pope under Mr. Freeman. Major Furnivall and Mr. Baker ran to Beckenham. Mr. John Eden still kept on with the Wycombe, but the Westerham road was deserted, and Mr. Sedgwick no longer occupied the Watford road. Mr. Bailey and Mr. Parsons kept to the St. Albans road during the summer; but in the winter Mr. Parsons ran the coach, with Selby as coachman, and H. Cracknell as guard. It was during this season, on September 9, that the unfortunate accident occurred to Mr. Cooper's coach. When within one hundred and fifty yards of Box Hill, the pole, an apparently sound one, which had been in use for some time, broke off short at the futchels; and the coach locking, eventually turned over. Three passengers besides Mr. Cooper were somewhat injured; but the remainder were able to go to London the same night. For the sufferers Mr. Cooper manifested the greatest anxiety, and everything that could be done for their benefit was done.

The opening of the season 1876 saw the Tunbridge Wells coach under the proprietorship of Lord Bective, Colonel Chaplin, and Captain Talbot, the latter of whom had succeeded Colonel Hathorn, Selby and A. Fownes being the professionals. The St. Albans was now an up coach worked by Mr. Parsons; Mr. Brand joined Mr. Praed on the Dorking road; but the Box Hill, owing to the indisposition of Mr. Cooper, did not run. The Windsor coach now went by way of Kew, Bushey, Hampton Wick, Staines and Datchet, the proprietors being Colonel Greenall, Mr. H. Bailey, and Captain Spicer; Mr. Hurman was too ill to take his turn. The Watford road, which had lain fallow in 1875, was now occupied by Mr. F. G. Hobson; while, as General Dickson had severed his connection with the Guildford coach, another, which in 1880 received the name of the New Times, was put on by Mr. W. Shoolbred, Mr. Luxmore, and Major Furnivall, the triumvirate engaging Tom Thorogood and E. Spencer as coachman and guard respectively. Colonel Clitherow joined Mr. Freeman in the maintenance of the Brighton coach, and Mr. Carleton Blyth, with Edwin Fownes for coachman and Blackburne behind him, ran from London to Oxford *viâ* Reading. From that place, however, to Oxford the horsing was undertaken by Mr. Mansell. The Maidenhead Criterion coach did not run in 1876, Mr. Eden gave up the Wycombe, the Westerham was taken off, and Colonel Kane having returned to America—where he set up a coach of his own, between New York and Pelham Bridge, taking A. Fownes with him as professional—the Virginia Water route was vacant, and so remained until 1879.

Before next May-day came round the ranks of coaching men had been thinned by the hand of death. In November 1876, Mr. Willis, the banker, joined the great majority. Though he never drove, he took great interest in the welfare of the Brighton road, and in Mr. Chandos Pole's time found the horses for the stage into Brighton, besides placing his fine stables in Farm Street Mews, London, at the disposal of the proprietors —a circumstance which was the cause of Hatchett's being the starting point in 1870, instead of the rendezvous at Charing Cross, as in 1869. Mr. Byng, too, who, besides taking great interest in everything appertaining to coaching, was instrumental in founding the Dogs' Home, died, and so did Mr. Eden, late of the Wycombe. Mr. Godsell, who had a house at Tulse Hill, and had had an interest in the Dorking and Westerham roads, though he never drove, also died towards the close of the year.

The season of 1877 witnessed a few changes. The St. Albans road passed from Mr. Parsons, who now ran between London and Watford, to Mr. Broadbent; Lords Bective, Cole, Helmsley and Castlereagh were associated with Colonel Chaplin in the management of the Tunbridge Wells, on which James Selby was still coachman, with Arthur Perrin, in lieu of A. Fownes, as guard; and the Dorking stopped short at Box Hill. The Windsor, Guildford, and Brighton went on as before, with John Thorogood and Ike Simmons as coachman and guard; but there were a couple of new ventures. Mr. C. R. Hargreaves and Mr. H. Wormald, with Edwin Fownes as professional, started the Rocket to Portsmouth, running down one day and back the next; and the Orleans Club put on a coach to Twickenham *vià* Richmond, with Adams as coachman; while, during the winter, Lord Arthur Somerset and Mr. C. A. R. Hoare ran the Rapid to Beckenham, an arrangement which found occupation for Selby when he had finished with the Tunbridge Wells.

The coaches which in 1878 ran in and out of London, and lent quite an old-time appearance to Piccadilly, were, in great measure, made up of old friends. Mr. Parsons ran to Watford and St. Albans; Mr. Shoolbred and Mr. Luxmore, with whom Major Furnivall made only a short stay two years previously, looked after the Guildford, having Sir H. de Bathe with them; while the Windsor remained in the hands of Colonel Greenall, Mr. Bailey, and Captain Spicer. Lord A. Lennox joined Mr. Freeman on the Brighton road; while visitors were carried to Dorking through the medium of the Perseverance now started by Mr. William Sheather, with Lord Aveland as his chief supporter; and this coach ran every year in the same hands down to the time of Mr. Sheather's death in 1885. As might have been expected, the horses were excellent, and the very liberal complement allowed no doubt accounted for their freshness at the season's end, when they were offered for sale. Mr. Sheather held to the idea that no horse should work more than once a day, and so the return journey was made with entirely fresh teams, an arrangement which materially lightened the work of the horses, for the coach invariably loaded well, be the weather what it might; Arthur Perrin was guard and Mr. Sheather's right-hand man. Lord Arthur Somerset and Mr. Hoare, having finished their winter undertaking to Beckenham, changed to West Wickham for the summer, Selby going with them; Mr. Hargreaves again ran to Portsmouth, having as companions Mr. H. Wormald, his old partner, and Mr. L. Blackett, who, it is believed, had had some practice driving on the Brighton and Arundel road. Mr. Carleton Blyth deserted coaching in 1877, but he this year (1878) again went to Oxford, and, changing his route, ran by Maidenhead and Henley; and the list of coaches was completed by that to the Ranelagh and Hurlingham, which made two journeys each way daily, the drive occupying thirty minutes. When all the above-mentioned coaches had finished for the season, another, which has since become famous, was started. This was the Old Times, which last season (1888) ran to Brighton on alternate days. The first proprietors were Sir Henry de Bathe, Mr. Carleton Blyth, Mr. H. Wormald, and Major Dixon; James Selby (subsequently sole proprietor) and Edwin Fownes, who since 1884 has also been a proprietor, being the professionals, the usual arrangement being for each of those concerned to drive one day a week. St. Albans was the destination fixed upon, and since November 4, 1878, when the Old Times made its first journey, it has never been off the road for a single day, except, of course, Sundays and Christmas Days. As will be seen, however, by the record for the years following, it has not always kept to one route.

On March 25, 1878, the coaching world lost one of its most respected members, Mr. W. H. Cooper—'Billy' Cooper he was always known as, both at B.N.C. and during the time he served in the 8th Hussars. He was taken ill in the previous January, while on a visit to Lord Fitzhardinge, and never recovered. The esteem in which Mr. Cooper was held at once showed itself by the immediate desire on the part of his friends to place some memorial to him in the church of Stoke D'Abernon, and this eventually took the form of a west window. When the window and design were determined upon, it was resolved that no one should be asked to subscribe, and that subscriptions should be limited to a minimum of 5*s.* and a maximum of five guineas—an arrangement which some imagined would prevent enough money being raised to pay for the window. So far from this being the case, however, Mr. A. G. Scott, who was as closely identified with the memorial as he had been with Mr. Cooper himself during life, found that, after paying 220*l.* for the window, and 11*l.* for a sketch thereof presented to Mrs. Cooper, there still remained a balance of 136*l.*, which was handed over to the Hunt Servants' Benefit Fund.

Having survived the winter, the Old Times ran to St. Albans during the whole of 1879, and the well-established coaches running to Guildford, Dorking, Brighton, and Windsor remained in the hands of their old proprietors. The Sevenoaks road was revived under Lord Helmsley and Baron William Schroder, who, with Ike Simmons as guard, started without a professional coachman, meaning to do the driving themselves; but Lord Helmsley becoming indisposed, his partner, fearing to tie himself down to a perpetual engagement, engaged Harry Ward (in November, 1888, a testimonial was organised) to assist him. Mr. Robinson, with F. Page as professional, ran a coach to Thames Ditton, the Ranelagh and Hurlingham coach was out again, and one ran to Hampton Court. The Virginia Water road was opened out, as already mentioned, by General Dickson and Captain Candy in 1871, and, after being deserted for three years, was taken for one season in 1875 by Colonel Kane, and was once more occupied this year by the Tally-ho, started by Captains Hartopp and Jacobson, having with them E. Cracknell, who, however, gave way to Evans in mid-season. The Box Hill coach was now put on the road by Mr. Seager Hunt, Lord A. Somerset and Sir Henry de Bathe, who took with them that neat coachman Ben Hubble. The West Wickham and Beckenham was still in the hands of its former proprietors; but the feature of the season was the undertaking of Mr. Carleton Blyth, who ran the Defiance from Oxford to Cambridge, a journey of 120 miles, for which 120 horses were kept. On Mondays, Wednesdays, and Fridays the Defiance left Oxford at 9 A.M., changing horses at Wheatley, Tetsworth, Stokenchurch, High Wycombe, Gerrard's Cross, Hayes, and Acton, the team from the last-named place running to Hatchett's, reached at 2.50 P.M., and where twenty minutes were allowed for lunch. A fresh team from Piccadilly worked to Tottenham Cross, the other changes being Waltham Cross, Wade's Mill, Buntingford, Royston, and Harston, fifteen teams in all; but rest horses were kept besides. On the intervening days the return journey was made. The Blenheim coach, which worked in connection with the Defiance, belonged to Mr. Augustus Craven, but on Saturdays the Defiance itself ran right through from Cambridge to Cheltenham, after leaving Oxford, where half an hour was allowed for supper, reaching the Plough Hotel, Cheltenham, at two on Sunday morning. On Monday the Defiance left Cheltenham at 4 A.M., 'the coach breakfasted' at Oxford, lunched at Hatchett's, and reached Cambridge at 9 P.M.

This somewhat herculean task, however, only lasted during 1879, as in 1880 Mr. Blyth ran the Defiance from London to Brighton, taking the long road by Sevenoaks, Tunbridge Wells, Uckfield, and Lewes; E. Fownes, Blackburne, and J. Banks being the professionals engaged. The route being a somewhat hilly one, five horses were used on three stages. On the coach arriving at Tunbridge Wells, three leaders abreast were employed; the same arrangement obtaining at the next two changes, till Lewes was reached. At the foot of the bridge on approaching Lewes the horses were stopped to let them get their wind, after which a fresh start was made, the horses galloping till the steepness of the ascent fairly reduced them to a walk. On the up journey another route was taken so as to avoid the hill. On one occasion, when E. Fownes essayed the task of coming down the aforesaid hill, the staple of the skid drew, but an accident was avoided. It was the custom, by the way, to carry on the Defiance a spare pole made in two or three pieces, the whole being screwed together when required. No change was made in connection with the Perseverance to Dorking, the New Times to Guildford, or the Box Hill coaches. The other Brighton coach now became a double one, with Mr. Chandos Pole, son of the former proprietor, as a new partner, Harry Ward and John Thorogood coachmen, with E. Spencer and Ike Simmons guards. Mr. Robinson was again on the road, but now ran on to Esher, while the Old Times went to Virginia Water during the summer. Captain Edwards and Mr. Noble put on a coach to York House, Maidenhead; and Captain Spicer having quitted the Windsor, was succeeded by Sir Thomas Peyton. In the autumn of the year the Old Times ran to Virginia Water and back on one day, and to Windsor and back the next; while during the

'The Defiance.'

winter months it ran between Windsor and London exclusively, another winter coach turning up in the St. Albans, run by Mr. C. R. Hargreaves.

In 1881 the Dorking, Guildford, Box Hill, and Windsor went on as before, except that Mr. F. Davis took Colonel Greenall's place on the Windsor, and the Old Times went back to Virginia Water till the winter came round, when it ran its original route to St. Albans, which road during the summer was taken by Messrs. Jones and Shaw. The Hurlingham and Ranelagh was again a convenience for the members of those clubs and their friends, and in August E. Fownes put on the Age to Brighton for a short season. At the end of the summer the Old Times stopped short at Oatlands Park.

Mr. Chandos Pole quitted the Brighton road in 1882, and on Baron Oppenheim joining Mr. Freeman, the coach was again a double one, horsed by Woodlands; for after the first few years Mr. Freeman preferred this system to that of buying his own cattle. E. Fownes and John Thorogood were the coachmen; E. Graham and E. Fownes, junior, were the guards. On one occasion when nearly opposite the Asylum on Banstead Downs a mishap occurred; and while the passengers and professionals were in painful confusion, a pedestrian on the road laughingly observed, 'What a capital picture this would make!' A Surbiton coach also ran in connection with the Brighton. The Dorking ran as usual, and so did the Old Times to Virginia Water; the Windsor, and New Times to Guildford; the Rapid worked between Esher and London; Mr. C. R. Hargreaves again ran the Rocket to Portsmouth, and the Wonder, Mr. Rumney's, went to St. Albans. The Maidenhead coach did not appear, nor did the Box Hill.

Hitherto the coaching revival had apparently been popular; but the year 1882 showed a falling off in the number of coaches, and 1883 was of less promise than the year before—a state of things for which it is not altogether easy to account. The wave of depression which affected every branch of sport and pastime doubtless had some connection with the waning of coaching; but there were possibly other causes, which it is not necessary to specify, at work. When the season of 1883 began the Perseverance still kept on to Dorking and Box Hill; Mr. Bailey and Mr. F. Davis stuck to the Windsor, the Old Times carried passengers to Virginia Water, and Mr. Rumney ran the Wonder to St. Albans, Sam Clark being the professional, as in the previous year. In the autumn the Wonder ran from Brighton to Eastbourne; but it was not till very late in the year that Mr. Freeman made any sign on the Brighton road, with John Thorogood as coachman, and J. Sullivan behind him.

Five coaches only ran out of London in 1884. Mr. Freeman did not put on the Brighton at all; but the Dorking Virginia Water, and Guildford went on as usual; the Windsor had Colonel Ferguson as one of the proprietors, the fifth being the Defiance, owned by Edwin Fownes, which this year ran to St. Albans *vice* the Wonder. In 1885 the Defiance was taken off the St. Albans road in favour of the Wonder, and ran to Bentley Priory, Edwin Fownes being still proprietor; there was no Brighton coach, and of the many roads which had at one time or another been taken, seven only were occupied, and the great coaching revival was now represented, in addition to the above, by the New Times, Perseverance, Old Times, and the Windsor, Colonel Ferguson now retiring from the last named. The new coach was put on to Eton, *vià* Hounslow, by Messrs. Beckett and M'Adam.

In 1886 there were several changes, though coaches were few. The Guildford, Old Times, and the Defiance remained as before; but, Mr. Sheather being now dead, the Dorking and Box Hill (the Perseverance) passed into the hands of Mr. H. Withers of Oxford Street, with whom were associated Messrs. Balding and Munday; the Wonder ran to St. Albans; but Mr. Freeman, instead of putting on the Brighton, ran the Royal to Windsor instead, with H. Thorogood as professional. A portion of the Sevenoaks road was revived, as Mr. Charles Webling put on the Excelsior between that place and New Cross. In the next year (1887), however, Mr. Freeman was again working between London and Brighton, the Windsor being now in the hands of Mr. King, with E. Fownes finding the horses and acting as professional. The Vivid, of which Fownes—who was presented by his friends with a new coach to celebrate his fifty-third year of connection with the road-was proprietor, though it was driven by his son Ernest, was put on to Hampton Court. There was no change on the St. Albans, Guildford, Dorking, or Virginia Water roads, and these, together with the Excelsior, were the coaches of the year.

In 1888 the Wonder, the Perseverance, the Vivid, now the property of Arthur Fownes, and the New Times held their way; the Defiance ran to Bentley Priory; and the Old Times, after its winter course was done, ran to Brighton on alternate days. Another coach of Selby's ran to Oatlands Park; it was called the Express at the commencement of the season, but it was subsequently renamed the Old Times, so that really there were two coaches of the same name, and owned by the same proprietor, running at the same time. Mr. Webling this year changed his plans, and ran from London to Tunbridge Wells. Mr. F. Davis, formerly of the Windsor, also ran the Surbiton coach. On the Brighton road, however, there was great opposition, for Mr. Freeman put on the Comet double coach, so that on three days in the week there were two coaches to Brighton, and on the remaining three days there were two up coaches. The Old Times kept to the 15*s.* fare; but the Comet charged only half a guinea, the same as the railway charge. When the summer season was over, Selby determined to run the Old Times to Brighton all the winter, and as Mr. Freeman, with whom Mr. M'Calmont was associated, resolved to keep on one of the Comets as well, there was every prospect of the Brighton road showing great activity. What the ultimate arrangements may be remains to be seen, as on Friday, December 14, the coaching world was startled by the announcement that James Selby, the proprietor of the Old Times, had breathed his last in the forenoon of that day. On Friday, the 7th, he brought the coach from Brighton, but complained of a cold. Bronchitis supervened, and, together with disease of the heart, proved fatal on the above day. Selby, who was only forty-five at the time of his death, was originally intended for an auctioneer, and was articled to that calling; but horses proved a superior attraction, and in course of time he managed Mr. Pawley's yard at Hastings. His connection with coaching, given in the foregoing pages, dates from 1872; but he was a busy man, and besides keeping commission stables in the Edgware Road, started a short time ago a business as coachbuilder in conjunction with Mr. Cowlard, who had formerly been in the employ of Messrs. Holland at the time that well-known firm miled nearly all the stage-coaches. Poor Selby was a genial kind-hearted man, and will be much missed in coaching circles. From having driven in and out of London, summer and winter, for so long, his face was perhaps better known than that of any other coachman. His effects were sold at Aldridge's on Wednesday, January 2, 1889, and realised phenomenal prices. The Old Times itself was bought for 290 guineas by Selby's subscribers, Messrs. H. L. Beckett, A. M'Adam, W. Dickson, A. Broadwood, and Carleton Blyth. Two pairs of whips brought 20 guineas, while 26 guineas were paid for two coach-horses.

Such is a brief outline of the coaching revival, and if the modern stage-coaches are not so numerous as they were a few years ago, no surprise need be felt at a period like the present when railway travelling is so expeditious and cheap, and the majority of travellers care much more about reaching their journey's end quickly than about the means of transit. Most people, for example, would probably prefer to go to Brighton and return in the newly-started and luxurious Pulman train to going down on a coach and cutting short their stay at the so-called 'Queen of watering-places.' Moreover, the running of coaches as mediums for advertising has not commended itself to many who would otherwise patronise the road. When the revival commenced in 1866, and for some years subsequently, the coaches were almost exclusively in the hands of those who remembered coaching in pre-railroad days; and those gentlemen had a strong personal following which materially helped to load the coaches. However, it is to be hoped that coaching will never die out; if it does, there is some chance of old traditions being forgotten. Like the war songs of the savages, and like the sea fisherman's 'marks,' the right and wrong way of driving four horses has hitherto been handed down orally. Few old coachmen, either amateurs or professionals, are alive, and those interested in the preservation of road traditions would regret to see the links with the past snapped at last. So far as what may be called the business coaches are concerned, the incorporation of 'subscribers' takes the place of the partnerships, in which the Duke of Beaufort, Sir H. de Bathe, Mr. Chandos Pole, Colonel Hathorn, and others, whose names have been mentioned, bore their share. The positions, however, of partners and subscribers are not identical; for, whereas the former share profits or losses as the case may be, subscribers pay a fixed sum for the privilege of driving one or more days a week. It is on this principle that Selby's and Fownes's coaches are run, so that if no passengers be carried, the working expenses are paid wholly or in part, and this accounts for the fact that both the Defiance and the Vivid will run through the winter.

A notice of modern coaching would perhaps be incomplete without a passing reference to the value of the horses employed, especially at a time when public attention is strongly directed towards the demand for and production of the general utility horse. It appears that, as coaching increased in popularity, and competition became more keen, better horses have been used, or it may be that purchasers have by degrees come to recognise the wisdom of buying animals whose daily work is some sort of guarantee for their soundness and condition. In 1870 the Brighton horses realised just over 30*l.* each; but in 1876 the St. Albans horses, 30 in number, realised 1,065 guineas, giving an average of 35½ guineas; a roan team brought 160 guineas, and four bays 210 guineas. In the same year the average for the Tunbridge Wells horses was 41 guineas, while the horses which had been working on the Brighton road averaged 88*l.* 4*s.*; the Guildford horses, 56½ guineas; the Wycombe 39½ guineas, and Mr. Carleton Blyth's Oxford horses 88 guineas. In 1877 the Brighton average was the capital one of 89*l.* 9*s.* for 43 horses sold, but one of them fetched 200 guineas, the total sum being 3,584*l.* 4*s.*, and 9 of the horses running to three figures. The Guildford horses, which have always sold well, averaged 80½ guineas for 19 lots; and 46 horses from the Portsmouth Rocket realised 1,928 guineas, giving an average price of 44 guineas. In 1878 the Brighton average was 57; the Guildford 65, and the Oxford 82½. In 1882, 25 lots from the Guildford coach sold for 2,207*l.* 2*s.*, yielding an average of 88*l.* 5*s.* 8*d.*; in the following year 74*l.* 2*s.* was the average, and in 1884 77*l.* 17*s.* 6*d.* During the last, mentioned three years the Windsor and Dorking horses averaged about 60*l.* each; while in 1883 and 1884, the Margate and Canterbury Champion horses brought about 60*l.* apiece. In 1885 the averages were as follows: Guildford (23), 74*l.* 10*s.*, the highest price 120 guineas; Dorking (13), 56*l.* 10*s.*; Eastbourne and Brighton (28), 44*l.* 15*s.*; Margate and Canterbury (10), 46*l.* 6*s.*; while in 1886 the Windsor averaged 61 guineas; and in 1887 the 31 horses from the New Times sold for 73*l.* 14*s.* 2*d.* each.

Although the coaching revival was first matured in London, the taste for driving ultimately extended to the provinces, though to a less extent than might reasonably have been expected. The purely business affairs which have always been in the country, running under the name of coaches—often omnibuses or breaks—do not come within the scope of these remarks. Though unquestionably useful as a means of communication, there is scarcely one, within the writer's knowledge, a journey on which can be said to have afforded pleasure. 'Well-whipped horses,' more than half worn out, a slow rate of progression, and a driver—they are not always coachmen—not possessed of the proverbial 'fund of anecdote,' do not conduce to pleasurable sensations. It is not pretended that this description applies to every public conveyance running in the country; but, unfortunately, it is too true in respect of many. The following remarks, therefore, relate only to those coaches started on somewhat the same footing as the London ones; and, considering the scenic attractions within easy reach of the most popular tourist resorts, and the number of tourists brought down by train, it is surprising that coaching should not have become a favourite means of locomotion in the provinces, and have proved a remunerative undertaking. Still, as will be gathered from the subjoined sketch, at one time and another a fair number of coaches have been started in various parts of England.

The younger generation have perhaps never heard of 'Mad' Wyndham, who, before the coaching revival was planned, committed what was then deemed the eccentricity of running the Cromer coach. The same vehicle—it weighed 30 cwt.—is, or was a few years ago, running between Bude and Holsworthy, in the West of England.

Prior to 1875 Mr. Platt ran a coach from Doncaster to Rotherham, his professional being F. Page, who, however, left to go with Mr. Lowther on the Scarborough and Bridlington Quay road. Mr. Hargreaves later on took up the road between Margate and Canterbury; Colonel Somerset, formerly master of the Hertfordshire hounds, used to drive his chestnuts between Enfield and Luton, his coach being named the Hirondelle; Mr. W. W. Crawshay was responsible for the Newnham and Gloucester coach; Mr. Carleton Blyth ran between Reading and Windsor; while Manchester and Altrincham were afforded coach communication by Messrs. Belcher, Mewburn, and C. Belhouse. Mr. Pryce Hamilton, who often turns out with the Coaching Club in Hyde Park, ran from Malvern to Ross; Mr. Nat Cooke—a well-known sporting character in Cheshire—started a coach between Woodside and Chester, with Purcell as professional; and Lord Mayo, with Ike Simmons as guard, ran between Brighton and Arundel. Captain Otway's coach joined Llandrindod and Kington, with H. Cracknell, formerly of the Windsor, as professional; Mr. Crawshay Bayley and Mr. T. Rosher ran between Brecon and Abergavenny, and Mr. Edwardes from Barmouth to Dolgelly.

In 1876 Captain Cecil Otway changed his route to Aberystwith and Presteign; Mr. Pryce Hamilton plied between Ross and Tintern; the Newnham, Gloucester, and Cheltenham coach was in the hands of Mr. Robert Chapman and Mr. Platt; a coach ran between Leamington and Stratford-on-Avon, and another between Cheltenham and Malvern; while Colonel Somerset in 1877 ran from Enfield to Hitchin. In the same year a coach was started between Cheadle and Manchester, while in 1878 Mr. C. B. E. Wright, master of the Badsworth, put on a coach from Buxton to Matlock, and Lord Aylesford one from Birmingham to Coventry, his horses coming from Charles Ward of the Paxton Stables. In 1879 Mr. Augustus Craven ran the Blenheim to Cheltenham in connection with Mr. Carleton Blyth's Defiance from Cambridge to Oxford; and Leamington had two coaches, one to Stratford-on-Avon, the other to Coventry, the Malvern and Cheltenham still keeping on.

Mr. Parsons, who had formerly been on the St. Albans road out of London, carried out, in 1880, his intention of running a coach between Reading and Brighton *viâ* Dorking and Guildford, changing in the succeeding year *viâ* Worthing, Arundel, and Chichester to Brighton and Portsmouth, while a coach was now running between Melksham and Bristol. Meantime at a previous period Colonel C. Rivers-Bulkeley, who as 'Mr. Charles' was well known between the flags on earlier days, ran from Rhyl to Bettws-y-Coed. In this year, too, Mr. Slater ran from Dover to Deal, and Mr. R. S. Hudson put on a coach between York and Liverpool, and while on its last stage, on the last day of the season, an accident occurred which was very nearly attended with fatal consequences to the passengers. While descending a steep hill between Prescot and Liverpool the horses bolted, and came into contact with a wall at the bottom. Two of the horses were killed and the passengers were severely shaken. In 1882 Captain J. R. P. Goodden and Captain W. W. Turnor, assisted it is believed by Captain Fife, started a coach from Sherborne to Weymouth; and in 1883

Mr. E. Cosier was running from Margate to Canterbury, Mr. E. Onslow Secker had put on the Quicksilver between Folkestone and Canterbury, while as soon as the Wonder had ceased running from London to St. Albans, it was taken into Sussex, and put on between Eastbourne and Brighton, taking Lewes on the way.

On the Continent a coaching venture was made in 1883, when Messrs. W. Forbes Morgan and H. Ridgway ran a coach from Pau to Lourdes, a distance of twenty-five miles. The English Club at Pau was the starting-point, and the Hôtel des Pyrénées the terminus at the other end, the journey occupying two and a half hours. Later in the season the route was changed from Lourdes to Oléron, the coach still starting from Pau. This road was four miles shorter than that to Lourdes, and was very picturesque, but as a set-off it was extremely hilly. Nevertheless good time was kept, and the coach loaded well. In 1885 Mr. Padelford joined the other two proprietors, the Pau and Oléron routė being adhered to; but, owing to the coldness of the season, the management met with indifferent success, the takings falling considerably short of those of the previous year. About the same time the Rocket was started to run to Biarritz, a journey of seventy-three miles, completed in eight hours, with six changes on the road. Edwin Fownes was coachman, and R. Graham guard. From Bayonne to St. Etienne a long hill was encountered, up which a 'cock-horse,' ridden by a lad in postilion dress, was used; but the road was wide, firmly made, and, with the exception of the hill aforesaid, well adapted for coaching.

A few seasons prior to 1885 Mr. James Turbett started a coach by Peters, and lent to him by Mr. Watson, a good man on the bench, and over a country between Dublin and the Wooden Bridge Hotel, Co. Wicklow; but it did not pay, and was thereupon discontinued; and in 1883 a venture was launched between Dublin and Avoca. On July 1, 1885, however, another attempt was made, as Captain Steed, whose horses were poisoned a year or two ago, got together thirty horses, and put on a coach built by Shanks, which started from the Shelburne Hotel, Dublin, at 11.30, and ran to Greystones. In 1887 the road was taken by the Tantivy, in the hands of Mr. Thompson, whose professional was Ernest Fownes. During the same year Messrs. Power and O'Reilly ran a coach they called the P & O between Dublin and Ballybrack; the same proprietors have run from Dublin to Bray by way of the Scalp.

In 1888 Mr. Thompson ran through Bray and Dalgany.

The Buxton to Matlock, Margate to Canterbury, Leamington to Stratford-on-Avon, and Folkestone to Canterbury coaches were in the hands of their former proprietors in 1884; while in the same year Mr. Woods ran between Petersfield and Winchester, having with him Ernest Fownes, then sixteen years old. Mr. Beckett ran the Express from Brighton to Eastbourne, the Wonder being taken off, and a coach was put on from Brighton to Worthing and Arundel. Things were much the same in 1885, in which year Lord Savernake (now Marquis of Ailesbury) put on the Star from Windsor to Henley

'The Red Rover in a gale.'

THE BRIGHTON, BATH, AND DOVER ROADS.

On these roads there were many coaches and many coachmen of high reputation, and I select them for description as it chances that my experiences of them date back many years, and have been constant and considerable. Castle Square, Brighton, in the morning and evening was crowded with people assembled to see the departure and arrival of the various coaches. The Square had as many coach offices as other houses. I will begin with the Times office, belonging to Samuel Goodman. He had the seven o'clock Times, which left in the morning and ran to the Golden Cross, Charing Cross, in about five hours and fifteen minutes. From Castle Square to the Elephant and Castle is fifty-two miles; thence a pair-horse branch coach took the passengers to the City. The coach was timed five hours to the Elephant. It returned from the Golden Cross at two, and reached Brighton at 7.15. A heavy family coach, called the Regent, left both ends at ten, and was supposed to do the journey in six hours, but it was really six hours and a half. Goodman had also the four o'clock Times, which left both ends at four and was due in London and Brighton at 9.15. He generally drove this coach himself, and as he had a farm six or seven miles out of Brighton on the roadside, he had a man who often took it out of and brought it into Brighton, Goodman getting down and sleeping at his farm. There was a very peculiar old fellow who drove the Regent. He was a very slow safe old coachman, who would not have liked to drive any faster than he did. In 1833, my mother not being very well, my father took a house at Brighton—Western House, which is next to the easternmost house of Brunswick Terrace. He was then in the House of Commons, and had to go up and down between London and Brighton often. Being a very fine coachman—very powerful, and with hands as fine on a horse's mouth as a woman's—he could drive any horses; indeed I have known him drive horses that went pleasantly and without pulling with him, when it had been declared that no man could hold them. He was in the habit of driving many of the coaches on the Oxford, Bath, Portsmouth, and Southampton roads, and was well known as a first-rate artist. Goodman—a surly cross-grained fellow—would not let him drive. My father, vexed at the uncourteous treatment he had received, went to Alexander's, a large horse and coach proprietor in the Borough. In the lapse of time I have lost the name of his large stables, but well do I remember that whilst business was being discussed I used to wait in the coffee-room. Coffee! save the mark—no whiff of the fragrant berry ever sweetened that den. Dog's-nose, gin, the smell of stale bad tobacco smoke, sand, sawdust, and spittoons offended the nose and eyes! All coffee-rooms all over England had boxes—fancy an old-fashioned church pew, only higher, say six feet high, a brass rod above it, another eighteen inches or two feet, and a dirty red stuff curtain (stuffy too), a narrow table in the centre of each, and a narrow ledge to sit upon against the side of the pew on each side, and you have 'the box presented to your view.' There would be five or six of these places on each side of the room, according to its size; they answered to the modern private room, and once taken were sacred to their occupants—the less favoured traveller having to share the still dirtier public table in the middle of the room. Oh! more fortunate youths of the present day who revel in the modern hotel, how little do you know of the discomforts of travelling shared not so very long ago with his contemporaries by him who writes these lines! You know not the perpetual 'Yes, sir! coming, sir!' (but he never came!) of the one unfortunate dirty, greasy waiter who had customers in the eight or ten boxes and at the middle table to wait upon. The memory of those days of my youth has, however, caused me to digress, so I must turn from the 'Chop, sir? yes, sir!' to our muttons, in the shape of my father and Alexander. Very little negotiation was necessary. It was settled that within a fortnight they should, between them, put on a coach leaving Brighton and London at the same time as Goodman's seven o'clock Times. Well can I recall it, a yellow coach, called the Wonder, and an afternoon coach leaving both ends at four, a dark coach with red wheels called the Quicksilver, both timed to do the journey to and from the Elephant and Castle in four hours and forty-five minutes. Capps drove the Wonder; Bob Pointer, as fine a coachman as ever was seen, drove one end of the Quicksilver.

All went swimmingly till one evening, going out of Brighton, a young coachman, son of one of the large coach proprietors whose office was in Castle Square, was driving the four thoroughbred chestnuts, as good and quick 'a Townend team' as could be found, when, for some never to be explained reason, they broke away from him, and he turned the coach over just opposite the New Steine Hotel. Several passengers were badly shaken, and two unfortunate ones were thrown on the spikes that surmount the railings of the New Steine. Happily, in time they all recovered, but it cost some money to cure them. Nothing daunted, the proprietors painted the Quicksilver dark brown, renamed her the Criterion, and she resumed her place on the road. Bitterly did Goodman repent his surliness and want of courtesy, for these coaches very sensibly diminished his takings. Poor Bob Pointer had one infirmity, and one very curious peculiarity. He could be depended upon to start at any hour perfectly sober, but it was necessary to have the stables at which horses were changed out of reach of a public-house, or he would get intoxicated before the journey's end.

Before I leave this coach I must relate a small personal anecdote. I was at a school where our creature comforts were well attended to as far as food went, for we were fed like fighting cocks, and in case of illness were tended by the kind wife of the schoolmaster as though we were her own children. As regards cleanliness, in winter I used to get a warm sea bath three times a week, which in those days, when I don't think people washed as much as they do now, was looked upon as rather an effeminate luxury, and in summer we bathed in the sea four or sometimes five days in the week. Now I, with some others of the boys, was idle and liked amusement better than learning my lessons, or doing those—to me, who am no poet—abominations called verses. The consequence of this combination of unfortunate circumstances was that I used to go home striped like a hyena, the various stripes representing by their difference of colour the different periods at which I had been caned. Yesterday's wheals would be red; two or three turning yellow denoted a thrashing of the day before, whilst the green and black and blue were relics of an anterior date. Learn we should, said the pedagogue, and if we did not take it in kindly at one end, we should have it knocked into us at the other. Two stalwart ushers had long thin canes which lapped round one's shoulders, or the small of one's back, and caught the tender under part of the upper arm, and that was indeed pain; but the doctor himself had a thicker, stiffer and more bruising weapon. He had a large school and charged a long price for tuition, yet he was always in debt. If he was worried by creditors or served with a writ he would come down to the school-room, and woe to any unfortunate small boy on whom his eye fell, or whom he called to bring up his verses or theme. We used to think it was his fancy that we stood in the bailiff's shoes. We knew by the twitching of his nose if he had been served with a writ that morning. Like a hawk swooping on a bird did he pounce from his chair, drawing the dreaded weapon simultaneously from his desk; his left hand was on the boy's collar and his knuckles in the boy's throat before he had time to say 'Oh!' and beginning at his heels he whacked him over the tendon Achilles all up the legs and up his back till he could whack no more, and dropped exhausted into his seat; from thirty to forty blows would he give, too severe a punishment with a thick cane for small boys.

On one occasion, early in November 1833, I, being then nine years old, had committed the high crime and misdemeanour of ending a pentameter with a three-syllable word, for which the usher caned me at eleven o'clock school. At five o'clock school the Doctor came in—I think he must have been served with two writs that day. His eye fell on me. 'Have you been caned to-day?' 'Yes, sir.' 'What for?' I told him. 'What, a three-syllable word again! Go and fetch my cane.' The usher was a good fellow, though passionate, and said, 'I caned him severely for it.' 'Never mind,' said the Doctor, 'he will remember two thrashings better than one.' His hand was on my throat, and I was writhing under his blows for fully three minutes. As he went out of the room he turned and said, 'After prayers to-morrow morning you shall have just such another thrashing.' And this threat brings us back to the Wonder coach.

Before six next morning I woke, dressed in the dark, and started, for I had made up my mind to run away, feeling that I had been quite sufficiently punished for my offence. The gate between the playground and the front approach swung and made a peculiar noise, and I was afraid to open it; but the dogs—there were half a dozen kept there—had scooped the ground out under, and through their private entrance I crept. Fourpenny bits, called Joeys after Joseph Hume, had just been invented; I had one of these in my pocket, the only coin I possessed. It was one of the bitterest, cold, foggy November mornings possible, and I had no greatcoat, and one glove. I knew where the Wonder put up—close to Mutton, the pastry-cook's. As I turned into the yard the horses were being put to. I saw Capps, whom I knew, and told him, with perfect truth, that my father had the gout and I was going up to him. Like a young idiot, instead of getting inside or into the front boot, I must swagger and go on the box. There were but three outside passengers. At prayers I was not missed; but the Doctor afterwards remembered his promise, and said, 'Now I will give that young gentleman an appetite for breakfast'—but I was not to be found. The son of the pedagogue, who was then home for a few days from Cambridge, got on to the Doctor's favourite horse and rode into the town, and a stupid porter told him that a little boy had gone on the box of the Wonder. Upon hearing this off went the Cambridge undergraduate, and performed the very extraordinary feat of catching the coach, though it had got a full hour's start. At Crawley, being so lightly clad, and having had nothing to eat since milk and bread and butter at six the night before, I was so cold I had got inside the coach. Just before we got to Horley, twenty-seven and a half miles from Brighton and five from Crawley, my pursuer overtook the coach and called upon Capps to pull up, but this he would not do, whereupon the undergraduate rode across the leaders, being nearly knocked over. Though his horse was dead beat, he followed the coach till it stopped to change at Horley; there a great palaver took place, and Capps was all for sticking to me, but at last reluctantly gave way, and I was delivered up. Some tea and some rashers of bacon and eggs were quickly put on the table, and we set off back to Brighton with a postboy, ride and drive, in an old Bounder, as postchaises were then called, from the fact that they bounded about on their Cee-springs, with the Doctor's animal tied on to the hand-horse. Poor old Vagabond! he never did another day's work, the ride finished him. All the Russells had been at school there: Lord Alexander, now a full General and C.B., was there with me; and Vagabond had been a present from the Duke of Bedford, John, sixth Duke, grandfather of the present and ninth

'Rode across the leaders.'

Duke, who succeeded his cousin. When we arrived I was greeted with: 'Well, so you object to a caning, do you? I shall respect your prejudices, and have prepared a very nice birch for you;' and sure enough he laid into me till he was so blown he could lay in no longer. Fortunately for him my father was in bed with the gout, for he was furious at the treatment I had received. However, Christmas came, and I went home and returned to the same school again, and remained there till I went to Eton.

The Wonder and Criterion flourished for many years. I should have mentioned the Age, as an older established coach, before these, but their origin arising from Goodman's surliness they followed the Times. The Age was started by Mr. Stephenson, a gentleman by birth. I suppose I must have seen him, but cannot say; his face and figure are familiar to me from the old coloured print of him standing by the side of his four greys in Castle Square just going to mount the box. Those connected with the Age that I remember well were Sir St. Vincent Cotton, a Cambridgeshire baronet, and Jack Willan, and on the baronet's retirement, Willan and Brackenbury—Bob I think his name was; he was the elder of two brothers, the younger of whom drove the London and Windsor Taglioni a few years later. The Age left both ends at noon, and took about five and a quarter hours. It was a very favourite coach, well horsed and driven, and all three coachmen were very popular. All these coaches ran to Brighton by the Elephant and Castle, Brixton Hill, Streatham, Croydon, Smitham Bottom, Red Hill, and Horley, and most of them by Crawley, Hicksted, Piecombe, and Patcham to Brighton; but some from Horley came by Cuckfield and Clayton Church to Piecombe, and so on.

Many coaches ran by Tooting, Sutton, Walton Heath, by Reigate, Hookwood Common, Crawley, and Hand Cross to Brighton; others by Smitham Bottom and Redhill to Reigate, and others again by Ewell, Leatherhead, Mickleham, Burford Bridge, Dorking, Horsham, by Henfield to Brighton; but this route was 61 miles as against 52½ the other way. Still there were passengers and fish and parcels to carry, so that, as all could not live on one road, each was considered, and residents in different localities kept the coaches going by patronising them.

Returning to Castle Square, I next come to the old Blue Coach office. Coaches from here were good and safe, but slower than the others described previously. From this office they ran not only to London but to Hastings, Portsmouth, and other places. Then there was the White Coach office, Snow's, at the north-east corner of Castle Square, with windows into the Old Steine. The coaches running from here were all white and belonged to Snow. There were several to London and other places from this office: one to London was called the Magnet, I remember. Also from this office ran the Red Rover, through Shoreham, Worthing, Chichester, Southampton, Salisbury, and Wells, to Bath. I often went to school and came home for the holidays by it. It was a very good fast coach, a dark body and red wheels, and the horses had red collars. I have forgotten the names of the coachmen unfortunately, and do not know who can tell me them—fifty years have passed since I travelled by it.

I remember leaving Brighton on the Red Rover one morning in such a gale of wind from the south-west as I have seldom seen; as we went along the road between the Bedford Hotel, then just newly opened, and Brunswick Square we saw two flys coming out of side streets blown clean over, and a poor woman coming along the bottom of Brunswick Square was caught in a squall, and her petticoats being whisked up were caught over the iron spikes on top of the rails above her head. Had anyone been in the square at that early and tempestuous hour I think he would have been reminded of a peacock, who puts up his tail in the spring and invariably turns his back to you. Fortunately some man coming along got to her and unhooked her. We had a very unpleasant drive to Worthing. The gale was, as a sailor would express it, on our port bow, and more than one of the passengers lost their hats for ever and a day. After leaving there we altered our course, and got it more abeam, and the wind subsided a little. I remember hearing that on that morning some elm-trees were blown across the London Road between Brighton and Preston, and that all the earlier coaches had to go up a very awkward narrow road on to the Down, and to come down another equally awkward one into the road beyond Patcham. There was an old fire-eating Irish major, some relation to an old Dowager Duchess who lived a good deal at Brighton. I remember his hat and wig well—beautiful silky brown curly hair it was—he lost them both off the coach on top of the Downs going to London that day. What was his name? O'Grady, I fancy.

After the Brighton Railway had run all the coaches off the road, and the Great Western Railway had done the same for the Bath and Bristol coaches, James Adlam, who for years had driven the Bath York House from London to Marlborough alternate days there and back, set up a four-horse coach on the long road to Brighton. Though I travelled by it a few times I forget the exact route he went. He was not a good coachman, but was the first that ever let me drive a public coach. When I was fifteen years of age and at Eton I had had hold of my father's horses several times for two or three miles at a time, so that I knew something about it, and was as handy with my whip then as any old coachman, and could both catch my thong or hit either leader without any difficulty. Jem Adlam did not get on well, which was his own fault. When people got sick of him and he gave up, George Clark started his coach and called it the Age. An ugly coach, very long, no perch, nut-cracker springs in front, and mail-coach springs behind; not a coach to my mind, but one of the best to carry a load I ever sat on. Clark was very short of money, and so was I, but I managed to find him three-fourths of the horses. We had no break on our coach; loaded tremendously: Monday, Wednesday, and Friday from Brighton; Tuesday, Thursday, and Saturday from London. Very long stages, some of them thirteen miles. Very weak, bad horses. It was splendid practice. Down some of the hills we only kept in the road by the use of the whip ; no use pulling at their heads --their heads only came, and not their bodies ; and to keep them and the coach out of the ditch, nothing but a smart smack over the neck or shoulder would do it. We ran from London by Kew Bridge and Richmond, pulled up at the Greyhound to water, and pick up passengers and parcels. George Clark– a very fine coachman—was over eighteen stone weight. If the coach was full I used to send him down by rail. One day, one minute before the clock struck, reins and whip in hand, I jumped on to the box and found an old gentleman occupying the box-seat. 'Come,' he said, 'this won't do. I am not going to be experimentalised upon.' 'What do you mean?' 'Why, that I am not going to be driven by a young chap like you.' 'Such will be your sad fate,' I replied ; 'the horses are mine, the coach is mine, and I am going to drive. You have only one alternative, and that is to get down and have your money back in the office (White Horse Cellar) ; but sharp's the word, for in ten seconds the clock will strike and the coach start.' He grumbled something, but did not move. When we stopped at the Greyhound, I was getting the waybill from the landlord, with very particular directions about some parcel to be delivered, when a passenger got down from behind, and touching me on the elbow, said, 'Young man, which is the way to the Star and Garter?' 'Turn to left at the end of the street and keep the uphill road.' 'Thank you,' said he, 'here is a shilling for you.' So I touched my hat and thanked him, and put it in my pocket—one I kept clear, and the contents of which were handed over to old George Clark. My box passenger had not uttered a word, but as I got on the box and started again he unclosed his lips. 'You have begun well, earned a shilling already,' he said. 'Don't you think I deserved it?' said I. 'I will tell you more about it by-and-bye,' said he ; 'and, look here, it will all depend how you drive how much *I* give you when we get to Brighton, if Providence ever permits us to get there.' 'All right,' I said, 'and if you are fond of coaching, I bet you sixpence you come and have another ride with me.' After a bit we got on, and chatted away. Our route from Richmond was under the Star and Garter, over Ham Common to Kingston-on-Thames, where we changed at the King's Arms, thence through Leatherhead, where we stopped at the Swan to water, and changed at the White Horse at Dorking; going then through Mickleham, we passed the Running Horse Inn, where old John Scott used to stay for Epsom, and in the stables of which many Derby winners have slept on the eve of and after their victory; and so by Burford Bridge, at the foot of the celebrated Box Hill. On our up-journey we dined at Dorking.

The first stage out of London was twelve miles from Hyde Park Corner. From Kingston King's Arms to Dorking fourteen miles, making twenty-six miles; by Westminster Bridge, Tooting, Merton, Ewell, Epsom, and Leatherhead it is twenty-three and a half miles. Our next change was at Horsham, thirteen miles, where on the down journey we dined at the King's Head. Thence we ran through Cowfold to Henfield, eleven and a half miles, and from there into Brighton, thirteen miles: a pleasant stage down, but up it was a twister; the first six miles out of Brighton uphill, and yet such a gradual rise a great part of the way that it took a practised coachman to find out it was uphill. Altogether it was about sixty-four miles; for I think it is impossible to get our route to Kingston in twelve miles certainly, from White Horse Cellar. When we arrived at Brighton my box passenger pulled out a golden sovereign. 'Young man,' said he, 'I never enjoyed a ride on a coach more in my life. Take this, and if the box seat is not booked I will ride up with you to-morrow,' and he did, and stood another sovereign, on receiving which second one I remarked, 'Thank you very much; this is a good job for old Clark.' 'Who is old Clark?' 'That fat old fellow standing down there; he is our ballast; when the coach is empty we take him down to make the springs ride pleasantly, when it is full we send him up to London or down to Brighton by luggage train in a truck by himself.'

'Is he your father that he takes all the money?' 'No,' said I, 'he's only my sleeping partner, and you know the sleeping partner in a firm gets all the money.' So he laughed, and said, 'I will come and have another ride as soon as ever I can;' and he often came after and we made great friends. Our existence depended on fish and parcels almost more than on passengers. We did very well till the branch rails to Leatherhead, Dorking, and Horsham ran us off the road. Poor old Clark got ill and bedridden, and we gave up the coach, after which for several years there was no coach to Brighton.

In 1866 there was no coach running regularly from London to Brighton, though Captain Haworth had been occasionally on the road, and in the year named he asked me if I would oin in putting a coach on by way of Croydon and Crawley.[1] The result was that we started the New Times—it was a yellow coach. Three or four people horsed it. The Captain used to go every day, but when any of us who horsed it went we used to drive a good part of the way. The first year he had no regular coachman, and, if I recollect right, one of the Cracknells was the guard. He drove some coach a few years later. This coach soon collapsed, and in the following year, 1867, the late Edward Sacheverell Chandos-Pole, of Radbourne Hall, Derbyshire, B. J. Angell, usually called 'Cherry Angell,' and I put on a two-end coach on the Croydon and Crawley road to Brighton. Pratt drove from London to Horley and Alfred Tedder from Brighton to Crawley, each taking the coach home from Horley. When any of us travelled by the coach, which was four or five days a week, we always drove. Angell horsed it two stages out of London, I horsed the middle ground three stages, and Chandos-Pole two stages out of Brighton. We had lots of fun and driving; the coach was very well horsed, and kept good time. There have been many Brighton coaches since; an American gentleman, Mr. Tiffany, ran for one or two years, and another American, Colonel de Lancey Kane, was a familiar figure on the road. In 1887, Selby's Old Times was put

[1] It was a three-days-a-week coach from each end.

on, making six stages. He drove it till almost the day of his death.

There were a great many coaches on the Bristol and Bath road to London. The one I usually travelled by was the York House coach from Bath, starting from both ends at seven A.M., and reaching London about seven, covering 110 miles. It stopped twenty minutes at Marlborough going up and at Salt Hill going down for breakfast, and half an hour at the Pelican at Speenhamland, better known as Newbury, both ways, for dinner. Old Mrs. Botham kept that hotel, and horsed the coach a couple of stages, and her nephews the Brothers Botham kept the Windmill at Salt Hill, where the coach breakfasted, and horsed it two or three stages. There was an hotel at Salt Hill, the Castle, where other coaches changed horses and breakfasted. Reilly, who kept the York House at Bath, horsed it some part of the way; I am not sure who horsed it out of London, but think it was Mr. Nelson. Their first change was nearly a mile short of Hounslow, close to where the railway arch now stands. That was the first public coach I ever drove, as I have mentioned before. James Adlam was not nearly so good a coachman as Jack Sprawson; the former was always going faster and taking more out of his horses than Jack. Adlam made his wheel-horses do all the work the first half of the stage, and when they were beat made the leaders pull both the coach and the beaten wheel-horses, so that he got the whole lot well tired before the end of the stage, and in spite of going faster he was always late—always a minute, sometimes five, sometimes more. Jack Sprawson made his horses work level, never seemed to be going so fast, and yet was always punctual to a minute. When they were run off the road Sprawson started a coach of his own from Reading to Devizes, and when the railway opened, first to Newbury and then to Hungerford; he ran from those places to Devizes through Marlborough, till finally the rail opened to Devizes and he had to shut up. He was universally liked and respected by every one, which I cannot say of the other man. They drove alternate days to and from London and Marlborough, seventy-four and a half miles—hard work every day—in the heat of summer and the cold of winter. Bath by Devizes from Marlborough was 107¼ miles, but most of the coaches came through Chippenham and Calne, 110 miles. The roads down from London parted at Beckhampton on Marlborough Downs, the right-hand road through Chippenham, the left-hand through Devizes. Old Edwards drove in the morning from Bath to Marlborough and back at night, thirty-one and a half miles each way, making sixty-three miles a day by figures; but ten miles each way over Marlborough Downs was equal to twenty miles; it was a fearful road in the snow. We sometimes went by the Regulator, half an hour later than the York House; Isaac Johnson, afterwards on the Quicksilver, Devonport mail (one of the three brothers elsewhere mentioned), drove from Bristol to Marlborough and back. Sometimes we came from London by the Emerald, a green coach leaving London at three P.M.; the Regulator was a dark coach with red wheels, the York House chocolate with yellow wheels.

I omitted, whilst writing of the York House coach from Bath, to state a circumstance which will give an idea to the luxurious first-class railway traveller, now usually wrapped from his chin to his toes in furs, of the discomfort in which people travelled by public conveyances in former days. Coming home once from Eton for the Christmas holidays in bitterly cold weather with snow on the ground, I was so perished with cold that, instead of going into the Pelican at Newbury, and falling to on the excellent boiled or roast beef or mutton provided for the coach dinner, I ran to the saddler's and invested twelve shillings in a large and thick horse-rug, and was much laughed at for my pains, not only by my fellow-passengers, but by my own family when I got home. However, that evening coming over the Marlborough Downs between that town and Calne I think I had the laugh on my side; and after I got home—mackintosh soft white stuff having then just been invented—I made the village tailor cover my rug with the patent, and this excellent warm wrap I had for years. No such thing as a railway wrapper or travelling rug was known in those days. No apron or rug belonged to a coach. At starting, or whenever they changed coachmen, the new comer appeared whip in hand and an apron over his arm—generally a stiff tarpaulin large enough for the box passengers as well as himself—the other passengers made shift with a bit of clean straw if they were lucky enough to get it. Our greatcoats were uncomfortable; they had pockets behind like an evening tail-coat, and on the hips with flaps over them; without unbuttoning the coat you could not get your hand in or out of them or withdraw anything you wanted; a small breast pocket was put for one's handkerchief and that was all. There was no such thing as a tab for the collar, only three long hooks and three eyes, through which the wind whistled into one's teeth. Before my time, I am told, even the coachman had no apron; this probably was the reason why so many of them wore knee-caps, and a night coachman was swaddled up something like a mummy—how he got on and off his box or could use his arms was a mystery. I must not forget dear old Mrs. Botham, of the Pelican, at Speenhamland, with her rich black silk gown and her high white, sort of modified widow's cap. She was always kind and hospitable. When the family posted up they dined there, and all were made to drink a little most excellent cherry brandy, each was presented with a cornet or screw of white paper containing brandy snaps of the very best, and when children travelled by the coach they had the same. The cherry brandy was noted for its excellence all over the country. Mrs. Botham died at a ripe old age, respected by all who knew her.

A coach ran from Salisbury to Chippenham Railway Station and back again, horsed and driven by a very respectable man and good coachman of the name of Stevens, who did both journeys—thirty-three miles each way. That it should pay between Chippenham and Devizes I can understand, but how he took anything except from 'through' passengers and parcels on the other two-thirds of the road I cannot think. About three miles out of Devizes you come to Red Horn turnpike on the edge of Salisbury Plain, and with the exception of the Bustard Inn, half-way and about two miles from Stonehenge, and the Druid's Head Inn and training stables about three or four miles further on, there is not only not a village, but not a house, in the twenty miles. The Great Western Railway branch by Westbury and Warminster drove Stevens off the road, and not long after the South-Western Railway opened their line from London through Basingstoke and Andover through Salisbury to Exeter.

The Dover road was always a very pleasant one to drive, excepting the fearful hill on the south of Chatham, not far from Brompton Barracks. Poor old Rickman, who was for many years stationmaster of the Midland Station at Derby, drove on this road. He was killed about the year 1879 or 1880 on the day they opened the loop enabling trains running from London and Trent to go through to Normanton or elsewhere without passing through Derby Station. He had walked along the line to see that it was being worked all right, and in coming back was run over and cut to pieces by a train. He was an excellent servant of the company, and most civil and obliging to the passengers. The three brothers Wright had many pairs of post-horses, and horsed several coaches. One kept the Ship Hotel at Dover, the principal hotel till the Lord Warden was built; another kept the Fountain Hotel at Canterbury, and was as well known and respected as the Cathedral; the third kept the Rose at Sittingbourne. When the Dover Wright died, he was succeeded by Birmingham, who had been commissioner to the hotel and used to take one's keys, and get one's luggage through the Custom House. When the Lord Warden was built, he took the hotel, and eventually became Mayor of Dover, and used to receive the potentates and princes who passed through. He was an excellent man and much respected. I knew him fifty years ago. He has not been dead above three or four years. When quartered in London I used often to go down by the Dover Mail, get on to the up Mail when we met her, and come back again with her to London. The spectacle of the Mails driving into the General Post Office, and coming out of it, arriving or starting, was very pretty and interesting. I used to get a good deal of driving, but never up or down that hill on the other side of Chatham. The coachmen were afraid of a drag-chain breaking and of being discharged if a stranger was driving, and an accident should happen.

'Two minutes to spare.'

OLD COACHING DAYS.

By Lord Algernon St. Maur.

AMATEUR REMINISCENCES.

The number of old coaching men—of those, that is to say, who were accustomed to drive when coaching was the speediest and most familiar form of locomotion—is gradually becoming fewer and fewer. It is because I had the advantage of being—or the misfortune to be?—an enthusiastic coachman in days of yore that the Editor has applied to me for a contribution, and I hasten to fulfil the request without further apology or preface.

My active experiences go back half a century. In 1830

Mr. Stevenson was driving the 'Brighton Age;' and I begin with him because he was the great reformer who set a good example to coachmen generally, as regards punctuality, neatness and sobriety. Before his day many were very slovenly. They drove without gloves or aprons; the old night coachmen frequently wore glazed hats such as sailors wear, and had bands of hay or straw twisted round their legs; they were uncouth and careless in appearance; rough in manner and language; much given to drink; and, if admitted as representatives of the profession, were likely to get the coachman a bad name which he did not deserve. The 'Age' left Brighton as the clock struck twelve, and a vast crowd assembled every day to see it start; it was well horsed and well driven. This has always been the most fashionable road for driving, and later on the late Duke of Beaufort, Lord Chesterfield, and several other gentlemen drove on that road. The professional drivers afterwards were Charles Jones, Sir St. Vincent Cotton, Dick Brackenbury, Jack Willan, Charles Ward, and Frank Jerningham. Willan had what was called a 'double load,' the 'Times,' which he drove from London to Brighton and back; it was said to be worth 700*l.* a year; but a man who drives one hundred miles every day, in all weathers, deserves to be well paid.

If I go back to my very earliest recollections of coaching, I must begin before the date I have mentioned.

In the year 1820, being then six years old, I was put into the old Frome coach, which carried six inside, to be taken to London. We left Frome at 6 P.M., and reached our destination at 12 next day—eighteen hours doing one hundred miles; but I have never yet forgotten that every time we changed horses the same question was always put to the guard, which was, 'Well, George, how is your brother Robert?' It turned out that shortly before, at some inn, the horses had been left to themselves, while the coachman and guard went in to drink; the horses started off, the guard rushed out, just in time to jump on to the coach, but as they were making for a pond he jumped off and broke his leg. Such instances of neglect were not

'THE LEADERS TOOK FRIGHT'

uncommon, and I remember an old coachman telling me that he once met two coaches in one night without any coachman, and that he managed to stop them both without any accident. From the age of six till twelve I was at school on Wimbledon Common, and went home three times a year in Mr. Dawnay's four-horse coach. This was a strange conveyance. It carried four inside; then, behind the body of the coach, there was a circular sort of basket which carried six passengers. A very few years previously, although the coaches were on springs, the box seat was not so designed, so that the coachmen were terribly shaken. State coaches were then built in the same manner. I was always very fond of horses, and when at this school I much envied our dancing-master, who came once a week in a tandem.

In those days Lord Spencer lived in Wimbledon Park, which abounded in game of all sorts. Wild ducks were by no means rare visitors, woodcocks were not seldom found, and there was also a heronry. Sir Francis Burdett lived upon the Common, also Tooke, Lord Melville, Count St. Antonio, and many more. At twelve years of age I went to Eton for four years; this was in 1826. Goodall was provost, Keate headmaster; Staniforth, captain of the boats. Here I first began to drive, having a gig occasionally or a phaeton from Bob Davis, who kept the inn next to Windsor Bridge. My next coaching experiences were from London to Peterborough and back three times a year, either by the Louth mail, which ran through Cambridge, or by the Stamford 'Regent.'

Ringrose drove the mail from Cambridge to Huntingdon and back. One fine summer morning, just at dawn, a donkey stood in the middle of the road, but as the mail drew near, he lay down and rolled, causing such a dust that the leaders took fright and upset the mail. Such an accident might, of course, have happened to anybody, but poor Ringrose was so chaffed, and was asked so frequently whether he had met the donkey that morning, that he was nearly driven off the road. There were some good inns in those days, the Cock Inn at Eaton, the Wheatsheaf at Atconbury Hill, the Haycock at Wansford, and the George at Grantham. Although I had no driving, I passed three very pleasant years in Peterborough, with five other pupils, at a tutor's. We read six or eight hours on most days; in summer we hired a four-oar from Cambridge and rowed on the Nene; we also sailed on Whittlesea Mere, then a lake about fourteen miles round, where we shot snipe, ducks, teal, widgeon, sheldrakes, ruffs and reeves, herons, and other birds. There were some very fine men in the Fens, who lived entirely by the gun, especially one Bate, six feet two. He shot with an old flint and steel gun, worth a few shillings, and for wadding he picked dry sedge as he walked along. I once asked him how it was that he scarcely ever missed a snipe; he replied, 'I never shoots at them, I always shoots where they're a-going, and then the shot meets them'—this, however, is a digression from coaching.

In 1833 I went to live in London, where I had such a seven years of coaching as I shall never forget. At that time all the mail coaches assembled once a year on the 1st of May, either in Lincoln's Inn Fields or some other roomy place, coachmen and guards all in their new liveries of scarlet and gold, all the horses in new sets of harness All the best horses in or near London belonging to the mails were put in on that day; several gentlemen, lovers of the road, such as Sir Henry Peyton, Sir Lawrence Palk, and several others, also lent their own teams to join in the procession, as the mails were driven through all the principal streets in the West End; but, before leaving London, all the regular mail teams were put in again. A dinner was always given at Westminster to the mail coachmen and guards; at this Mr. Chaplin (afterwards member for Salisbury) presided, and he generally gave 'shouldering' as a toast, which was considered a capital joke. As the meaning of the word will be little understood by the present generation, I may explain that it referred to a system in vogue which was rather against the interest of the coach proprietors. Coachmen were allowed to pick up 'short passengers between the different towns, charging them a shilling or half-a-crown, according to the distance, and to put these small sums into their own pockets; and as these short passengers handed the money to the coachman over his shoulder before alighting, this custom was called shouldering. Foreigners were much struck with this procession of the mails. I and other gentlemen who were interested in coaching always rode round with them on horseback. The last procession took place in May 1838; there were then twenty-seven mail coaches in London; the Earl of Lichfield was Postmaster-General, and Mr. George Louis was Superintendent of the New Post Office.

I belonged to the B.D.C., or Bedfont Driving Club; an association which had about thirty members. We dined there, at the Black Dog, three times during the summer. The Club was formerly held at Benson, near Oxford, but Bedfont was much more convenient. It was a pretty sight, about eleven at night, when starting for London, to see all the coaches in the yard, all the lamps lit, and teams of divers colours. I regret that I have not retained the list of the members of the Club, but it included Lord Sefton, Sir Henry Peyton, Messrs. Villebois, Bunbury, Kenyon, Spicer, Sumner, and many others. We also had a very pleasant coach dinner in Botham's, at Salt Hill; the Duke of Beaufort, Lord Chesterfield, Counts d'Orsay and Batthyany, and a host of others, sat down to the number of about fifty; the hours were small when we reached Kensington Corner.

The Bath road was in excellent order, as there were pumps at short intervals for watering the road all the way to the western city. There were several excellent coaches on this road—the 'York House' to Bath, the 'Berkeley Hunt' and 'Tantivy' to Cheltenham. About this time some of the coaching men [1] put a very smart Windsor coach on the road called the 'Taglioni,' with a picture on the hind boot of the *danseuse*

[1] The Earl of Chesterfield and Count (afterwards Prince) Batthyany. It was a two-end coach. Charley Jones (a brother of the former Sir Henry Tyrwhitt) and young Dick Brackenbury were the coachmen.—B.

as she appeared on the stage. The horses, all piebalds, were supplied by Mat Milton, a noted character in those days, and they were splendidly driven by Charles Jones. I must also mention a first-rate pair-horse coach, the 'Wonder,' put on the road by Lovegrove of the Bear at Maidenhead. It was full every day, and did the twenty-six miles to London in two hours and a half to a minute.

Among my own early experiences was driving the 'Age' to Oxford by way of Uxbridge and Beaconsfield. There was much racing and opposition on this road between the 'Age' and the 'Royal William'—indeed, with such energy was the coach conducted that the driver told me he once drove the whole distance, fifty miles, in three hours and sixteen minutes. The 'Age' ran from the Green Man and Still in Oxford Street to the Mitre at Oxford, leaving London at one, reaching Oxford at half-past six. Major Fane, a fine coachman, often drove the 'Royal William.' Such was the jealousy between these two rival coaches that the horse-keepers of the 'Age,' which happened to be first and was changing horses, put a number of stable buckets across the road, thinking to delay the 'Royal William;' but Major Fane, who was driving and galloping at the time, the moment that he saw their little game, caught all his horses fast by the head, and giving them a smack all round, splintered the buckets into pieces and went on his way rejoicing. At first I used to drive to Oxford and return the next day, but I soon wished for more work; so after dining at the Mitre I used to send for one or two friends who happened to be in the city, and we sat together till eleven, when I drove the Gloucester mail back to London, by Henley and Maidenhead, reaching London at six; then to bed for two hours, after which I passed the day as usual. I was very fond of driving by night, as horses are always so lively; to hear the ring of their feet on a sharp frosty night, the rattle of the bars, and the clatter as they rose and surmounted the tops of the hills, was to me the sweetest of music. Sometimes I drove the Gloucester mail from London nearly to Benson, where we met

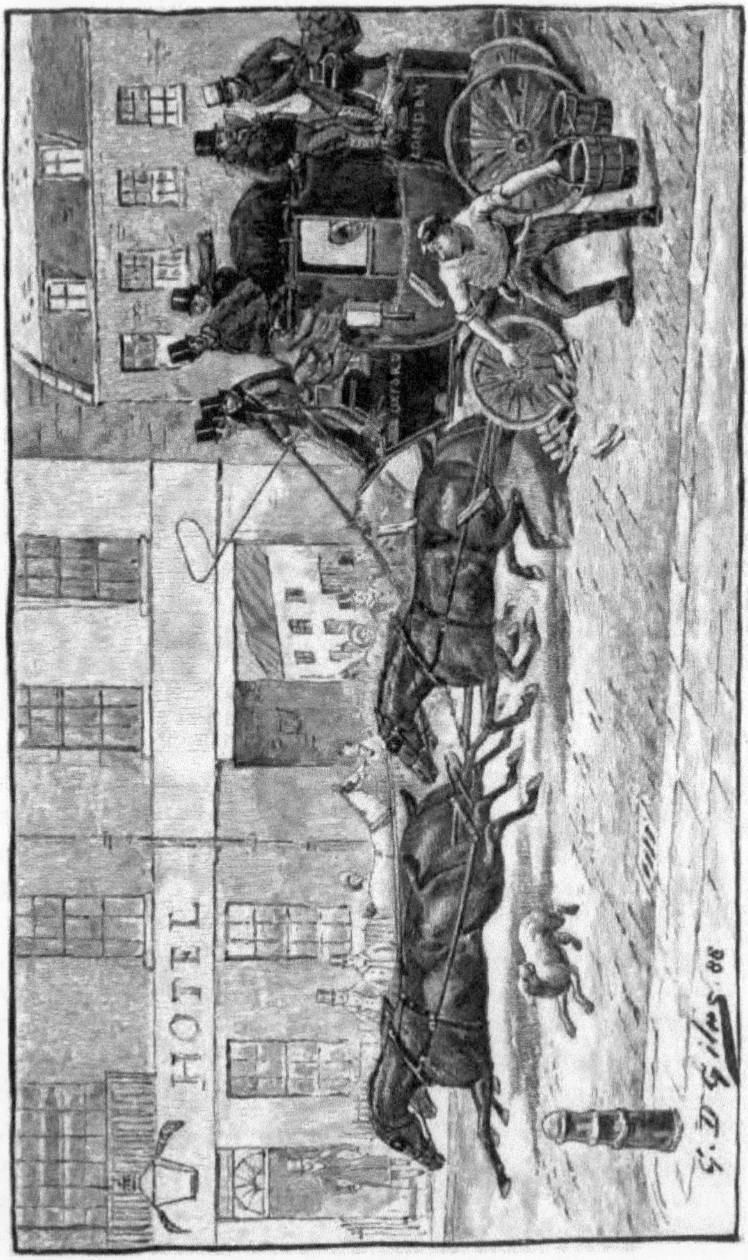

SPLINTERING THE BUCKETS

the up-mail, when I got on to that and drove back again. The first night that I drove this mail out of London the old coachman would drive with short-wheel reins, which just came round the middle finger. He called the usual reins 'a newfangled French fashion.' It was a dark, wet night, and rather foggy. When half-way down Henley Hill he began chirping at the leaders, which set them pulling. All he said was, 'It's a nasty hill with a bridge at the bottom, but we must go along, only mind what you're at, as this is just the spot where my partner was killed this day week; he ran up the bank and turned her over.' Some of these men were terribly reckless. I soon left this road for the Basingstoke or Exeter, which I much preferred to any other, and I never left it as long as coaching lasted. The 'Quicksilver,' or Devonport mail, and the Exeter 'Telegraph,' were simply perfection—such coachmen, such guards, and such horses! How well I remember the four blood chestnuts, with ring-snaffles, out of London! Then there was a grey leader over Hounslow Heath, who refused to start at all unless he had ear-caps on. These looked very odd when the ground was covered with snow. I often wondered who found out this horse's peculiarity, for it was such a strange remedy for a bad starter.

We left Paine's Old White Horse Cellar, opposite Hatchett's, at half-past eight; we changed at Hounslow and at Bedfont Gate (invariably called Bellfound Gate, but I never knew why), and reached Bagshot at a quarter before eleven—twenty-six miles. Here I slept, was called at half-past three, left at four, reached London at half-past six; then to bed till eight or nine, as the case might require. Sometimes I drove right down to Whitchurch, near Andover, met the up-mail and drove it back again, thus driving all night.

On two coaches, the 'Quicksilver' and 'Telegraph,' we had no side-reins or check-reins, never crossed or lapped the traces, nor throat-lashed the leaders; four reins in one hand and whip in the other was deemed sufficient. The mail-coaches carried four passengers inside and three outside, the guard having a small seat behind all to himself; he also had a sword and a blunderbuss, and a 'yard of tin,' which he could blow with sufficient expertness to make himself heard at a great distance. The motto on the forepart of the mail was 'Nemo me impune lacessit.' A coachman one day asked me what it meant, and I explained to him; but I added, 'On the "Quicksilver" it means, "Nobody ever gives me the go-by,"' and nobody ever did; for even when we were last out of London we were nearly always first into Hounslow. When going into Devonshire I got on to the mail at half-past eight in the evening, and got off it again at four the next afternoon, thus occupying twenty hours, driving all sorts of distances. When I went to Exeter by the 'Telegraph' we left London at five in the morning and reached Exeter at half-past ten at night —176 miles in seventeen hours and a half! We breakfasted at Bagshot, dined at Deptford Inn, and had tea at Ilminster. We changed horses nearly twenty times. There were three guards belonging to the 'Telegraph,' all first-rate men, who carried small twisted horns in their pockets, as the passengers were troublesome in trying to blow the usual long horns. These guards frequently managed to jerk the drag from under the wheel without stopping the coach, but this was very dangerous; a guard on another coach was killed in attempting it. There was a four-mile stage from Wincanton to Last Gate. A friend of mine, a first-rate coachman, asked the professional the shortest time in which he had ever done the distance, and he replied fifteen minutes. My friend, who was driving, said, 'I think it might be done in twelve.' He started at a gallop and did the four miles just under twelve minutes. The next day the professional tried to do the same, but, unfortunately, when at full speed one of the horses put his foot into a hole near the side of the road and broke his leg, which spoiled all. I never heard that he tried it again.

When I went into Dorsetshire I used to go by the old Exeter mail. I drove to Salisbury, eighty-six miles; sometimes to Dorchester, 120 miles. One evening I met this mail at

Dorchester. The only passenger was the coachman's wife, so they both got inside and I drove them to Salisbury, where Billy Chaplin, as he was called, got into the mail, which he horsed himself, and, of course, the professional ought to have been driving. I was just mounting the box when the guard said to me, 'I don't know what to do with the calf.' 'Calf,' I said; 'what calf?' He replied, 'I did not tell you before, but veal is cheap in Dorchester and dear in London, and there's a crown to be got out of that calf, only the London butchers like them alive; but now that Billy is inside perhaps I had better cut its throat, as if he hears it "bah!" I might get into trouble for carrying it in the hind boot.' I replied, 'Leave the calf alone. I will drive very steadily out of the town, and in less than twenty minutes our only inside, barring the calf, will be fast asleep.' I think it only fair to add that both our insides behaved very well, as we heard no more of either of them till we reached Piccadilly, when Mr. Chaplin jumped into a cab, the calf was dropped into the bottom of the mail-cart under the bags, and carried off to Newgate Street.

I was often asked in those days why, being so fond of driving, I did not keep a coach and team of my own. My reply was: 'In the first place, consider how much more practice there is in driving road-coaches with all sorts of horses; a man must become a judge of pace, which is not only useful but necessary; and then again one learns how to put horses together.' A man's own team is all very well for ten or twelve miles, but in driving a hundred miles he has the variety of ten or twelve teams, likewise of all sorts of ground, and again of driving horses with all sorts of mouths, all sorts of tricks and all sorts of tempers. I drove the Basingstoke coach whenever I could, frequently three days a week. It ran long stages. The coach stood at Gerrard's Hall, near St. Paul's, and ran from there to Bedfont, fifteen miles; thence to Bagshot, thirteen; Hartley Row, thirteen; Odiham, four; Basingstoke, six. It was considered a slow coach, but it was not so in reality. It left the Cellar at half-past nine, reaching

Basingstoke at three, doing fifty-two miles in five hours and a half; but there was much road-work to be done, picking up a great many 'short passengers.' We also stopped ten minutes at Virginia Water for refreshments, and generally more than ten minutes at Odiham, where the proprietor of the coach lived, and he always had a very nice luncheon laid ready on the table. It was my invariable practice to keep time to a minute. We had roan horses nearly all the way, and it was, of course, not always easy to supply deficiencies. One day, after changing horses at Hartley Row, on nearing Odiham the coachman said to me: 'Do you find any difference between this team and the others you generally have?' I replied that I thought that they rather wandered about the road just at starting. 'Well,' he said, 'I did not like to tell you before, but they have not an eye among them.' On reaching Basingstoke I remained till five, when I got on to the Weymouth 'Magnet,' and arrived in London at nine, nearly a hundred miles. There were many amateurs on this road—Sir John Rogers, Sir Lawrence Palk, Sir Walter Carew, Lord Willoughby de Broke, Mr. Wadham Wyndham, and many others.

There was much life on the road in those days, as those who could not afford post-horses went by coach; occasionally four ladies would engage the inside from Exeter to London. One night the guard said to me, 'Be sure not to turn her over to-night, as we have four members inside,' and I found that these were four members of Parliament. The day after the Coronation, I was just leaving the White Horse Cellar, with a very heavy load on the Basingstoke coach, when a clergyman came running up, and asked if I had any room. I replied that I was very sorry, but that the coach was more than full already. He exclaimed, 'I really must go, or I shall be in a sad scrape; cannot you make room for me somewhere? I am ready to jump into the boot or anywhere, sooner than be left behind.' 'Well,' I said, 'both boots are full I know, but sooner than you should get into trouble we will try what we can do.' So I told one of the porters to take a large trunk out of the front boot and pile it up on the top of the other luggage, and then the clergyman scrambled into the boot. Of course I left the door open that he might breathe, and I actually left London the day after Her Majesty's Coronation with four in, eleven out, a ton of luggage, and a clergyman to boot, and in the boot! Strange to say, we were liable to be fined for carrying one extra passenger, also if the luggage was piled up beyond a certain height; whereas, at present, omnibuses, with only a pair of horses, appear to carry any number of passengers.

Now as to pace. It often struck me that coachmen seldom knew at what pace they were going, unless they were driving themselves. I will give an instance of this. The Exeter 'Defiance' left the Cellar every evening at half-past four, loaded very heavily—I was always very fond of a full load. It was well horsed with four dark browns, all sixteen hands, which trotted much faster than they appeared to do. The usual coachman kept on telling me that I was losing time, and repeated this so often that I resolved to play him a trick if I could; for, driving as much as I did in those days, I began to think that I knew something of pace. So I trotted along, making all possible haste I could, but, of course, without galloping. When we reached Basingstoke, the ostler stood at the inn door with his hands in his pockets. It was a fine summer evening, and the town clock was exactly opposite the inn. The coachman said, 'Well, Jim, where are the horses?' 'Lor! bless ye, master, I haven't put the harness on yet,' was the man's reply, 'for you be here forty minutes sooner than you've a ben for six months.' I looked another way, and slipped off the coach, as my journey ended there. Soon after, being invited to shoot in Norfolk, I went there by the 'Phenomenon,' which left Mrs. Nelson's inn at the East End of London at seven o'clock. I had never been that road; the distance to Norwich is 116 miles, of which I drove eighty; the coach was well horsed, but we had no guard. Mrs. Nelson was a good business woman, and all the passengers were asked to pay their fares when on the coach before it left the inn yard. We had a very smart team into Sudbury—three piebalds and a grey. Just as we entered the town there was a man with a wheelbarrow in the middle of the road, with his back towards the coach. I ex-

The Sudbury barrow.

pected him to move, but he did not do so till we were close to him; he then ran away with his shovel, leaving the barrow, luckily lengthways, in the middle of the road. As it was downhill and I had a heavy load (nearly all Quakers), it was impossible to stop, so I opened out the leaders as well as I could; they were not throat-lashed or coupled very close, and fortunately did not shy. I managed to clear the barrow with the wheelers also, but the near hind wheel caught it, smashing it to atoms, with a loud report. The Quakers at the back, behind the luggage, all jumped up much alarmed, asking what had happened, as, of course, they had seen nothing and most likely thought that the coach had given way.

I returned in a day or two, driving a hundred miles. It so happened that I did not go that way again for two years. I then met this same coachman coming towards London, who made a sign for me to stop; after a few observations, just as we were both starting again, he remarked with a smile, touching his hat at the same time in the most respectful manner, 'I beg your pardon, sir, but you didn't happen to meet with the Sudbury barrow again, did you?' These long coachmen loved a joke dearly, and never forgot to name it if you happened to touch anything when driving.

I may here add a few words about the patent, or pressure, drag. That this drag is a great boon I cannot deny; but as to treatment, I know nothing that has been so much abused. In the days of the mails and fast coaches it would have been invaluable. Stopping to put the drag on, or take it off, would have been quite unnecessary; whereas, formerly, if behind time, a coachman was often tempted to run down a hill with a heavy load, without the drag, to save time, and this caused several sad accidents, the coach getting the better of a weak team of horses who could no longer sustain the weight behind them. There is also another great advantage in this drag, as some hills are only steep just at the top, so that after descending a short distance all pressure can be removed, and the rest of the descent being gradual, you can run down the hill at the rate of ten or twelve miles an hour. With the old drag and chain, when once it was on, it could not be removed till level ground was gained, as no horses could *back* a coach uphill.

The drag, however, may be, and often is, greatly abused. What do we see now? We may note a well-appointed coach being driven about London, but when necessary to pull up, the horses are no longer expected to stop the vehicle; the coachman's duty is to put on the patent drag. It is also often kept on after the coach has been stopped, lest the horses should move again. As the team descends, either in town or country, or even when going over the London bridges, on goes the drag. But the place of all others in which to see the popularity of the patent drag is the top of St. James's Street; here it goes on with a jerk, a pressure and a noise, that would almost lead one to think that the coach had arrived at the top of Henley Hill, with 'eleven and four,' and two tons of luggage; whereas, for years, we formerly trotted down St. James's Street, full in and out, with many loads, bound for Mr. Hart's hospitable Trafalgar Hotel at Greenwich or elsewhere, without any skid at all. But then horses knew their business. The drag is still more abused in the country, as every flyman makes use of it down gradual descents, where it is not the least required, causes a most unpleasant noise, and wears away both itself and the tires of the wheels to no purpose.

Now, I beg to state that I am not finding fault with the coachmen of the present day; no doubt there are excellent men among them, and I think it marvellous how few accidents have happened to coaches, especially in and about London, since railways opened, as modern drivers could not have had the opportunity of driving all sorts of horses, by day and by night, as had to be done formerly. The fact is, that horses are not taught to hold back, as every horse ought to be; but, of course, if dealers and horse-breakers can sell them when ignorant of this useful accomplishment, they will continue to do so. The drag should never be used excepting when absolutely necessary. I have heard much about the drag saving horses' legs; it may do so to a certain extent, but not nearly so much as some people imagine. I have not found that horses last any longer; and two of my oldest friends, who have driven four horses all their lives, still take a pride in descending steep hills without any drag at all, and declare that their horses last quite as long as other people's. Of course, in driving a pair of groggy wheel-horses the drag may save them from coming on their heads when going downhill. Living in a hilly country, I still retain breeching and bearing-reins, and the old drag and chain swung under the coach, as in old days, but I employ the pressure drag as well. There may be many changes yet; for,

> What can escape Time's all-destroying hand?
> Where's Troy, and where's the May-pole in the Strand?

as somebody wrote years ago.

But Troy's in Wales, there's no question about that. I quite forget who sang,

> The team trots merrily o'er the road,
> The rattling bars have charms;
> Eleven and four is our average load,
> And we change at the Coachman's Arms.

There was one team in the Brighton Day Mail quite perfection, three chestnuts, and a brown near wheeler who could trot while all the others galloped, but the horn upset him, and unless held hard he was off like a rocket. Such were some of the quaint experiences of horses which one gained on these old coaches.

The love of driving was so strongly developed in many enthusiasts, that when coaching came to an end as a business it began to be followed as a sport or amusement, and I now propose to make a few observations about the pleasure road-coaches, London teams, the meets at the Magazine, and driving generally.

In 1839, finding that railways would soon put an end to coaching, I was one day much surprised by two old friends calling upon me, and inviting me to purchase their coach, which they had kept between them for some years, stating that they could no longer afford to keep it, and that they were both going on to the turf to make fortunes. I begged them to reconsider their decision, adding that if they really intended to leave the road for the turf I thought it quite likely that I should see them 'both out,' which I regret to say has long since come to pass, nor did I ever hear of those fortunes to which they then looked forward.

I bought their coach, however, which proved to be an old mail. These mails, made by Ward about 1835, ran better than any coaches that I have ever driven; they travelled very steadily, followed well, galloped without rocking, and I have never heard of any one of them being upset.

Having bought a coach, I had no team; in fact, I never really had a team, as I was always driving odds and ends, perhaps a cabriolet horse and a hunter at wheel, and two buggy or gig horses as leaders, or some equally eccentric combination. Occasionally this was not all pleasure, but it was grand practice, nor can I ever forget the kindness of my friends in lending me all sorts of horses, and sending them on with servants and helpers, when I wished to drive twenty or thirty miles; one of the best and pleasantest teams that I ever drove consisted of four gig horses, each belonging to a different owner. I soon began to drive large parties of friends to Greenwich, Richmond, Windsor, Henley, Hampton Court, and Virginia Water; also to Epsom, Ascot and Goodwood, and the latter, as we arranged it, made a most enjoyable outing. We were generally a party of ten; we left London on Monday morning, sent horses on, had four teams in all, stayed the whole week with a kind friend about twelve miles from the course, so that we had a twenty-four-mile drive every day, and drove back to London, some sixty or seventy miles, on Saturday. We also used to attend the races at the Hoo, then held in the park, some six miles below Welwyn, and thirty-three from London.

I cannot help regretting that there should have been a sort of interregnum between the stage-coaches and pleasure-coaches.

The road came to an end in 1840, but it was not till some ten years had elapsed that the Tunbridge, Brighton, and Dorking coaches were put on the road. During these years everything appeared to have got out of gear. The new coaches were badly built, good crops or whips were not to be found, and nearly everything connected with coaching cost more than double, especially horses. I have had a few drives on these pleasure-coaches, but must confess that I never had the same joyous sensation as of yore, when mounting the box of the 'Quicksilver' Mail or the Exeter 'Telegraph,' for a journey of two hundred miles. It seemed so very tame by comparison, just driving a few miles out of London and back again; but I am very glad that good coaches and horses have not altogether disappeared, and that the love of the road survives so strongly as it evidently does. Some of these coaches load well, are well horsed, and well driven; the chief fault to be found is with regard to the time lost in changing horses, sometimes five or ten minutes, which time the horses have to make up. In old days, two minutes was deemed quite sufficient. Till invited to do so, it never entered my head to write about driving, but now I wish I had retained one half of the coaching songs, anecdotes, and other matters, which might have interested or amused those who still care about coaching. I remember a few lines of a coaching song, written by an old friend in 1835, as under:—

Some people delight in the sports of the turf,
  Whilst others love only the chase;
But to me the delight of all others is
  A coach that can go the pace.
There are some too for whom the sea has its charms,
  And who sing of it night and morn,
But give me a coach with its rattling bars,
  And a guard who can blow his horn.

How the girls all doat on the sight of a coach,
  And the dragsman's curly locks,
As he rattles along with eleven and four
  And a petticoat on the box;

His box is his home, his teams are his pride,
And he ne'er looks downcast or forlorn;
And he lists to the musical sound of the bars,
And a blast on the old mail horn.

There was another song, 'The Tantivy Trot,' which had a great popularity.

THE TANTIVY TROT.

Here's to the heroes of four-in-hand fame,
Harrison, Peyton, and Ward, sir;
Here's to the dragsmen that after them came,
Ford, and the Lancashire lord, sir.

Let the steam-pot
Hiss till it's hot;
Give me the speed
Of the Tantivy trot.

Here's to the arm that holds them when gone,
Still to a gallop inclined, sir,
Heads to the front with no bearing-reins on,
Tails with no cruppers behind, sir.

Let the steam-pot
Hiss till it's hot;
Give me the speed
Of the Tantivy trot.

Here's to the dear little damsels within,
Here's to the swells on the top, sir;
Here's to the music in three feet of tin,
Here's to the tapering crop, sir.

Let the steam-pot
Hiss till it's hot;
Give me the speed
Of the Tantivy trot.

The subject of accidents seems to be an interesting one to those who are fond of reading about coaching in the old days.

My own luck in this respect was great, personally. During all the years that I drove, I never witnessed any accident, but I will try to describe some of which I have heard, as such description may serve to teach the young coachman what to do and to avoid doing.

The Edinburgh Mail on leaving London one foggy night was driven by an old man named Penny; he became nervous, and asked Jack Webb the guard (a first-rate man, and very active) to come over the roof and drive for him, which he did; but the fog was so dense that in a few minutes he turned the Mail over, and poor old Penny was killed. Webb saved one or two mails from accidents by letting himself down from the foot-board, either on to the pole or on to one of the wheel-horses, and collecting the reins which had been accidentally dropped, and was thus enabled to stop the horses; this feat required great nerve and activity, and I am pleased to add that he was liberally rewarded.

A coachman named Bollin, in Northamptonshire, was driving down a steep hill when the near leader's rein broke. Of course he could not stop, but he had the presence of mind to do the only thing possible to get out of the scrape; he gave his off leader a smack under the bar, put them all into a gallop, over the bridge at the bottom of the hill, and managed to stop them going up the next hill, which was fortunately steep. The passengers were so delighted that they all clubbed together and made him a very handsome present, as they quite expected to be killed, and no wonder; for I must admit that it requires some nerve, nor is it all pleasure, to sit still on a four-horse coach with a Christmas load when galloping down-hill, with a bridge at the bottom, and only three reins to the four horses; but all's well that ends well, as this gallop did.

Sydney Robinson, who drove from London to Basingstoke, had his leg broken in a most unfortunate manner, he being a steady man and a good coachman; he left Bagshot with only one passenger who was on the box-seat. After passing the

Jolly Farmer, a small public-house on the road, a brewer's dray, with empty barrels, went by the coach at a trot, and the barrels made such a noise that the coach-horses started off. The box passenger was so alarmed that he quite lost his head, and frantically clutching the two near-side reins, pulled the horses out of the road, and overturned the coach. This silly fellow escaped unhurt, but Robinson's leg was badly fractured; he was laid up for many weeks, and felt the accident for the remainder of his life.

Wignell, who also drove on the Southampton road, was upset, and broke his leg so badly that it was taken off above the knee, after which he wore either a cork or a wooden leg; he was upset twice afterwards, and broke his leg each time, but luckily the wooden one. During the seven years that I drove on the road, I had two horses down. We changed at Bagshot, when a most miserable off-leader was put into the coach. I exclaimed, 'What is that?' The coachman replied, 'I have often complained of that horse, but the master will not change him.' 'Well,' I said, 'my belief is that he will be on his head before he has gone a mile;' and it so happened: in less than half a mile we left him by the roadside and went on with three. Another day I was driving a coach called the Forester through the New Forest; on descending a hill, down came the off-wheeler; the coachman burst out laughing and exclaimed, 'That's just where it is! I was a watching you, you know, how you pulled them together and came gently off the brow of the hill as a coachman had ought; but that horse would never have fallen had I been a-driving, for I never interferes with them old cripples, for if you goes fast enough down them 'ere 'ills, they are afraid to fall.' Now I never forgot that lecture, as there is much truth in it: always go fast with unsound horses if you can.

One night, the mail from Salisbury to Southampton being rather behind time, they were having a merry gallop through the Forest, when the horses bolted out of the road, having taken fright at the cover of a carrier's cart which had been blown off and left by the roadside. The mail was overturned, and the coachman was killed; the guard, a ready and active man, went on with the mails as soon as he could, and on reaching Southampton, had some bills printed describing the accident, which he distributed at all the inns and public-houses, and in a few days the sum of 500*l.* was collected for the coachman's widow and children.

There are certain things that nearly all horses dislike and shy at. I remember one of the mails being upset in the same manner, through the cover of a cart being blown off between Egham and Staines, at early dawn. I never was on the Worcester Mail, but I have heard that it has been seen 'the other way up' more often than any other mail out of London.

I have always been given to understand that the late Duke of Beaufort, Lord Chesterfield, Mr. Probyn, Mr. H. Villebois, Sir Walter Carew, and Lord Willoughby de Broke were reckoned among the best coachmen between the years 1830–40.

Mr. Charles Jones, Age, Brighton; Bob Brackenbury, Age Brighton; George French, Tunbridge Wells Telegraph; Williams, Light Salisbury; Charles Ward, Devonport Mail; Tim Carter, Exeter Telegraph; Jimmy Witherington, Oxford and Cheltenham; Bill Harbridge, Exeter to Plymouth: these are a few of the best coachmen that I can remember, about the same time.

I have heard it stated that, if a set of four-horse harness were taken to pieces and thrown upon the floor, very few coachmen would be able to put it together again. This may be so, but I found enough to do in learning how to bit and harness four horses properly, and to put them together, taking care that the bridles or headstalls did not pinch their ears, which is often the case; that the bits were not too high nor too low in their mouths; bearing-reins, cruppers, pole-chains or pole-pieces not too tight or too loose; that the pads fitted well to their backs, and were well stuffed; all traces the right length; throat-lashes rather tight if no bearing-reins; the pole-hooks downwards, not to catch the bar of the bit, coupling-reins the right length. Be sure that the reins of your four-horse harness are cut properly; many sets of reins are sent out from the saddler's cut all wrong.

After driving seven years on the road by day and by night, I began to think that I knew most part of my lesson, but I was very soon undeceived, as, when I began to drive about London, I soon found that I still had a great deal to learn. In the country, going straight ahead, your chief duty was to make each horse do his own share of work and to keep time; but in London, so to speak, a man must be all eyes and ears; horses all well in hand, and ready to stop in a moment. I found it a good plan to couple my leaders a little closer, and to pole up my wheelers a link or two, when squeezing through the City in the afternoon. I have seen a few meets of both clubs at the Magazine in Hyde Park, and have been glad to notice a few good coachmen, some very well-built coaches, and many excellent horses. At first, the horses were too often very badly put together, traces much too long, and pole-chains generally much too tight; nor have I seen much improvement in these matters lately. I dislike carriage-horses in a coach; they are quite different animals from coach-horses; both are excellent in their proper places, but not by any means interchangeable.

I will now imagine that some young man who has never yet driven, but is attracted by the revival of coaching and is anxious to learn, desires to know how he may best set about it. First, I would buy a second-hand coach, or a strong break, having had it carefully examined; the harness, if second-hand, should also be looked over most carefully, the reins and hame-straps particularly. Horses could be bought at Tattersall's, or at Gray's Inn Lane, or St. Martin's Lane, or at any well-known dealer's. The best sizes for horses is perhaps about fifteen three, and they need not be too well bred. If the team only requires holding and not hitting, you will never learn to use your whip, the proper use of which is among the novice's greatest difficulties. He is nearly always to be met twisting his whip round and round, trying to catch up the thong, and looking at that when he ought to be watching his horses. He should learn to use his whip at home, before getting on to a coach at all. Let him sit on a table or high stool, in a large room, or, perhaps, a garden is better still. He should drive a short split stick, about six inches long, into the ground, at a proper distance from his chair, insert a small piece of card or paper into the cleft of the stick, and slash at it and try to hit it with the whipcord or point of the whip. This he will soon learn to do; then let an old hand teach him how to catch up the thong instantly; for the moment you hit a leader, some wheel-horses hang back, and should have a reminder at once, smart and effective. The next thing to be done is to learn how to put your team together, so that you may be well able to teach your servants, who generally know little or nothing about it. Then the novice will do well to take some lessons in driving from some one who thoroughly understands the art, always taking his whip and reins in his hands before mounting the box; when there, he must place his knees and feet close together, without any apparent stiffness, and be sure to cover his legs and feet with an apron: light jean in summer, strong cloth in winter.

Teach your horses to stand still after you are on the box, till you wish them to move; having all your reins properly in hand, raise it gently, and they will all start at once; you should never have recourse to that horrible new custom of crying out 'Hold up,' [1] in a stentorian voice, which is most unseemly and quite unnecessary, only intended for Bath wagon-horses in the olden time. Begin by driving a few miles into the country, then round the parks, and as soon as you can shift your reins properly, and use your whip, take a turn in the streets before twelve o'clock. Having gained confidence, begin at the Marble Arch, drive down Oxford Street, Holborn, round St. Paul's, and back by the Strand and Piccadilly; this was a favourite

[1] Or more commonly 'Pull up,' which is ridiculous.—B.

drive of mine, and should you take this drive about four o'clock in the afternoon, you will find plenty to do, and have a really good practice.

Do not stoop or lean forward, but sit quite upright on the coach-box; not at all stiffly. Hold your whip well up across your body; do not hold it close to the end, in the present fashion, but some distance from the end, otherwise you have no power to strike when necessary, and are very likely to let the whip fall altogether. As to your reins, they should be held as near your heart as possible, if you happen to have one; if not, where your heart ought to be. When you arrive at the top of a hill, pull your leaders gently back, as their traces should then be slack, and the bars should 'chatter.' When about to rise a long steep hill, catch hold of all their heads and trot up as far as possible, no matter how slowly, as in walking, few horses step together; consequently they will work better together and rise the hill more easily at a slow trot. The Scotch, or pressure drag, is an admirable and most useful invention; how glad we should often have been of such assistance some fifty years since, on dark or foggy nights when among steep hills with heavy loads and weak wheel-horses! But I must add that it is now most absurdly abused, as country flymen put it on on all occasions, whether the hill is steep or not; and I also see young raw-boned coachmen using it continually, even when they stop or wish to do so; whereas all horses should be taught to stop the coach themselves, also to run down any ordinary incline without any drag at all. My drag-chain has broken more than once when half down a steep hill; but, with a strong sensible pair of wheelers, and sound breeching, I never got into trouble.

In old days, when wishing to shorten, or take up the reins when driving, it was customary to seize the reins with the right hand behind the left, and pull them back through the fingers of the left hand; but this is a slow process. You should learn to take your reins back from the front, by placing the right hand in front of the left, and pushing them back as quick as possible, but taking the greatest care not to *drop* a rein in so doing, which is most dangerous; in fact, a beginner should practise this, either at first in the house, or on the coach-box without horses, or when the horses are standing still. If you build a coach, employ one of the best coachmakers, and do not try to build it too light, as light coaches are failures. I never knew one under 18 cwt. fit for all sorts of work or to carry a load well without rocking; most coaches weigh quite one ton. Be sure to build it with the foot-board well over the horses; when on the box you should not be able to see the part of the wheelers from the hips to the tail; let these horses be as near the splinter as possible with safety. Your pole should be rather a short one, as the nearer your leaders are to the coach in reason, the better, as the draught is less, and they are more within reach should they require your right hand; and be sure your traces are not too long; in this way you will have all snug and under control. When driving about the streets of London take care to keep your leaders well in hand, and never allow them to pull when turning a corner, or you will soon be in trouble; take plenty of room, and time also, when possible; in fact, it should be a case of 'eyes everywhere'; and, above all, remember that you must practise often, as is the case with chess, whist, or billiards. Study pace, which is most useful, especially in the City: suppose that you wish to pass a vehicle going the same way as yourself, and that another vehicle is meeting you at some little distance, you should know your own pace, and, at a glance, the pace that the vehicle you wish to pass is going, also the pace of the carriage approaching; in fact, a judge of pace can squeeze through the City in half the time of an ordinary mortal. I believe that I have now ventilated the four-horse coach pretty freely; and if I have only interested or amused for a few minutes any past, present, or future coachmen, I shall be more than repaid for these feeble efforts, made for the road, which is still dear to me. But ten times more shall I rejoice if, from the hints which I have given about driving four horses, I have been able to teach the rising generation of coachmen how to get on comfortably and avoid accidents, from which I myself had the good fortune to be totally exempt from 1833 to 1887, some fifty-four years.

THE OLD NORTH ROAD.

What pleasant nights and days I have passed on the old North Road, when going to shoot on the Moors in Yorkshire or in Scotland!

'Over the moors.'

Two or three friends and myself used to secure the whole of the Edinburgh mail about a week previously; we went in hackney-coaches with our servants and luggage to Sherman's Bull and Mouth Inn, opposite the New Post Office, and here was a grand sight about eight o'clock in the evening, as the yard was filled with mails and stage-coaches with enormous loads, starting for the North; teams of magnificent horses, mail-guards and coachmen in their liveries of scarlet and gold lace; horse-keepers busy with the horses, porters helping to load the heavy night-coaches, some of which carried from two to three tons of luggage, as besides the roof and the two boots there was a scrole from behind the back seat, on which was often placed a heavy trunk, and occasionally a sack of oats. Some coaches also had a cradle under the coach, which consisted of a large square piece of wood, suspended from the perch by ropes or chains, on which luggage was also carried; add to this fifteen passengers of twelve stone each, and we must not be surprised that the cattle sometimes sobbed a little when going over the brow of the hill.

I had often driven this mail, and one night it was proposed that I should begin at once, take the reins in the Bull and Mouth yard, drive into the Post Office yard, take up the mail-bags and drive out again. Now this was very unusual for an amateur; however I did it, and nothing was known or said about it, so we trotted off at once, and I drove 146 miles, the longest drive that I ever had at one sitting. I then began to grow sleepy, as we had had heavy rain all night, and the sun came out very hot the next day. About midday the coachman begged me to go on driving, declaring that the next team was the best between London and Edinburgh; but having driven about seventeen hours, I declined. I once went to Fort William, returning by the Pass of Glencoe, and the coachman told me that, as nearly all the harness happened to be worn out at the same time, new harness had been ordered for the whole seventy miles at once, but it had arrived without winkers. Strange to say, no accident happened, as not one horse in all the seven teams appeared to miss anything. I regret that coaching did not last a few years longer, as in 1830 it had scarcely reached perfection, and in 1840 it came to an end, as railways in all directions were opened that year. I also regret that the Government did not forbid the opening of more than a few lines at first, to see how they answered, as in that case those connected with the road would not have suffered as they did, many being utterly ruined. Few people are aware of the misery caused by railways to innkeepers, coachmen, guards, postboys, ostlers, and horse-keepers, as it all came to pass so suddenly. Nor could anybody foresee exactly the effects they would have, as the proprietor of a coach on the Western Road was offered 800*l.* by the railway company to take his coach off the road within a year of the opening of the railway; and those who have read the life of George Stephenson, the chief inventor of railways, may remember that he thought it likely that railways would only be used to carry heavy goods, or that, if they carried passengers, it would only be at the rate of twelve miles an hour, as most people would fear to go faster, whereas very shortly I found myself being carried to Bath, 110 miles on the broad gauge, in two hours and twenty minutes. At first railways met with much opposition, for not only were companies made to pay fabulous prices for land, but several large landed proprietors ordered men to watch day and night to prevent levels and measurements being taken on their property, and there were many free fights in consequence. Then we suddenly fell into the other extreme, many people being most anxious that a branch railway should be brought almost to their doors, or, at any rate, to the small town or village near which they happened to reside.

I think it was Charles Dickens who told the touching story of the two coachmen (brothers, if not twins) who met daily on the road, just raising their whips, or waving their hands to each other, but scarcely ever having time to stop or exchange a word. One died, after which the brother complained how dull the road had become, adding, 'I never see Tom's cheery face now, all life seems to have left the road;' and in a very few months he followed his brother.

Let me conclude these remarks by mentioning the requisites for driving, which are good eyes, strong arms, light hands, good nerves, good temper, and plenty of practice.

PROFESSIONAL REMINISCENCES.

Any account of old coaching days and matters appertaining to them must necessarily be interesting to those fond of the road, and the fact that these reminiscences were supplied by Philip Carter, a coachman of more than fifty years' experience commencing from the year 1828 and continuing almost up to the present time, will, it is hoped, tend to give them value.

The Belle Sauvage, Ludgate Hill, fifty-eight years ago was the property of Robert Nelson, son of Ann Nelson, of the Bull Inn, Aldgate, and was justly celebrated for being one of the most extensive and popular establishments of its kind in the metropolis. Among the most noted of the fast coaches was the Defiance, which ran from London to Oxford, and the honour of driving it was divided by two very well known coachmen, Adams and Foreman. It was horsed out of Oxford by Christopher Holmes, who had for some years strongly opposed a wealthy firm of that town, by name Coster and Waddall. Mr. Nelson was at the same time proprietor of the fastest and most popular mail in England, the Devonport Mail, commonly called the Quicksilver. In 1828 Mr. R. Nelson instructed one of his coachmen to give young Carter all possible advice and information that he might go to work as soon as he was capable, and after a few weeks Carter drove the Leeds Courier out of and into London from the Belle Sauvage.

On his first day out with him, his mentor took the opportunity of having him 'sworn at Highgate,' stating it was a very essential form to go through in order to become a qualified coachman. His curiosity to know the nature of such an oath induced him at once to assent. He immediately pulled up at the Wellington Hotel at Highgate, where he was duly sworn, 'not to drink small beer when he could get strong; not to kiss the maid when he could kiss the mistress, and never to pass that house without calling to have a bottle of champagne,' and the landlord was bound to give him credit if he had not the wherewithal to discharge his liability. Carter continued on this coach until 1829, and next drove the Stroud Water mail as far as Benson in Oxon; he was then fortunate enough to be appointed to drive the Red Rover to Brighton, a coach started conjointly by Messrs. Nelson and Holmes, the latter having sold his business at Oxford. It began to run at the time of the proclamation of William IV., whose residence was at the Pavilion in Brighton, and in consequence of performing the journey in half an hour less time than any other coach, it had a capital season. This coach left London half an hour later than any other and arrived at the same time as the rest, leaving at 4 P.M. and reaching its destination at 9 P.M.

In order to advertise and give notoriety to the coach, on the occasion of the King opening Parliament the coach conveyed his maiden speech to Brighton in the short time of 3 hrs. 35 mins., Philip Carter driving, Mr. Holmes having made strenuous efforts and obtained the speech in shorthand notes.

Soon after this Carter had a most miraculous escape from a fatal accident. He carried a full load of passengers, and Captain Barclay (of pedestrian notoriety) was on the box. He was a man well known in the coaching world, and was in the habit of driving a great deal with the Brighton coachmen, many of whom were part proprietors; not being one himself, however, Carter could not allow anyone to drive. On leaving the office at the Clarence Hotel he had twelve outside passengers all booked and loaded. A gentleman who was a regular customer came up at the last moment, and being the last coach from Brighton, Carter was prevailed on to take him on his consenting to ride on the roof and pay the expenses of an information in the event of there being one. The accident occurred by the pole breaking close to the futchels at the top of the hill going off Thornton Heath down into Streatham. Immediately the pole broke it fell down between the horses, and they commenced the descent with fearful rapidity. Carter had some difficulty in preventing Captain Barclay from trying to pull the horses up, as he knew it was an impossibility, and he managed to get round the very awkward turn at the bottom of the hill with only a slight concussion which threw the aforesaid gentleman off the roof on to the ground; but he fortunately escaped with a severe shaking. The impetus with which they were going carried them up to the top of the other hill, where, with the assistance of the Captain, he pulled up near the Pied Bull, a pair-horse coaching establishment. Here they were furnished with a new pole and continued their journey to London.

When the coach became well established, soon after Christmas, both proprietors sold their horses. Carter then went on to the Hope, a coach running to Sheffield and Halifax, and this he drove to Hockliffe and back for about two years. In consequence of the Hope being removed to the Bull and Mouth, he went on to a coach called the Stag to Shrewsbury, put on by the proprietors of the Wonder coach, which also ran to Shrewsbury, with a view of running a coach called the Nimrod off the road. They succeeded in doing this in about a year, after a very strong opposition during the whole time; each coach used to gallop for the lead of the road, leaving the Wonder going at its usual pace and time. Carter had strict injunctions not on any account to allow the Nimrod to be in advance of the Stag. Mr. Sherman, who was at that time increasing his coaching establishment, had just finished building the hotel in St. Martin's-le-Grand, now called the Queen's, which was first opened during that year; it was then called the Bull and Mouth, and was carried on for some years on his responsibility entirely managed by a Mrs. Sanderson. When the Stag was taken off the road Carter went to Oxford to drive a coach put on by the tradesmen of that town, who had formed a company, and horsed by Major Fane, who contracted with the proprietors. The coach started from the Three Cups, Oxford, leaving at 8.30 A.M., arriving at the Gloucester Coffee House at 2, going to the Old Bell, Holborn, leaving the Gloucester Coffee House on its return journey at 3 P.M., arriving at the Three Cups at 8.30 P.M. This Carter drove up and down as long as the coach was on the road, about twelve months, daily except Sundays, without the assistance of either guard or break. He then went back to Nelson's, of the Bull Inn, Aldgate, and drove the Exeter Telegraph to Basingstoke and back daily, until the railway interfered with it, leaving Piccadilly at 5.30 A.M., arriving at Basingstoke at 9.55 A.M., stopping at Bagshot to breakfast; leaving Basingstoke on his return journey at 6 P.M., arriving at Piccadilly at 10.15, and the Bull Inn, Aldgate, at 11 o'clock. This he did for some years without ever missing a day except Sundays, and he is always pleased to think it was undoubtedly the best-appointed and fastest coach in England up to its last journey. The entire distance (176 miles) was performed in seventeen hours; they stopped one hour for meals.

Carter never remembers being late at the Bull Inn, Aldgate, during the whole time he drove, except once, and then only seven minutes; but he was told of it by Mr. Nelson. This happened to be a coach that he was more particular about than any other in his establishment, having gone to great trouble and expense in bringing it to the perfection it reached. All other Exeter coaches being very slow, the people who horsed them ridiculed the idea of his success, and declined horsing it over the same ground, although they horsed his other Exeter coach. He was not to be discouraged, sent horses all the way to Exeter, and horsed the coach himself the entire journey from London to its destination. By making punctuality the primary consideration the coach became a very good property, and enabled Mr. Nelson to sell all his horses, with the exception of two London stagers, at a remunerative price.

For some months before this coach ceased running to Exeter the proprietors took advantage of the South-Western Railway being open as far as Basingstoke by contracting with the company to carry the coach and passengers as far as they were open, the proprietors paying the ordinary first and second class fare for all passengers, the coach and either coachman or guard to be conveyed free of charge. By this arrangement the coach performed its journey to Exeter in two hours less time, leaving the South-Western Railway Station, which was then at Nine Elms, one hour later than it had left London theretofore, and arriving in Exeter one hour earlier, during the whole of which time, until the Great Western Railway opened throughout, the coach loaded better than before.

Curtis Brothers being the proprietors at Basingstoke, they placed the London coachman on the coach to drive from Basingstoke to meet the coach coming from Exeter, and on one occasion an extraordinary incident occurred. The coach passed many miles over a very extensive tract of country then and now known as Salisbury Plain, remarkable for very long ranges of hills and deep valleys, extending many miles right and left of the road, and in the month of February of that year a very rapid thaw set in immediately after an exceptionally heavy fall of snow. The ground was frozen very hard, the water from the hills descending so rapidly that in seven or eight hours there were streams of a great depth in the valleys where a drop of water had never before been seen, and the current in some in tances was so strong that it did a great deal of damage. Changing horses at Amesbury about twelve o'clock, the coach should have passed Stonehenge, standing on the summit of a steep hill, a deep valley approaching it. At this time the water was running down the valley, and was headed by an embankment at the bottom of the hill, which had been thrown up by reducing the hill. On the return journey, about three hours later, changing horses at the next village called Winterborne

Left behind.

Stoke, a small trout stream there had so much swollen that it had destroyed a great part of the village, in which was the stabling the coach-horses had just vacated, and the horses taken off were about to enter. On reaching the hill at Stonehenge, about half an hour later, the water had so much increased that it was just running over the embankment. The coachman, having some doubt as to the safety of crossing the embankment, pulled up. Two or three of the passengers got off the hind part of the coach, intending to follow over on foot. On getting safely over, the coachman had just pulled up when the whole bank gave way. The passengers that had got off were left behind, without a possible chance of getting to London that night, the coachman making the best of his way to the Star Hotel at Andover, where the coach stopped half an hour for dinner, and reached Basingstoke at 7 P.M., the time it was due, to be conveyed by the last train to London.

A comprehensive idea of the life and work of a coachman in former days may be gathered from the sketch of the career of Mr. Charles Ward (one of a family well-known on the box), written by himself, and published for private circulation a few years back. The Editor takes the opportunity furnished by the author of quoting the following extracts.

My father was a coach proprietor as well as a coachman, and, I am proud to say, one of the best whips of his day. He gave me many opportunities of driving a team. I will not, however, enter into all the details of my youthful career, but proceed to state, that at the early age of seventeen I was sent nightly with the Norwich and Ipswich mail as far as Colchester, a distance of fifty-two miles. Never having previously travelled beyond Whitechapel Church, on that line of road, the change was rather trying for a beginner. But fortune favoured me; and I drove His Majesty's mail for nearly five years without an accident. I was then promoted to the Quicksilver, Devonport mail, the fastest at that time out of London. It must be admitted that I undertook this task under difficult circumstances—involving, as it did, sixty miles a night—since many had tried it ineffectually, or at all events were unable to accomplish the duty satisfactorily. It is gratifying to me to reflect that I drove this coach more than seven years without a single mishap.

Getting at length rather tired of such incessant and monotonous nightly work, I applied for a change to my employer, the well-known and much-respected Mr. Chaplin, who at that time had seventeen hundred horses employed in coaching. His reply was characteristic. 'I cannot find you all day coaches,' said he; 'besides, who am I to get to drive your mail?' I must say, I thought this rather severe at the time, but, good and kind-hearted man as he was, he did not forget me.

Not long after this interview, the Brighton day mail being about to start, he made me the offer to drive the whole distance and horse the coach a stage, with the option of driving it without horsing. Like most young men I was rather ambitious, and closed with the former conditions. The speculation, however, did not turn out a very profitable one, and, the railway making great progress, I sold my horses to Mr. Richard Cooper, who was to succeed me on the box. I was then offered the far-famed Exeter Telegraph, one of the fastest and best-appointed coaches in England. My fondness for coaching still continuing, and not feeling disposed to settle to any business, I drove this coach from Exeter to Ilminster and back, a distance of sixty-six miles, early in the morning and late at night. After driving it three years, the railway opened to Bridgewater; this closed the career of the once-celebrated Telegraph. But those who had so long shared its success were not inclined to knock under. My brother coachman and myself, together with the two guards, accordingly started a Telegraph from Devonport to London, a distance of ninety-five miles by road, joining the rail at Bridgewater, thus making the whole journey two hundred and fifty miles in one day. At that time there was a coach called the Nonpareil, running from Devonport to Bristol.

The proprietors of this vehicle, thinking that ours would take off some of their trade, made theirs a London coach also, and started at the same time as we did. We then commenced a strong opposition. I had a very good man to contend against—William Harbridge, a first-class coachman. We had several years of strong opposition, the rail decreasing the distance every year, till it opened to Exeter. The Nonpareil was then taken off, and they started a coach called the Tally Ho! against the poor old Telegraph. Both coaches left Exeter at the same time, and this caused great excitement. Many bets, of bottles of wine, dinners for a dozen, and five-pound notes, were laid, as to which coach would arrive first at Plymouth. I had my old friend Harbridge again, as my competitor. The hotel that I started from was a little farther down the street than the one whence the Tally Ho! appeared, so that as soon as I saw my friend Harbridge mounting the box, I did the same, and made the running. We had all our horses ordered long before the usual time. Harbridge came sailing away after me; the faster he approached, the more I put on the steam. He never caught me, and, having some trifling accident with one of his horses over the last stage, he enabled me to reach Plymouth thirty-five minutes before he came in. My guard, who resided in St. Albans Street, Devonport, hurried home, and as the other coach passed he called out and asked them to stop and have some supper; they also passed my house, which was a little farther on, in Fore Street. I was sitting at the window, smoking, and offered them a cigar as they passed—a joke they did not, of course, much relish. The next night they declared they would be in first; but it was of no use, the old Telegraph was not to be beaten. Thus it went on for several weeks; somehow they were never able to get in first. We did the fifty miles several times in three hours and twenty-eight minutes (that is, at the average rate of a mile in four minutes and nine seconds, including stoppages), and for months together we never exceeded four hours.

Still, in every contest one party must ultimately give in; that one, however, was not the Telegraph. We settled our differences, and went on quietly for the remainder of the time, occasionally having a little 'flutter,' as we used to call it in those days, but we were always good friends. Should this narrative chance to meet the eye of some of those who used to travel with us in bygone times, they will doubtless well remember the pace we used to go.

After a few years the railway opened to Plymouth, and many gentlemen asked me to start a fast coach into Corn-

Rivals.

wall, promising to give it their patronage. I accordingly started the Tally Ho! making it a day coach from Truro to London, joining the rail at Plymouth; this was a very difficult road for a fast coach, but we ran it, till Government offered the contract for a mail; we then converted the Tally Ho! into a mail, and ran it till the rail opened to Truro. It will have been seen that I kept to coaching nearly as long as there were any coaches left to drive.

I had for some years given up driving regularly, having taken the Horse Bazaar at Plymouth, where I used to supply officers of the garrison with teams, and give them instructions in driving; this I still continue to do, and in every variety of driving. It gives me, indeed, much pleasure to see many of my pupils daily handling their teams skilfully; not a few of them giving me good reason to be really proud of them, as I know they do me credit. In my description of my driving career, I stated that I had never had an accident; I ought to have said, no serious casualty, never having upset or injured anyone; but I have had many trifling mishaps, such as running foul of a wagon in a fog, having my whole team down in slippery weather; on many occasions I have had a wheel come off, but still nothing that could fairly be termed a bad accident.

During the last twenty-five years I have been engaged keeping livery stables and breaking horses to harness, and in that period I have had some very narrow escapes. In one instance, the box of a new double break came off and pitched me astride across the pole between two young horses; I once had the top of the pole come off when driving two high-couraged horses; a horse set to kicking, and ran away with me in single harness. As I was of course pulling at him very hard, my feet went through the bottom of the dog-cart, he kicking furiously all the time. Fortunately I escaped with only a few bruises. On another occasion, in single harness a mare began kicking, and, before I could get her head up, she ran against the area railings of a house in Princess Square, Plymouth, broke both shafts, and split the break into matches; myself and man nearly went through the kitchen window, into the arms of the cook; she did not, however, ask us to stop and dine.

I could mention many little events of a similar kind, and consider myself very fortunate in having never had anything more serious than a sprained ankle or wrist during my tolerably long career.

Before concluding, I will relate some of the difficulties we had to encounter in foggy weather.[1] We were obliged to be guided out of London with torches, seven or eight mails following one after the other, the guard of the foremost mail lighting the one following, and so on till the last. We travelled at a slow pace, like a funeral procession. Many times I have been three hours going from London to Hounslow. I remember one very foggy night, instead of my arriving at Bagshot (a distance of thirty miles from London, and my destination) at eleven o'clock, I did not get there till one in the morning. I had to leave again at four the same morning. On my way back to town, when the fog was very bad, I was coming over Hounslow Heath when I reached the spot where the old powder-mills used to stand. I saw several lights in the road, and heard voices, which induced me to stop. The old Exeter mail, which left Bagshot thirty minutes before I did, had met with a singular accident; it was driven by a man named Gambier; his leaders had come in contact with a hay-cart on its way to London, which caused them to turn suddenly round, break the pole, and blunder down a steep embankment, at the bottom of which was a narrow deep ditch filled with water and mud. The mail-coach pitched on to the stump of a willow-tree that overhung the ditch; the coachman and outside passengers were thrown over into the meadow beyond,

[1] These words remind me of a good plan for driving on a foggy night, which it may be well to mention here. I have often when driving at night been obliged to pull up and put my lamps out, and was able to get on better without them than with them. The lights shine on to the fog and back again into the coachman's eyes, so that he can see nothing, and is fairly dazzled. So far as he is concerned he is better without lamps, but a light at night is desirable in order to prevent other vehicles from running against one. It is therefore a great object to have a light and to prevent it from shining in the eyes of the coachman, as it is apt to do in a fog. In the coach wallet or the pockets of coach or carriage should be a thick bit of leather fitting over the square or circular lamps, coming down just so far as to cover rather more than half the flame, and firmly strapped or buckled on. This shows the ditch or fence on either side, lights the road, and does not come back off the fog into the driver's eyes. It shows a certain distance, and keeps other people from running against you.—B.

and the horses went into the ditch; the unfortunate wheelers were drowned or smothered in the mud. There were two inside passengers, who were extricated with some difficulty; but fortunately no one was injured. I managed to take the passengers, with the guard and mail-bags, on to London, leaving the coachman to wait for daylight before he could make an attempt to get the mail up the embankment. They endeavoured to accomplish this with cart-horses and chains. They had nearly reached the top of the bank when something gave way, and the poor old mail went back into the ditch again. I shall never forget the scene; there were about a dozen men from the powder-mills trying to render assistance, and, with their black faces, each bearing a torch in his hand, they presented a curious spectacle. This happened about thirty years ago. Posts and rails were erected at the spot after the accident. I passed the place last summer; they are still there, as well as the old pollard-willow stump.

I recollect another singular circumstance occasioned by a fog. There were eight mails that passed through Hounslow. The Bristol, Bath, Gloucester and Stroud took the right-hand road from Hounslow; the Exeter, Yeovil, Poole, and Quicksilver, Devonport (which was the one I was driving) went the straight road towards Staines. We always saluted each other, when passing, with 'Good night, Bill,' 'Dick,' or 'Harry,' as the case might be. I was once passing a mail, mine being the faster, and gave my wonted salute. A coachman named Downs was driving the Stroud mail; he instantly recognised my voice, and said, 'Charlie, what are you doing on my road?' It was he, however, who had made the mistake; he had taken the Staines, instead of the Slough road out of Hounslow. We both pulled up immediately; he had to turn round and go back, which was a feat attended with much difficulty in such a fog. Had it not been for our usual salute, he would not have discovered his mistake before arriving at Staines. This mishap was about as bad as getting into a wrong train. I merely mention the circumstance to show that it was no joke driving

AFTER THE ACCIDENT

a night mail in those days. November was the month we dreaded most, the fogs were generally so bad. A singular event happened with the Bath mail that ran between Bath and Devonport. Its time for arriving at Devonport was eleven o'clock at night. One eventful evening, they had set down all their outside passengers except a Mrs. Cox, who kept a fish-stall in Devonport Market. She was an immense woman, weighing about twenty stone. At Yealmpton, where the coachman and guard usually had their last drain before arriving at their destination, being a cold night, they kindly sent Mrs. Cox a drop of something warm. The servant-girl who brought out the glass, not being able to reach the lady, the ostler very imprudently left the horses' heads to do the polite. The animals hearing some one getting on the coach, doubtless concluded that it was the coachman; at the same time, finding themselves free, and being, probably, anxious to get home, they started off at their usual pace, and performed the seven miles in safety, passing over the Laira Bridge and through the toll-bar, keeping clear of everything on the road. Mrs. Cox meanwhile sat on the coach, with her arms extended in the attitude of a spread-eagle, and vainly trying to attract the attention of those she met or passed on the road. She very prudently, however, abstained from screaming, as she thought she might otherwise have alarmed the horses. They, indeed, only trotted at their ordinary speed, and came to a halt of their own accord at the door of the King's Arms Hotel, Plymouth, where they were in the habit of stopping to discharge some of the freight of the coach. The boots and ostler came running out to attend to their accustomed duties, but, to their astonishment, beheld no one but the affrighted Mrs. Cox on the coach and two passengers inside, who were, happily, wholly unconscious of the danger to which they had been exposed! The coachman and guard soon arrived in a post-chaise. Poor Mrs. Cox drank many quarterns of gin to steady her nerves before she felt able to continue her journey to Devonport, where she carried on a prosperous trade for many years. Many people patronised her, on purpose to hear her narrate the great event of her life. I often used to chaff her, and hear her repeat the history of her memorable adventure.

I will add a little anecdote of Bob Pointer, who was on the Oxford road. Giving his ideas on coaching to a young gentleman who was on the box with him, on his way to college, he said :—

Soldiers and sailors may soon learn to fight; lawyers and parsons go to college, where they are crammed with all sorts of nonsense that all the nobs have read and wrote since Adam—of course, very good if they like it—but to be a *coachman, sir*, you must go into the stable almost before you can run alone, and learn the nature of horses and the difference between corn and chaff. Well can I remember the first morning I went out with four horses; I never slept a wink all night. I got a little flurried coming out of the yard, and looking round on the envious chaps who were watching me—it was as bad as getting married—at least, I should think so, never having been in that predicament myself. I have escaped that dilemma; for (he concluded) when a man is always going backwards and forwards between two points, what is the use of a wife? A coachman could never be much more than half married. Now, if the law—in the case of coachmen—allowed two wives, that would be quite another story, because he could then have the tea-things set out at both ends of his journey. Driving, sir, is very like life; it's all so smooth when you start with the best team, so well-behaved and handsome; but get on a bit, and you will find you have some hills to get up and down, with all sorts of horses, as they used to give us over the middle ground. Another thing, sir, never let your horses know you are driving them, or, like women, they may get restive. Don't pull and haul, and stick your elbows a-kimbo; keep your hands as though you were playing the piano; let every horse be at work, and don't get flurried; handle their mouths lightly; do all this, and you might even drive four young ladies without ever ruffling their feathers, or their tempers.

Shortly before the publication of this volume, in December 1888, the sudden and unexpected death of James W. Selby shocked lovers of the road, to few of whom he was unknown;

for Jem Selby was without doubt the most widely popular of modern professional coachmen. Selby's white hair gave a suggestion of age which was not borne out by the calendar, for he was only in his forty-fifth year. His energetic career shows that even in these modern days a coachman may work hard

The late James Selby.

and lead an extremely busy life. Born in 1844, Selby seemed to have appeared out of due time, for at that period railways had driven coaches off the road and the coaching revival had not begun. The lad was sent into an auctioneer's office, but he found many opportunities to follow the occupation in which he delighted, his father being proprietor of the Railway Hotel, Colney Hatch, to which a large livery-stable business was attached. James Selby's professional career opened about 1870, when he began to drive the Tunbridge Wells coach, owned by Lord Bective, and on this he continued for five summers, occupying his winters on the St. Albans road. In the summer of 1876 the late Lord Helmsley, Colonel Chaplin, and Lord Arthur Somerset ran the coach to Tunbridge Wells, Selby retaining his position; in 1877–8 he drove from Beckenham to London and back for Mr. Charles Hoare, and in the autumn of the latter year Selby's own coach, the Old Times, was put on the St. Albans road. The venture was highly successful, and in 1879 the Old Times did a double journey, starting from West Wickham at 8 A.M., going through Beckenham to London, and arriving at Hatchett's at 10.30. It then left for St. Albans at 11 A.M., and reached the Cellar again at 6 P.M., when Selby once more took up his passengers for the return journey to West Wickham. This was hard work, for he had to reach his home in St. John's Wood to sleep, and to leave not later than 6 A.M. the next morning. In the winter of 1880–81 the Old Times coach went to Windsor, and in the summer of the same year it was put on to Virginia Water, on which road it continued until the summer of 1888, going in the winter only as far as Oatlands Park. Last winter (1888), however, the Old Times started for its journey to Brighton. Major Dixon, Sir Thomas Peyton, and Sir Henry de Bathe were his first subscribers on the Old Times coach in 1878, Major Dixon remaining with him, his firm friend and patron, until his death in 1886. On January 18, 1881, the Old Times had a memorable journey, the only passengers being Major Dixon and Selby. They drove to Windsor in a severe snowstorm, Selby being forced on his return home to have his hat thawed, it being 'frozen to his head.' The coach ran these eleven years without intermission, Sundays and Christmas Days excepted. In the spring of 1879, Selby went to Paris and started a coach for Captain Cropper, which ran from Paris to

Versailles, but only for a short time. He visited Ireland in 1883, at the request of the late Captain Chaine, to see if it was possible to put a coach on from Larne to the Giant's Causeway, but he considered the expense of working too great.

Selby's name will be memorable in the annals of coaching in consequence of his having beaten the record by driving from London to Brighton and back in 7 h. 50 min. At the Ascot meeting of 1888 a bet of 1,000*l.* to 500*l.* was offered and taken that the journey could not be done in 8 hours. On July 13 Selby started from the White Horse Cellar punctually at 10 A.M., having on the coach Messrs. Carleton Blyth, McAdam, Beckett, Walter Dixon, W. P. Cosier, and Alfred Broadwood. Passing along Piccadilly, Grosvenor Place, and Buckingham Palace Road, over the Chelsea Suspension Bridge, the Horse and Groom at Streatham was reached at 10.28, and here the first change occupied 47 seconds. West Croydon was passed at 10.45 o'clock. A pace of thirteen miles an hour was maintained to the Windsor Castle, Purley Bottom, where another change, occupying 1 min. 5 sec., took place. Horley was reached at 11.51½, the coach having travelled some of the distance between Earlswood and that town at a speed of 20 miles an hour. At Crawley the time was taken 12.11, a couple of minutes having been lost by a delay at some level crossing gates which were open to let through a train. Fresh teams were taken on at Peas Pottage, Cuckfield, Friars Oak—the galloping stage between the two last-named places being covered in admirable style—and Patcham. The coach drew up at the Old Ship, Brighton, at 1.56.10—that is to say, 3 min. 50 sec. under four hours.

Of course there was no delay at Brighton; the coach was turned round, the return journey begun, and the Cellar reached at 5.50.

One other notable performance may well conclude this chapter. In 1834 opposition coaches—the Oxford Age, driven by Joe Tollit (one of four brothers, John, William, George, and Joe), and the Royal William, driven by Snowden—ran from Oxford to London, starting at the same time. There was keen rivalry between the two. The Age usually reached London first; but on the evening of April 30, Snowden gave out that next day he was determined to have the best of it, and he had prepared the way for a remarkable achievement by ordering horses to be ready and waiting for him at the different changes, these orders having been given as he drove back to Oxford on the afternoon of the day named. Joe Tollit was no less resolved not to be beaten, and the result was that the Age accomplished the journey from Oxford to Oxford Street in 3 h. 40 min. Tollit started from the Vine Hotel, High Street, at 11 o'clock on May 1, and thus describes the journey :—

I was just two hours going to Wycombe (25 miles), leaving that place exactly at one o'clock, and one hour and forty minutes going from Wycombe to London (29 miles). The Old Blenheim Coach left the Star Hotel at 9 o'clock, and we passed it at Gerrard's Cross, 20 miles from London, although we had to wait at Uxbridge, for the horses were not harnessed, and at Acton I had to drive the same team back to town that had just come down, and also to help harness them. I had a lady just behind me, and I asked when at Notting Hill if she had felt at all alarmed? She said not in the least, her only fear was that her friends would not be at the Bell and Crown, Holborn, to meet her. This turned out to be the case, so I put her into a 'growler' and sent her home. Sir Henry Peyton, of four-in-hand renown, met Mr. James Castle, the driver of the Blenheim, in Oxford Street, and said, 'Well, what's become of the Age and Royal William; I thought they were to be in town before you to-day?' 'Well,' he said, 'so they are, I should think, for they passed me while I was changing horses at Gerrard's Cross, and I have not seen them since. If they have not had a jolly good dinner before this time, they have been very idle.'

A more remarkable achievement than this has rarely found a place in coaching annals. It was said of Joe Tollit that he could get more out of four horses than any man in England. The following instance of coolness and daring must have somewhat astonished anyone of weak nerves who happened to be on the coach at the time. Black Will, as the people used to call him, a well-known whip, went to London with Tollit on the box-seat one day, and just after he changed horses at Beaconsfield, and was going down Dupree's Pitch, as it was called, one of the leaders began kicking and got one of her legs over the inside traces. Black Will asked Tollit if he was not going to stop, but he replied, 'No, not till I get to Gerrard's Cross, for if I do she will begin again.' 'Well,' the other said, 'I have been driving for forty years and never dared to do a thing of the sort.' Tollit drove the animal right through to London, and she never kicked afterwards.

MODERN CARRIAGES.

By George N. Hooper,

President of the Institute of British Carriage Manufacturers; Member of the Council of the London Chamber of Commerce.

Much has been written of late years on this subject, but as most of the information is strictly technical, and is widely scattered, it is proposed to place before the reader a *résumé* of the subject, mainly from a popular point of view, and chiefly extending over the reign of Her Majesty Queen Victoria, and the period that has witnessed the introduction of travelling by railways and tramways; for these agencies have been the main factors in the necessary changes that have taken place, by reason of the absolute revolution in land locomotion.

The design, construction, and weight of carriages must, in almost every case, depend greatly on the state of the roads over which they are to be used; and the coachmaker, however clever, scientific, practical, or artistic he may be, must inevitably sooner or later adapt his work to the wants of his supporters. In the interest of himself and others, the sooner he realises the fact, the better for all concerned. From the first introduction of carriages into England they had to be made to use on the roads (or no roads) that were available, and from the time of Charles II., when they became an ordinary article of manufacture, till the time of George III., when Englishmen woke up to the advantages of good roads, the progress in the art of carriage-building was slow, notwithstanding the efforts of the

Coachmakers' Company of London, to whom King Charles II. granted a charter of Incorporation. This charter conferred very extensive powers, and corresponding duties, on the master, wardens, and court of assistants, who were empowered to search for badly-made carriages and destroy them, and to train up apprentices and workmen to perform their work skilfully. Each workman, after serving a satisfactory apprenticeship, became by right a freeman of the company, with a vote for members of Parliament for the City of London, and a right to claim relief and assistance if unable to provide for himself in sickness and old age. Thus were rights and responsibilities duly balanced by the Government in those days.

The carriages then, and subsequently, built prove to us by the examples still preserved, that artistic skill, as well as good handicraft, was encouraged by those who ordered and those who made them, for all carriages in those times were invariably built to the order of the buyer. Fashions changed but slowly, and improvements were equally slow. With the improvement of English roads by the great engineer and road-maker MacAdam, an absolute revolution occurred in the design, construction, and weight of carriages, and the English nobility, landed gentry, and middle classes awoke to the advantages of rapid transit from place to place of persons and merchandise (for up to that time a great deal of the passenger and goods traffic was conveyed by saddle and pack horses, carrying their loads on their backs, and at a very costly and slow rate); the coachmakers of those days threw themselves with ardour into the work that lay before them, in improving the carriages that the new roads required, by reducing their weight, by a more skilful arrangement of parts, and improving the springs and axles. Among these may be mentioned the following London firms who rapidly and industriously provided the new order of vehicles:—

Hatchett & Co., Long Acre; Winsor & Co., Long Acre; Barker & Co., Chandos Street; Baxter & Pearce, Long Acre; Birch & Co., Great Queen Street; Collingridge, Cook, Rowley,

& Co., Liquorpond Street; Adams & Hooper, Haymarket; Hobson & Co., Long Acre; Houlditch & Co., Long Acre; Coates & Blizard, Park Lane; Tilbury, Marylebone Road; Howard & Parker, Long Acre; Messer & Co., Margaret Street; Hopkins, Davies Street; David Davies, Wigmore Street; Thrupp, Oxford Street; Williams, Oxford Street; Waude, New Kent Road; Windus, Bishopsgate Street; Robinson & Cook, Mount Street; and Booker, Edmonton.

These were well supported by—

1. John Collinge, with his patent improved axles to carry oil for three months, in place of the old axles that required the black grease removed and renewed every day.

2. Obadiah Elliott, of Westminster Bridge Road, who invented and patented in 1802 his improved method of building four-wheel carriages without a perch, resulting in the introduction of elliptic springs, and great reduction in weight. Birch, of Great Queen Street, Lincoln's Inn, about this time also patented improvements in the heads of landaus, which had been invented in the town of that name in Germany.

3. Thrupp & Glover, with improved springs made from English steel, in place of those hitherto made of German steel.

4. At the same time scientific men were writing essays and treatises on traction, and the best form for wheels, as regards durability and ease in draught.

During the latter part of the reign of King George III. and the regency of George IV., English carriages rapidly improved, the attention of the public being incessantly directed to the subject; the Prince Regent taking great personal interest in their construction, and frequently personally conferring with his coachmaker, William Cook, who from his frequent intercourse with the Prince Regent (subsequently king) became familiarly known as 'King Cook.' Sir John Lade and Count d'Orsay subsequently suggested many improvements, from their own use of carriages and acquaintance with the work required. Their example was followed by others.

Palmer patented inventions and improvements in the stage

and mail coaches, letters being now carried with greater speed and safety in four-horse coaches, instead of as in former times in saddle-bags by mounted postmen. Highwaymen and footpads had been almost driven off the road, partly by arming the guards of the coaches carrying the mails, and by a more speedy administration of justice on offenders. The less frequent breakdown of coaches on the improved roads, and the more rapid pace of travelling, also rendered the highwayman's calling more uncertain.

During the reigns of Georges III. and IV. it was the custom to serve out the new scarlet and gold-laced liveries to the drivers and guards of the royal mail-coaches on the King's birthday, and the coaches were driven in procession through the London streets. It was a pretty sight, that Londoners dearly loved; they turned out in large numbers to admire and criticise the horses, men, and coaches, and there was great emulation among all concerned in obtaining a favourable opinion from those who were proud of them, and almost gloried in their achievements and the punctual performance of their duties.

At the commencement of the reign of Her Majesty Queen Victoria, travelling on English roads had undergone a vast change; posting for the upper classes, and stage-coach travelling by the middle classes, had reached a punctuality and perfection that could hardly have been imagined a generation or two before. Working men travelled from town to town (always on foot) in search of employment, acquiring an amount of knowledge and experience they could not otherwise have obtained.

At this time, the great day for seeing and being seen in one's carriage was Sunday, and on a fine Sunday afternoon the road from the Marble Arch to Hyde Park Corner was filled with the chariots, coaches, landaus, barouches, britzskas and cabriolets of the nobility and gentry of England who spent the season in London, and on other afternoons the same road was almost as well filled with hundreds of well-appointed carriages of the same class.

So great a fascination did the art of four-horse driving at this time possess for gentlemen of the upper classes, that many practised it under the expert and experienced drivers of mail and stage coaches, and often ended by excelling these professionals in rapid, skilful, and exact driving, and knowledge of the habits, tempers, and qualities of the teams, so that their establishments of horses and carriages derived many advantages from the knowledge they had acquired on the road.

Hobson greatly improved the two-wheel gigs of his time, and Tilbury invented the pretty vehicle that bears his name, and was greatly in fashion among the young men.

The travelling carriages of the nobility and gentry had received great attention, and had been immensely improved, so much so, that the best of them were used for very long journeys through England and Scotland, and across the continent of Europe from Calais to Rome, Calais to Vienna or other distant capitals, requiring only the renewal of the worn iron tires of the wheels, and new soling the drag-shoes as they became worn by the contact with the road.

When Her Majesty and the late Prince Consort built a castle for themselves in the highlands of Scotland, they had still nearly a hundred miles of road to travel from the nearest railway station at Aberdeen. The Royal travelling carriages were old but sound, and it was not worth while to build new ones that might not long be wanted: accordingly the then Crown Equerry (the late George Lewis, Esq.) would year by year have the old vehicles carefully overhauled by the most trusted and careful of the Court coachmakers of his day. A number of men, equivalent to the weights to be carried on the journey, were placed inside the body and on the outside seats; they rocked and swayed the carriage up and down, to test to the utmost the steel springs, they examined the leather braces, and the strapping, the steps, doors, glasses, blinds, and all the multitude of etceteras that might fail on the road. Exact lists were made on the spot of every large and small repair that was needed, the drag-shoes were put in their places to ascertain that the soles were thick and strong enough, and the chains the proper length for service—not too long nor too short—the tool-boxes were opened and ransacked, to ascertain if every necessary tool was there, with spare clips and bolts and strong cord. In fact, nothing was left unexamined even to the packets of nails and screws, and an exact estimate of cost had to be submitted before the carriages left the royal mews, and the order was given to proceed with the work. With such an organisation and such precautions, the old carriages conveyed their precious charges safely, and no unnecessary expense was incurred under conditions of transition in the manner of travelling.

At the time when the Emperor Napoleon III. was in the height of his prosperity, many of his best carriages were made in London: they were copied in Paris, where the adoption of London fashions did much to improve French carriages.

In any Imperial gala procession the Imperial coachmaker accompanied the procession on horseback, in a well-appointed and handsome uniform, attended by his workmen (suitably clad in gala dresses) in case their services were required. It is probable that the general public were quite ignorant of the reason for their presence. In fact, they were the counterparts of the breakdown gang, held available by modern railway companies in case of accidents on the line.

The contrivances for comfort, safety, and conveyance of luggage had attained a perfection that was greatly appreciated by well-to-do travellers. Capacious and neatly fitted boxes, with covers to exclude rain and dust, were carried on the roofs of closed carriages; some were placed under the cushions, others in and on the front boot. At the back of the rumble that carried servants behind, a capacious cap-case contained ladies' bonnets and head-gear, while a row of hat-boxes was attached behind the upper part of the rumble; two wells, secured to the bottom of the carriage, contained provisions, accessible from trap-doors in the carriage flooring; the sword-case projecting from the back of the body (easily accessible from the interior) contained arms for those inside the carriage, while the courier was provided with pistols placed in holsters at his side of the rumble. The front of the body was furnished with a folding sunshade and Venetian blinds with movable laths for sultry weather; spring curtains kept off the sun's rays, and a lamp with one or two candles, fixed at the back of the carriage, lighted the interior; the heat, burnt air, and smoke of the wax candles passing away outside the carriage. Some of these elaborate private carriages were provided with *dormeuse* boots, and from them could be developed beds affording accommodation for sleeping during night journeys. Veritably Pullman's sleeping cars were anticipated, and in use long before he was heard of.

Some of the most complete, compact, and hardworking of these noted travelling carriages were used by the king's messengers to his ambassadors in foreign capitals. The safe custody and rapid delivery of important Government despatches from one end of Europe to another entailed great responsibility and care on the part of those entrusted with them. These messengers were generally retired military or naval officers, or other hardy and adventurous gentlemen. Occasionally, the incessant and continuous rapid travelling of many days was so exhausting, that they had to be lifted out of their carriages on reaching their distant destination. In very hot or very inclement weather their suffering was sometimes acute.

These carriages were provided with strong safety ropes under the body, extending from one C-spring to another, in case a much-worn leather spring brace should break at an inconvenient place or time, and arrest further progress: they were also provided with two drag-shoes and chains, and in addition a wheel-hook and chain, in case a bad piece of road should displace one or both of the drag-shoes; also a drag-staff to let down in ascending an Alpine road, to prevent a jibbing horse, or one with sore shoulders, from backing, and sending the carriage, its occupants, horses, and servants, down a precipice. In addition, there was a box (or tool budget) provided with

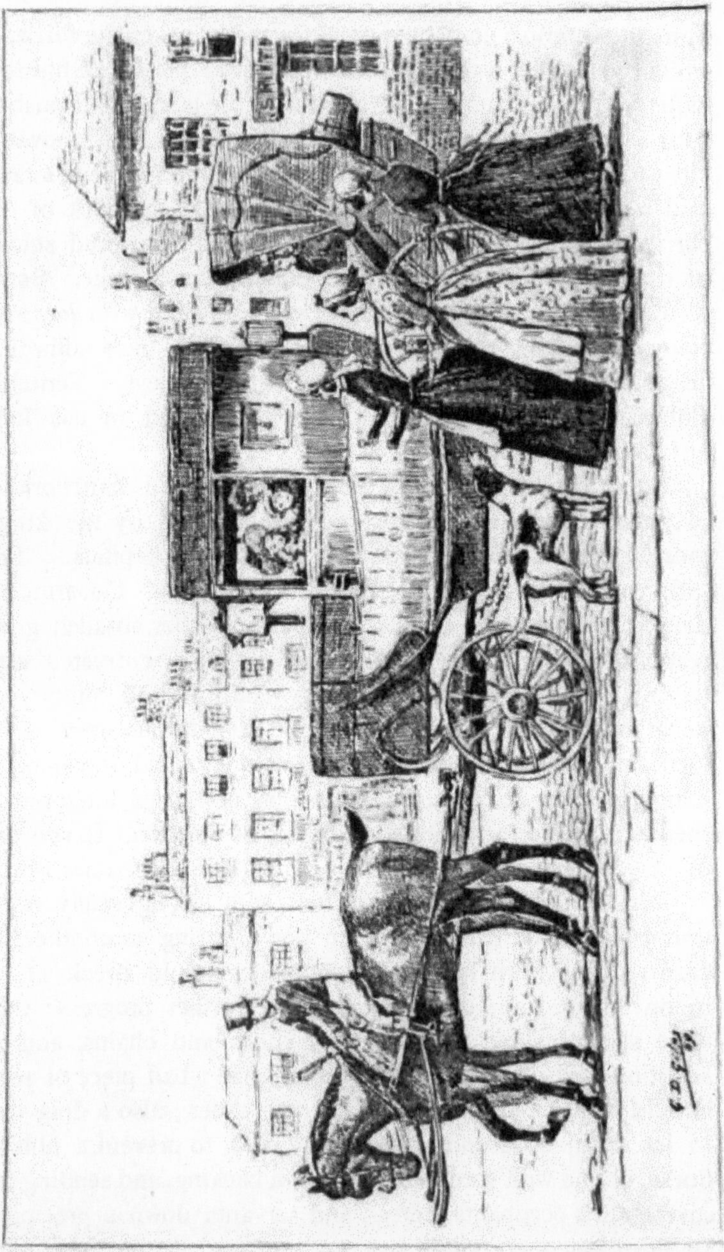

The Dormeuse.

all necessary tools, with spare bolts and clips in case of a breakdown in the open country; and a good courier was expected to be able to use the tools effectively, to replace a broken bolt or secure a broken tire with a tire-clip.

Carriages for continental travelling had always to be provided with loose swinging splintrees attached to the splinter-bar—so that each horse pulled from a centre—easing the horse's collar, but rendering accurate guidance more difficult and less precise than when the traces are attached to fixed splinter-bars, as is usual in England—where, consequently, with ordinary care, collisions were less frequent, by reason of greater certainty in steering.

The couriers who accompanied noblemen and great families on their continental journeys were almost invariably foreigners—Swiss, Italian, German, or French. They required a combination of qualities to perform their duties to the comfort and satisfaction of their employers, for on the good management and knowledge of this functionary depended much of the pleasure of a continental ramble. It was, of course, necessary that he should speak three or four languages, if not to perfection, at least so as to be well understood in the roadside inns and hotels. He had to organise the route, the length of the day's journey, provide for punctual relays of post-horses, order rooms at hotels beforehand, if his party were large, settle the bills, pay all expenses on the road, and duly render periodical accounts of the money supplied to him. With a bachelor employer his duties were comparatively light, but with a large party his responsibilities were heavy, though diminished somewhat if his employers were considerate.

If a long tour were arranged for, and there were a large proportion of ladies who entered much into society and gaiety, the baggage was proportionately extensive, and would be carried in a compact *fourgon*, half carriage, half van, the fore part having a cabriolet body with folding hood, carrying the courier and lady's-maid, while in the rear were tiers of neatly numbered and arranged wooden boxes, the leather-covered imperials, hat-cases, or portmanteaus, being put outside and protected with a capacious waterproof tarpaulin cover.

This vehicle often preceded the party in the family coach, landau, or britzska, by some hours, so that, on their arrival at the hotel chosen, all was comfortably arranged for their reception.

But this was not the only manner of travelling, although it was that usual with the wealthy nobility and gentry of England. On the Continent the system of posting was conducted in a way which differed from the English plan; for while, in this country it was left to private enterprise, abroad it had been organised as a sort of semi-state affair, with regulated tariffs. Post-horses were supplemented, however, by private enterprise of a convenient kind.

The Italians had a class of 'vetturini' who owned carriages and post-horses, and were ready to drive you from Naples to Paris, or anywhere else, at short notice, if terms could be arranged to suit both parties.

There was less responsibility, but at the same time less comfort, with such an arrangement; for the owner of the carriage and horses was master, and, to a certain extent, paramount on the journey.

In England post-horses and post-carriages could be had at the town hotels and at the country inns, and were invariably attached to houses of entertainment, the charge per mile being regulated much by the gradients and conditions of the neighbouring roads. The innkeepers as a body were enterprising, proud of their horses' condition, harness, speed, and punctuality; the public carriages (mail and stage coaches) mostly belonged to them, and they kept up a keen competition among themselves, especially as regards speed of journeys, and fares for travelling. The best coaches were run on the roads leading north and west of London; to York, Manchester, Liverpool, Bristol, Exeter, and Plymouth. So remarkable was the punctuality, that although the guard with his London-made watch brought the exact London time, many people considered they could well set their clocks by the arrival of the coach from London.

The box-seat next the coachman was considered a place of honour, generally reserved for some local magnate, if it was known that he intended to travel by the coach. Frequent contact and conversation with highly-educated gentlemen was a training to these coachmen, softening and refining their rougher natures, and polishing off their angularities of character; they were looked up to and consulted on many matters, and the consideration bestowed on them as a class attracted more cultivated men to the calling than would otherwise have presented themselves. The isolation of the drivers on the public conveyances of the Continent, while driving, tended always to keep them among the peasant class, from whom they came. At this time one of the travelling carriages common on the roads of France was the heavy two-wheel cabriolet, hung on C-springs and leather braces behind, and carrying four persons inside under the hood; the luggage was roped on a board behind, and the rate of travelling was about four miles an hour. In Cornwall, not a very great many years ago, the public carriages consisted of light one-horse covered vans travelling at about the same rate.

In France the through traffic on the high roads was carried on by 'diligences' and 'malle-postes,' the latter conveying the mails, owned by companies under the patronage of the State, starting from Paris and traversing the great roads to the frontiers of Belgium, Germany, Switzerland, Italy, and Spain. The diligences were huge heavy conveyances of a type totally different from the English ones, which were unlike those of all other countries as regards lightness, compactness, and general arrangement of seats; for whereas the English carriages had most of their passengers outside, the continental ones placed most of theirs inside. This arrangement was probably adopted by reason of the greater equability of our climate, the summer not being so hot, nor the winter so cold, as in most continental states.

In France the first front portion was the *coupé*, carrying three persons, looking on the horses and exposed to the dust, mud, smell, and neighing of the great stallions usually employed. Next came the *berline* (or coach proper), carrying six inside transversely, and face to face; after this came the *rotonde*, or omnibus, carrying eight persons, also sitting face to face, but on each side as an omnibus. The *banquette* was on the roof of the *coupé*, and carried three or four persons, protected from the weather by a leather hood, with folding glass windows in front.

On the floor of this was carried treasure—heavy sacks of silver five-franc pieces, being consigned to bankers or for making payments in connection with the business of the 'diligence' company, and sadly incommoding the feet and legs of travellers on a long journey. The fares varied in respect of place. 1. The coupé; 2. berline; 3. rotonde; 4. banquette. The last, affording the best view and most fresh air, generally attracted young Englishmen on their travels.

Screw-breaks, to retard the speed of the carriage down mountain roads, were general on the French carriages long before they were taken up in England—the steep Alpine gradients probably led to their use. The journey from Paris to Geneva would occupy three days and two nights, the longest rest being at Dijon; a halt of twenty to thirty minutes was made at intervals for meals, and the horses were generally changed very rapidly. The diligence leaving Paris early on Monday morning reached Geneva on Wednesday night.

The same guard (or 'conducteur') would go through, getting down from his seat on the banquette at every change of horses, sleeping as he could at intervals; but the driver, a peasant in a blue linen suit, would drive his team of five horses one stage, and be replaced by another, so that on such a journey there may have been sixty different drivers, each driving about an hour.

Five horses was the regulation allowance for such a diligence, which, besides the passengers, carried a large quantity of luggage on the roof behind the banquette, and over the berline and the rotonde. There were two wheelers, and three leaders, driven from a high box, supported by strong iron stays in front of the banquette, about half-way forward over the backs of the wheelers. The driver held little conversation with the guard, and none whatever with the passengers. He was ill clad and ill protected from the cold at night—fortunately for him, his exposure rarely exceeded an hour. In former times the near-side wheeler was ridden by a gaily-uniformed postilion, with high and heavy jackboots and a cocked hat, who managed the team of five horses; but probably from motives of economy he was afterwards replaced by a more humble and less costly successor. The horse-collars were of great size and weight, and fitted well; the traces were nearly always of rope, but neither the harness nor carriages were so well cleaned and kept up as in England.

But there were two accessories, one appertaining to each country, that differed entirely: the whip, and the coach-horn (or 'yard of tin,' as it was sometimes familiarly called).

The English coachman carried in his right hand a work of art in a neat, jaunty, highly-finished whip with a thong skilfully plaited, and he used it with grace, sometimes with an elegant flourish just enough to remind a highly bred-horse that he was not doing his best, or to remove a troublesome fly; at other times with resolution, to chastise a sluggard who wished his mate to do all the pulling, while he trotted along with a loose collar and traces.

The French driver carried an elastic stick with a long and taper thong, but he had a marvellous knack of so using his whip on entering a town, as to imitate the detonation of percussion caps, and so announce his arrival. The English guard cleared the road of a sleeping waggoner by a blast or octave on his long copper horn, but in so merry and pleasant a way as to cheer all hearts, and many were the children in the towns who turned out to greet the coach.

In Germany the *eil-* and *schnellwagen* performed the duties of keeping up communications on the roads, but the service was greatly in the hands of the Prince of Turn and Taxis, who for some reason in a former age had been granted a sort of monopoly. If the postilions of the olden time in France were gay in colours, the German postilions were gayer still: some wore canary-coloured suits, others blue, with a multitude of gold-coloured tassels, aiguillettes and white plaited ornaments, resplendent with buttons, buckles, and head-gear, and some in scarlet. But neither the French nor German service was so rapid as the English; for the vehicles were heavier, the breed of horses coarser, and the men not animated with the desire to show off to advantage, as was the case in England.

In Switzerland a light narrow four-wheeled vehicle differing from those of all other countries was in general use. It is difficult to describe to the uninitiated, and somewhat doubtful whether an English coachmaker could make one from any written description, though he might do so had he a full-sized working drawing made by one who had graduated in any of the good modern technical schools, such as we now have in England.

Its name was a *char-à-côté*, and the body was like that of a tilbury; but, instead of carrying two persons, it carried three—instead of going forward like a tilbury, it was suspended on four wheels coupled together by two elastic poles, the body being fixed sideways; the driver sat 'somewhere,' probably on the luggage over the front wheels, if there was any; if not, then on the head of the perch-bolt, his face on a level with the horse's hind-quarters, and his feet dangling close to the surface of the road; luggage was also carried on a board between the hind wheels. There was a fixed panelled head over the seat part of the body, and with a leather apron, a step and a pair of shafts, the trap was complete absolutely—but not perfect, as some of our readers may have found out to their cost, in days gone by. It was generally so suspended that the passengers entered the carriage and looked out on the near (or left) side, which was all very well if the view on a mountain road was on that side; but it sometimes happened that the view nearly all day long was on the right side of the road, and in that case the travellers had to admire as best they could the walls of rock close to which they travelled.

There were, nevertheless, some advantages on the score of safety in these long narrow carriages, for they cleared one another on the somewhat narrow mountain roads of Switzerland, and this is not always the case with the modern and wider carriages now in common use in that country.

When the Swiss engineers laid out the improved roads of their country, they did not foresee that Switzerland would sooner or later be compelled to move with the times, and to bear on her roads the carriages of other countries, as well as the little narrow ones common to their own, and the passing of ordinary vehicles on the narrow mountain roads requires the utmost care to avoid accidents. One hears of omnibuses, diligences, private carriages, and carts toppling down the precipices by reason of collisions, horses taking fright, jibbing, and other causes, and fortunate are the occupants if they ever again—alive, or not seriously injured for life—reach the road from which they fell.

Passing through the Engadine from St. Mauritz to Finstermunz, and slowly climbing the mountain-side to the Austrian territory at Nauders, after passing for many miles along the narrow roads and tortuous narrow main streets of the Swiss villages, one almost suddenly emerges on the wide and truly imperial roads of Austria, laid out with a width, boldness, and grandeur that are in great contrast to those left behind. Perhaps (and probably) they are roads of a later date, and laid out by men who were aware of the difficulties and dangers of the adjoining narrower roads.

A few words more, and we have done with the roads and carriages of continental Europe. In Russia they have the 'tarantass' and the 'kibitka.' In Norway tourists travel in a carriole that only carries one person, and has a board behind for luggage, shafts for a hardy little horse, a pair of springs and two wheels.

The Irish, like the Swiss, have carriages unlike those of

any other nation. The outside car, so common in the land itself, has made little way elsewhere. It may roughly be described as a dog-cart body hung sideways, but the similitude goes no further, for it is suspended on a pair of low wheels which revolve inside, or rather under the body. The seats are provided with cushions and stuffed backs, and the footboards turn up when not in use. The driver sometimes sits on a separate seat in front, and at other times on one of the side seats.

'Advised to hold on.'

To ride on or drive an Irish car requires a certain amount of teaching, training, or practice. Visitors from other countries are very apt to be thrown off into the road, if the driver is humorous, or lively, and turns a street corner quickly; any stranger who rides on an Irish car ought to be advised to hold fast, and not relax his hold till he has safely ended his drive.

Ireland was much indebted to the enterprise of an Italian named Bianconi, who had settled in one of the small towns, and gradually overspread the country with a regular service of two and four wheel cars, well horsed and organised. Many of the latter were drawn by four horses driven from a high seat, and enabled travellers to see the country to advantage. They were all, however, open carriages, and exposed the travellers to the full influence of the rainy climate of the Emerald Isle.

American ingenuity has for many years been directed to carriages, and with the object of precisely adapting means to ends, but with some remarkable contrasts in design, construction, proportion, and finish.

Many Englishmen have from time to time seen the light spider phaetons that have been brought over to England; but in 1887, during the American Exhibition at West Kensington, people had the opportunity for the first time of seeing a genuine American stage coach. This was the 'Deadwood' coach, daily and nightly attacked by Colonel Cody's party of wild Indians in the 'Buffalo Bill' performances.

It may surprise our readers to hear that similar coaches may still be seen in New York, where they are used for journeys outside the city, to places not served by railways. They are neither like an English stage coach, French diligence, nor German schnellwagen. They have no springs, but the coach bodies are suspended on perch carriages with leather braces of heavy make and proportions, and seem to answer the purpose intended.

The reason of the very heavy stage-coach and very light ordinary road vehicles is consistent, strange as the assertion may appear at first sight. It happened that at a particular period of development in the United States railways and tramways were made in advance of ordinary roads, and it was never found to be worth the expense of developing the latter, as had been done in Europe, for twenty or thirty years before railways became general. This will probably happen in all new countries and colonies, where facility of communication is extended on the system that has found favour in America. It therefore follows that carriages &c. drawn by horses would always (or nearly always) be used on rough and ill-kept roads, and would have to be made to suit the conditions available for traffic.

To carry heavy loads on bad roads it has been found in America, as in Europe, that the carriages must be strong and weighty; but for light loads, light carriages, hung low between light and high wheels, do the work required in a satisfactory way. But it must not be expected that such carriages provide all the comfort and convenience of European carriages which have been criticised, improved, and remodelled time after time and year after year by all the makers of Europe, who have competed among themselves for nearly forty years at numerous great international and other exhibitions.

Changes of ideas, tastes, and fashions take place in most countries, and although thirty years ago European carriages taken to the States were condemned by reason of their weight, that is not so now, for as the upper classes of Americans came over to Europe in thousands and travelled not only over the most accessible but over remoter parts, they found that the European types of carriages had so many merits and advantages, that they bought and ordered them freely, and took them home for ordinary use in their own country.

To such an extent did this happen, that the coachmakers of America had to adapt their work to the altered tastes of American buyers, and one now sees in New York, in Chicago, and in the cities on the Pacific coast, that London taste prevails as regards carriage fashions.

About fifty years ago gigs on two wheels swarmed on the suburban roads round London, mornings and evenings, for the bankers, merchants, and traders who lived in the outskirts, drove up to their offices in the morning in their gigs, returning in the same way in the evening. Where the establishment was small and the gig the only carriage kept, the gig-house built at the side of the residence was indispensable, and many of these diminutive gig-houses may still be seen on some of the roads leading into London, just as a few of the 'torch extinguishers' still remain in some of the older squares of London, attached to the area railings—one on each side of the principal entrance—reminding one of times when footmen carried torches, and ran beside the carriages, before London had any lamps, gas, or electric lights.

Closely connected with carriages and roads were the inns of former times, which have undergone almost as much change in condition, use, and customs as the carriages we have been considering. The inns, even in villages and small towns, had to be used occasionally by the nobility, landed gentry, clergy, professional men, and upper class of merchants and manufacturers in the course of their journeys, as well as by labouring men, and were chiefly kept by steady, orderly, and hospitable landlords and landladies, who prided themselves on their clean linen, well-aired beds, and orderly households. The servants had mostly been long in the same house, and knew the guests personally, and in a friendly way. The cooking and provisions, though plain, were fresh and wholesome. The landlord brewed his own beer, and got credit or the reverse, according to the result. The middle and lower classes relished their home-brewed table beer or cider, while the upper classes kept to orthodox port and sherry, there being little demand for sparkling wines and claret. Of spirits there was but a moderate demand, and then only as an occasional fillip, not to be repeated till next day. With the withdrawal of the custom of the upper and middle classes, the character of a large proportion of such houses gradually fell, and many are now places for the sale of drink—lodging and other entertainment seems now to be relegated to some other classes of the community.

Returning to the main purport of our chapter; not very long before the accession of Her Majesty Queen Victoria, hackney-coaches were the only carriages plying for hire in the streets of London. They were invariably the old family coaches of the nobility and gentry, and frequently bore the arms, coronets, and heraldic devices of their original noble owners. They were, however, despoiled of their gorgeous hammercloths that seated the coachman in front, and the carved stands that supported one or two footmen behind in their former halcyon days. They had their whip or full C-springs, leather braces and perch, but the carpet was replaced with straw. The folding iron steps were deprived of their soft carpets and trimmings, and being uncovered showed their bare iron limbs; the windows rattled and let in rain and cold air. The hackney-coachman was a man fond of his beer or gin, wearing a heavy box coat with about ten cloth capes, one over the other; encumbered with the weight of his protection from rain and cold, he was generally slow, seldom civil, and usually grumbled at the fare given in return for service. Starting in a hackney-coach was very different from hailing a modern London hansom cab. Now, by raising an umbrella or walking-stick, you may be off in thirty seconds; then—it took a good five minutes to remove the horses' nose-bags, stow them away in the boot, unfold the body steps, get in the passenger, tuck the loose straw neatly in, refold the steps, close the door, gather up the reins, inquire for the route and destination, and mount the high driving seat. If five or six miles per hour were accomplished, the pace was considered fair; but the interior was odoriferous, the smells somewhat mixed, and if fever of some sort did not lurk in the corners, so much the better for the passengers; for little was then done to enforce the most primitive sanitary regulations and precautions.

About the year 1830 a light two-wheel cab, with a fixed panel top, and carrying two persons inside, was introduced; the driver sat on a little seat over the off-side wheel; it was hung high, and was dangerous if the horse fell, but it prepared the public for faster, less cumbersome, and less costly vehicles than the old coaches.

About 1835 the first four-wheel cabs, carrying only two passengers inside, and drawn by one horse, appeared in London. It was soon found that they could be made to carry four persons inside with a very small increase of weight.

The following story, current in 1837 at the time of the introduction of broughams, may here be related: The late Lord Chancellor Brougham, who was not only a great lawyer, orator, and writer, but also an innovator, and an originator of many ideas on many subjects, grasped the idea before anyone else, that a refined and glorified street cab would make a convenient carriage for a gentleman, and specially for a man of such ideas of independence as one who carried his own carpet-bag on occasions when time was important and his own servant otherwise employed.

The Chancellor called on his coachmakers, Messrs. Sharp & Bland, of South Audley Street, and proposed to them that they should build a small close carriage, like the street cabs that carried two persons inside, and had just been introduced in London. They were evidently not the men to carry out a new idea that was destined to overspread the world, wherever good carriages are now used. They were in the habit of building family coaches, landaus, barouches, britzskas, and chariots, which function carried with it certain ideas of rank, ceremony, dignity, independence, and we may add prejudice. They threw so many difficulties in the way, that it was hopeless to get them to carry out the work satisfactorily, so his lordship called on some neighbours of theirs in Mount Street. Messrs. Robinson & Cook had not been so thoroughly trained in the school of crystallised habit, obstruction, and prejudice as their neighbours; they accordingly accepted the idea, and the order for construction, with alacrity, civility, and energy.

They did their best; they pleased their customer; he was delighted with the result, and in his turn he did his best to influence the world of fashion. He began with his personal friends, advising them to order carriages like his new one, and he so influenced the carriage-buying public that they flocked to the coachmakers who had worked out successfully the idea which was destined to revolutionise the old method of carriage-building as regards lightness, handiness, ease of access, and economy.

Shillibeer introduced omnibuses about the same time; they ran for some years from Paddington to the Bank of England and back, and for a long period the owners did not seem to realise the fact that riders required to go in any other direction.

By degrees, as new and wider thoroughfares and streets were opened up, other wants arose, and were gradually provided for by the competition of younger and newer traders seeking employment for brains and capital.

Omnibuses have been greatly improved of late years, especially as regards the ventilation of the interior, which for many years was extremely defective, and probably led to the spread of disease, much illness, and loss of health, strength, and energy in those who habitually used them. Now that London has so much excellent wood pavement, with a chance of its further extension, it is probable that the same class of horses now used could draw a vehicle affording rather more space per passenger; but those who travel outside have far better accommodation than in former times, and the convenient staircases and better outside seats now attract many female passengers, who prefer the fresh air and sight of the busy traffic of the streets, to having their feet trodden on by some heavy boor in the interior.

A singular vehicle appeared about the year 1840; it was called 'slice of an omnibus.' Imagine twenty inches cut off the end of an omnibus, suspended on two wheels, and a pair of shafts attached to the front part, the driver sitting on the roof and the passengers entering or leaving by a door behind. They were ugly, cramped as to accommodation, and soon went out of use; but they had one good effect: they taught people to look, hope for, and expect something better; and Mr. Harvey, a linen-draper of Westminster Bridge Road, did improve on the idea. He made a more roomy body, cut a gap in the off hind upper portion, and put in it a seat for the driver; it carried three persons inside, protected from rain and storm, but not comfortably, and besides it was too weighty.

The idea which has made the name of Hansom so well known was the application to two-wheel vehicles of the system of suspension that had not long before been applied to the four-wheelers; he lowered the body by placing the axle under the seat instead of below the floor line, as had hitherto been usual. But, although he accomplished improvements so much needed in a public vehicle on two wheels—low suspension, for safety in case of the horse falling, and facility of entrance and exit—he had not the skill to utilise his materials to the best advantage, such as is expected of all carriage builders who are masters of their craft.

He had, as an architect, been brought up in the use of materials where weight was of no consequence, and his patent for some years prevented others showing him the way to do better; in fact, after his death, the cab-builders copied his designs, using a low standard of materials and workmanship—making up in substance and weight what was deficient in quality and skill. When, about 1873, the Society of Arts offered prizes for improvements in street cabs for London, coachmakers turned their attention to the matter, and Forder, of Wolverhampton, showed how the weight could be reduced by the use of better materials and more skilled workmanship. He mounted his vehicles on lighter wheels, reducing the weight of the undergear, and making the body correspondingly lighter. His neater and more comfortable interior fittings suited the public taste in this country, and led to an export trade to other countries, where hansoms have since been adopted and copied. The laying of better road surfaces of wood and asphalte in London has induced many of the cab-owners to go a step further and put indiarubber tires on the wheels.

Messrs. Laurie & Marner of Oxford Street had, about the year 1842, introduced a close carriage midway between a brougham and a coach, which they called a 'clarence,' 'sovereign,' or 'carriole.' It had very curved and rather fanciful lines, seated four persons inside, was entered by one step from the ground, carried the coachman and footman on a low driving seat, and was used with a lighter pair of horses than the family coach required. They afterwards made such carriages with landau heads, and David Davies introduced a novelty in such carriages by providing the front windows with bent plate glass. They were all hung on elliptic or other combination of springs that did not need a perch to sustain them. The celebrated novelist

Sir E. L. Bulwer took up the fashion, and had his 'sovereign' fitted with a miniature hammercloth; but they were a passing caprice, and have not retained the public favour like the brougham.

About this time King Louis Philippe of France presented Her Majesty with a four-horse *char-à-bancs*, a long open carriage hung high, and having four seats following one another all facing the horses, and each holding three persons. Taking this as a type, the late Prince Consort had one designed on a smaller scale with three seats only, the body being much lower, and furnished with a light, movable roof, and waterproof silk poplin curtains provided with silk canvas openings, so as to afford a view without the use of the usual little heavy plate-glass windows in bronze frames. He also ordered a design to be furnished of a carriage with a similar driving seat, but the hind part arranged with the seats sideways—omnibus fashion—this being the first wagonette. These were the two carriages that enabled the then Royal couple to take many pleasant country drives accompanied by the youthful members of their family. At the same time the Prince had some sleighs designed from descriptions furnished by himself, and carefully criticised and amended them where they did not quite carry out his ideas, many of which he had derived from the museum of ancient sleighs made for and used by his ancestors and still preserved at the Feste (or castle) that overlooks the modern town of Coburg.

A carriage which has seen its best days is the curricle, although it was, in the times of the Prince Regent, the most stylish of all conveyances. The body, like that of the cabriolet, was hung on C-springs behind and elbow springs in front, but it was used with a *pair* of horses; the pole being supported by the 'curricle-bar,' a stout rod of turned iron placed transversely on roller fastenings attached to the pads. A strong leather brace connected the spring fixed below the pole with the oval slit in the middle of the 'curricle-bar.' There is still one of these carriages to be seen in London; it belongs to, and is frequently used by, a highly esteemed Cheshire landowner and peer.

About the early part of Queen Victoria's reign, Count d'Orsay, a man of fashion and some taste in carriages, turned his attention to the cabriolet, and, aided by Mr. Courtney (of the firm of Barker & Co.), greatly improved on the original French pattern, which had already been much refined and improved in London. He raised the wheels, shortened the long elbow springs, and stiffened the hind end of the shafts, gave more slope and smartness to the lines of the body, showed people that the head should be set back in front, but never entirely lowered, placed the 'tiger' nearer the body, and selected such high-stepping grand-action horses as made the new and refined carriage look worth twice as much as its predecessor.

The groom or 'tiger' was an important feature of the turnout. He was light of weight, short of stature, self-possessed, and well able to manage the high-mettled horse under whose head he stood when his master alighted. This class of lads and men was tolerably numerous for the thirty years that such carriages were the fashion, but they have disappeared, like the race of mail and stage coachmen and guards.

In 1845 the first C-spring brougham was made by George Hooper for the lately deceased Marquis of Donegall (then Earl of Belfast), who had previously had his brougham hung on W. B. Adams' patent equi-motive bow springs. They, however, did not satisfy him. Then he had C-springs applied to the hind part, but without a perch. This also was not satisfactory. He then said: 'I must have a perch undercarriage with regular C-springs and leather braces.' This was constructed, with a wrought-iron perch made of carefully faggoted iron. It went to work, the maker almost trembling lest it should fail and cause an accident. However, it proved a great success, and has been adopted for carriages of various kinds all over the world where any pretence to refinement or fashion is made. The proportion of parts required the most careful and thoughtful arrangements to get the best possible results with greatly reduced bulk and weight of materials; and though great diversities of form, shape, and size have to be provided for, it is astonishing how little material change has been made since the inventor first introduced the system.

At this time London swarmed with the handsome chariots, coaches, landaus, barouches, and britzskas of the nobility and gentry. Many were hung on perches with C-springs, and almost as many with under as well as C-springs, for they had been added in the reign of George IV., much to the alarm of the London artisans of that day, who considered that the vibration and consequent wear and tear of the under works would be so much reduced, and their durability so much prolonged, as to deprive the workmen of the means of living. Like most other improvements, they tended to the enjoyment of the buyers and likewise to the welfare of the men, who were kept busily employed making the carriages that had been so greatly improved. It may here be mentioned that London carriages were then being rapidly improved, and that wealthy foreign nobles and merchants visiting England, ordered or bought handsome and costly carriages to be sent to their own countries. The best London carriages and their makers' names became well known in all the great capitals of Europe, where English carriages were copied with more or less success by the coachmakers carrying on business there.

Mail-phaetons hung on mail springs and perches were much used by noblemen and gentlemen; the late Earl of Chesterfield generally had the credit of turning out with one of the best, if not actually the best. They were frequently used by bachelors for long posting journeys in England, as well as on the Continent. They are still a favourite carriage (hung on elliptic springs), and have almost reached perfection in the hands of Peters.

The carriages generally driven by ladies are mostly park and pony phaetons. This type of carriage owes its origin and fashion to the Prince Regent (afterwards George IV.) In the course of his studies in coachmaking with the late Mr.

William Cook, he worked out the idea of a comfortable, low, elegant, and stylish carriage which he could drive with a pair of ponies of about fourteen hands; and many of our readers may have seen engravings, lithographs, and prints with a portrait of the Prince driving his favourite ponies. If a Prince Regent, or King, could drive and liked the amusement or exercise, others less exalted in station might do the same without loss of dignity, and they accordingly followed the King's example.

Two-wheeled dog-carts had long been used by sportsmen when going out for a day's shooting, to convey themselves, servants, dogs, and guns to their destination; but with improved roads, and the establishment of railways, they were put to many other uses, and were adopted for carrying persons with comfort and safety, rather than for the special conveyance of dogs.

The use of lancewood for shafts offered an excellent elastic material to increase the easy run of these vehicles. The various patterns of bodies might be reckoned by hundreds, almost by thousands, each maker adopting one of his own, which differed in some respects from his neighbour's. About fifty years ago, the fulcrum shafts were patented by Fuller of Bath and George Hayman of Exeter, and applied to many two-wheeled carriages. Their chief aim was to suppress the jolting (or knee action, as it was called) caused by the rise and fall of the shafts at each step of the horse, and the plan is now adopted for nearly all two-wheeled carriages when the construction permits the application, so that such carriages now run much more pleasantly than those of the olden time. Many vehicles of this type are made of small size, hung low, and are much driven by ladies and even by children. They are balanced, according to the load they carry (two or four), by allowing the body to travel back or forward on polished iron slides fixed on the shafts, and regulated by a screw with crank handle behind. Where the fulcrum shafts are used, the lever arm acts on the seats only, instead of on the whole body,

Many years ago Hooper & Co. made one for Captain W. G. Craven in which the opening and closing of the hind door adjusted the balance. They have now a very simple plan of regulating the balance with a lever having a handle beside the driver's seat.

Most of the gigs of the olden time were hung (Stanhope fashion) with four springs (two side and two cross), forming a square, and they carried the body only, the strong iron-plated ash shafts being connected with the axle by span-irons. This system of construction and suspension gave comfort to the two occupants of the body, but the shafts being wholly without spring action vibrated terribly when used with a fast horse, and the vibration was mitigated as far as the horse was concerned by a capacious and well-stuffed saddle-pad. With very fast driving, it was almost impossible to keep the iron plates and stays sound for any length of time, even with the utmost care and precaution. When, about fifteen years ago, gigs were again inquired for, the comfortable four-spring arrangement of the old Stanhope gigs was combined with the improved method of using the lancewood fulcrum shafts with elegantly tapered hind ends. By applying neat chains to the axle flaps under the springs, and attaching the splintree in front, an even pull was secured from the axle and wheels. By attaching the shafts to fulcrums near the front step, they were connected with the body, and by supporting the tapered hind end between two cylinders of Indiarubber, free play was permitted without risking a rattling noise. Adding a curved iron to give the appearance of the Stanhope shafts to the elastic ones, the altered construction and arrangement was scarcely perceptible. The best points of two systems of construction are combined in the neatest possible manner, giving ease and comfort to the rider as well as the horse.

The introduction of the game of 'polo' of late years among officers and civilians has created a demand for gigs of small size, to use with the polo ponies at times when they are not required for saddle-work.

For some years the young men of fashion have driven a small Stanhope phaeton with compassed rail and sticked body in front, and seat for the groom behind, under the name of 'T carts,' usually drawn by a horse of 15 to 15½ hands. They are now giving place to 'Spider Phaetons,' a sort of tilbury body on four wheels, with a neat little seat for the groom behind, supported on branched irons; most of them have a folding head over the front body. Those first made, although light looking from the substitution of iron stays for solid wood construction, had a trembling and vibrating motion; but with more solid construction, and the suppression of the vibration, they have become not only comfortable, but with more refined designs and construction, more stylish in appearance. They carry a lady and gentleman on the front seat comfortably, and the hind seat is made of such size as to carry only one person, and the groom runs no chance of having his dignity hurt by his master or one of his friends having to sit beside him.

'Victorias,' 'mi-lords,' and 'ducs' were used in continental capitals, especially in Paris, long before they became fashionable in London. Although cab-phaetons had been introduced forty years ago by Mr. David Davies, and more recent attempts had been made with partial success to induce people to use them in England, it was not till H.R.H. the Prince of Wales ordered one for the use of the Princess that English people came to understand their handiness and advantages. Set off by Her Royal Highness they became irresistible, and people at once understood that it was 'the correct thing' to ride in them.

It is probable that few people reflect on the causes of changes of fashion, but they are sometimes worth considering. The facts are sometimes singular and unexpected, but seem to follow a regular course, at least in one respect: as soon as a carriage has been developed, improved, perfected, and apparently no longer capable of improvement, it falls out of use, being superseded by some invention, change of circumstances, or other sufficient and inevitable reason that cannot be turned aside.

The rough and heavy travelling and other carriages that preceded 1830 fell out of use as the new and better roads of McAdam were made. The mail and stage coaches had just reached perfection in design, durability, lightness, and handiness, when the introduction of railways literally drove them off the high roads that seemed to have been made for them; so the gigs and phaetons, kept in large numbers by the London bankers and merchants to drive to and from their suburban houses, were driven off the roads by omnibuses, tramcars, and suburban railways.

The death of the late Prince Consort, and the withdrawal of the Court from London, rendered the dress carriages of the nobility almost useless; but fortunately not altogether, for the Royal State and dress carriages are still kept up for drawing-rooms, levées, and State ceremonials as suitable appendages of Royalty. The great nobles have also in many cases retained or renewed theirs, to the delight of sightseers in London, when they make their appearance in St. James's Park on their way to and from drawing-rooms and levées. If the days are fine on such occasions, these works of art are shown to advantage.

The foreign ambassadors in London have latterly been renewing their ceremonial carriages, notably those of Russia, Germany, and Italy; and the Royal dress carriages used by Her Majesty and her guests in the procession to Westminster Abbey on the Jubilee Thanksgiving Day were previously renovated, providing welcome employment to coachmakers and their men after a long spell of trade depression.

The depression in agriculture in England and Ireland, and the reduction in the profits of trade and manufactures, have also affected the use of carriages, more especially 'barouches.'

These carriages had, by the firms of Peters & Sons, Hooper & Co., and others, been brought to a perfection hitherto unapproached, but in many cases they required special horses to draw them. Reduced incomes, and the advent of 'victorias' drawn with one horse or a pair of ponies, have almost put an end to the building of such barouches as were redeeming features to the drive in Hyde Park, now usually teeming with second and third rate vehicles—very different from the days when there were leaders of fashion who knew a great deal about horses and carriages, and could criticise with sound sense and judgment. With the vast increase in the wealth of the inhabitants of the British Empire, it seems strange that so many people should nowadays begrudge a liberal or even fair expenditure on their horses, carriages, and equipments, while willing to pay lavishly for pictures, sculpture, furniture, pottery, or bric-à-brac.

Great is the rage and demand for 'shoddy' carriages (fortunately for some people, for their sale affords a far larger profit than genuine and conscientiously well-made ones), and the supply naturally keeps pace with the demand. Accidents happen, buyers get bitten, and cry out (when it is too late) after the bill has been paid.

The system and method of taxing carriages is also very prejudicial to the coach-building business. Like all other taxes on raw products or manufactures, the carriage tax tends to limit the consumption, demand, and use. People will not pay forty-two shillings a year for the privilege of keeping their old carriages for use in rainy weather and for rough work, but prefer to hand them over (instead of cash) to the seller of a new or other second-hand carriage, who has to warehouse them till he can find purchasers. The innkeepers and livery-stable keepers, who would otherwise buy them to let for hire, will not encumber themselves with one more than they absolutely need, as their profits would every year be reduced by the amount of the additional carriage tax. Besides, many of the vehicles could only be let for two or three months each year, although the tax would have to be paid as if they were earning money all the year round, as do omnibuses, tramcars, and town cabs. The capital of the coachmaker is locked up with a large stock of carriages, of which the sale is impeded

LIST OF FASHIONABLE CARRIAGES USED IN 1888.

Name of Carriage	Size of horse	No. of wheels	No. of persons carried	Open	Closed	Folding leather head	Approximate price in guineas	Approximate weight	Government licence
								cwt.	£ s. d.
Pony cart	1 pony, 12 to 14 hands	2	2	open	—	—	20 to 50	3 to 4	0 15 0
Dog cart	1 horse, 14½ to 16 hands	2	4	"	—	—	25 " 60	5 " 7	0 15 0
Gig	1 horse, 15½ hands	2	2	"	—	—	40 " 90	5 " 7	0 15 0
Hansom cab . . .	1 " 16 "	2	3 {2 inside & driver behind}	half closed, sliding windows in front		—	90 " 145	8 " 10	0 15 0
Phaeton	1 " 15 "	4	4	open	—	—	45 " 90	5 " 7	1 1 0
Road phaeton . . .	1 " 15½ "	4	4 {2 in front, 2 behind}		—	—	45 " 80	5 " 7	1 1 0
T cart	1 " 15½ "	4	4 {2 in front, 2 behind}	"	—	—	45 " 90	5 " 7	1 1 0
Park phaeton . . .	2 ponies, 14 "	4	3 {2, 1 behind}	"	—	to cover 2 persons	80 " 150	6 " 8	1 1 0
Victoria phaeton . .	1 horse, 15½ "	4	4 {2 in front, 2 inside}	"	—	to body	90 " 150	6 " 8	1 1 0
Double victoria . .	1 " 15½ "	4	6 {4 inside, 2 in front}	"	—	"	90 " 170	7 " 9	1 1 0
Stanhope phaeton . .	1 " 16 "	4	4 {2 in front, 2 behind}	"	—	"	90 " 150	7 " 9	1 1 0
Mail phaeton . . .	2 " 15 "	4	4 {2 in front, 2 behind}	"	—	"	100 " 180	8 " 10	2 2 0
Pair horse wagonette .	2 " 16 "	4	8 {6 behind, 2 in front}	"	—	—	80 " 150	8 " 11	2 2 0
Pair-horse break	2 " 16 "	4	10 {8 behind, 2 in front}	"	—	—	90 " 160	9 " 12	2 2 0

Miniature brougham .	1 „ 15 „	4	4 {2 inside, 2 in front}	—	„	—	90 „ 150	7 „ 9	1 1 0
Single „ . . .	1 „ 16 „	4	4 {2 inside, 2 in front}	—	„	—	90 „ 160	8 „ 10	1 1 0
Circular-fronted brougham	1 „ 16 „	4	6 {4 inside, 2 in front}	—	„	—	95 „ 175	9 „ 11	1 1 0
Double brougham . .	1 or 2 horses	4	6 {4 inside, 2 in front}	—	„	—	100 „ 185	9 „ 11	1 1 0
Single brougham (on under and C springs)	1 horse, 16 hands	4	4 {2 inside, 2 in front}	—	„	—	140 „ 220	11 „ 13	1 1 0
Double „ „ .	2 „ 15 „	4	6 {4 inside, 2 in front}	—	„	—	145 „ 235	12 „ 14	2 2 0
Sociable	2 „ 15 „	4	6 {4 inside, 2 in front}	open	—	{to cover 2 persons}	90 „ 180	11 „ 13	2 2 0
Barouche sociable . .	2 „ 15½ „	4	6 {4 inside, 2 in front}	„	—	„	100 „ 200	11 „ 13	2 2 0
„ on elliptic springs	2 „ 15½ „	4	6 {4 inside, 2 in front}	„	—	„	100 „ 200	11 „ 13	2 2 0
„ on under and C springs . . .	2 „ 15½ „	4	6 {4 inside, 2 in front}	„	—	„	180 „ 280	13 „ 17	2 2 0
Light coach, on elliptic springs . . .	2 „ 15 „	4	6 {4 inside, 2 in front}	—	closed	—	150 „ 230	11 „ 14	2 2 0
Light coach, on under and C springs .	2 „ 15½ „	4	6 {4 inside, 2 in front}	—	„	—	190 „ 260	14 „ 17	2 2 0
Shelburne landau . .	2 „ 15½ „	4	6 {4 inside, 2 in front}	open or closed		{(self-acting) to cover 4 persons}	180 „ 250	11 „ 15	2 2 0
Sefton „ . .	2 „ 15½ „	4	6 {4 inside, 2 in front}	„		„	180 „ 250	11 „ 15	2 2 0
Landaus, on under and C springs . .	2 „ 16 „	4	6 {4 inside, 2 in front}	„		„	200 „ 280	15 „ 18	2 2 0
Dress chariot . . .	2 „ 16 „	4	3 {2 inside, 1 in front}	—	closed	—	300 „ 600	18 „ 20	2 2 0
„ coach . . .	2 „ 16 „	4	5 {4 inside, 1 in front}	—	„	—	320 „ 650	18 „ 21	2 2 0
Four-in-hand drag . .	4 „ 16 „	4	12	—	„	—	200 „ 350	18 „ 24	2 2 0

by the method of taxation. It is only in England that such a state of affairs exists, and where coachmakers' warehouses and factories are encumbered with old carriages. Till this year (1888) the imposition of a duty of fifteen shillings on vehicles weighing less than four hundredweight encouraged the production of such small carriages as enabled people to save twenty-seven shillings per year in the tax—hence the demand for small carriages that required but little skilled labour, and material, and compel a pony to draw a load of people that should really be drawn by a large horse. Carriages drawn by one or more horses and subject to a forty-two-shilling tax have been given up by thousands in order to save twenty-seven shillings of yearly tax, and such carriages block up the factories (chiefly in provincial towns), because the taxation is not only heavy, but continuous, and oppressive, intensifying the trade depression that exists by reducing the quantity of skilled labour that formerly did (and would again) find suitable employment under more fair and just conditions. While other articles of convenience and comfort were taxed, carriages were not exceptionally treated, but now those who find employment and profit in their production are placed on a different footing from the rest of their fellow-countrymen, the products of whose industry have been freed from taxation.

By reference to the tabular statement on pages 376, 377, a very fair idea may be formed as to the general character of the carriages mostly in use at the present time, and useful information obtained by those about to buy carriages for the first time. The columns are arranged as follows:

1. The names.
2. The proper size of horses.
3. The number of wheels.
4. The number of persons carried.
5. The amount of shelter provided.
6. Whether open, closed, or provided with folding leather heads.
7. The approximate price for various qualities and sizes.

8. The approximate weight, varying much according to size and the requirements of buyers.

9. The Government licence payable annually for each sort of carriage.

A short description of each carriage will probably afford some assistance in the choice of a suitable vehicle.

And here, *en passant*, we may mention that carriages of all kinds should really be proportioned both to the size and weight of the persons who use them, and of the horse or horses intended to draw them ; proportion and fitness are all-important for a satisfactory result.

The pony-cart is generally small, is hung low, and carries two, and occasionally four, persons. It is mostly driven by ladies and young people, and more frequently in the country than in London.

The dog-cart is almost always made to carry four persons ; its hanging varies according to the taste of buyers—some preferring high, others low ones ; the balancing is arranged by a screw acting behind, or by the action of a lever, or by simply moving the seats by hand, the body being hung back for carrying two persons, and forward for four persons.

Gigs vary much. The old style of Stanhope gig has four cross springs, and the bent ash shafts are strongly plated with iron. They are sometimes made with folding heads. Many gigs are now made with elastic lancewood shafts with tapered hind ends, and with fulcrum action. Many of the polo ponies are now used in light small gigs made especially to suit these smart little animals.

Gigs are considered equally suitable for London and country use.

Mr. C. J. de Murrieta has recently had a very successful gig made for him. By taking the old curricle body, refining the lines, and reducing the proportions, mounting it with a folding head, and suspending it on a Stanhope gig carriage, he has succeeded in producing not only a novelty, but a new type of carriage, not only very comfortable, but very stylish and gentlemanlike in appearance, and already the criticisms of those well able to judge have pronounced it a success. It is well to remember that, unlike dog-carts, gigs seat only two persons, and consequently when a groom is taken he must ride beside his master.

The hansom cab is so familiar to all Londoners and persons visiting London, that little need be said beyond that it has been greatly reduced in weight, refined in appearance, and is so comfortable a mode of conveyance that many prefer it to most other carriages.

Phaetons are carriages on four wheels that carry four persons, who generally all sit looking forward. Their pattern is multitudinous, and their style and price equally so.

Road phaetons and dog-cart phaetons are on four wheels. They are almost always used out in the country. The persons occupying the hind seat generally sit with their backs to the horse. Their style is generally of a somewhat sporting character. They carry luggage, or dogs inside the body. Many have been made of late years, and merely varnished, not undergoing the usual process of painting. The painting, however, adds durability to the carriage by more effectually keeping the moisture from the wood, iron, and steel.

Of late years the name buggy has been adopted to indicate a low-hung gig with a folding head. H.R.H. the Duchess of Connaught had one specially built for her own driving in India, and this type is now called the Connaught buggy.

T-carts are phaetons on four wheels; the front of the body resembles a gig with round-cornered seat. The persons occupying the hind seat face the horse.

Park phaetons are mostly considered ladies' carriages, the principal body being in front, generally provided with a folding head, leather wings to protect the steps from mud, and a seat for one servant behind.

Victoria phaetons have the body of curved form with a head over the principal seat, which is behind, and carries two persons. The driving-seat also carries two persons in front. The body is provided with four wings, to protect the steps and the occupants from the mud thrown by the wheels. It is always entered by a single step; many are provided with a little seat, for children, which folds into the back part of the front boot.

Vienna phaetons are in most respects like the victoria, but are of angular form and have higher wheels.

Of late years many victorias have been suspended on iron perches with under and C springs and leather braces; they are of various patterns and sizes, and look well when used with a pair of cobs of from fourteen to fifteen hands.

Double victorias are a combination of a victoria and sociable, rather more like the former as regards size and weight, and like the latter in form and accommodation; they are made with folding head to the hind part of the body, have a more comfortable seat for the third and fourth persons in the body than a victoria, have no doors, but are provided with wings over the wheels to protect the steps from the mud. They are becoming a favourite carriage, and look well with a pair of fourteen-hand ponies.

Stanhope phaetons have a curved panel seat in front provided with a folding head, and railed seat large enough for two persons behind, but generally occupied by one servant. They are hung on four wheels and elliptic springs, are mostly driven in England with one horse, but on the continent of Europe almost always with a pair.

Mail-phaetons differ from Stanhope phaetons in being always made for pair-horse work, and rather larger and stronger. Some are suspended on under-carriages with perch and mail springs, much in the manner of four-horse coaches, and this mode of construction is much favoured by driving men as the correct thing. Many more, however, are hung on four elliptic springs with an arch cut in the boot to allow the front wheels to pass under and facilitate turning the carriage.

Those having outside futchels (straight bars of wood to support the splinter-bar) are preferred by connoisseurs, as giving a character not possessed by those having merely the iron stay support.

Wagonettes have one general feature, being suspended on four wheels and carrying four or more people behind, sitting sideways and face to face. Many small ones are made with the hind seat removable, so that they can be readily converted into phaetons, carrying two persons in the principal seat in front and two persons facing the horses in the railed seat behind.

The wagonette break is of larger size than the one-horse carriages of that type ; it is always made with a high driving-seat, and fitted for two, and sometimes four horses.

Chars-à-bancs are more various in form than most other carriages ; they are generally high and strongly made, to carry a good many persons. Some have four seats, each carrying three or four persons, on the top of a high and long boot ; the seats are reached by convenient folding and sliding steps concealed in the boot and shut in by a small door. Others have the central seats kept low ; the four persons sit as in a coach, facing one another ; doors and folding steps provide easy access. The front driving-seat is made high in this class of carriage, and frequently the hind seat for the grooms is also high, being carried, as in the case of drags, on strong ornamental irons ; at other times this seat is kept low, and the grooms sit with their backs to the horses. Most of the large carriages of this type are used with four horses and are suspended in various ways, some on perch under-carriage with mail springs, others have in addition under-springs, while others again have four ordinary elliptic springs. Some are now made on a smaller scale and go well with a pair of horses. A char-à-bancs is essentially a carriage for a 'grande maison,' and for country use, and it is rarely found where a coach-house has not room for more than four carriages.

Beaufort phaetons have been made in recent years to meet a special want ; they carry six persons on a compact and strong carriage to hunt-meetings. They are strictly a gentleman's carriage, and, although provided with doors to facilitate reaching the middle seat, do not profess to provide such accommodation as ladies expect.

Private omnibuses are now essential to all large country establishments, and are made of many sizes, and with varied accommodation, from the light one that carries four persons under cover, to the capacious two or four horse carriage. Of late years the proportions and lines have been greatly refined, and the weight reduced, and although they can never aspire to be elegant carriages, they have gradually become much more agreeable to look at than was the case formerly. With high front wheels, low step to enter the body, spring-lock to the door, external side-lamps that light the interior from the outside, ventilators, hat and umbrella straps and nets, pockets, cupboard, &c., they now combine the utmost accommodation with the minimum of weight.

Broughams are of all sorts and sizes, from the smallest miniature which carries two small persons inside and two smaller ones on the driving-seat, and are drawn by a cob of fifteen hands, to the large, roomy, or weighty ones that are used in the royal establishment with a pair of coach-horses.

The medium-size single broughams carry two persons inside and two servants on the driving-seat.

Circular-fronted broughams carry three inside, the third person being carried in the bow-window that projects from the body over the back part of the boot, and forms a segment of a circle, allowing the bent windows to slide over one another.

Double broughams carry four persons inside and have straight fronts, generally with one large window, which may be lowered if desired, and two smaller front side windows, which are almost invariably fixed.

In many establishments of the nobility and gentry, when a brougham is kept, it is suspended on an iron perch, with under and C springs and leather braces, giving greater ease to the motion of the carriage, and suppressing the vibration that is inseparable from carriages hung on elliptic springs.

Sociables are low-hung carriages of angular form that have

a well-doorway, entered by a single step; they carry four persons inside, have a folding head over the hind part of the body, and a low driving-seat in front. They are generally driven with a pair of horses of from 15 to 15·2 hands. This is a favourite type of carriage with H.R.H. the Princess of Wales.

'Barouche sociables' differ from those already described in several important features; in form they resemble two cabriolet-shaped bodies placed facing one another; they are entered by two steps, have four long wings over the wheels to protect the occupants from mud, and always have a light driving-box supported on curved irons. They were chiefly used in establishments of the first rank; but for some unexplained reason are gradually going out of use, although elegant and stylish carriages.

Barouches have for more than fifty years been considered an indispensable open carriage for nearly all first-class establishments. Originally made with full deep panels and suspended on wooden perch and C-springs; afterwards with panels much reduced in depth, and with the front panels scooped away to allow the passage of higher front wheels; then hung on wooden perch carriages with the addition of under springs to the C-springs; subsequently on forged iron perches, with very shallow panels, and reduced in size and weight, always with the driving-seat fixed on curved ornamental ironwork, they have reached a refinement and elegance that seems to have almost exhausted the chance of further improvements.

Many such carriages have been hung on elliptic springs, rendering them available for country as well as London work, for which the C-spring barouches have in recent years been almost exclusively retained. But the taste of the day sets in favour of C-spring victorias rather than of the stately and lordly barouche.

The old type of family coach has, as an ordinary carriage, gone out of use, but there is still need for close carriages to carry four full-grown persons comfortably inside. This want has been met by a reduction in size, and by a refinement of proportions; cutting through the doorways; carrying down the doors, and providing single steps with covers opening with the doors. The body being hung lower than formerly, enables persons to enter or leave the carriage more rapidly, and when large numbers of carriages are assembled to take persons home from operas, theatres, balls, concerts, or any other assemblies, this facility is of great public advantage, as the company, instead of being detained that *mauvais quart d'heure* in the lobbies, crush-rooms, and entrances (the ladies generally in light dresses and sometimes in a cold draught or cutting east wind), can be more rapidly dispersed without the tiresome discomfort of former times. They are made with curved and also angular outlines to suit the taste of purchasers. Some have black panels to the whole upper part, while most have windows in the upper side panels.

Landaus carry four persons inside, have folding heads that protect all from the rain and weather, and are mostly made of two patterns: some with curved lines approaching that of a barouche, others with a well, and angular lines, more like the carriages known as sociables. Those with curved lines are known as 'Sefton' landaus, from the present Earl of Sefton, who had the first one built for his own use. Those with angular lines are known as 'Shelburne' landaus, from the late Earl of Shelburne, who had the first of that pattern built.

No other carriages have had so much care, attention, and inventive talent bestowed on them as landaus, and the agreeable feature in the matter is, that all the important improvements that have been effected and permanently adopted are English: they have been made in vast numbers, and have been surpassingly useful in our rainy and damp climate. If the coachmakers of the beginning of the century could but inspect the best landaus of the present day, side by side with their own productions—good of their kind as they were—they would marvel at the improvements effected by their successors.

Many of these landaus have been suspended on forged iron perches, with under and C springs and leather braces. The first attempts were heavy and cumbersome, but more elegant and refined types were produced and have held the public favour for years. Latterly Shelburne landaus have been similarly suspended, and they offer considerable advantages to elderly or infirm persons. They are open and closed carriages combined. Being hung low, they can be entered with a single step as a brougham, and the mechanism of the heads is so perfect that they can be opened and closed in case of rain almost as readily as an umbrella. If better known, they would be more appreciated.

The dress-coach carries four persons inside, while the dress-chariot carries only two persons inside. Such carriages, produced under able hands, are not only triumphs of mechanical but also of artistic skill, for they combine more than any other vehicle that is produced the most diverse materials; the artificers carry on the most varied occupations, and the manufacturer has so to design his work, arrange his materials, and control the whole construction, that in the end they shall produce a result of the utmost harmony, whether mechanical or artistic; for it is of little use to produce a fine mechanical work and mar it by coarse or inappropriate decoration; or to ornament with the utmost refinement and taste a work that is mechanically incorrect. All the proportions, the suspension, the equipments, and decorations must be in harmony; but the whole effect of a very perfect work may be marred by a pair of coarse-bred horses, badly-fitted harness, servants of ill-proportion as regards figure, or untidy and slovenly bearing, or with incongruous liveries or hats.

No wonder so few fine equipages are now to be seen. Their production requires a combination of qualities in the owners, producers, coachmen, and all connected with them, that needs to be kept in practice, and they deserve and should receive appreciation in those who are critics or even spectators; for the owners of fine pictures, a fine house, a fine horse, or even a good suit of well-fitted clothes, derive some satisfaction and encouragement from the approval of friends and the outside world—for all are mortal, and moved by somewhat the same sentiments and tastes—refined or blunted according to surroundings or other circumstances.

That there is a satisfaction in gazing on such equipages is evidenced by the crowds of critics and sightseers who throng St. James's Park on drawing-room and levée days. Were the elegant ladies, gallant officers, stately nobles, and great statesmen who attend such Court ceremonies conveyed thither in omnibuses or London four-wheel cabs, it is probable that many sightseers would stay away. And what shall we say about the Lord Mayor's procession on each ninth day of November? His state coach is eagerly looked for as the outward and visible sign of his rank and dignity as chief magistrate of the City of London. The eye of the public has to be pleased and satisfied; it wants sentiment and glitter to enable it to realise the rank and station of the occupants, for what the handsome uniform is to the officer and soldier, the state carriage is to others who have to take prominent positions in the eyes of their fellow-men.

Last, but not least, is the mail-coach, or four-in-hand coach, however now best known as a 'drag,' a small coach body with large and deep boots, carrying four persons inside, hung on a wooden perch under-carriage, with mail-coach springs, frequently with mail-coach axles. Each boot has a high seat, the front one carrying two persons, the driver being on the right or off side, seated on a deep wedge-shape driving cushion. The hind seat is elevated on curved irons, and carries two or three persons; two seats on the roof, one at each end, carry three or four persons according to the taste or requirements of the owner; a break, actuated by a long lever handle to the right of the driver's seat, and having two arms provided with wood or India-rubber blocks which are pressed on the tires of the hind wheels to retard the speed of the carriage when descending hills. Such carriages are (or should be always) provided with a strong pole made of the finest and toughest ash from young and well-grown trees, five splintrees for the leaders (three for use, and two spare ones in reserve in case one of the three becomes disabled from any cause).

Many of these carriages, especially those sent to foreign countries, are provided with numerous additional fittings to carry luncheons and picnic arrangements, but so contrived as to be little observed when in use.

This list and description might be much extended by describing carriages occasionally made for special purposes, and may be closed with a description of a few carriages used as public conveyances and plying for hire on the streets of London and large provincial towns.

The hansom cab, as a private carriage, has been already noticed. Those used on the streets much resemble them, and, although of somewhat rougher build, these new vehicles may be favourably compared with those of any other great city. And with improved cabs have come an improved class of drivers, greatly encouraged by the managers of the Cab-Drivers' Benevolent Association and those other benevolent ladies and gentlemen who have latterly provided the cabmen with comfortable shelters, where they are protected from the rain and storms, and obtain wholesome refreshments at moderate rates.

The four-wheel cabs are small closed carriages holding four persons inside and with a low driving-seat on the boot for the driver, with space for another person at his side, seldom, however, used. They are hung low, are entered with a single step from the ground, and are provided with an iron rail round the roof and a chain to prevent luggage from falling off, or being removed by unauthorised persons. When carrying a full load of luggage on the roof and full complement of passengers, it is a marvel how easily a cab-horse can draw it and take it to a distant destination.

These vehicles cannot, however, be compared with the hansoms for style, comfort, and finish. A large proportion of them are still coarse, noisy, odoriferous, and jumpy as regards the springs. When, however, it is considered to what uses they are put, some excuse may be offered for their shortcomings. For they take Jack and his mates on their arrival from Sheerness or Portsmouth; Tommy Atkins and his friends, perhaps fresh from camp life at Aldershot or Colchester; or Mary Jane and her boxes to her new place in a distant suburb; and as it is often cheaper to hire a cab than a cart to remove goods (other than personal luggage), it is hardly to be wondered at that the varnish is not as brilliant as on the duke's brougham or the countess's victoria.

The omnibuses of London, whether used, with two or three horses, are compact, useful, and handy carriages, carrying from twelve to sixteen persons inside and twelve to sixteen outside. It is probable that, comparing weight of passengers carried with weight of vehicle, there are no carriages used in any part of the world superior to them. They have been greatly improved as regards ventilation, and ease of access, specially to the roof seats; and many being now provided with lever breaks pressing on the two hind wheels, and actuated by the driver's foot, he is able to ease the horses of much strain otherwise inevitable from the frequent stoppages in taking up and setting down passengers.

A few words may be added regarding second-hand carriages, for the guidance of persons of moderate means or of economical inclination.

There are not many articles of manufacture that vary so much in quality, durability, and style as carriages; for by the judicious use of putty, paint, and varnish, much that is not strictly good, sound, or honest may be made to shine and look attractive to innocent eyes. It is therefore necessary to be cautious in buying smart-looking second-hand carriages. On the other hand, some of the best London carriages are so soundly made that it is difficult to thoroughly wear them out. There are, however, reasons that cause them to change hands from time to time, such as death of owners; diminution of income through various causes; departure of temporary residents to colonies or foreign lands; changes of fashion; and, in addition, the effect of the carriage taxes in England is to keep down carriage establishments, in order to minimise expenditure on carriage licences. Thus, year by year, there is a constant flow of a number of first-rate carriages into the hands of the best London carriage-builders; and by applying to respectable firms, reliable second-hand carriages can be had on contract, or purchased by those who from choice or necessity desire to limit their yearly expenditure.

There is only one rule for the guidance of would-be purchasers of second-hand carriages even when a reliable builder's name is plainly seen on the axle-caps. The rule is a negative one, but still is valuable: 'Do not purchase any second-hand carriage unless you have ***implicit faith*** in the ***vendor***.'

Changes of fashion have this effect—that, however good a second-hand carriage may be, if it is even a little out of the fashion, people are unwilling to buy it; such carriages the coach-builders are generally anxious to sell at almost nominal prices, and to those persons who do not object to what may be a little out of fashion, such carriages offer an excellent investment; for many years' use may be had out of them with a very small outlay for repairs.

We should weary our readers were we to attempt to givef descriptions of the various improvements that have been taking place from year to year. The use of concealed hinges, whereby the neatness of the suspension and wider opening of the doors is secured; spring door locks and improved inside handles, rendering shutting and opening easier; and the saving of many nice dresses and lace by suppressing the projecting inside lever handles, are among minor improvements.

Landaus have during the last thirty years had more ingenuity bestowed on them than any other carriage: in extreme reduction of weight and size, and by contrivances to provide available sitting accommodation in bodies of small external dimensions; in improved arrangements of the folding heads to enable them to fall flatter, and afford more view and air to the occupants of the carriage; in the concealed and ingenious mechanism which facilitates the closing and opening of the heads, almost as simple in action as the opening and closing of an umbrella or parasol; in the application of single steps, with covers to open with the doors; in improved weather plates to effectually prevent rain entering through the joint of the roof; in the use of mild steel in place of iron plates, increasing the stiffness and reducing the weight of the body; in securing the standing pillars on the sides of the solid rockers, instead of framing them into the bottom sides, whereby doorways are rendered much stiffer, and the doors and glasses more easy and certain in action.

The interiors of carriages have also been much improved by spiral springs of thin steel wire in the cushions and backs, morocco-covered trays, card-case pockets, portable mirrors, whistles and bells to communicate with the coachman; the lace is better woven, and the interiors have an air of greater comfort, neatness, and high finish. It is singular to what an extent silk linings for carriages have been abandoned during the last twenty years, in favour of morocco leather with a dull grained surface; it may be on the score of the greater durability of leather.

Lever breaks to retard the speed of carriages descending hills, by pressing a block of iron, wood, or India-rubber on the tires of the hind wheels, were introduced about thirty years ago. Screw breaks had been used on the continent of Europe for some time before, probably necessitated by the requirements of travelling on the steep gradients of the Alpine ranges of Switzerland and Italy; their action, at first weak and uncertain, has been greatly improved, but the lever is almost invariably preferred in this country. Some coachmakers cleverly conceal most of the working parts, and thereby prevent disfigurement to the outlines of good carriages. The late Prince Consort had a screw break applied to one of his *fourgons*, in which the screw had so rapid a pitch that one or one and a half turns applied the pressure on the wheels.

Here it may be not inappropriate to refer to the increasing use of India-rubber tires. Applied to the wheels of the best London carriages (although expensive), they afford ease and comfort, and moreover suppress noise, a great consideration to very many persons in delicate health or of nervous temperament; also, by reducing the concussions on the carriage and springs, these tires tend to curtail the cost of repairs, and to prolong the working life of the carriages to which they are applied. As one improvement often leads to others, this one would only be feasible on roadways with wood or asphalte surfaces such as London now possesses. With hard and rough stones India-rubber tires would fare badly; but, in view of their extended use in other towns and countries where roads may be expected to be improved, merchants will do well to encourage the growth and import to this country of large and regular supplies of the raw material. Already there is a great demand for India-rubber mats, which are a modern introduction, and have recently been greatly improved in neatness of pattern and appearance, almost superseding those of cocoa-nut fibre, wool, &c.

International and home exhibitions have exerted a considerable influence in stimulating changes and improvements, the former much more numerous than the latter. They have, however, to be entered on with caution by carriage-builders; for it sometimes happens that the inviting country retains the best positions for its own manufacturers, and politely places foreign competitors in such a remote position, and with such incongruous surroundings as ploughs, harrows, and farm carts, as to disgust visitors, and lead them to infer that the carriages are in company suited to their deservings. Even a gold medal will not compensate for an unfavourable impression on possible buyers; and with the pattern and measurements neatly and accurately taken by one or more manufacturers of the country that invites others to send their carriages in competition, and with the customs tariff arranged at a sufficiently high rate, the foreign exhibitor undergoes the process of 'easy shaving,' with little chance of business resulting after all his trouble, expenditure, and enterprise.

One outcome of international exhibitions was probably little anticipated on their first being held. The frequent meetings of exhibitors at one of the great international exhibitions led to the establishment of the Master Coachbuilders' Benevolent Institution, which has already collected upwards of 27,000*l.*, chiefly from those engaged in the manufacture. It maintains thirty-five pensioners, has an annual income of 800*l.*, and at its monthly committee meetings unfortunate coach-makers, their managers and clerks, are helped in times of trouble and distress.

Technical schools have been established in London, Manchester, New York, and Sydney; and with a little more encouragement from some of the now worse than wasted old endowments, would rapidly rise in efficiency and importance. Annual examinations in the technology of carriage-building are held under the auspices of the City and Guilds of London Institute; and it may here be mentioned that when proposed and founded about fourteen years ago by the Council of the Society of Arts, General Donnelly, R.E., was directed to consult the writer with the view of including the art of carriage-building in the five subjects (or industries) on which the plan should be tried. After many consultations, a scheme was worked out and organised, and of the total number of candidates for the first five examinations, one-half were coach-builders. After holding the office of examiner some seven or eight years, the writer resigned in consequence of impaired health and pressure of other duties.

These technical classes, and annual examinations of the pupils to test the results of the teaching of carriage drawing and designing, and technology of construction and finish, are exerting a very favourable influence on the industry both in London and in the provinces, inducing a friendly rivalry among the competitors, exciting them to renewed exertions, improving them professionally, morally, and socially, so that they are able to better their position both from a monetary and social point of view—a move forward highly to be valued now that so large a proportion of working men are entrusted with the government of the country through the votes they exercise at elections.

The result of the technical classes has been to turn out some hundreds of more or less skilful carriage draughtsmen, who, being able to make full-sized working drawings of carriages, greatly facilitate the production of more elegant and better proportioned vehicles, and are likely in the near future to exert a favourable influence on the whole trade. But instead of passing the apprentices and young workmen through the classes by hundreds, it is to be hoped that at no distant time they will be passed through by thousands, to the benefit of themselves and their country. Some have been instructed in the art of perspective drawing, and a few can produce drawings of carriages in perspective with facility. Already lithographers and printers are able to supply illustrations of carriages in perspective very fairly, an accomplishment that an older generation of coachmakers said was not only difficult but impossible, and never would be done. It has, however, been done in our time, notwithstanding.

Associations of carriage-builders have existed in England, France, and in the United States for some years, the American being the most active and enterprising, holding its meetings in a different town each year, and numbering about four hundred members at each meeting, some travelling one or two thousand miles to be present and take part in the proceedings, for mutual aid, support, and protection. The French one consists solely of Paris coachmakers. It has exercised a great influence in the development of the carriage industry in France, and has been carried on with very considerable skill, intelligence, and patriotism.

The London Coachmakers' Company holds its charter of incorporation from King Charles II., and in its day has done good service to the industry it was founded to foster and encourage. From a state of almost entire torpor about twenty years ago, it has been urged and pushed on to a condition of greater influence and usefulness; but its pace was too slow for the times we live and move in, and another establishment, the Institute of British Carriage Manufacturers, had to be founded about six years ago on a popular basis, where all the officers have to undergo an election every year at the annual meeting. It has already done a large amount of work that ought to have been done by the chartered company, which holds ample funds for trade purposes.

It may here be mentioned that in one of the rooms of the offices of the royal mews at Berlin formerly occupied by General Willison, Master of the Horse to the late Emperor Frederick William, there was a first-rate collection of about eighty oil paintings of royal carriages of various countries, with their horses and harness, &c. The collection is, in many respects, a valuable one, and it is to be hoped it may be long preserved, where it may be seen and admired by Englishmen visiting the now important capital of the German Empire.

About fifteen years ago the Science and Art Department at South Kensington, through the British Foreign Office and British ambassadors in foreign capitals, made an excellent collection of photographs of the ancient state carriages of the sovereigns of Europe. The photographs are now the property of the Coachmakers' Company of London. They were shown at South Kensington in 1873, at Liverpool in 1886, and at Newcastle in 1887. The Institute of British Carriage Manufacturers (having its head-quarters at the New Town Hall, Westminster) possesses a unique collection of illustrations of ancient carriages, including working designs prepared, some 200 years ago, for a former Duke of Saxe-Coburg, an ancestor of the late Prince Consort.

In relation to carriages, heraldry plays a somewhat important part in indicating ownership, pictorially and by signs and emblems, sometimes historical, and often otherwise interesting. But its use is much diminished with the reduction of the number of dress and state carriages now kept. At the present day the art of monogram designing and painting gives almost as much employment as heraldic drawing and painting.

In London there has long existed a system of contracts for the supply of new and second-hand carriages by coachmakers, whereby for a certain yearly payment one or more carriages are supplied, and kept in sound repair and nice order with little or no trouble to the lessee or person hiring. The system would not be so extensively developed had it not many advantages to recommend it to those who keep carriages.

It is specially convenient to persons enjoying fixed incomes, and who are disinclined to pay a large lump sum to purchase a new carriage: to ladies who prefer a definite annual payment rather than the uncertainty of bills for repairs: to persons who have not paid much attention to the selection of carriages, there is considerable relief of trouble and anxiety: there is also the satisfaction of using a carriage always kept in nice order, as the coachmakers provide a good substitute for temporary use, while repairs are being effected, free of charge.

Of course the charge varies according to the value of the carriage (whether new or second hand), and the term for which the contract is agreed to run. These contracts are made for one, three, five, seven, and ten years; the yearly rate of hire being proportionately reduced as the term becomes longer; printed and stamped agreements are generally signed by both parties.

It is perhaps little known to strangers that many of the best carriages in the London parks are contract carriages, and that many persons of wealth and station, whose carriages are all that can be desired in style and finish, simply pay an annual fixed sum to the family coachbuilder.

It may be said, this is easy enough for persons living in London all the year round, but not to those who spend the greater part of their time in the country. But to any large London firm it is very rarely difficult to make arrangements with respectable persons in the provincial towns to do such small repairs as are from time to time necessary, whilst for thorough restorations the carriages come to London for a few weeks.

CURRICLE AND CABRIOLET

AMONG the number of two-wheeled carriages two important vehicles of the past stand out in places of their own. In the dignity of their appearance as in the distinction of their history and associations, the Curricle and the Cabriolet were the aristocrats of the two-wheeled tribe; one succeeding the other as *the* fashionable vehicle of its day for the owner's own driving.

To the curricle belonged the unique distinction of having been the only English two-wheeled carriage to which a pair of horses (abreast) could be driven. In it the pole and bar took the place of the shafts* of all other vehicles with two wheels. On occasion in days gone by leaders would be added, making it a four horse carriage, but normally a pair was its complement, its lightness and sporting appearance when well turned out making strong appeal to men of wealth and leisure.

Vehicles built on the same principle, first seen in Italy and later improved in France, were in use quite early in the eighteenth century, but not until the Regency was it that the English curricle really 'caught on,' proving at first a rival and then a supplanter in fashionable esteem of that odd four-wheeled favourite, the Highflyer phaeton. The extreme height of so many Regency vehicles characterized the curricle in earlier forms that were not long in giving place to a design of moderation and elegance. A neatly rounded body was provided with a folding leather head (hood); from the footboard a high dashboard of stiff leather inclined gently outward over the horses' quarters, the series of graceful curves being completed by the

* A pair of horses are driven one on each side of a pole; a single horse is driven between a pair of shafts.

big cee springs supporting the body at the back. Cee springs took their name from their resemblance to the letter C; in such a vehicle as the curricle they repeated almost perfectly the curve of the body and contributed greatly towards its harmonious lines. As in all such vehicles the seating was for two, one beside the driver, with — usually, but not always — a groom's seat between the springs behind. The principle of two wheels with a pair of horses made the curricle the closest descendant among carriages of the classic chariot of ancient history which, otherwise, it so little resembled. The method of attachment of the horses, common to no other vehicle, was by means of a curricle-bar, a burnished steel rod lying transversely over the horses, attached by roller fastenings to their pads (saddles); the head of the pole was suspended from the centre of this bar by a strong leather brace fastened under a spring in the former. Always provided that the horses were well matched in size and action, and that the balance of the vehicle was correctly adjusted with due allowance if a groom was carried, for his weight at the back, the result was a jaunty and extremely comfortable carriage with an easy, buoyant motion.

Curricles were 'easy' on horses, too, and for that reason as much as for their smartness were much in favour with Corinthian whips of the Regency, and with their successors of a later day, for driving long distances as well as for town and park use. Their popular innings was a long one, and even after the fashion for them had passed they continued to be used well into the latter half of the nineteenth century by many of the older school. Lord Tollemache was still driving one in the late 'eighties, and the first Marquis of Anglesey drove his up to the time of his death in 1854. The latter formed the subject of a delightful but rare lithograph that gives us perhaps the best surviving illustration we have of a perfectly turned-out curricle of the day, as well as containing a characteristic portrait of the veteran field marshal. Somewhat surprisingly its original design was the work, not of one of the accepted artists of sport, but of an amateur.

Many other great names were particularly associated with curricle driving in days not too distant. Thrupp mentions that, 'Charles Dickens drove one as soon as his writings procured him the means, and Count D'Orsay and Lord Chesterfield had new curricles from Messrs. Barker's as lately as 1836.' In the history of carriages the name of Count D'Orsay crops up frequently, more than one vehicle owing as much to his interest as a leader of fashion as to his coachmanship and an amateur knowledge of carriage design and structure that he added to his varied accomplishments, artistic, social and sporting. His curricle was often enough to be seen at the entrance of Gore House in Kensington when London talk was concerned with nothing so much as the receptions Lady Blessington held there, and with her particular association with D'Orsay; but thinly veiled by the pretext of his marriage to her unfortunate step-daughter, Lady Harriet Gardiner. At the time when the new curricle by Barker was built for 'the last of the Dandies', Lady Blessington, some seven years a widow, had in fact just moved into Gore House, which stood where is now the Albert Hall; and that period was beginning in which it became the almost nightly meeting place of the world of fashion, wit and talent, and for a time a serious rival to Holland House itself in the brilliance of its gatherings. The triumphant success of one of the most accomplished women of the age had begun with her marriage to Lord Blessington, when, 'Royal dukes and statesmen, Burdett, Castlereagh, Scarlett, Erskine, Charles Kemble, Charles Mathews, and Lawrence and Wilkie the great painters, crowded to her conversaziones and for three years she kept a sort of mimic court. Young, beautiful, witty, graceful and good humoured, she was able to hold her own with the elite of London Society.'

For much of the lavish extravagance that brought an eventual end to the greatness of Gore House, with the sale of its treasures and the flight of its hostess to France, D'Orsay was as responsible as he was for much else that was unfortunate in Lady Blessington's career from the day, in 1822, when she saw him first. 'The first man', she said after this meeting, 'I saw wearing pale lemon coloured gloves, and devilish well they looked.' Whatever his failings, though, D'Orsay's sporting achievements and associations illustrated the better side of his character; beyond his taste for carriages and driving was the undeniable fact of his having been a superb horseman, excelling either across a country or on one of the perfectly schooled hacks he rode in Town; as an artist too, he made not a few of his contemporaries in sport the subjects of his gift for portraiture.

Lord William Pitt Lennox, who wrote much on sporting matters and had a particular fondness for driving in all its forms, has left us a reminder that the curricle had another very important patron in the Duke of Wellington, who drove one in France as well as at home; and S. Sidney, in his exhaustive *Book of the Horse*, recalls that, 'It was somewhere about 1846 that I saw the great Duke of Wellington driving himself in a sulphur-yellow curricle with silver harness and bar, over old Westminster Bridge, to take part in a review at Woolwich; the late bridge was very steep, and he walked his horses up the ascent from Westminster.' The cost and difficulty of finding horses in pairs so closely matched in size and pace and of such quality that they were suited to curricle work put the carriage beyond the means of any but the well-to-do, and its associations would be almost entirely with the great names of the period were it not that it was also an age richly provided with eccentrics; inevitably a vehicle of such possibilities must attract at least one of them.

Certainly it was absurdity, not greatness, that distinguished 'Romeo' Coates, the owner and driver of a nightmare among curricles. It was as much on account of this freak vehicle of his as because of the burlesque appearances on the stage that earned him his nickname that the 'caricature dandy' became such a widely known figure of fun at first in Bath and later in London. A fortune inherited from his father enabled him, when a middle-aged man, to give his extravagances full rope. Descriptions of the shape of his famous curricle do not all agree, but that of William Bridges Adams may be assumed authentic, having been published as early as in 1837: 'The shape of the body was that of a classic sea-god's car, and it was constructed in copper. This vehicle was very beautiful in its outline, though disfigured by the absurdity of its ornamental work.' About this ornamental work and the appointments in general, only one opinion seems to have been held, by those who described the thing as looking like a polished kettle-drum as well as by its few admirers. A profusion of shells, and frequent repetitions of the owner's crest — a crowing cock — and motto — 'While I live I'll crow!' — adorned the bodywork, and more cocks, of polished brass and of generous size, were mounted on all suitable and unsuitable parts of the harness. This monstrosity was drawn by a pair of white horses and driven by 'Romeo', of whose appearance it is recorded that a good figure was marred by a sallow countenance much seared with wrinkles: 'In the daytime he was covered at all seasons with enormous quantities of fur, but the evening, as the time when he went to the balls, made a great impression, for his buttons as well as his knee-buckles, were of diamonds.'

Driving in the park, Coates was often followed by a pack of urchins loudly crowing 'Cock-a-doodle-do!'; his appearances as an actor caused minor riots in gallery and pit, and cat-call greetings of 'Old Cock-a-doodle!', 'Old Turn Coates!', or 'Driving Coates!' were flung at him rather than the title of his own choice — 'The Amateur of Fashion'. The last was the description given him in play, bills announcing his playing of Lothario in 'The Fair Penitent' or the part of Shakespeare's Romeo. As the former he made his London debut at the Haymarket Theatre in 1811; the latter he played in Bath and in London in a manner never seen before or since that was the subject of a passage in Captain Gronow's Reminiscences.

'The very first appearance of Romeo convulsed the house with laughter. Benvolio prepares the audience for the stealthy visit of the lover to the object of his admiration; and fully did the amateur give expression to one sense of the words uttered, for he was indeed the true representation of a thief stealing onwards in the night . . . His dress was *outre* in the extreme; whether Spanish, Italian, or English no one could say; it was like nothing ever worn. In a cloak of sky-blue silk, profusely spangled, red pantaloons, a vest of white muslin, surmounted by an enormously thick cravat and a wig *a la* Charles the Second, capped by an opera hat, he presented one of the most grotesque spectacles ever witnessed upon the stage. The whole of his garments were evidently too tight for him; and his movements appeared so incongruous that every time he raised an arm or moved a limb it was impossible to refrain from laughter; but what chiefly convulsed the audience was the bursting of a seam in an inexpressible part of his dress, and the sudden extrusion through the rent of a quantity of white linen sufficient to make a Bourbon flag . . . The total want of flexibility of limb, the awkwardness of his gait and the idiotic manner in which he stood still all produced a most ludicrous effect; but when his guttural voice was heard and his total misapprehension of every passage in the play, especially the vulgarity of his address to Juliet, were perceived everyone was satisfied that Shakespeare's Romeo was burlesqued on that occasion. Much more in the same vein describes succeeding absurdities in the performance, until, with the death scene; I question if Liston, Joey Knight or Munden was ever greeted with such merriment; for Romeo dragged the unfortunate Juliet from the tomb much as the washerwoman thrusts into her cart the bag of foul linen. But how shall I describe the death? Out came a dirty silk handkerchief from his pocket, with which he carefully swept the ground; then his opera hat was carefully placed for a pillow and down he laid himself. After various tossings about he seemed reconciled to the position; but the house vociferously bawled out, "Die again, Romeo!" and obedient to the command he rose up, and went through the ceremony again. Scarcely had he lain quietly down, when the call was again heard, and the well-pleased amateur was evidently prepared to enact a third death; but Juliet now rose up from her tomb and gracefully put an end to this ludicrous scene by advancing to the front of the stage and aptly applying a quotation from Shakespeare:

"Dying is such sweet sorrow,
That he will die again tomorrow."'

Coates' eccentric fame has survived him largely because of his carriage; and carriages, it so happened, were the cause of his death. He was crushed between two of them in a street in Covent Garden in 1848, and died soon afterwards at his house in Montagu Square.

To early days of the curricle, when greater height gave it greater risk, and consequently greater merit in the eyes of the Corinthian whips of the Regency, belonged a few with particular records and associations of their own. One of them, well known on the Old Steyne when the Prince Regent's presence in Brighton brought there the owners of so many distinguished vehicles, was the brown curricle of Lord Petersham. Its horses, too, were brown, so was the harness and the groom's livery ; an all-brown turn-out in fact, and a delicate compliment to the object of his lordship's devotion, a certain Mrs. Brown. To the same original genius belonged the designing of the ' Petersham ' coat, the blending of ' Petersham Mixture ' snuff and a connoisseurship in snuff and tea that included the laying down of collections of both on the same principle as cellars of wine.

History has never disclosed the identity of a gentleman who, driving a pair of blood bays to a curricle in Hyde Park in the year 1802, came to such grief as to earn the accident a description in the old *Sporting Magazine*, and to move the writer of it feelingly to express himself in the words : ' The groans of the horses and the lamentations of the driver exceed the power of the pen to describe, and never can be obliterated from the writer.' Somewhere near the Magazine the horses took fright and bolted, the groom was pitched out of his seat at the back when one of the wheels struck against a stone, and the owner, quite unable to pull up, apparently thought that his best chance of checking them was in guiding them to the edge of what was then called the Canal, later to become the Serpentine. For the moment this succeeded and a passer-by was able to take hold of the bridles ; but, making off a second time, the horses threw him on one side. The driver, as a desperate resort, turned their heads into the deeper water, where both were drowned and the curricle submerged ; the owner himself was rescued with difficulty by a number of bystanders.

Such an accident could as easily have befallen a four-wheeled carriage, and for the reputation for its risk that once attached to curricle-driving there seems to have been little justification when the height of the vehicles was not exaggerated. Brakes that in any carriage the driver could apply to retard the wheels were an invention of later days, though, and the safe driving of anything depended entirely on the coachman's ability to control his horses by his skill with reins and whip and in the preliminaries of correct putting together, harnessing and bitting. Any danger there was in a curricle greater than in a four-wheeled carriage

Geoffrey Bennett Collection — *Hon. Henry Graves*

Plate I. The Marquis of Anglesey driving his CURRICLE. *See page* 27

H. Arthurton Collection *John E. Ferneley*

Plate II. Mr Massey Stanley driving his CABRIOLET. *See page* 40

Author's Collection *J. F. Herring senior*

Plate III. CABRIOLET HORSE AND TIGER. *See page* 41

lay in horses falling, bringing the pole to the ground and pitching out the occupants. With this in mind, and the added risk of a horse slipping on modern smooth road surfaces designed for motors, the owner of one of the only two curricles one remembers seeing used in London within the last twenty-odd years, made use of the system of attachment associated with the Cape-cart of South Africa — the bar supporting the pole being attached in front of the horses and below the collars — instead of the bar supported by the pads and over the horses which takes its name from the curricle and is its correct accompaniment.

Both these recently-driven curricles, by the way, had a groom's dickey seat at the back, as in the case of the one in the print of the Marquis of Anglesey; some other old prints and paintings show curricles without it, and a fine surviving example of this type, once owned and used by the Kemp family in Suffolk, is still to be seen at the Stranger's Hall at Norwich.

Though a single-horse vehicle, the Cabriolet had, in the form and general appearance of the body, much in common with the curricle. Employed in England from about 1810, and before that in a cruder form in France, it made its true début as a vehicle of fashion, the curricle's successor in favour, with the opening of Queen Victoria's reign. Count D'Orsay here makes another appearance in the story of carriages as the cabriolet's sponsor. In collaboration with the coachbuilding firm of Barker and Company he evolved a refined and improved carriage — the cabriolet of dignified lines and delicate finish — from the existing type; this was rapidly adopted as the most correct and appropriate carriage for the personal driving of the man-about-town; the Count's taste in such matters was paramount, where he led others followed.

At the beginning of its fashionable career, W. B. Adams wrote of the cabriolet: 'The principal reason why this carriage is so much liked is its great convenience. It carries two persons, comfortably seated, sheltered from sun and rain, yet with abundant fresh air, and with nearly as much privacy as a closed carriage if the curtains be drawn in front. It can go in and out of places where a two-horse carriage with four wheels cannot turn; and a boy is carried behind, cut off from communication with the riders.' With a pleasing naïveté Mr. Adams adds : ' This is a very convenient vehicle for unmarried men to go out in at night.'

The cabriolet body was elegantly curved, its nautilus-shell shape being carried out in the folding leather head — normally kept half closed — the sloping splash-board and the gracefully bent shafts. A rigid apron of leather, or sometimes wood, enclosed like a door the lower part, protecting the legs of the occupants. The springing and method of suspension on the two large wheels were similar to those of the curricle. But unlike that vehicle the cabriolet never had a seat for a groom, and one of its particular distinctions was the little padded platform between the cee springs at the back, on which stood the ' tiger ', holding on by two straps attached to the body.

No cabriolet was complete without its tiger, a diminutive groom, either a boy or a man of almost midget size, immaculately turned out in livery — usually a belted frock coat, white ' leathers ', ' tops ', and a silk hat that bore a cockade if the master's rank warranted it. The smaller the tiger, the more highly was he prized as the attendant of the appropriate horse, which was invariably a big one, as big and powerful as consistency with the highest quality would allow. Perfection in a cabriolet called for a tiger so small and a horse so large that the former could only just reach the latter's bridle when standing at his head. Everything about the fashionable ' cab ' was the ultimate word in smartness ; a vehicle that had to be and always was irreproachably appointed. Never a turn-out for the man of limited means, when one considers that the combination of size and quality in horseflesh has been ever hard to attain and consequently expensive, and that a cabriolet in regular use in London must demand the keeping of at least two, if not three, such horses in the stable. One of the minor distinctions of the cabriolet was the custom of hanging a bell to the collar, introduced by those who did most of their driving at a fast pace and were much on the road at night, later adopted by the hansom cab. The use of the cabriolet head was unusual in that this was very rarely folded right back to leave the carriage entirely an open one ; if this were done the folded head left no room for the tiger to stand on his platform and one of the characteristic elegances of the turn-out was lost. Fully extended, the head came far enough forward to shield the faces of the occupants in bad weather. Between the two extremes was the position of normal use, in which it stood vertically in front to give driver and passenger unobstructed forward vision; to the sides they could look out through little oval-shaped windows set in the leather. In this position, one of the improvements said to have been thought out by the ingenious D'Orsay, the head was described as 'set back', or 'half-struck'.

Like the curricle the cabriolet had its day. Its elegance gradually gave place to the simplicity of the dog-cart in its various forms and only a faithful few continued to drive their 'cabs' in the London streets and in the Park, though it was a long time before they disappeared altogether. At the end of the century the late Lord Rosebery was driving what was then a solitary survivor among cabriolets, and this actual vehicle was, up to the outbreak of war in 1939, to be seen at the London Museum, among other carriages there. Probably the only one driven in Town since was that used for a short while by the late Alfred Vanderbilt, who between 1908 and 1914 ran the *Venture* and *Viking* coaches on the Brighton and London road, having at one time as many as 100 horses at work, and who lost his life in the *Lusitania* disaster.

Even in 1876, Lord William Pitt Lennox was lamenting the cabriolet as something belonging to the past: 'I own myself that I regret cabriolets are no longer the fashion', he wrote, 'for a man that can afford to keep a number of carriages, a victoria and brougham are all very well; but the former is only available in fine weather, whereas a cabriolet with a projecting head could defy most showers of rain. A well-appointed cabriolet was a comfortable and gentleman-like conveyance, and for the bachelor, did the duty of a close carriage at half the expense. A perfect cabriolet horse, however, costs money, and the equipage must be well turned out. A seedy looking cabriolet and horse to match are abominations not to be endured.'

The Duke of Wellington was an advocate and regular user of cabriolets long before they became generally fashionable in London, and Lord William, who was attached to his staff in his younger days and who often used to drive him, has left us an anecdote unique in its personal recollections of the Duke and his sporting associations:

'The late Duke of Wellington, when Ambassador to the newly-restored monarch, Louis XVIII, in 1814–15, seldom, except on state occasions, made use of any other vehicle, [than a cabriolet] the carriages being devoted to the service of the Duchess. This I can vouch for, for at that period I was attached to his Grace's staff, and was always in the habit of driving him when occupied in paying visits in the morning or of attending dinners and parties in the evening.

'Never shall I forget one evening at Paris, when driving my chief in his cabriolet from the Hotel Borghese to the Theatre Francais, I very nearly upset the vehicle; and as the accident occurred in a very crowded street, it might have been attended with serious consequences. It was an eventful day in my life; and, to explain my distraction on that occasion, I must enter at some length into the cause of it. This I do most readily, as the whole transaction reflects so much credit on the Duke's kindness of heart.'

There follows an account of the Duke's lending Lord William his best hunter, *Elmore*, for a day with the Royal Staghounds, meeting at Versailles; business having at the last moment prevented the Duke himself from riding. This valuable horse carried Lord William perfectly and, 'it was hinted to me that the Duke could command almost any sum for him.

'A party of young men headed by Count D'Orsay, afterwards so well known in London, proposed a steeplechase home for a sweepstake of one Napoleon each, which, had *Elmore* been my own property, I should gladly have entered him for; but I remembered the Duke's injunction ['Don't knock him about!'] and declined.

'Delighted with the character the new purchase had obtained, I started to ride quietly home by myself, when, within half-a-league of Paris, in crossing a small grip, I found that my horse went lame. To dismount and inspect his foot was the work of a moment, but I could see nothing. No alternative was then left me but to lead the limping animal home, which I did among the taunts and jeers of the rabble.

'No sooner had I reached the stables than I sent for the head groom and the Duke's state coachman, to whom I explained all that had occurred.

'"Well you have gone and done it", said the latter, who was a most eccentric character. "We wouldn't have taken three hundred guineas for that horse."

'This knight of the ribbons, be it remarked, always spoke in the plural number, and talked of what *we* had done in the Peninsula, of *our* triumphal entry into Madrid, and of how *we* had beaten Ney and all the French marshals.

'Happily for me the Duke, who had been occupied all day, was out riding, and I did not see him until we met at dinner. I had fully made up my mind to tell him of the accident before going to bed, but waited until I received a further account of the horse's state. As a large party was assembled little was said about the hunt until the ladies left the room, when I was called upon to give an account of the run, which I did. I then mentioned the brilliant manner in which *Elmore* had carried me, and the panegyrics he had received from all. "A splendid animal", said Wellington, "I hope to ride him next Monday at Fontainebleau." My heart quailed within me. The hours glided on, and when driving the Duke to the theatre that night in his cabriolet, so distracted was I that I grazed the curb-stone and was within an inch of knocking over one of the gendarmes as we approached the theatre'.

Later, 'Upon leaving the theatre I became so thoroughly distracted that I scarcely knew what I was about; unluckily a young horse who was a little skittish, had on that evening taken the place of the one that I had been in the habit of driving . . . With great difficulty I threaded my way through carriages of all descriptions, and was approaching the Rue de Rivoli when I heard a clattering of horses' hoofs behind me and the cheers of some hundreds of people assembled near the Palace of the Tuileries.

'"It is the King returning from the Louvre, where His Majesty has been dining with the Duke D'Orleans", said my companion. At the moment my thoughts were engrossed with *Elmore* . . . So, instead of pulling the left rein to enable the royal *cortège* and the cavalry escort to pass me, I pulled the right one, and very nearly brought my chief to grief . . . we had not proceeded many yards when a *gamin* with a taste for pyrotechnic exhibitions let off a cracker, which so frightened the animal I was driving that he bolted across the street, came in contact with a lamp-post and as near as possible upset the cabriolet. What made it worse was that the escort above referred to was returning at a brisk trot to their barracks, and had we been overturned, the Duke might, for the first time in his military career, have been trampled upon by French cavalry.

'"Lucky escape!" was the only remark Wellington made, and as the danger to which I had exposed him had completely roused me from my lethargy, I at once "screwed my courage to the sticking place" and told him the whole of my day's adventures with hounds.

'"Can't be helped", said he in his usual quick manner, "accidents will happen."'

'Upon the following morning my worst fears were realised; *Elmore* was dead lame, and when I reported this to his Grace his only answer was, "I cannot afford to run the chance of losing my best horses; so in future you shall have the brown horse and the chestnut mare, and if you knock them up you must mount yourself."'

With the passing of the cabriolets the race of tigers disappeared as well. Part and parcel of the vehicles to which they were indispensable, they were characters of their day, very full of that wit and self esteem which is supposed to compensate many little people for what they lack in stature. 'A special London product', G. N. Hooper called the tiger, in a neat pen picture, 'he was produced in no other city, British or foreign; all the genuine tigers hailed from London. His age varied from fifteen to twenty-five. Few there were that were not perfect masters of their horses, were they ever so big. In shape and make he was a man in miniature, his proportions perfect, his figure erect and somewhat defiant; his coat fitted as if it had been moulded on him; his white buckskin breeches were spotless; his top boots perfection; his hat, with its narrow binding of gold or silver lace, and brims looped up with gold or silver cord, brilliant with brushing, was worn jauntily. As he stood at his horse's head, ready to receive his noble master, you might expect him to say, "My master is a duke, and I am responsible for his safety."'

The first of all tigers, whose name was Alexander Lee, won distinction in his later years as a composer and a musician. His master, who takes his place as the ' inventor ' of tigers, was none less than that desperate whip, Lord Barrymore, onetime boon companion of the Prince Regent and distinguished always as ' Cripplegate ' from his brothers ' Hellgate ' and ' Newgate ' and his engaging sister ' Billingsgate'. In contemporary fiction as in history the race of tigers have their places, with among their representatives Tiger Tim of the *Ingoldsby Legends* and Dickens's precocious Mr. Bailey, who, you will remember, arrived at the full dignity of tigerdom to the metamorphosed Montague Tigg, leaving behind him the squalor of Todgers's.

' I've got the right sort of governor now', said Mr. Bailey, ' You can't see his face for whiskers, and can't see his whiskers for the dye upon 'em. That's a gentleman ain't it ? ' Nor was the horse of Mr. Tigg's choice out of keeping, as Mr. Bailey described him : ' Why he's own uncle to Capricorn and brother to Cauliflower. He's been through the winders of two chaney shops since we've had him, and wos sold for killin his missis. That's a horse I hope.' But the tiger's greatest moments were those in which he assumed the reins in his master's absence : ' Mr. Bailey, junior, just tall enough to be seen by an enquiring eye, gazing indolently at society from beneath the apron of his master's cab, drove slowly up and down Pall Mall about the hour of noon, in waiting for his ' governor.' The horse of distinguished family, who had Capricorn for his nephew and Cauliflower for his brother, showed himself worthy of his high relations by champing at the bit until his chest was white with foam, and rearing like a horse in heraldry ; the plated harness and the patent leather glittered in the sun ; pedestrians admired ; Mr. Bailey was complacent, but unmoved. He seemed to say " A barrow, good people, a mere barrow ; nothing to what we could do if we chose ! " and on he went, squaring his short green arms outside the apron, as if he was hooked onto it by the arm pits.'

Passages like these from authors whose knowledge of such vehicles as the cabriolet was close and personal give revealing glimpses of their uses, of the atmosphere, background and characters that belonged to driving a century ago. The very spirit of coaching and road travel with horses lives in some descriptive pieces that were among the finest achievements of Dickens or de Quincey. Yet a greater power of making such things survive was commanded by painters and illustrators of that day; their art could exactly capture and hand on the vehicles themselves, not only their atmosphere and surroundings but their details of form and appearance, and niceties beyond written interpretation. The best years of coaches and many carriages coincided happily with a time both of great writers and gifted sporting artists, who found in driving a subject of endless possibilities and conscientious treatment. More recently many others have recognised the possibilities, while dismissing conscientious treatment as superfluous. Nineteenth century vehicles depicted in twentieth century art generally are provided with wheels of some kind and are attached to horses, also of some kind, and to that extent are accurate. Few modern writers introducing the name of a carriage or coach fail to choose one that is inappropriate to their purpose, period or setting. The better the writer the bigger the bloomer, seems to be the rule; it certainly was in the classic instance of Conan Doyle and the tandem in *Rodney Stone*. Any English two-wheeled carriage might conceivably be used as a tandem cart, except only the curricle; barred because of its structure; but nothing save a curricle would suit the creator of Sherlock Holmes, who gave a final touch of originality to the whole turn-out by supplying the bay mares with yellow manes. Dr. Watson himself could not have done better.

One of the most convincing cabriolet pictures ever painted is one that was on loan to the Tate Gallery. It is by John Ferneley, the Melton Mowbray artist known best for his hunting portraits of 'Meltonians,' the personalities of the 'Shires, and their horses, for contemporary hunting scenes and a few racehorse portraits. Commissioned by Mr. Massey Stanley, a member of the New Club at Melton and a prominent figure in the world of hunting, it depicts him driving in Hyde Park, passing the Achilles statue, in what perhaps was one of the first cabriolets with the elegance of many that were to follow within so short a while. The horse is a tribute to Ferneley's skill; a height of as much as seventeen hands is suggested without any of the fine breeding being lost to size, and all the quality of a blood 'un is accentuated and shown to full advantage by harness that is an adornment in its neatness. A little more movement, perhaps, and a little less of the statuesque pose, could have added to the effect; but the picture must be considered as what it is — a portrait; horse, owner, tiger, and even the dog are portraits, and vehicle and harness precisely reproduce what Ferneley saw. If instead it were a mere illustration of a typical fashionable cabriolet, some minor points like the painting of the whip and the tiger's leg-wear might be criticised.

To both J. F. Herring and the younger Marshall belong other paintings that depict splendid and characteristic cabriolet horses, and each has been engraved. The print after the former artist is well known by its title *The Cab Horse, St. James's*, and shows a magnificent grey, ready harnessed in the most luxurious of stables, with his immaculate cigar-smoking tiger beside him. A companion print, *The Cab Horse, St. Giles's*, as full of character, gives a glimpse of the opposite extreme; in a sordid slum stable a cabman, who might well be the identical one who wanted to fight Mr. Pickwick, is about to lead out the broken-down slave of a very different cab — the hackney cab of the London streets.

OTHER TWO-WHEELED CARRIAGES

REDUCED AS FAR AS possible to groups, two-wheeled carriages become less formidable in number and variety than they seem as a disorganised mass, in general intended for the owner's, rather than the liveried coachman's driving. The curricle and the cabriolet being allowed their place of privilege, and hackney-cabs — including the hansom, occasionally a vehicle of private ownership — being segregated as in a class of their own, there remain those of Gig type, those of the Dog-cart species, and some miscellaneous traps.

Like most vehicles dating from the eighteenth century, the Gig in its earliest forms had a weight and crudeness later eliminated, and a loftiness given it by large wheels, straight shafts and high springing. Popular about 1790 was the Chair-back gig, having a small cabriolet-like body of rounded form suspended by leather braces, after the manner of the more important carriages of that time, from cee or whip springs at the back and with elbow springs in front. The Whiskey was a gig of the same period with a little caned body like a chair fixed upon the shafts above horizontal springs. The leather brace-suspended gig failed to maintain favour far into the nineteenth century, but the Whiskey type in an improved and more finished form, but similarly sprung, presented itself under the name of a Dennet. It is said to have been the product of a Finsbury coachbuilder named Bennett whose initial became mysteriously altered in the name of his vehicle.

All these gigs were, at their best, the work of good coachbuilders, mainly London ones. In country places many early gigs were made with no springs at all, simply with seats fixed above the shafts or hung by leather from wooden frames, and were sold to farmers and others for very small sums; if they cost less than £12 and had 'Taxed Cart' painted on them they were subject to a yearly tax of only twelve shillings, while that for other two-wheeled vehicles in 1790 was £3.17.0. What were called Rib Chair gigs were completely springless carts of this kind, with a solid board seat shaped to a semi-circle and enclosed by a rail with upright rib supports.

Not so easily defined is the one-horse chaise met with in literature; the term seems to have been a rather general one, loosely applied to various vehicles of the chair-back type of body, with or without heads and sometimes with four instead of two wheels. Even Oliver W. Holmes' inimitable verses on the *One-Hoss Shay* are no guide to its appearance, though as full of wheelwright's lore as they are entertaining:

"Have you heard of the wonderful one-hoss shay,
That was built in such a logical way,
It ran a hundred years to a day,
And then of a sudden it — ah! but stay,
I'll tell you what happened without delay:
Scaring the parson into fits,
Frightening people out of their wits —
Have you ever heard of that, I say?
Now in building of chaises, I tell you what,
There is always somewhere a weakest spot —
In hub, tire, felloe, in spring or thill,
In panel or crossbar, or floor, or sill,
In screw, bolt, thoroughbrace — lurking still,
Find it somewhere you must and will —
Above or below, or within or without,
And that's the reason, beyond a doubt,
A chaise breaks down, but doesn't wear out.
But the deacon swore (as deacons do,)
With an 'I dew vum,' or an 'I tell yeou,'
He would build one shay to beat the taown,
'N the keounty 'n all the kentry raoun;
It should be so built that it couldn' break daown,

'Fur,' said the deacon, ''ts mighty plain
That the weakest place mus stan the strain;
''N the way to fix it, wy, I maintain,
Is only jest
To make that place as strong as the rest.'
So the deacon enquired of the village folk,
Where he could find the strongest oak,
That couldn't be split, nor bent, nor broke —
That was for spokes, and floor, and sills;
He sent for lancewood to make the thills;
The crossbars were ash, from the straightest trees;
The panels of white-wood, that cuts like cheese
But lasts like iron for things like these;
The hubs of logs from the 'settler's ellum,'
Last of its timber, they couldn't sell 'em,
Never an axe had seen their chips,
And the wedges flew from between their lips,
Their blunt ends frizzled like celery tips;
Step and prop-iron, bolt and screw,
Spring, tire, axle and linchpin, too,
Steel of the finest, bright and blue;
Thoroughbrace, bison-skin, thick and wide;
Boot, top-dasher, from tough old hide
Found in the pit when the tanner died.
That was the way he 'put her through.'
'There,' said the deacon, 'naow she'll dew.'
Do! I tell you, I rather guess
She was a wonder and nothing less!
Colts grew horses, beads turned gray,
Deacon and deaconess, dropped away,
Children and grandchildren, where were they?
But there stood the stout old one-hoss shay.'

Over long to be quoted in full, the tale, you will remember, goes on to tell of the shay's hundred years of life, until:

'First of November, "fifty-five,"
This morning the parson takes a drive . . .'

When:

'All at once the horse stood still,
Close by the meet'n-house on the hill,
First a shiver, and then a thrill,
Then something decidedly like a spill;
And the parson was sitting upon a rock,
At half past nine by the meet'n-house clock,
Just the hour of the earthquake shock!
What do you think the parson found,
When he got up and stared around?
The poor old chaise in a heap or mound,
As if it had been to the mill and ground!
You see, of course, if you're not a dunce,
How it went to pieces all at once;
All at once, and nothing first,
Just as bubbles do when they burst.'

One thing the poet did not exaggerate was the care and thought in choice of materials, and time and skill given to building, that distinguished the old craftsmen of the wheelwright's and coachbuilder's trades; work of some of them that still survives puts mass production and modern methods to shame.

Two outstanding gigs to gain favour in the first half of the last century were the Tilbury and the Stanhope. The Tilbury was remarkable for having a cut-away chair body with no boot foundation at all — or in another form, merely a very small box-like protrusion beneath the seat — and an elaborate system of suspension on seven springs. Sometimes it was spoken of as the Seven-Spring gig. The front or foot-board part was hung to the shafts, or a cross-bar above them, by elbow springs and leather braces; the back of the body received support from a gallows-like erection of three iron rails rising from the back cross-bar. In the Stanhope, the railed box-seat rested on the more solid foundation of a neat boot, or locker, to the underside of which the shafts attached, and was carried by a simple arrangement of two side and two cross springs. It is not surprising that, with its more compact appearance, greater simplicity and valuable luggage space (in the boot), the Stanhope should have achieved the more lasting popularity. Allowing for modern improvements in springing and design, the elimination of superfluous weight and unnecessary metal belonging to earlier road conditions, and the use of rubber instead of iron for tires, the main characteristics of the Stanhope are to be traced in most of the more recent gigs.

Both Stanhope and Tilbury gigs were produced in the first instances by a coachbuilder named Tilbury working on designs suggested by the Honble. Fitzroy Stanhope. The former insisted that, as the first of the two vehicles to appear was to bear his name, the other should be called after his patron, who was in fact a personality of considerable importance in driving history. Apart from his influence on carriage design — one of the phaeton group bearing the name of Stanhope as well as the gig— he was reputed one of the most accomplished four-horse coachmen among the earlier amateurs on the road, and had much to do with the inauguration of driving clubs that were the forerunners of the Four-in-Hand and Coaching Clubs. Contemporary reminiscences pay such tributes to his social as well as sporting popularity as : ' Few men had seen more of the world in all its phases than poor Stanhope ; but under whatever circumstances you met him, whether at the social board, in the race-course, on the box of a ' drag ', in the snuggery of the Garrick Club, or in the shooting field, he was ever the high-bred gentleman. His nerve and head when on the box were equally good '. A lengthy illustration of his ability as a coachman concludes with a reference to another very highly rated accomplishment in days of coach travel : ' Stanhope's vocal powers were of the first-rate order, as all will bear testimony who listened to his merry and musical voice when he carolled ' The Swell Dragsman,' ' The Bonny Owl,' ' The Days that we got tipsy in a long time ago,' and other convivial songs. Poor Fitzroy ! his loss was deeply felt by a large circle of friends '.

The old chroniclers of the Road gave much space to recalling songs with driving as their theme and to remembering the men who were particularly noted for their singing of them. ' The Swell Dragsman ' was but one of many such songs : in days when railways became an active threat to the continuance of driving Egerton Warburton wrote what became the most popular of them all, 'The Tantivy Trot'. A character once as well known on the Western road for his singing as for his driving was a certain Mr. Prouse who appealed to the convivial *Nimrod* (C. J. Apperley), and earned a place of honour in his recollections: 'After five bottles of hock, which he could put under his waistcoat at a sitting without the smallest inconvenience, he has often been seen to fill a bumper and place the glass on his head, during the time he would sing a song, in which not only every coachman's, but every innkeeper's name between London and Plymouth was introduced. At the same time also he would go through the manoeuvres of hitting wheeler and leader,* without spilling a drop of the wine; and after he had drunk it off, he would run the empty glass up and down the large silver buttons on his coat with very singular effect.'

To return, though, to gigs. With the development of business with the aid of bagmen, who did not in those days aspire to the title of commercial travellers, a need arose for a compact vehicle of light weight able to accommodate a representative quantity of samples, that could be drawn by one horse and driven by the bagman himself. A gig with a sufficiently large boot was the obvious choice; and bagman's gigs, by the end of the first quarter of the nineteenth century, were among the commonest vehicles on all the roads of England. With men of business and farmers as with private owners in town as much as in the country, the gig's popularity became almost universal; and its commonest form was the Stanhope, subject of course to much elaboration, modification or adaptation to suit individual needs or tastes. Wholesale alteration of original design greatly complicates the definition of most carriages, whether on two or four wheels; various names were so freely bestowed by coachbuilders or private designers who produced vehicles of their own that differed in detail only from a distinct species, as to present a confusing assortment of names attached to variations of one carriage. Often the name of the individual responsible was chosen, or that of the place of his and his vehicle's origin. The student of old sporting prints can find depicted in them quite a number of gigs that were variations of usual types, and driving

* Leaders, the foremost pair of horses in a team of four; wheelers, the pair nearest the coach.

enthusiasts of later times have had some of them faithfully reproduced, christening the resultant sporting vehicles, 'Something Slap', 'Very Spicy', or 'Park Gate' gigs after the Alken or Pollard prints from which they were culled. Americans added considerably to these complications when they took up driving on the English principle and brought to it all the enthusiasm they usually devote to their hobbies ; which they began to do much earlier than is generally supposed, for as long ago as in 1852 Thackeray wrote of 'the fashion of rapid driving [having] deserted England, and, I believe, trotted over to America'.

Henry Alken showed a particular fondness for drawing gigs in scenes that illustrate the days of driving on the road. His lively depiction of a gig of Stanhope type in *Something Slap* portrays an entertaining character once well known 'down the road' ; he was a certain Mr. Barclay who indulged his taste for gig-driving to the extent of keeping relays of the highest class of gig-horse — nearly all odd-coloured (skewbald or piebald) — stabled the whole length of the London to York road at intervals close to the places where the York mail coach changed its teams. Leaving London, or York, at the same time as the mail, he would, it was said, almost always beat its time over the whole journey and be first home. This would have given Mr. Barclay some enlivening gig-drives of little less than twenty hours each, allowing for almost two hundred miles covered at about ten miles an hour including stoppages, a pace very hard to maintain over so long a distance even if all his horses were up to the standard of the skewbald in the print and his companions invariably as encouraging as the lady of the bonnet. To Alken, too, among so much else that is excellent in sporting art, belong the illustrations to Nimrod's *Life of John Mytton*, of all sporting personalities the most desperate. Gigs were to Mytton an appealing and frequent means of endangering his neck and frightening his friends : 'As he was one day driving one of them in a gig', wrote Nimrod, 'who expressed a strong regard for his neck, with a hint that he considered it in some danger, Mytton addressed him thus : "Were you ever much hurt, then, by being upset in a gig ?" "No, thank God," said his companion, "for I never was upset in one." "What ! " replied Mytton, "*never* upset in a gig ? What a d——d slow fellow you must have been

Author's Collection *Henry Alken senior*

Plate IV. Mr Barclay driving his STANHOPE GIG. *See page* 48

Author's Collection — *C. B. Newhouse*

Plate V. TANDEM COCKING CART. *See page* 50

all your life ! " and running his near wheel up the bank, over they both went, fortunately without either being much injured'. It was a gig, too, but with two horses driven tandem, that Mytton drove straight at the closed turnpike gate at Hanwood, to find out, as he told the unfortunate horse-dealer who sat beside him, if the leader was a good timber-jumper.

For either single-harness or tandem work the gig had a tremendous following among sporting undergraduates of Oxford and Cambridge, the finding of suitable gig-horses never being a very difficult or costly matter, whether they were jobbed (hired) or purchased. Lord Algernon St. Maur, a famous coachman, as fond of gig-driving as he was of four-horse work in his younger days, recalled in his reminiscences in the Badminton book on *Driving*, that, 'About the year 1835, a dealer, George Carrington, who lived near Tyburn Gate, where the last execution took place in 1812, was invaluable, as he could generally find you a first-rate gig or buggy horse in twenty-four hours, usual price twenty-five pounds'; a price that put gig-driving within the reach of anyone who could afford to drive at all. The same writer had some awkward moments to relate when driving a gig, which help to prove the truth of an old saying on the Road to the effect that more four-horse coachmen met their deaths trying to drive one horse to a gig than in any other way. Of many stories that associate the undergraduate with the gig, perhaps the palm goes to one of a nervous old gentleman returning from a visit to his nephew at Oxford: the latter had prevailed upon his uncle to save the cost of posting back to London by allowing him to drive him in a gig — driving, of course, a horse of guaranteed quietness and good manners. A mile or two on the road ; 'Do you know, nephew', said uncle, 'this is but the second time in my life I have been in a gig ?' 'Well, anyway,' replied nephew, 'that's once more often than this horse has been in one ! '

The most obvious distinction of the gig in almost any form was that it seated but two people, one passenger beside the man who drove. Among the rare exceptions to this rule were some of the older vehicles of gig type intended for tandem driving, which had a single seat for a groom added behind the box. Such a vehicle was the Cocking-cart, an extremely high tandem cart more like the front boot and box-seat of a coach, on two wheels (with the groom's seat added), than anything else. The size of the boot would have provided space for fighting cocks driven to a Main by sporting owners, or, on shooting occasions, for gun-dogs ; the ultra-sporting appearance of such a vehicle is well illustrated in a print, *Going to the Moors*, after C.B. Newhouse. In a yet earlier and more exaggerated form, a trap of this kind with the groom's seat behind built three feet higher than the already high box-seat, appropriately earned itself the title of a Suicide Gig. Not as high as the one in Newhouse's print — although described in the catalogue as 'the actual vehicle from which C.B. Newhouse painted his famous picture' — was a tandem cart of similar type driven in the Parade of Carriages at the International Horse Show, Olympia, in 1920. To those who remember that wonderful show — the last occasion on which a large and representative collection of old and historic carriages were shown to the public, driven and turned out as nearly as possible as they appeared on the roads in days gone by — this vehicle, driven by that prince of tandem-coachmen, the late Alfred Butcher, will always stand out as one of the most striking among so many that were nearly perfect.

Gigs naturally might be of any height, from those that could be used with a horse of sixteen and a half hands down to some of pony size, but the bodies of most were prevented from being over high from the ground by that graceful curvature of the shafts which was a usual feature of those other than the earliest, and which tended to counteract the comparatively large size of the wheels. Like other vehicles, they have of later years been driven from a lower box than in the days when coachmen favoured an almost straight-legged driving position and achieved it by means of high and steeply sloping box-cushions. What became known as the Liverpool gig, or at its most elegant the Lawton gig, represents the most recent type, having a neat box mounted on a modified boot foundation, up-to-date springing and rubber tires. Lawtons found much favour in the horse show ring for tandem driving, and sometimes were provided with a folding hood, when they became liable to the name of Lawton buggies as well as of hooded-gigs.

The practice of adding a head, or hood, to a gig was of course anything but a recent innovation, and a Buggy, as understood in England was really only a hooded gig — usually the term was given to those of rounded body-form, while those of the squarer form were called simply hooded gigs. In America the name of buggy was applied to varying vehicles, four-wheeled driving waggons among them.

In another of the gig tribe, the Sulky, the seating was for one person — the driver — only. Sulkies of considerable height with very large wheels and straight shafts were used in the old trotting matches on the roads in the first half of the last century; in substance they were built as light in weight as it was possible to make a vehicle, with practically no body-work and a mere skeleton frame supporting the little single seat like a perch. Yet lighter, of course, are those low-hung metal affairs with two pneumatic-tired wheels used in modern trotting racing and still keeping the name of sulkies.

Of more recent origin than the gig was the Dog-cart, having its first examples within the nineteenth century. Much more than the gig — as popular for town use as on the roads — did the dog-cart belong to the country, developing in its various forms into the accepted country house vehicle used for practically every purpose that did not call for a carriage driven by a coachman in livery. Dog-carts proper were made to seat four people, those at the rear sitting back-to-back with the driver and the passenger beside him, and having their feet on a tailboard let down for the purpose, but kept closed when only the front seat was in use. Originally built, as the name implies, with a sporting intention, dog-carts, in their earlier forms were built very high on a capacious boot; this was ventilated at the sides by venetian blinds — a small series of slats slightly overlapping one another — and designed to hold gun dogs or greyhounds. Such a vehicle enabled the country sportsman to transport himself, his friends and his dogs to distant shoots or coursing meetings with the aid of only one horse, or, if he wished, to indulge a taste for tandem driving.

Later modified by reducing the height of the trap and the size of the boot to dimensions that were still big enough for a dog or two, or a fair quantity of baggage, and given more modern springing, the dog-cart found what was perhaps its perfect form for either single or tandem work. A workmanlike simplicity was a characteristic of the vehicle, whether the work of a country maker or the most exclusive London firm ; a square straight-sided body — often improved by an outward slant downwards of the panels, giving smarter and more rakish lines — with or without venetian slats, shafts straight rather than bent, lamps square or dial shaped — the former giving the more sporting appearance, cord covered cushions, plain iron rails, and everything built for service without unnecessary embellishment. Seat backs or 'lazy-backs' added to the passenger seats but not to the coachman's box, which kept a higher level, ensured a practical, sporting effect. Variations in detail were many. The Oxford, the Newport Pagnell, the Malvern and the Norwich were all types of dog-cart differing slightly one from the other but preserving the same general characteristics. What may be termed the versatility of the Victorian dog-cart was well illustrated by Sidney in what he had to say of the once-popular Whitechapel dog-cart ; this became 'more favourably known, since the Prince of Wales [King Edward VII] made Sandringham his country seat, as the "Norfolk shooting cart", the most capacious of all two-wheeled sporting and family carriages ; which may be built plain enough to take pigs to market, and handsome enough to convey a party of cavalry subalterns to the meet of a crack pack, or with dogs and guns to a shooting party at the "Duke's"'.

In the lowering of the height of dog-carts, noticeable in most of the more recently built, axles bent downwards beneath the body played their part as well as smaller wheels. One of the lowest hung types appeared, for pony use, with the initial popularity of polo in this country — when polo ponies were ponies in fact and not the horses they became later — and was given the name of Polo cart. A tendency in some other later dog-carts, so called, was to build them in almost tray-like form, departing altogether from their original sporting purpose. Such vehicles were really in many cases little more than elaborated two-wheeled trade carts, like those commonly used by country butchers and bakers, but light-built, more highly finished and provided with the back-to-back seats typical of the dog-cart. Traps of this kind in their lightest forms, sometimes with open slat sides and with lazybacks extending to the box as well as the seats, were given names like Rustic carts or Village carts. A common failing with two-wheeled traps was cocking, a tendency to tip up when in use so that the shafts pointed upwards and the tailboard down, making matters hard for the horse, uncomfortable for the passengers and spoiling the look of the turnout. Frequent causes of this were the horse being too big for the cart or the wrong adjustment of the tugs, but more often the disturbance of balance caused by carrying back-seat passengers. To correct this balance a contrivance was added to many improved dog-carts, which, worked by a lever, moved the position of the seats on slides, or sometimes adjusted the whole body of the vehicle.

So much ingenuity devoted to varying, improving or modifying the dog-cart to suit different tastes was a proof of its popularity. In Victorian country life it became ubiquitous; the vehicle of endless functions. The master or his groom drove it to or from the railway station when guests arrived or departed; the mistress took it into the nearest town on her shopping visits; the son of the house claimed it for his sporting occasions; in it the doctor went the rounds of his rural practice; the ambition of the small farmer or tradesman was to own an up-to-date dog-cart, though in his case a gig like the one his father drove might answer as well — for it was, after all, the ownership of a gig and not a dog-cart that was advanced as evidence of the respectability of a witness at a famous murder trial! Playing so big a part in Victorian life, the dog-cart appeared often in contemporary literature as a 'property' doing much to suggest the country atmosphere and even, when well handled, conveying an impression of its owner as good as a portrait of the man himself:

'In these ingenious days one cannot but be struck with the many devices that exist for the discovery of character. One man finds you out by your handwriting; another by the tone of your voice; a third judges exclusively by the shape of your hat; . . . I think I should myself be inclined to judge a man's style by the sort of carriage he drives. This tendency — superstition — call it what you will, prompts me to take rather a careful si such vehicles as I come across, and therefore it was that, observing a strange dog-cart in the inn yard as I traversed its stones, with an unlighted cigar in my mouth, I paused to examine more minutely, the unfamiliar equipage.

'So slang a turn-out it has not been my fortune to meet with, before or since. Imagine a very high box, narrowing considerably towards the top, on which, judging by the cushions and hand-rail, it is fair to conclude the driver is supposed to sit, perched on a pair of extremely tall wheels, painted red, and picked out with a staring yellow. Imagine the shafts of this contrivance, perfectly straight and of great strength and substance, nearly on a level with the withers of the unfortunate animal that has to draw it. Imagine the old machine, wickered, and lacquered, and glazed, and polished to the most dazzling pitch of brilliancy, attached to the person of a well-bred, crop-eared, vicious-looking bay mare, herself wearing as little harness as is compatible with the fact of her being attached to anything at all, and that little of the colour and appearance of untanned leather. Add to these, a tall whip with a yellow crop, long enough to drive four-in-hand, a pair of enormous lamps, and a white bull-terrier coiled on the foot-rug, licking his lips, with a bloodthirsty expression of countenance, and winking hideously with his ominous and ill-looking eyes.

'The proprietor of such "a trap", as he would probably call it, could not fail to be a study in himself. Loud accents from within smote on my ear as I approached the bar . . .'

But after such a description of 'a trap' by that punctilious author Whyte Melville, you really need to be told little more about its owner; you know nearly all there is to know about him; that he is a young man of 'flash' and 'slangy' appearance with manners to match; almost you might guess his name, which was, in fact, Plumtree.

Tandem, of course, might be driven to almost any carriage on two wheels, with the one obvious exception of the curricle, and even — though it were considered *infra dig* — on four wheels for that matter. Even Hansom cabs at times have been used for tandem work. Recent tandems virtually have been only those of the show ring, a mere alternative means to pair harness for exhibiting the action of two hackneys, and with their showmen a light modern gig, often a Lawton, has become the usual choice of vehicle. When serious tandem-driving was practised on the roads the early gigs gave place to dog-carts as the more appropriate vehicles ; Victorian lovers of tandem finding in various dog-carts a suitability beyond that of any gig, a better balanced, more road-worthy turnout with room for four people to travel. And, when all is said, there could be no vehicle so appropriate to the purpose as a dog-cart, provided it were one of true sporting type with the essential coachmanlike attribute of a raised and backless driving box.

An offshoot of the dog-cart family of comparatively recent date that still survives in limited use was the Ralli cart, having similar seating but with the body brought to rather a lower level by the shafts being rooted inside the body, instead of under it as was the case with the dog-cart. The Ralli body, too, often though not invariably was made to differ from the rectangular shape of the parent vehicle in the rounded sides curving outwards over the wheels.

The popular and useful Tub cart or Governess car is probably the best known of what may be termed the miscellaneous two-wheeled traps. In origin one of the most modern of English vehicles it was made, as the name implies, tub-like and low to the ground. A little door at the back gave access to a usual capacity for four people seated sideways and facing each other, with their backs to the wheels, the driving being done by the occupant of the rearmost off-side (right-hand) seat. Having been built in large numbers all over the country in quite recent times, tub carts are still common enough, particularly those of pony size, though many of the country-made examples seen about are of such rough workmanship as hardly to come under the heading of carriages. On the other hand many beautifully finished coach-built ones were produced in London some forty-odd years back, notably those turned out by the Paddington firms of Offord and Mills. Though found of every size, governess cars were suited best to ponies and when used, as they were originally intended to be, by children and elderly people, had the obvious advantages of safety, lowness and accessibility. Having said which, there appears little to add on the subject of tub carts ; they have little history, were never vehicles of sport or long travel, and by reason of the fact that good driving could not best be practised in a sideways-on position, never appealed to those who drove for the sake of the art. The Princess car, introduced towards the end of the last century by a Suffolk coachbuilder, was an improved version of the governess car not nearly so often met with. A more elaborately furnished vehicle than the average tub cart, it was made on the same principle with the main difference of being entered by a step in the front. The absence of a door at the rear gave the great advantage of a forward-facing driving seat, which also was made movable for adjustment of the balance.

Superior to tub carts from the driving point of view and equally safe and unassuming may be counted those low-hung, two-wheeled Floats in which the forward-facing driving seat is only a step from *terra firma*. Similar vehicles to these, but with a head and usually in a more finished coach-built style, used to be known as Ladies' Chaises and had their origin in France. Another float that has become a rarity, though it was never a carriage in the true meaning of the word, was intended solely for breaking horses to single harness, and known as a Long-shafted Breaking cart, or sometimes as a Single-break; in this a pair of exceedingly long shafts kept the float body and its occupant at a comfortably safe distance from the heels of a young horse being schooled, and gave the driver better control and greater security.

Quite unlike any other vehicle, entirely peculiar to the country of its origin and only occasionally seen in England was the Outside Car or Jaunting Car of Ireland. Passengers sitting back to back on narrow seats above a pair of unusually small wheels, faced the sides of the road; shelf-like footrests fell outside the wheels and were hinged so that they could be folded up when necessary to move or house the car in a narrow space. Though most cars were provided with an additional little seat intended for the driver, facing forwards, it was, and still is in Ireland, a rare thing to see a jarvey sitting in it; crouched on one of the side seats he could share the discomfort of his passengers and increase their danger by sideways driving.

Reproduced by Gracious Permission of H.M. the King *George Stubbs*

Plate VI. The Prince of Wales's HIGHFLYER PHAETON, with horses and Thomas, the State Coachman. *See page 59*

International Horse Show *Lynwood Palmer*

Plate VII. LADY'S [or GEORGE IV] PHAETON (1910). *See pages* 61 *and* 68

Author's Collection *Cooper Henderson*

Plate VIII. MAIL PHAETON meeting STAGE COACH (1848). *See pages 62 and 70*

Author's Collection *Lynwood Palmer*

Plate IX. SPIDER PHAETON driven by Harry Milton (1910). *See pages* 67 *and* 68

Athol Maudslay, who travelled much on Irish roads in the last century and who wrote of driving in 1888, may be referred to for a first-hand opinion of the outside car of that time:

'The Irish car is inseparably connected in our minds with Ireland and the Irish; there is an eccentricity about it that appeals to our sense of the ludicrous. Both to the theoretical and practical coach-builder it is possessed of no good quality when balanced on two wheels, as the balance is rarely, if ever, true. In the dog-cart the weight is distributed almost over the axle, but this is not the case with Irish cars.

'Sometimes someone, enthusiastic about all that is Irish, exports one of these vehicles, and it is seen standing in a coach-house side by side with sober and precise English carriages like a clown or a pantaloon amidst a gathering of Church dignitaries in sober canonicals; or wending its way along our quiet English country lanes'.

FAMILY OF PHAETONS

THE name of Phaeton, first applied to a carriage in 1788, came in time to distinguish a whole tribe of carriages, the varieties of which were added to by coachbuilders and designers for more than a century. Collectively, phaetons represented a considerable proportion of the sum total of English carriages; individually, they differed widely enough in appearance and purpose to leave no characteristics common to them all except those of being four-wheeled, open, and meant mainly for the personal driving of owners or amateurs.

That carriage of exaggerated height and eccentric appearance known best as the Highflyer, or Perch-High phaeton belonged to the first years of phaeton driving and owed much of its favour and fame to the fact that George IV, when Prince of Wales, kept one for his own driving. Four horses were as commonly driven as a pair to this 'monstrous-looking vehicle', as the practical W. B. Adams called it; hastily adding that his reason for alluding to it at all was 'to serve as a standard to show the great progress which a comparatively short period has developed in the art of the carriage constructor.' Writing within some thirty years of the time of the Highflyer's popularity, the same author devoted to it two pages of criticism and description which may be abbreviated to: 'The vehicle looked like a mechanical illustration of the play, *Much Ado About Nothing*. It was a contrivance to make an enormously high and dangerous seat for two persons inconvenient to drive from, and at the same time to consume as much material and mix up as many unsightly and inharmonious lines as possible. The framework of the carriage was constructed with two iron perches, the outline of which was hideously ugly . . . The shape of the body was as though the rudest possible form capable of affording a seat had been put together'. A wealth of technical detail and stringent disapproval given to the analysis of the pillar supporting so high a body, the curved iron stay needed to hold it together, the box or locker fitted beneath it, the huge carved hind-spring and brace occupying half the vehicle's length and the placing of the springless servant's seat behind, end with the opinion that, 'To sit on such a seat, when the horses were going at much speed, would require as much skill as is evinced by a rope-dancer at the theatre. None but an extremely robust constitution could stand the violent jolting of such a vehicle over the stones of a paved street'. Forty years later than Adams, Thrupp provided a more concise and less biased description that included essential measurements, better than any words illustrating the excessive height of the Perch High phaeton: 'It was shaped like a curricle and had a leathern hood. The centre of the body was hung exactly over the front axle-tree, the bottom of the body was 5 ft. from the ground, the front wheels were 4 ft. high, and the hind wheels 5 ft. 8 ins. The hind wheels were far behind, as we see them in a horse-dealer's skeleton brake. There was a large platform board over the hind axle tree for servants or luggage'.

Such was the phaeton immortalized by Stubbs in the beautiful painting at Windsor that includes a pair of the Royal phaeton horses, appropriately harnessed, and the portly figure of Thomas, the State coachman; of all pictures of the Highflyer the most pleasing and much the most important. The very peculiarities that made such a vehicle seem ridiculous to a coachbuilder like Adams have left it with a distinctive Regency character and an interest of associations. History of the time links it intimately not only with the Prince but with many of those whose original sporting tastes added such a spice to the age. Tommy Onslow — the Colonel Honble. Thomas Onslow — whose fame lives mainly in the couplet:

What can Tommy Onslow do?
Why, drive a phaeton and two.
Can Tommy Onslow do no more?
Why, drive a phaeton and four.

Sir John Lade, the Prince's Master of the Horse, who not only drove, but looked, like a stage-coachman and who married the light of love of a highwayman who had been hanged — that lively Letty Lade whom Stubbs portrayed on horseback, whose coachmanship was said to equal her husband's and whose command of language was at least comparable with that of 'Billingsgate', sister of 'Cripplegate' Barrymore. And Barrymore himself, one of the founders of an early driving club, who 'drove four splendid greys, unmatched in symmetry, action, and power', and shared with his brother 'Hellgate', as Henry Angelo recorded, tastes that in any other age would have been considered very poor: 'Lord Barrymore's phaeton was a very high one; and after our midnight revels in town, I have often travelled in it with him to Wargrave. One dark night, going through Colnbrook, he kept whipping right and left, breaking the windows, delighted with the noise as he heard them crack..' How the householders of Colnbrook described this harmless pastime one cannot say, but Barrymore called it 'fanning the daylights'.

Dated a few years earlier than his Windsor phaeton picture (1793), is another by Stubbs in the National Gallery, showing a perched* but head-less phaeton which, though very high, has a body less exalted than that of the Highflyer and placed more reasonably 'amidships' with its weight distributed between the two axles. For all its quaintness it suggests something of a comfort befitting the worthy couple who occupy it. Popular at the same time — the last years of the eighteenth century and the first of the nineteenth — was a modest phaeton for one horse; this was built with a hooded gig-like body for two, mounted well back between the rear wheels, the small front wheels being set far enough forward to separate the driver from his horse by a great deal of space and rather give the vehicle the look of a hooded gig with two front wheels added to it. Ungainly though it was, this carriage had merits that, improved upon, were inherited by most succeeding and superior kinds of phaeton.

In the later years of George IV, the hazards of such vehicles as the Highflyer having lost their charm, the King wanted a low-hung carriage, safe and easy of access, to which he could drive

*Built on a perch, see Mail Phaeton, page 63.

a pair of ponies. His coachbuilders produced for him, in 1824, a neat little carriage conforming to these requirements, luxuriously appointed, having beautifully rounded lines ending in a forward curving splashboard and built very close to the ground on little wheels not much bigger than those of a Bath chair. Four years later a similar small phaeton was made for Queen Victoria, when Princess. Later varied and elaborated forms that became very popular for ladies' driving were called after both sovereigns, George IV phaetons and Princess Victoria phaetons.

So much did coachbuilders exert themselves in the development of this important type of phaeton that its variations were as diverse as the names given to it when no longer necessarily confined to pony size. With wheels of varying size and substance; with rounded or angular body, but usually with the folding head; on cee springs and a perch (main support of undercarriage, timber or metal, connecting front and rear axles), or on elliptic springs with no perch; with or without a groom's seat behind; with or without a rail above the dash to support the reins; it claimed the names of Park Phaeton, Lady's Phaeton, or when produced by the firm of Peters, Peters Phaeton, as well as the two of Royal association. Later Victorian times found it *the* fashionable vehicle for a lady's own driving, its shape making so excellent a background for the crinoline which in many carriages was something of an embarrassment. Only the last word in neatness and studied detail in its appointment was good enough for the Park phaeton seen at its best in Hyde Park on a summer's morning, or, as Sidney spoke of it, 'in perfection including the fair drivers, at cover side in the pasture counties'. More than any carriage did it impress that authority, its contemporary, and move him to an unwonted enthusiasm in recording what it should be, and was, at its most brilliant:

'It has no room for luggage of any kind, and must be attended on by a single groom sitting on the rumble behind, who may be a very neat lad or an equally neat slim old man, but must be in very correct costume, or on state occasions by two grooms. In former times great ladies, like royalty, were attended by outriders, with harness bridles of the same colour and stamp as the pair in harness; but the custom is so nearly extinct that when it occurs it creates a great sensation. The park phaeton is one of the most expensive carriages in use, not excepting the pair-horse victoria, as well as the most delightful; because, although a groom replaces the gorgeous coachman and attendant Jeames, the horses or ponies must be of the most expensive character. Of whatever size, they must have quality, action, proud carriage, irreproachable heads, necks and tails; in a word the symmetry of the ideal Arab, with the true action that 'steps and goes'. They must be a perfect match in colour, height, and action; admirably broken, yet full of courage. In a word, they must have the appearance of fiery dragons, with the docility of trained chargers, and, while they step freely up to the bit, over the ground, shaking their long manes, must not pull an ounce. The long parasol whip should be borne, like a flag, aloft, for ornament, not for use'.

Those were days, let it be remembered, when the world followed the English manner implicitly in all that appertained to carriages and the driving and harnessing of horses. A suggestion of the care, forethought and attention to every detail that lay behind the perfection of a fashionable London turnout is contained in that description. Incidentally, the Victoria referred to, a carriage which takes its place more properly in the category of coachman-driven vehicles, probably traced its origin to the elaboration of the park phaeton. The parasol-whip, an elegant Victorian toy for lady drivers, had, fitted to the crop of a very light phaeton whip, a miniature parasol which when open might have shaded slightly the user's face or bonnet while certainly ensuring that the lash could only be 'for ornament, not for use'. John Leech, in one of his illustrations in Surtees' *Plain or Ringlets?* depicted the fair Rosa McDermott carrying one when driving a little single-pony carriage with a basket-work body, itself one of the most humble poor relations of the phaeton family.

In sharp contrast to the ladylike qualities of the Park or George IV phaeton were those of its extreme opposite, the dignified, massive, high-built and, by about 1830, very fashionable Mail phaeton. Essentially was this a man's carriage, sporting of appearance but versatile in its uses, as correct for park driving and town work as it was for all country purposes, and often employed, too, for long distance travel. Allowing for the usual changes in weight and detail, it proved its practical attributes by surviving into quite recent years in occasional examples driven by connoisseurs of the sporting carriage — usually coaching men who found in it the vehicle most appropriate to driving their coach horses in pairs — and can be considered the unquestionable head of the phaeton family.

Though often confused with other phaetons superficially similar in appearance, the true mail phaeton's characteristics were distinctive and should be unmistakable. A pair-horse carriage, it was built on an undercarriage that was in every respect a replica of that of the mail coach from which it took its name, having a wooden perch, mail coach springing, the mail axle boxes secured by bolts — introduced to coaches for their safety — and, as in a coach, a quarter lock. The body was in the form of a long box foundation with rectangular sides supporting, in front, a comfortable hooded double seat and, at the rear, a rumble seat large enough for two servants. In early days two liveried servants were its complement, the outcome of its use occasionally as a travelling carriage, but later one only was carried as was usual when a pair of horses were driven, two grooms becoming accepted as essential only with four horses as on a drag. A strong coaching association belonged to the mail phaeton in its appointment and method of turning out — what the old school of driving men used to call ' a Down-the-Road flavour '. Steel pole-chains were used, never the leather pole-pieces* of the majority of pair-horse carriages; the pole often had at its head the steel pole hook that could carry the bars (swingletrees) if leaders were added and a team driven instead of a pair; the black harness, substantial and brass-mounted (plated mountings belonged only to some coachman-driven or jobmasters carriages) would be used with collars of brown leather or plaited straw like those of road coaching, and the wheelers' harness of a team set was appropriate. In the painting, plain unlined wheels of red or yellow would contrast with a body of more sober hue, and all such finicky embellishments as thin

* To attach a pair of horses to the pole, leather pole-pieces (straps), running from pole-head to kidney-links at the bottom of the horses' hames, are used with most carriages; but in coaching and with some sporting carriages chains are used.

lines painted on the spokes would be avoided as smacking of the Park and the ladylike carriage rather than of the serious work of the Road. In town a pair of big stepping horses might be driven, but for travel and in the country the choice was with those more blood-like, for performance rather than ostentation.

As a travelling carriage it could be, and often was before railways became general, used with post horses* on prolonged journeys by bachelor owners who eschewed the closed chariot or post chaise. Having a perch undercarriage, like that distinguishing coaches of all kinds and all post chaises and travelling carriages of those days, made the mail phaeton a suitable carriage for the postboy's driving, as no later phaeton or other carriage built without a perch would have been. The Duke of Beaufort who was so experienced a road traveller and a great personality in driving history, made plain this point (in *Driving*) after having mentioned the iron guards worn by postboys on right leg and foot to protect them from injury from the pole : ' Even with this, observant travellers must often have wondered, when they have seen the wheel-boy's foot bent or caught under the pole, how it was he did not get more hurt. Fortunately for postboys all carriages were built with perches, so that the pole rode steady. Had they driven with the modern carriages without perches, every time they went over a crossing or a gutter they would have stood a good chance of having their knee-cap or thigh fractured. It is a matter for speculation how many horses' teeth are knocked out by the flying up and down of the pole in the present day '. While the transition from perched to perchless carriages effected an important reduction in weight and an increase in neatness in those introduced mainly for town work and smooth going, it brought too a certain loss of dignity that the perch gave to the older carriages of the road. So sharp a line of demarcation did the change make in the progress of carriages that coachbuilders were wont to divide all four-wheeled carriages into two main kinds, those with perches and those without, though so many types were subject to both methods of building as and when fashion or individual choice dictated.

An instance of the mail phaeton's occasional use with post

* Driven by a postboy riding the nearside horse of the pair.

Author's Collection *Cooper Henderson*

Plate X. FOUR-WHEELED DOG-CART used for posting. *See pages* 69 *and* 70

Plate XI. FAMILY WAGONETTE (1900). *See page* 71

Plate XII. PRIVATE OMNIBUS for a single horse (1920). *See page* 81

horses was recalled by the Duke of Beaufort in one of his many Road anecdotes: 'I once witnessed a most laughable scene with a sulky postboy, who could drive very well but would not go along. It was posting through Oxfordshire on a mail phaeton in the year 1834. The owner of the phaeton, a very fine coachman, had driven his own horses the first stage, and was going to drive others further on in the journey. The post-horses were good and the gentleman was in a hurry, but nothing would induce the boy to go on. The gentleman's driving whip was in the bucket, so he took it out, laid into the horses, put them into a gallop, and kept them in it until they got to the town where they were to change. The postboy was furious, and invited the gentleman to get out and have his head punched, which he immediately did; but when the boy saw six feet one, as upright as a dart, descend from the phaeton, he took his hat off and apologised, pulled his forelock and said he hoped he would not be reported to his master'. In fairness to those important Road characters, the admirable and long extinct race of postboys belonging to every posting inn in the country, let it be remembered how very few of them apparently were otherwise than as civil as they were capable; generally they were the 'Jolly Postboys' immortalized in the old song, in spite of all the hardships of a life of constant riding and exposure to all weathers. Boys in name only, they were a hardy little breed of men whose small size and light weight was as essential to their profession as to that of a tiger or a jockey; very neat and, like most of the old Road fraternity, taking great pride in their appearance, nearly all were artists in their difficult craft of ride-and-drive. 'The "boys" were brought up to it from childhood', the same authority wrote: 'They learnt how to drive by riding the leaders, the wheel-boys* talking to them and instructing them as they went along. They were generally the sons of older postboys; many of them were what are popularly called 'characters' in their way and they were very good judges of the company they had to drive . . . In the old days they all wore hats made of beaver — real fluffy beaver; generally white hats but sometimes black ones. Their

* When four horses were used for posting, two postboys drove, a wheel-boy and a lead-boy, riding the two nearside horses.

jackets were light blue or yellow — at some of the houses they were scarlet cloth — made of a sort of moleskin stuff, with only one row of buttons; their breeches were of the whitest corduroy, and their boots brown-topped . . . A postboy was like a soldier in those days. Everything he had, his pocket handkerchief and anything else he wanted, went into his hat . . . Posting in private carriages with post horses in England on the main roads was by far the most comfortable and convenient method of travelling, and the riding and driving of the postboys was a science that had reached as near perfection as possible'.

The wide uses to which mail phaetons could be turned were added to in the case of those — and there were many of them — made with the seats interchangeable, enabling them to be transformed at will into coachman-driven carriages, the rumble seat becoming the driving box and the comfortably-cushioned and hooded seat taking its place behind. A few, built almost as big as small char-a-bancs, were given a third seat for two, seating six in all, the additional seat sometimes having access by doors in the boot foundation. Generally used for driving to meets and seldom seen except in hunting countries, these were known as Beaufort phaetons or Hunting phaetons.

Lighter than the mail phaeton but built without the characteristic perch, with elliptic springing, and often with Collinge's axles,* was the Demi-Mail (sometime called Semi-Mail) phaeton; later Victorian times saw many of this type in use, and having the limited lock of the original mail extended by an arch cut in the forepart of the body to admit the front wheels, while still remaining a pair-horse vehicle with the same arrangement of seating; though the name of demi-mail was also given, at a much earlier date, to one as early of origin as the true mail and differing from it only in the method of springing.

To the complexities of carriages of this kind the Stanhope phaeton added its quota by its resemblance, for the casual observer, to the demi-mail. Its body, really that of a Stanhope gig extended by continuation to a groom's seat behind and mounted on four wheels, was light enough to be as often employed with

* Axles with removable hub-cap, to facilitate greasing, used on most recent carriages.

a single horse as with a pair, and its lock was a full one making possible turns in a small space. Again, modified and lightened to a degree best suited to single-horse driving and built without a head, the T cart was an offshoot of the Stanhope that enjoyed a run of popularity towards the end of the last century.

It was as successor of the T cart that the Spider phaeton made its debut in this country, where it was to achieve greater success than other American designs of carriage. G. N. Hooper, in 1888, provided a note on both T cart and Spider phaeton, showing that at that date the popularity of the one was giving place to the other: 'For some years the young men of fashion have driven a small Stanhope phaeton with compassed rail and sticked body in front, and seat for the groom behind, under the name of "T carts", usually drawn by a horse of 15 to 15½ hands. They are now giving place to "Spider Phaetons", a sort of Tilbury body on four wheels, with a neat little seat for the groom behind, supported on branched irons; most of them have a folding head over the front body. Those first made, although light looking from the substitution of iron stays for solid wood construction, had a trembling and vibrating motion; but with more solid construction, and the suppression of the vibration, they have become not only comfortable, but with more refined designs and construction, more stylish in appearance. They carry a lady and gentleman on the front seat comfortably, and the hind seat is made of such size as to carry only one person, and the groom runs no chance of having his dignity hurt by his master or one of his friends having to sit beside him'.

Though of varying degrees of lightness spider phaetons were all much lighter than phaetons so far used in England; at their best, they were delicate and graceful little carriages having none of the crudeness of so many of American design, like those of the 'Runabout,' Surrey and Road-waggon types, of much practical use but very little grace. Neat metal stays performed in the spider functions that called for substantial timber in earlier phaetons; American spider wheels could be made with spokes of elastic wood that need be only a fraction of the thickness of English oaken spokes, and need not be dished (i.e., set in the hub at a slight angle and upon an axle arm bent to give them an outward pitch) as were English wheels. Rubber tires, coming into use in the 'eighties, added to the general effect of the Spider and much helped its appeal to owners who no longer had to consider strength and travel-worthiness of primary importance. As a single-horse vehicle or with a pair, pole and splinter bar* of course being interchangeable with shafts, it earned a popularity that, in so far as driving continues at all, has never quite deserted it for Park and show-ring use.

Driving men of late Victorian years and those who followed on, undeterred by the motor car, in Edward VII's reign lacked none of the enthusiasm of their predecessors. As coachmen, either amateur or professional, they brought a skill and understanding comparable to their fathers' to the driving, horsing and appointing of their vehicles. The thriving continuity of the revival of stage coaching on the Road, the interest kept up in the Four-in-Hand and Coaching Clubs — with full memberships holding regular meets of private drags in Hyde Park and elsewhere — and the advent of the greater horse shows — like Royal Richmond and the International at Olympia — added a spirit of competition to the encouragement of coachmanship and its attendant arts. Many turnouts seen in the Park and the West End reached something nearer perfection in neatness and ultra-smartness than ever before; a flicker, perhaps, before the candle went out, but a very brilliant flicker as it is seen reflected in some of Lynwood Palmer's pictures. Look, for instance, at his picture of a superb pair driven to a spider phaeton by that ever immaculate whip, Harry Milton, in about the year 1910 — faultless as a turnout — with all its spirit and 'go,' its accuracy, its acknowledgment of the importance of detail, translated into water colour by an artist who had made driving a personal study. In oils, another painting of his recalls some of the charm of the early years of the International Horse Show; that of a then well-known lady whip driving a spirited pair, just out of the arena, to one of the few lady's, or park, phaetons still to be seen at that time.

Less widely known and less numerous than his portraits of great contemporary racehorses and those of a hunting interest, Lynwood Palmer's pictures of coaching and other aspects of

* To which the traces attach in a pair-horse carriage.

driving were as invariably portraits, differing in this from the work of Charles Cooper Henderson, foremost among the painters of driving of pre-railway times but belonging to the illustrative or scene painting school. In other respects a close parallel exists between the two artists. Henderson succeeded in surrounding his Road subjects with an atmosphere of authority and conviction greater than that attained by any of his contemporaries — brilliant as several of them were — because he combined with naturally great artistic gifts and unbounded enthusiasm a close personal association with his subject. To Palmer, who was born only some nine years before Henderson died, horses were an all-absorbing interest from boyhood, and of all forms of horse activity driving was nearest to his heart. His driving pictures reflect an observation and understanding as acute as Henderson's and an enthusiasm for all that appertained to the Road which made him in later life its leading authority and one of the few amateur coachmen of his day to equal professional skill. A full tale has been told by both these artists of many vehicles beside the coach and four, and each in his time found in the phaeton an object of beauty to be faithfully treated; the one in the forms of mail phaeton and four-wheeled dog-cart, the other in the graceful lady's phaeton inherited from the time of George IV and the dapper spider of American origin.

To trace the origin of the Four-wheeled Dog-cart one would have to go nearly as far back as to that of its two-wheeled kinsman. The name is self explanatory, the body having the back-to-back seats and let-down tailboard typical of the dog-cart proper, and otherwise having been subject to almost as many variations and modifications. By custom and association it was allowed always the distinction of belonging to the phaeton tribe, and in various forms and at different times it claimed such alternative names as Dog-cart phaeton, Dog phaeton and Road phaeton. A distinctively sporting character belonged to four-wheeled dog-carts of the best types, and while out of place in town, their country uses were many, for all sporting and country house occasions, marketing and station work. Adaptability to either a single horse or a pair added to the attractions of what was one of the most useful general purpose carriages, and even, on occasion, would a four-wheel dog-cart serve for tandem driving. Cooper Henderson has given us one of true sporting type pressed into use in yet another role, that of a substitute posting vehicle, in that exhilarating print, *Late for the Mail.* The occasion was one of those episodes in the old life of the Road that appealed so strongly to Henderson, bringing out the best of his talent for depicting fast travel, and horsey character on four legs or two; a would-be passenger by mail coach has, with his servant and his dog, missed it at a changing place; no post chaise is available in which to give chase but there is a four-wheeled dog-cart, a pair of old blood posters and a postboy, together showing a turn of speed equal to overtaking Her Majesty's Mail. The companion print, *In Time for the Coach*, shows the mail phaeton at its best, used by its owner to pick up on the road the stage coach on which his journey is to

WAGONETTES, BRAKES AND OTHER INFORMAL CARRIAGES

None among the more modest carriages as commonly driven by their owners as by coachmen or grooms gained more general favour in the last century, retaining it into the present one, than the Wagonette. No beauty in its simple form, single or pair horse, its appeal was a strictly practical one ; its general usefulness made it for the country dweller almost the perfect family vehicle. In its open body, behind the usual driving box carrying one passenger beside the driver, it carried from two to four, sometimes more, on either side, sideways and backs to the road with the access by a rear door and step.

The wide use of wagonettes began only with the International Exhibition of 1851, though a coachbuilder at Amersham was said to have built one for Lord Curzon in the early eighteen forties, about the same time that the Earl of Chesterfield had one from his coachbuilders at Derby. Royal favour did much to popularize them in their early days, the Prince Consort having been among the first to appreciate their usefulness and to order one from a London firm, it afterwards became a favourite vehicle with the Queen and her children. Within a few years coachbuilders great and small all over the country were at work on this popular means of transport, and even rural wheelwrights were producing humble vehicles of wagonette type, appealing, with the large accommodation provided, as much to the farmer and the country flyman as to the private owner. In their most utilitarian form removable seats made way for goods when necessary, and the body finish was merely that of varnish applied direct to the woodwork without painting. Sometimes a solid roof could be attached to a wagonette, the roof made with side and front windows in the form of a detachable top, usually kept suspended by a pulley arrangement from the coachhouse roof when not in use; this, when lowered into place on the carriage, transformed it into a closed vehicle with much of the appearance of a private omnibus.

Comprehensive utility could hardly be carried further than in a wagonette, at once a family, business or sporting carriage or a goods carrier, open or closed, for one horse or two, that anyone might drive. Its country uses were almost endless and in some cases not without their humour, as when its virtues were discovered by the flymen or carriers who were usually among the characters of any small town or sizeable village. One of these whose memory survives him was a certain Charley whose wagonette was almost as well known in a rural part of Dorset some forty years ago as were his Newgate fringe and his independent opinions of, and attitude towards, life in general. Whatever others might call him, Charley aspired to the title of Jobmaster, and had this description painted up in large letters after his name above his stable door; beneath appeared the words, 'Open and Closed Carriages and Commercial Vehicles for Hire.' Charley's stud consisted of one horse, perhaps a few years younger than his owner, and his vehicles also added up to one — a wagonette. If you ordered an open carriage, the wagonette arrived with Charley on the box, if a closed carriage was wanted the detachable top was added, if it were a commercial case the seats were removed; and if Charley and his wagonette were not good enough for you, you could always walk.

In the hands of the greater town coachbuilders, the wagonette became a neat, if not dignified, carriage of rounded rather than angular lines, and subject to much elaboration. The Portland wagonette, a large pair-horse vehicle, a superior form that was provided with a folding hood, was introduced by the Duke of Portland, and made its appearance about 1894. One of several earlier variations was one that provided direct access to the boxseat from the body of the vehicle, designed by a builder at Halesworth. Different ideas for incorporating a hood found perfection in the 'nineties with the Lonsdale wagonette, perhaps the most polished vehicle of any of wagonette form, lower hung in the body than most, beautifully finished, luxuriously cushioned and with the hood folding back over the wheels. The late Lord

Lonsdale, as much an authority on all that appertained to carriages as he was on every other matter concerning the horse, was its sponsor, and made much use of it on shooting, country racing and other sporting occasions as a postillion-driven vehicle.

Now that that picturesque but practical and important figure in English carriage history, the postillion, has become virtually extinct, surviving only in the Royal Mews where ride-and-drive carriages are still turned out on rare occasions, he calls for some explanation. What the postboy did on the Road in long-distance travel, the postillion did in private service, driving from the saddle of the near horse of a pair, two postillions working if four horses were used. An immaculate figure in white 'cords,' or 'leathers,' and tops, he wore the little close-fitting waist-length postillion jacket ornamented with three rows of small brass buttons and often bearing on the left sleeve a large embroidered badge incorporating his master's crest or a design significant of his rank. A narrow-brimmed, light-coloured tall hat of beaver or silk was usual, though Royal postillions wear velvet caps; and his whip of closely plaited leather on a whale-bone core, bore at least half-a-dozen equidistant silver bands between ferrule and thong. Generally the carriages so driven were some of those belonging to formal occasions but among the old school of Englishmen were a few who kept alive the posting tradition with varied carriages into recent times. The last were Lord Lonsdale, at Lowther and Barley Thorpe, and the late Lord Rosebery, at The Durdans, Epsom, whose posting turnouts were still to be seen in the nineteen-twenties. Lord Lonsdale's carriages, whether for his own driving, his coachmen's or his postillions', were always irreproachably turned out — 'pictures of spit and polish,' as one of his old coachmen used to say — and among stable employees there was no higher qualification than to have been trained in his service. Each of his varied types of carriage was precisely appointed in the manner appropriate to it, all were painted in the distinctive Lonsdale yellow, and the horses — all chestnuts, as were his hunters — are still cited by older horsemen as patterns of a perfection belonging to the past.

If wagonettes in their diversity of quality could embrace such apparent incompatibles as the magnificent Lonsdale postillion turnouts and such rural 'convaniences' as Charley's, they were equally inconsistent in their size. For ponies one remembers them so small as to have really the body of a governess car mounted on four wheels, with a box added, while at the opposite extreme their size and uses brought them into the category of Brakes*.

The Wagonette Brake for four horses or a pair, and often used in the country with a unicorn team (three horses, one leader with two wheelers), was in fact the most popular form of brake in both private stables and jobmaster's yards, for exercising and breaking-in harness horses as much as for the carrying of passengers. Its box hardly lower than that of a coach, its long wagonette seats taking as many as seven passengers on each side — except in occasional examples in which this seat length was curtailed to make room for an additional forward-facing seat at high level, parallel with the box, and taking up to four persons — it sometimes followed the coach principle of being built on a perch foundation, but more often was perchless. As a four-in-hand vehicle for the amateur's driving, the wagonette brake became accepted as the commonest alternative to the private coach for use on informal occasions when the latter was considered too 'dressy,' as for country picnics, coursing meetings or hunt race meetings. Unlike a coach, it could just as well be used with a pair if a team was not available, and the family coachman could drive it when a station or shopping vehicle was wanted or simply to exercise the carriage horses. It had, in fact, its place in every driving establishment of any size.

When, in the last great driving match ever seen on English roads, the late Lord Lonsdale covered twenty miles in fifty-five and a half minutes with four separate turnouts, each driven five miles, he chose a sporting brake as the vehicle for his four-horse lap. That was in March, 1891, in bitter winter weather when the chosen length of road, between Reigate and Crawley, had to be cleared by a snow plough before the race, already once abandoned and then run by Lord Lonsdale alone.

* Apparently the most usual spelling, though the alternative — break — has been used by some writers, and helps to suggest one of the vehicles main uses — to break horses to harness.

One of the sporting sensations of the age, arousing world-wide excitement, the match had been arranged to decide a bet of £100 between Lord Lonsdale and Lord Shrewsbury, the former to drive galloping horses and the latter his fast trotters, each contestant to cover five miles of road four times, once driving a single horse, then driving a pair, then a team (four-in-hand), and finally to ride and drive a pair as a postillion. When on the appointed day Lord Shrewsbury withdrew at the last moment, his horses not appearing, his opponent, whose faith in the superior speed of his galloping horses had never wavered and who had spent endless time, patience and money — many times the amount of the modest stake involved — on careful and elaborate preparation, was loath to abandon the match and to disappoint the crowds who had turned out in snow and icy weather to see it run. He decided to race alone, against Time, and so prove that twenty miles, with four separate turnouts, including the time spent in changing from one to the other, could be driven within an hour. His success, in spite of a half-hearted police attempt to interfere during the first lap, was one of the triumphs of the most remarkable sporting career of recent times. Vehicles of American type, chosen for their lightness, were used on the pair and single stages, the best of which took less than thirteen minutes. It was, though, on the high box of the brake, sometimes with its wheels barely touching the ground, that Lord Lonsdale made his name as a coachman, flying the five miles in fifteen minutes and a fraction of a second, behind a team made up of thoroughbred leaders, and wheelers that had learnt their work in a London fire-engine.

In another role wagonette brakes figured commonly as the tripper-carrying vehicles of the seaside town or of the Londoner's outing or beanfeast. Alternatively popular for these purposes were large vehicles with a succession of forward-facing seats set one behind the other, quite commonly known as 'brakes' but properly belonging, like all big vehicles with this arrangement of seating, and capacity, to the genus Char-a-banc. Public char-a-bancs for sight-seeing or tourist use were massive and rather ungainly of appearance, often with fixed staircases at the rear leading to high placed seats that would take as many as thirty passengers, and sometimes having an awning or canopy top. Regular ships of the road in fact, but delightfully steady road-holding vehicles to drive, and the means of many a young would-be coachman ' having a handful ' and getting a little practice with a team. Country proprietors and the men they employed as drivers, in the Lake district and elsewhere, sometimes had a weakness for describing or advertising char-a-bancs as ' coaches,' which they certainly were not ; other resourceful geniuses in the north even went to the lengths of fitting such things with dummy coach-bodies to heighten the illusion, earning for them the apt but unflattering name of ' Bastard coaches'.

In contrast were Private Char-a-bancs, generally beautifully finished sporting carriages built as high as coaches with the seats facing forward, favoured for team-driving in the larger country house establishments or, as an informal alternative to the regimental drag, by army officers. With so much association with public vehicles the name of char-a-banc has almost lost its significance as describing also some of the neatest large carriages produced in Victorian times, having a distinction as well as a variety in building and seating that led Hooper to write of them in the 'eighties as :

' More various in form than other carriages, they are generally high and strongly made, to carry a good many persons. Some have four seats, each carrying three or four persons, on the top of a high and long boot ; the seats are reached by convenient folding and sliding steps concealed in the boot and shut in by a small door. Others have the central seats kept low ; the four persons sit as in a coach, facing one another ; doors and folding steps provide easy access. The front driving-seat is made high in this class of carriage, and frequently the hind seat for the grooms is also high, being carried, as in the case of drags, on strong ornamental irons ; at other times this seat is kept low, and the grooms sit with their backs to the horses. Most of the large carriages of this type are used with four horses and are suspended in various ways, some on perch under-carriage with mail springs, others have in addition under-springs, while others again have four ordinary elliptic springs. Some are now made on smaller scale and go well with a pair of horses. A char-a-banc is essentially a carriage for a ' grande maison,' and for country use, and it is rarely found where a coach-house has not room for more than four carriages'.

Nothing, perhaps, better exemplifies the elegance that could be attained by one of the char-a-banc tribe than the one presented, in about the year 1844, to Queen Victoria by Louis Philippe of France. Having four forward-facing seats, each for three passengers, it was often used for shooting parties at Windsor as a postillion-driven carriage, and can still be seen at the Royal Mews at Windsor; as can so many other interesting carriages, mainly of the more formal types, examples of which it would be very hard to find elsewhere in these days. This particular carriage, which, incidentally, the Prince Consort had reproduced in smaller form with three seats, does not, of course, represent a type or species, probably being unique in its design like some other of the Royal vehicles of great historic interest. Many more at Windsor or Buckingham Palace are the best preserved survivors of once widely used classes of carriages; not a few of them still in limited use there, and nowhere else in England today, turned out and driven to those old standards of perfection that Royal servants have not forgotten.

A very neat, very sporting little brake of picturesque lines and intended for private use in the country with a team or a pair, was the Shooting Brake, which had, behind its high box, a strong suggestion of the dog-cart in its bodywork. Suppose a four-wheeled dog-cart body of the most sporting type to be extended forwards to a box like that of a coach, at a much higher level than the other two seats and with foot-board over the horses, the whole vehicle well above the ground on fairly high wheels and given a full lock, and you have an idea of its form but none of its neat effect and finish. In the panelled sides of the capacious boot under the box were set the venetian-blind panels of dog-cart association, repeated again in smaller form in the well between the rear seats, which were made reversible, so that their four passengers could sit face to face, two with the backs to the horses, and well sheltered by the high box, and two as at the back of a mail phaeton or a coach; or else back to back as in a dog-cart, the tailboard being let down to support the feet of those behind. Seating but six in all and therefore without any commercial uses, this distinguished type of brake was as rare as the wagonette variety was popular, and its owners were to be found mainly among connoisseurs of the sporting carriage.

Coaching men were usually those in whose stables such carriages survived until quite recently, who kept up in diminishing numbers the old tradition of the Road turnout for their own and their friends' driving. The distinction that existed between niceties of horsing, harnessing and turning out of carriages of this kind and those of coachmen-driven carriages and the like was a sharp one; the coaching or Road way of doing things differed much from the strictly Carriage way, as has been mentioned in the passage dealing with the mail phaeton; beyond this again were essential differences in the appointing of coaches even, the Road and the Park each demanding their own methods, and almost every important type of vehicle had its own peculiarities of appointment, the understanding of which was a source of pride and interest to driving men — and, quite often, a source of heated argument. To record the existence of these points that were so important to carriages when in use is perhaps sufficient in dealing with the carriages themselves, without pursuing the subject as far as the endless details of appointment that have been dealt with in exhaustive works on driving, particularly American ones glorying in the intricacies of English harness lore.

Among latter day private stables, in which the park coach and its subordinate vehicles, the brake and phaeton, divided the work of the stud with coachman-driven carriages like the brougham and victoria, were to be counted some of those — particularly in London — of members of the Coaching Club, where a great deal of responsibility and experience were called for in the head coachman. In addition to all his other duties as manager of an often considerable stud such a coachman would have to be prepared to turn out one day a team to the drag for his master's driving, another day perhaps a pair to a brougham, or a pair or single for a phaeton, bearing in mind always the precise appointment and harnessing for each, and being able to drive all of them himself when needed. The daily exercising of all the horses in pairs to a brake, when they were not otherwise at work, would certainly fall to him, and in many cases as well the initial buying of young horses and breaking them in. The stables and harness room of such an establishment were usually a miracle of smartness under a head coachman of the old school; stable dicipline was as exacting as that of a ship of war and 'spit and polish' came before everything. In the coach-house you could use as a mirror the panels of any one of the assorted carriages lined up there and all painted in a uniform colour — whatever the 'stable colour' might be. If now no such stables survive, with their brilliant vehicles giving a little interest to a West End and Park monotonously mechanised, it is still not many years since a few of them were kept up to standards as high as, for instance, those of the late Sir Edward Stern's stable. All of one colour — blue roan, of one size and one stamp, his horses were one of the sights of London, driven to the quietly painted brown drag, wagonette brake, brougham or victoria according to the occasion, or standing in that immaculate stable within a few yards of Hyde Park Corner, presided over always by that most polished, precise, and perfect of head coachmen, 'Alf' Bennett, of whom it used to be said that he might have been taken for a duke except that he was much too well dressed.

The tradition of coaching and sporting driving survived later still in one private stable that was the pattern of its kind. At the home of the late Lynwood Palmer, an old country house tucked away near the Bath Road and not far out of London, there were always to be seen blood horses kept and used for fast driving — often at night when busy days left no time to drive by light. There, ranged about a yard that in itself was a picture of old world perfection, were stables that had never been empty in the more than forty years the artist owned them; a harness-room in which hung team, single, double and tandem sets of harness in uniform and dazzling lines of polished leather and brass, and glazed bit-cases full of steel that shone like silver; a long, low coach house housing the vehicles in regular use, all perfect of their kind, and most with stories of their own. Next to the road coach, which had begun its long history running daily out of London as a public coach well back in the last century, stood the private drag, then, successively, the wagonette brake for exercising, a shooting brake with a history that would fill a book, a mail phaeton that once was Lord Lonsdale's, a high dog-cart, spider phaeton and one or two more survivors of sporting driving, all, except the light-painted road coach, conforming to the 'stable colour' of blue and each in its neatness, like everything about that stable, speaking of the owner's enthusiasm and good taste.

To have anything to say of harness stables in which smartness ranked high among the virtues and to overlook those apostles of elbow grease and pipeclay, the West End jobmasters, would be unforgivable. Those there were whose yards, stables and turnouts outshone all but the best of those of private owners; some in a way of business calling for the keeping of scores, even hundreds, of horses, whose names were household words; others, though by comparison 'little men,' who turned out pairs and teams equal to the best in London, which was a very good best indeed. Many people found the system of jobbing preferable to maintaining their own carriages, horses and servants: a jobmaster provided them by the year or shorter period, the responsibilities of a private stable were thus avoided with the troubles attending sick horses or unsatisfactory servants, the jobmaster being under contract to maintain continuous service, the better firms finding complete turnouts of almost the same quality as the most distinguished in private ownership.

Great users of brakes of various kinds were jobmasters, for the morning exercise of horses not otherwise at work and the breaking, making and accustoming to traffic of youngsters and fresh horses up from the country. Most horses being broken to harness would be put-to in the first place in double harness to a brake with an old and reliable 'brake horse' or 'schoolmaster'. Some of the West End firms made a point of turning out their exercise brakes to look as immaculate and ultra-smart as possible, thus combining advertisement with essential work, and made with them a great show; knee-capped pairs 'stepping up to their eyebrows' looked all the more impressive for having such finishing touches as the knee-caps of white buckskin and pipeclayed. Much used by the jobmaster and horsedealer was the Skeleton Brake, now almost as great a rarity as a shooting brake. The appearance of the skeleton explained its name; a high-placed box, taking of course one person beside the driver, was set well forward on a massive perch foundation boasting no other bodywork whatever except a little platform, where a

Plate XIII. PRIVATE WAGONETTE BRAKE (1930). *See page* 74

Plate XIV. SHOOTING BRAKE (1930). *See page* 77

Plate XV. TOWN COACH (Dress or State Coach). *See page* 83

James Pollard

Plate XVI. TRAVELLING (Posting) CHARIOT (1817). *See page* 85

stable-helper could stand holding on behind the box, which allowed him to jump easily on an off when the high spirits of a fresh 'young one' demanded it. Pole and splinter bar would often be heavily padded with leather and designed, like the large, dished, wide-set wheels, to defeat as far as possible every artifice known to young horses. Many skeleton brakes were used, too, in the larger private stables, as well as being very widely employed by the horse bus companies for the preparatory schooling of their animals. Some idea of the magnitude of the latter task can be gained when it is remembered that some forty-five years ago, when horse buses were at their best, there were some 3,700 of them at work in London and that each omnibus claimed the services of a stud of ten horses, or twelve if working a hilly route.

Though the public omnibus of the London streets was hardly to be considered a carriage, in the ordinary sense of the word, most certainly the Private Omnibus, a very different vehicle, was one of the most popular of informal carriages. It shared to a great extent the wide popularity of the wagonette and had, although a closed vehicle, much in common with it. The arrangement of seating was the same but enclosed by a neat body of solid coachwork, with windows at the sides and front and in the door at the back, while the roof was fitted with a low railing for carrying luggage. As a single or pair horse vehicle of private use it was intended for the driving of the coachman in livery, and served as a convenient and less formal alternative to smarter closed carriages like the brougham for station and theatre work; uses which gained it sometimes the name of Station Bus in this country, and Opera Bus in America, Commercially the small-sized bus became popular with hotel proprietors for railway work, and with town commercial travellers who found the large amount of covered space useful for carrying bulky samples.

The largest forms of private omnibus — and the most uncommon — were those intended for four-in-hand work, when they became vehicles for the owner's driving as well as the coachman's. To these, and occasionally to the smaller kinds. would be added an outside roof seat, seating up to four people, placed immediately behind the box as on a coach, thus providing yet another alternative to the private four-horse drag for informal country and sporting occasions. At coursing or race meetings such vehicles made admirable grand-stands, and could claim at least one advantage over the coach in the shelter of the comfortable inside accommodation, wherein a central folding table played a useful part at lunch time in the bad old days when hospitality and driving both flourished.

DRESS AND TRAVELLING CARRIAGES

THE year 1838, it has been said, saw the climax of the building of Dress and State carriages. It was natural enough that the time of Queen Victoria's coronation should produce some of the finest examples of these vehicles of formality and magnificence before the tide set in the direction of those that were simpler and less cumbersome; the new reign opened with occasions for the use of splendid equipages in Town, and with a demand still existing for travelling carriages. Before long, fashion and the spread of rail travel had the coach-builders busy on new ideas.

From the heavy family coaches, for town use or travelling, of the eighteenth century had emerged what is best known to us as the State Coach or Town Coach (though in various forms it claimed several other titles), examples of which are still to be seen occasionally in a few coach-houses of the greater country homes, in the windows of West End coachbuilders or making rare appearances on occasions of ceremony in the City of London, provincial cities or assize towns. Ponderously impressive, as was becoming to the vehicle from which the coach-building trade derived its name, the Town coach was cee spring hung by leather braces on a perch foundation, managing to combine cumbrous strength with a graceful finish; great dished wheels were set off by axle boxes of burnished brass. The body, seating four, was enclosed above richly painted panels by blind-fitted windows of plate glass, and sumptuously lined within with cloth, or even silken material, that carried out the colour scheme of paintwork and liveries. Chased and elaborate gilt or plated metal work was used for door handles, furniture and lamps, in harmony with the metal furnishings of the harness;

the lamps in particular often being very heavily ornamented and hexagonal or octagonal in shape. The accompaniments essential to its completeness were, on the huge hammer cloth covered box, a coachman in state livery of white wig, three cornered, gold braided hat, heavily braided, frogged and gold-corded livery coat of coloured cloth or velvet, silk knee-breeches, hose and silver-buckled shoes; standing on the platform between the rear springs, two similarly liveried footmen, bewigged and wearing cocked hats — the whole theme of the liveries being carefully studied and subject to much detailed elaboration. Horses, preferably Yorkshire bred, of bay colour and at least seventeen hands high, wearing massive, heavily ornamented harness with housings matching the coachman's and lackeys' liveries, the hammer cloth and coach panels. On the last of which finely gilded armorial bearings repeated those of either silver-plated or gilt metal on hammer cloth and harness.

Akin to such a coach, of similar uses and of no less dignity, but with lines that gave it an appearance of even more elegance, ranked the State or Dress Chariot. Here the seating was for two only, on one forward facing seat, the coach body being curtailed to eliminate the second seat with its back to the horses, and giving a front line nearly perpendicular or slightly sloped inward from base to top and having a forward facing window. When, as was often the case with such dress vehicles, a detachable coachman's box made conversion to a postillion-driven vehicle easy, this front window had its obvious advantages in giving the occupants an unobstructed view of the road ahead. When coachman-driven, a state chariot commanded the same magnificence in all its appointments as the coach seating four, and was in no way its inferior in importance; nor was it usually, in spite of its appearance, much lighter in build, the undercarriage being similar, and what was saved in weight of the body woodwork was made up in additional plate glass. Weight saving in such closed vehicles of early date, as substantial in their roofwork as elsewhere and with doors and panels of solid mahogany, was discouraged as entailing a loss of essential strength and dignity, and most perch-built carriages, although designed in the first place with bad roads in view, were found when used in later years on smooth surfaces, to be so perfectly contrived and balanced as to follow the horses with the minimum of pulling effort.

That these dress coaches and chariots of the past survive in such numbers as they do, is a fact not without its wonder and something of a tribute to the quality of the craftsmanship put into them. Either because they were so well built as to have proved almost indestructible or because their beauty saved them from the vandalism or neglect that have left us without examples of many less spectacular carriages, they are more often to be seen in good preservation than any other types. Almost every provincial museum of any size that can boast having a carriage at all can exhibit its Town coach or chariot still bearing the arms of some local family or important personage. In use, though, on occasions of ceremony, they will have been seen scarcely more often in late years than such purely ceremonial, walking-pace vehicles as the carved and gilded Royal State Coach, the coach of the Lord Mayor of London, the rarely used Speaker's Coach or others unique in character, historic vehicles rather than carriages.

Otherwise than as dress vehicles, chariots were built both for town use, driven by a coachman, and for travelling with post horses. Of the former one of the neatest introduced for less formal private use and with the appointments and accompaniments correspondingly modified, was the Chariot D'Orsay. The Count's excellent taste in such matters was here exemplified in a comparatively sombre chariot without unnecessary embellishments, with a simple box in place of the sumptuous hammer cloth, with unadorned panels and the accompaniments of plain harness and dark liveries. Private Posting Chariots were among the most generally used of long-distance travelling carriages, figuring frequently in prints of the Road, after Pollard and Newhouse, as the representatives of the most luxurious and rapid private travel with four horses and two postboys. In this form a rumble seat at the back usually provided room for two servants, and space between the front springs could contain a platform to carry luggage, attributes common to most travelling carriages whether chariots, coaches or vehicles that could be used open or closed with hoods.

Compared to all that has been left on record of stage and mail coach travel before railways, by those who themselves experienced it, private travelling carriages have been given less than their due. In fact there were among all old English carriages none more interesting than these varied vehicles, designed for the wealthy and so built of the finest materials as long to outlast the days when they carried their owners countless hundreds of miles; not only travelling all over Britain but covering the Continent on the Grand Tours of English families, through France, Italy, Belgium and Germany of many months duration. The ingenuity of the London coachbuilders responsible for vehicles that thus often became their owners' homes for long periods contrived as much for the occupants' comfort as for their safety, space being found in some cases for books, provisions, bullion, or money needed for travelling expenses, carried in a well beneath the floor. Even the means of heating and preparing food on the road and, when the carriage was of the Dormeuse variety, of sleeping at full length with an extension into the forward boot for the feet. For prolonged continental tours of important personages one carriage was not always adequate for the family, servants and baggage; the journey would be planned and organised in advance to the last detail, a courier on horseback preceding the party and making all arrangements for changes of horses and inn accommodation, and servants and baggage travelling in a supplementary vehicle, the Fourgon.

'If a long tour were arranged for, and there were a large proportion of ladies who entered much into society and gaiety, the baggage was proportionately extensive and would be carried in a compact fourgon, half carriage, half van, the forepart having a cabriolet body with folding hood, carrying the courier and lady's maid, while in the rear were tiers of neatly numbered and arranged wooden boxes, the leather covered imperials, hat-cases or portmanteaus, being put outside and protected with a capacious waterproof tarpaulin cover. This vehicle often preceded the party in the family coach, landau or britzska, by some hours, so that on their arrival at the hotel chosen, all was comfortably arranged for their reception'.

So wrote the builder of many travelling carriages, G. N.

Hooper, of Adams and Hooper of the Haymarket, a firm specialising in the larger private carriages of travel and state. Writing in the 'eighties, some forty years after the demand for such vehicles had disappeared, he recalled their distinctions and uses from memory and personal association, and to quote him further is to quote an impeccable authority.

'The travelling carriages of the nobility and gentry had received great attention and had been greatly improved, so much so that the best of them were used for very long journeys through England and Scotland, and across the continent of Europe from Calais to Rome, Calais to Vienna or other distant capitals, requiring only the renewal of the worn iron tires of the wheels and new soling of the dragshoes [skidpans holding hind wheels when going down steep hills] as they became worn by contact with the road.

'... The contrivances for comfort, safety and conveyance of luggage had attained a perfection that was greatly appreciated by well-to-do travellers. Capacious and neatly fitted boxes with covers to exclude rain and dust were carried on the roofs of closed carriages; some were placed under the cushions, others in and on the front boot. At the back of the rumble that carried servants behind, a capacious cap-case contained ladies' bonnets and head gear, while a row of hat-boxes was attached behind the upper part of the rumble; two wells, secured to the bottom of the carriage, contained provisions, accessible from trap-doors in the carriage flooring; the sword-case projecting from the back of the body — easily accessible from the interior — contained arms for those inside the carriage, while the courier was provided with pistols placed in holsters at his side of the rumble. The front of the body was furnished with a folding sun-shade and Venetian blinds with movable laths for sultry weather; spring curtains kept off the sun's rays, and a lamp with one or two candles, fixed at the back of the carriage, lighted the interior; the heat, burnt air and smoke passing away outside the carriage. Some of these elaborate private carriages were provided with dormeuse boots, and from them could be developed beds affording accommodation for sleeping during night journeys. Veritably Pullman's sleeping cars were anticipated, and in use long before he was heard of.

'Some of the most complete, compact and hardworking of these noted travelling carriages were used by the King's messengers to his ambassadors in foreign capitals. The safe custody and rapid delivery of important Government despatches from one end of Europe to another entailed great responsibility and care on the part of those entrusted with them. These messengers were generally retired military men or naval officers, or other hardy and adventurous gentlemen. Occasionally the incessant and continuous rapid travelling of many days was so exhausting, that they had to be lifted out of their carriages on reaching their distant destination. In very hot or inclement weather their suffering was sometimes acute.

'These carriages were provided with strong safety ropes under the body, extending from one c-spring to another, in case a much worn leather spring brace should break at an inconvenient place or time and arrest further progress: they were also provided with two drag-shoes and chains, and in addition a wheel hook and chain in case a bad piece of road should displace one or both of the drag-shoes; also a drag-staff to let down in ascending an Alpine road, to prevent a jibbing horse or one with sore shoulders from backing and sending the carriage, its occupants, horses and servants down a precipice. In addition there was a box or tool budget provided with all necessary tools, with spare bolts and clips in case of a breakdown in open country; and a good courier was expected to be able to use the tools effectively, to replace a broken bolt or secure a broken tire with a tire-clip.

'Carriages for continental travelling had always to be provided with loose swinging splintrees attached to the splinter bar — so that each horse pulled from a centre — easing the horse's collar, but rendering accurate guidance more difficult and less precise than when the traces were attached to fixed splinter bars as is usual in England — where consequently, with ordinary care, collisions were less frequent, by reason of greater certainty in steering.

'The couriers who accompanied noblemen and great families on their continental journeys were almost invariably foreigners — Swiss, Italian, German or French. They required a combination of qualities to perform their duties to the comfort and satisfaction of their employers, for on the good management and knowledge of this functionary depended much of the pleasure of a continental ramble. It was of course necessary that he could speak three or four languages . . . he had to organise the route, the length of the day's journey, provide for punctual relays of post-horses, order rooms at hotels beforehand, if his party were large, settle the bills, pay all expenses on the road and duly render periodical accounts of the money supplied to him'.

Posting on the continent while varying much in different countries in methods and efficiency always differed entirely from the English system. Everything in foreign travel was, to the inexperienced visitor, fraught with complications and — Britons journeying abroad in their own carriages usually being accepted a 'milords' of unlimited wealth — impositions in the matter of charges; hence the importance to travellers of a trustworthy courier. As a class, couriers were admirable and remarkable, earning the praise of many for whom they made foreign travel not only possible but comfortable. Hooper referred to them as travelling usually in the fourgon or sometimes in the carriage itself; more often, though, they carried out their arduous advance work in the saddle; as that experienced road traveller, the Duke of Beaufort explained when writing of French posting and paying his tribute to the race of couriers.

'These were an extraordinary race of hardy men, capable of any fatigue', he wrote, 'who had all the routes of the continent at their fingers' ends, and knew which hotels to avoid as well as those to be patronised. Supposing a traveller had landed at Calais and was going right through to Marseilles. When the carriage was brought ashore from the steam packet and the horses were put to, off went the courier, on a little horse provided by the maitre de poste, but always on his (the courier's) own saddle, with his cloak rolled on it; and he made such haste as to get to the change in time to have the horses out ready to be put to on the arrival of the carriage... The courier rode all the way from Calais to Marseilles. The writer has known three couriers who have ridden from Rome to Calais night and day without stopping, and to the best of his recollection it took nine or ten days and nights to do the journey. It sounds incredible, but it is an actual fact that it has been done several times and no stoppage of more than two hours ever occurred. This, considering the inevitable wranglings and quarrels with postmasters, postillions and douaniers, is a very extraordinary feat. The couriers had a very good idea of their own importance, and got themselves up very smartly. They wore a blue jacket with short tails, with red facings, leather tights, jackboots and spurs, and jackets much bedecked with gold lace; a hard stiff glazed cap, with a gold lace band, a chin-strap for windy weather, and a fall-down to go over their ears and keep their necks dry in rain'.

As entertaining as authentic on Road matters, the same author added to his reminiscences of travel abroad a note on that most intriguing of carriages the Dormeuse, mentioned also by Hooper; the Duke's definition being; 'A dormeuse — i.e., a travelling chariot with a long boot in front into which one could, by letting down the front of it, put one's legs, the front fixing under the seat — made a good bed. A rolled-up mattress was carried in the boot, and this joined the cushions the travellers sat on. Imperials, bonnet-boxes, cap-boxes, and wells under the seat held the luggage. On the dickey behind was a cabriolet head to keep the servants warm and dry'.

That *hooded* dickey or rumble, affixed behind the carriage body like a little separate carriage joined to a greater one, added much to the unusual lines of the dormeuse, which otherwise contained so much that was unique among carriages. One dormeuse, at least, survives still — the same one, no doubt, of which the Duke wrote, for it was built in about the year 1820, by Adams and Hooper, for the seventh Duke of Beaufort and was used by him on many long journeys, including the one he made from Badminton to Vienna when representing the Court of St. James' at the Emperor of Austria's coronation. Its last public appearance behind four horses and two postboys was at Olympia, London, in 1920, when it left Badminton on loan to take its place in the Parade of Historic Carriages, the brilliant feature of the International Horse Show of that year and the last serious attempt to show such vehicles completely and accurately turned out as they used to be on the roads. Seen then with all its original features in perfect preservation and as they were mentioned in the writings of the Duke and of Hooper — pillows, leg-rests, strong-box, the hidden well beneath the floor provided in King's Messenger's carriages, swordcase, and even some of the original trunks — it made a particularly impressive appearance in the daily drives of a long procession of vehicles, each appropriately horsed and with its suitably dressed passengers and servants, and many having the added interest of authentic histories and records of travel before railways.

Among other travelling carriages used for posting that were shown on that occasion — when, as someone said, 'coaching prints came to life' — were two posting chariots built at about the same time as the dormeuse chariot, one with a rumble seat for servants and the other with a rear platform; one or two hooded carriages of landau type (for dress use or travel), and a britzska; these last, if properly classified, being counted in the ranks of the open-bodied carriages. Each, lent for the period of the show by its owner, was a perfect example of its kind and a proof in its survival of the wonderful quality of the workmanship of English coachbuilders. To what an extent some of the latter specialised in certain types of work was exemplified by all the private travelling carriages in the show having been built by one or the other of two firms, Adams and Hooper or Peters and Sons.

From their association with the long and arduous journeys of King's Messengers, to which Hooper referred, travelling carriages derived much of their romantic interest. One of these adventurous official travellers has an important place otherwise in driving history, as a well known amateur coachman, one of the leading figures in the revival of stage coaching in England, and an author. He was Captain M. E. Haworth, whose love of four-horse driving led him to organise and eventually to run, in 1866, and with the support of the Duke of Beaufort and several other enthusiasts, the first London to Brighton coach to mark the return of road-coaching years after the rail had killed it as a business. His two books, *The Silver Greyhound* and *Road Scrapings*, commemorate his experiences as traveller and coaching man. One journey that he had particular cause to remember was made in a travelling carriage from Turin to Paris; it entailed going over Mont Cenis by a track on which horses were out of the question and mules were used — nine of them, under conditions that, as the traveller himself described them, provide an illustration of what foreign travel could be.

'It was in the month of December, and at the time I left Susa, at five p.m., the snow was falling so thickly that by the time I had completed half the ascent, the road or track was completely obliterated. It was a beautiful moonlight night. I was lost in admiration of the manner in which the nine mules, attached to a light travelling carriage, wended their way over the trackless snow. The stupendous mountains, clothed in all the sombre grandeur of their winter attire, surged up before me, peeping as it were into the deep chasms beneath, on the very verge of which the mules moved cautiously along. It was wonderful to watch, where the road twisted and turned almost at right angles, the careful manner in which each animal in turn dropped out of his work until they were again in the straight running.

'Notwithstanding the beauty of the scenery and the interest with which I watched the long string of mules, which appeared at times to be actually balancing themselves upon the narrow ledges, I was not without anxiety, partly perhaps on account of a friend to whom I had given a seat in my carriage. He had recently broken his leg at Turin, and was taking the earliest opportunity of a safe escort to London. The driver had no more direct control over the mules than could be conveyed by his voice, though I must do him the justice to say that when he did open his mouth, he did so to some purpose. His mules, however, did not require reproof often, and a short grunt, with the name Garibaldi or Emanuel sufficed to make them spring forward as if they were ashamed of being named before strangers. The driver himself frequently makes short cuts across the angles of the road as he plods through the snow, leaving the mules to thread their way entirely according to their own judgment.

'It was on one of these occasions, when the driver loitering out of sight, perhaps to cut his tobacco, was absent somewhat longer than usual, that the mules appeared to be feeling their way with more than ordinary caution, while the uneasy motion of the carriage indicated that we were not travelling upon a plain surface. Almost instinctively, I ejaculated at the top of my voice, imitating as near as I could the driver's intonation : "Wo-a-a-h!" Every mule stopped dead short. If they had not done so, or moved on one single inch, this incident would never have been recorded by me!

'Opening the door of the carriage I beheld a frightful precipice, over which we were literally hanging; while, turning round in order to step out with greater caution, I found that the weight of my body perforated the lightly packed snow and that I could not feel the ground beneath it. Had it not been for the firm grip I had of the wing of the carriage, I must inevitably have been precipitated into the abyss of snow-covered boulders many hundred feet deep below'.

Ensuing pages tell of the outcome of this situation; of the carriage being regained from the edge of the precipice by attaching the mules to its body and turning it over; of the captain and his crippled passenger eventually reaching one of the Refuge huts then maintained at intervals on Mont Cenis by Piedmontese peasants; of their being held up there for two nights by fresh falls of snow that made movement impossible; and ultimately of their escaping from the abject discomfort of this lodging to continue the journey by sleigh, the track having become impassable to anything on wheels.

By contrast with such travelling as that, posting on English roads was luxury; at its best, bowling along good McAdam 'turnpikes' at ten or eleven miles an hour, behind post horses and postboys changed at frequent intervals at posting inns, in a comfortable private carriage; at its worst, making use of all the same well organized facilities but riding in hired Post Chaises of less comfort and subject to the objection of as frequent changing as the horses and the 'boys.' As a vehicle, the old post chaise or hack chaise supplied at every English posting house could be described as the simplest form of chariot. Its body, like other chariots, seating two, was hung in the same way by leather braces from cee springs — this and its almost invariable colour earning it the popular name of 'yellow bounder'. Windows in front and in each door gave it plenty of light; luggage could be carried on a little forward platform between the front springs, and the tops of these springs were connected by a bar which Harris described as, 'somewhat resembling in shape a milkman's yoke, but not nearly so large in the centre — in fact about three or four inches was the extreme width of it'. This bar was a unique feature of the post chaise and was put to frequent use by the postboys as a means of rest from the saddle when returning to a posting house with an empty chaise. On such occasions, when they knew beforehand that a return would have to be made without passengers, they would take with them a pair of long reins and use these to drive back, sitting on the forward bar and resting their feet upon the luggage platform.

Chroniclers of road travel who eulogised the pleasures of posting were mainly those who experienced it in their own comfortable travelling carriages, though not all of them have made this fact clear. 'If I had no duties and no reference to futurity, I would spend my life in a post chaise with a pretty woman'; so said Dr. Johnson, in whose travelling days posting was a long way from being the well organized and rapid means of travel it became later; substitute luxurious private chariot for post chaise, and you have an idea of what the doctor was probably thinking about. Lord William Pitt Lennox, writing of posting days far more advanced than Johnson knew, was more explicit: 'In bygone days it was very agreeable, albeit rather expensive, to travel post, especially in your own light chariot or britchka; but to be dependent upon hack chaises on the road was far from pleasant. These chaises were not very well hung on springs, the windows seldom fitted closely, and the rattling noise reminded one of a dice-box in full play upon wheels. There was generally straw enough at your feet to hold a covey of partridges. Although these vehicles were light and followed well, a great deal of time was wasted in shifting your luggage from one to the other at every stage, or, at most, every other stage'.

More than one of the authorities quoted has mentioned — without always agreeing as to its spelling — the Britzska, thereby introducing one of the most liked and widely used of private posting carriages, although one — unlike those so far dealt with — of open body. In its form it was as distinctive as elegant: 'The body and seats all swing alike on cee springs. The boot [rumble seat] behind will accommodate two persons. The body, when the knee-flap is open, will hold four; but in wet weather it is only fitted for two. The front part of the head

[hood] has a calash attached to it, which is easily put up and down. The access of rain is carefully guarded against; and in case of cold weather, there is an ingeniously contrived glass shutter which folds up in a recess in the head, and which when let down will fill the whole front, closing with an air-tight joint in front of the knee-flap. The sword-case behind is large and convenient; and the leg-room in the interior is abundant.' That description was given by W. B. Adams, in 1837 when britzskas for some ten years had been built in this country in numbers that bore testimony to their merits. Where they differed most noticeably from other comparable carriages was in departing from the curved bottom line of body with one that was perfectly straight. Lighter than most English carriages of their day, they were developed from a German design introduced to this country by the Earl of Clanwilliam, and soon became known to postboys and coachmen as 'Briskers' or 'Briskies,' names which managed to suggest something of their pleasing appearance as well as getting over difficulties of spelling and pronunciation.

The adaptable nature of all such vehicles must always be given full allowance in considering their appearance. A britzska, for example, a popular open posting carriage as Adams described it, was still as much a britzska, though hardly recognisable as one, when someone fitted a box to it and used it as a town carriage with a coachman to drive it; or when some up-to-date coachbuilder built it with simple elliptic springs, its look entirely changed by the absence of the perch and the sweeping cee springs. In that last form it became very like, and has been often taken for, a Russian Droitzschka; which, seating two only, in an open body much lower hung than the britzska's, also became a favourite carriage in England under the name of 'Drosky.'

More often driven from the box than from the saddle was the stately Barouche, of mainly regal or aristocratic associations, though used in its day for many purposes. Among open vehicles it could be counted almost the equal of what the town coach was among closed ones; at its most magnificent it called for the same big upstanding horses, of which a pair, four or even six might be used. Its body, sometimes so shallow as to be almost tray-like, was of family capacity, usually hung high on cee springs and following in its lower line the half circle of the coach body; the box when present was yet higher and often supported by ornamental scroll ironwork. Its popularity dated from the eighteenth century and persevered throughout the nineteenth in spite of the competition of so many more economical carriages. In the Royal Mews it is still represented among the carriages of occasional ceremonial use. In literature the barouche makes many appearances, in many roles, as a vehicle of great occasions, of family use and of sporting associations.

'In an open barouche, the horses of which had been taken out, the better to accommodate it to the crowded place, stood a stout old gentleman, in a blue coat and bright buttons, corduroy breeches and top boots, two young ladies in scarfs and feathers, a young gentleman apparently enamoured of one of the young ladies in scarfs and feathers, a lady of doubtful age, probably the aunt of the aforesaid, and Mr. Tupman, as easy and unconcerned as if he had belonged to the family from the first moments of his infancy. Fastened up behind the barouche was a hamper of spacious dimensions — one of those hampers which always awakens in a contemplative mind associations connected with cold fowls, tongue, and bottles of wine — and on the box sat a fat and red-faced boy, in a state of somnolency, whom no speculative observer could have regarded for an instant without setting down as the official dispenser of the contents of the before-mentioned hamper, when the proper time for their consumption should arrive'.

The owner of that barouche, the stout old gentleman, was, of course, Mr. Wardle, and the occasion that of the memorable military manouevres at which Mr. Pickwick made his acquaintance. In earlier years another stout gentleman had set a precedent in the use of a barouche as both vehicle and grand-stand on like occasions, when Sir John Lade drove him and his guests from his palace, the Pavilion at Brighton, to Lewes races; six horses were used for this royal barouche, known then as a German Waggon. That barouches were much used by their owners as vehicles for their own, rather than their coachmen's, driving, gave them a distinction unshared by other comparable carriages. In the earlier days of amateur four-in-hand driving they were often put to this use, and among the first of the driving clubs was one, in being in 1808, which demanded of its members the driving of barouches rather than drags. Landau characteristics in some barouches were so marked as to earn them the name of barouche-landaus; while single-horse carriages modelled on the lines of the barouche, rarely built later than at the opening of Queen Victoria's reign, were called Barouchets.

For the rest the open carriages employed for dress occasions and travel, mainly postillion-driven, were Landaus — the senior members of the landau tribe. ' An open and closed carriage in one', Felton called the landau, with its jointed heads that could be closed over the four passengers to enclose them as snugly as in a dress coach, or folded back to provide a vehicle comparable with a barouche as an open carriage. But for the essential difference of the heads taking the place of a permanent roof, the landau of state differed little from the coach of state. At its most magnificent it was an equally impressive vehicle, subject to the same formality in its appointments, and, dating from mid-eighteenth century, it had had almost as much time in which to develop varieties of form. It belonged in truth to a race apart from the less formal landaus — some of them very modest little vehicles indeed — which shared its name and for the greater part were introductions of Victorian times, to take their places with contemporaries and equals like the brougham and victoria.

Formality in an equipage reached no higher point than in a Landau Grande Daumont drawn by four horses, driven by two postillions, and attended by two outriders, whose livery coats matched the postillions' jackets and whose horses were of the same colour, size and quality as those drawing the carriage, the blinker-bridles and cruppers of all six horses being en suite. When, on ceremonial occasions, state landaus attended by outriders are turned out at the Royal Mews they are probably the only ones to be seen in the world today. The royal outriders forming a solitary link with the mounted men-servants whose function long ago was to protect the occupants of important travelling carriages from the dangers of the road.

ROYAL LANDAUS

In the coach-houses of Windsor and Buckingham Palace landaus are represented in every degree of state and semi-state magnificence, their uses, past or present, depending on the formality of the occasion and accompanied by varying niceties of appointment in harness and liveries. In stately importance few carriages of any kind exceed the 18-foot long postillion landau built within this century for King Edward VII, which follows in its lines the form of the old travelling landaus, on perch, cee springs and braces, but has every embellishment possible to add to its regal appearance. In contrast is the quiet elegance of those dapper, much lighter postillion landaus that have their place in the Ascot procession. In these, light wheels, Collinge's axles and neat modern springing replace the perch and cee spring under-carriage, and gracefully shallow bodies with the panels finished in plain grey are a departure from the usual painting of royal carriages.

VICTORIAN COACHMAN-DRIVEN CARRIAGES

THE first and most important fresh idea in carriage building to come with Queen Victoria's reign was that of a simple private carriage of permanently closed body that could be drawn by one horse. The first, because the original carriage of this type was designed within almost a year of the Queen's accession; the most important, because hitherto closed carriages had been of the majestic order of coaches and chariots, as costly as they were formal and confined to the ownership of the wealthy, whereas one horse driven to a neat vehicle that might, at its simplest, cost less than a hundred pounds was a propostion that could and did, make 'carriage folk' of a much greater number of families and professional or business men.

Lord Brougham, Lord Chancellor of England, in designing the first of such private carriages and commissioning its building, all unwittingly made his name a household word universally applied to the most popular and the longest to survive of closed carriages. Various simple cabs of closed body, four wheels and one horse had been known for some time in northern British cities, and in Paris, as hackney vehicles for hire, and for a few years in London. These suggested to Lord Brougham the possibility of a neat, well-finished private carriage on the same principle, or what was described as 'a refined and glorified street cab which would make a convenient carriage for a gentleman, and especially for a man of such ideas as one who carried his own carpet-bag on occasions when time was important and his own servant otherwise employed'.

With that still surviving Brougham, the first one of its race, have survived also some details of its history. With a design for it Lord Chancellor Brougham approached his family coach-builders, Sharp and Bland, of South Audley Street, whose failure to grasp its possibilities, and the resultant triumph of a rival firm, are best left to the tactful pens of fellow members of the trade.

'They [Sharp and Bland] were evidently not the men to carry out a new idea that was destined to overspread the world, wherever good carriages are now [1888] used. They were in the habit of building family coaches, landaus, barouches, britzskas and chariots, which function carried with it certain ideas of rank, ceremony, dignity, independence, and we may add prejudice. They threw so many difficulties in the way that it was hopeless to get them to carry out the work satisfactorily, so his lordship called on some neighbours of theirs in Mount Street. Messrs. Robinson and Cook had not been so thoroughly trained in the school of crystallised habit, obstruction and prejudice as their neighbours; they accordingly accepted the idea and the order for construction with alacrity, civility and energy. They did their best; they pleased their customer; he was delighted with the result, and in his turn he did his best to influence the world of fashion. He began with his personal friends, advising them to order carriages like his new one, and he so influenced the carriage-buying public that they flocked to the coachmakers who had worked out successfully the idea which was destined to revolutionise the old method of carriage building as regards lightness, handiness, ease of access and economy'.

Thus Hooper combined a neat expression of professional feeling with his acknowledgment of the brougham's importance among carriages; some ten years earlier Thrupp had paid his tribute and given dates and measurements:

'I think it was in 1839 that the first vehicle that was nearly the shape of the present Brougham was built by Mr. Robinson, of Mount Street, for Lord Brougham. Messrs. Thrupp built one in the following year, 1840, of the same shape. In a few years they were built by nearly all coachmakers, and proved so convenient that they superseded even the cabriolet for gentlemen's use. The size of the first Brougham was much as is now in vogue, about 4 feet long in the body, and the same breadth outside measure, the wheels 2 feet 11 inches and 3 feet 7 inches, the driving boot was without any arch, in a single sweep from the body to the foot-board; it was hung on elliptic springs in front, and five springs behind without any body steps'.

Before it found its eventual way to the South Kensington museum that historic original brougham could claim as its successive owners Sir William Foulis, Lord Henry Bentinck and Lord Bathurst; and among the great men who had driven in it as passengers, both Disraeli and Gladstone. Though highly finished in olive green paintwork and originally lined with silk tabaret, it did little more than foreshadow the extreme neatness and elegance of later broughams. It was in fact comparatively clumsy, an obvious initial attempt to refine a hackney cab, made needlessly heavy with iron plates to strengthen the body, iron stays, a board called an opera board at the back as a protection against collision from other carriages following in a crowd, wheels that were too small and too heavy and lines marred by the body being narrower behind than in front. The presence of a swordcase proved a lingering of the old traditions of the travelling carriage, and with such things as the 'driving boot without an arch' was very soon to be eliminated as the real possibilities of lightness were accepted.

Improvements on that first example produced in time the miracle of neatness that was the true Victorian brougham, the general favorite in town, the family carriage of the country house and the product of countless coachbuilders. At first the seating was confined to two as in the little Bachelor's brougham; the nick-name of 'Pill-box' derived as much from diminutive size as from the carriage's popularity with doctors. Soon Family broughams and Double broughams became as general, and in many the single horse gave place to a pair. Low enough hung to be but a step from the ground, the highly finished bodywork attained lightness hitherto undreamt of in a closed vehicle; the cloth or leather upholstered seats were no higher than the floorboards of earlier carriages, raised above the axle level only by the height of the neat elliptic springs; up-to-date inside fittings like mirrors, ashtrays, a clock and a speaking tube communicating with the coachman appeared; and with the coming of rubber tires for slender wheels silence and easy running were attained by London broughams. On the lightly railed and cushioned box sat a coachman in quiet livery, usually without a second servant but with room beside him for a carriage-groom, footman or pageboy if occasion demanded. Collinge's axles (those that allowed of the wheels being greased by simply unscrewing the hub-caps) had become general in light and non-sporting carriages and to most carriages was fitted an unobtrusive brake for the coachman's use, either by foot-pedal or hand-lever, acting by pressure of blocks on the tires of the hind wheels. A detachable tray-like basket, shaped to the roof, could be strapped on to most broughams when wanted for luggage.

Variations in the form of broughams might fill a book of their own. While most designers and builders held to simplicity combined with neatness as a guiding principle, and perfection in the brougham was generally allowed to be found in those built by the noted firm of Barker, there were plenty who strove to make of it a much more formal vehicle. Lord Lytton, the author, in days when he was Mr. Lytton Bulwer and the brougham still a comparative newcomer among carriages, formalised it with a hammer cloth box and rear platform for footmen and produced a kind of hybrid chariot-brougham.* Much later in the Queen's reign were brougham bodies mounted on perches and cee springs ; a compromise with earlier, statelier ideas, but hardly representative of what that knowledgable Victorian, Sidney, considered typical of the everyday brougham of his time :

'For the owner of a carriage who does not make driving a pleasure, for a family, a single lady or a bachelor, whether for town or country use, the brougham occupies the first place. It is the only close carriage that looks well with one horse and one man. It looks equally well with a pair, if their size harmonizes with the carriage. It may be light and single for the Park, or capacious and double for the happy pair with a full quiver. It is the warmest carriage in winter, and is cool with all the windows open in summer. In the Park and at other assemblies of the fashionable the windows of a brougham are so 'hung on the line' as to present a fair face at the very best point of view for admiration and conversation . . . Although by occasional flashes of fashion broughams are painted in bright and even gay colours, where only one is kept it is better to adhere to sombre

* Called a Surrey Clarence. A carriage described as 'midway between a brougham and a coach' was introduced in 1842 and given the name of Clarence.

shades. Where taste or fashion is an object, the colour of the carriage and livery of the coachman should harmonize. Gaiety may be given to the more sombre hues by harness rich in metal ornament, by gay-coloured saddle-cloths and rosettes. Gaudiness, however, should be avoided'.

In the eighteen-seventies and afterwards the Victoria came to fill much the same place as an open carriage that the brougham did as a closed one. King Edward VII, when Prince of Wales, set the fashion for victorias in this country in 1869, when he introduced one from Paris. Queen Victoria, often appearing in it — or rather in others copied and developed from it by English coachbuilders — set the seal on its success in London, and it was not long before victorias were being used and built all over the country. In establishments running to two or more coachman-driven carriages a victoria was the perfect opposite number to a brougham; the former doing duty mainly in summertime and for daytime drives, the latter when the weather or evening work called for more protection than was given by a victoria's hood. If all the niceties of correct turning out were observed, however, as in a good town stable they always were, victoria harness differed much from brougham harness in being lighter made, in keeping with the lighter appearance of the vehicle, though in the main the same rules of quiet appointment applied to both carriages. In both, too, were to be found as great and as tortuous variations of form when once the coach-making trade realised the victoria's possibilities in this direction.

All these varieties sprang from a simple victoria that could be described in brief as a George IV or Lady's phaeton with a box added so that it could be driven by a coachman in livery. At first coachbuilders liked to call it a Victoria phaeton, but outside their trade the word phaeton always implied a carriage for personal driving, and the shortened description — victoria — became general. The body of the victoria proper, like that of the George IV phaeton, was low-hung, generally following a neat curve in shape but sometimes angular, door-less, with a neat folding head sufficient to ward off showers and wings as a protection from mud thrown up by the wheels. On the box — a very light one — was room for a second servant when wanted.

On elliptic springs and rubber tires it looked all over what it was, the neatest of ladies' carriages. In elaborating the victoria from one carriage into a dozen or so, great ingenuity was shown, original features of the carriage often coming off worst in battles with personal taste. A catalogue of victorias with no pretensions to being a complete one would contain those having a little folding seat for a third occupant sitting with his back to the box, added to many which otherwise retained the original form of a forward facing seat for two only; also Double Victorias, big enough to seat four as in a double brougham or coach; and some of either kind having low doors. Any kind might be adapted to the work of either one horse or a pair, and various alternatives to the elliptic in the springing included the old combination of cee spring and perch, and the Morgan cee spring (a modified form rising to less height but with leather braces to carry the body) used without a perch. Those of stately use were made with a footman's rumble seat behind.

More than with other carriages is there disagreement among knowledgable authorities who were contemporaries of the victoria as to its origin. For the world of fashion the fact that the Prince of Wales bought in Paris the vehicle that inaugurated its popularity in this country was sufficient evidence that it could be written down as French; it was, says one writer, 'as a fashionable carriage, a creation of the French Empire'. Others, who went deeper into the facts, traced it to English designs, including that of a coachbuilder, J. C. Cooper, who is mentioned in the *Coachbuilders' Art Journal*, of 1885, as having designed 'both the curved and the angular victoria, and the original drawings remained for some time in his portfolio, condemned by the conservatism of English coachbuilders; they at length found favour in the eyes of his continental clients, and we believe we are correct in stating that the first little vehicle built from them was purchased by the Prince of Wales in Paris, in 1869, whence it was brought to England and copied as a novelty of French design'. Probably both countries contributed to the victoria's final perfection, something being owed to the Four-wheeled Cabriolet built in Paris about 1845, the Pilentum of English building (having a similar low-hung open body and being used occasionally with one horse or two before the Queen's

Longmans Green & Co. Ltd. *G. D. Giles*

Plate XVII. DORMEUSE CHARIOT. *See pages* 86 *and* 90

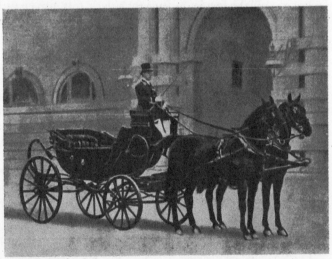

Raphael Tuck & Sons Ltd.

Plate XVIII. BAROUCHE, still in occasional use at the Royal Mews. *See page* 95

Author's Collection *George Garrard*

Plate XIX. Town Coach Horses and Coachman (1798). *See page* 84

Author's Collection *George Garrard*

Plate XX. Chariot Horses and Postillions (1798). *See pages* 73 *and* 85

Raphael Tuck & Sons Ltd.

Plate XXI. Modern SINGLE BROUGHAM in the Royal Mews. *See page* 101

W. W. Rouch, photo

Plate XXII. H.M. Queen Alexandra in a Cee-spring VICTORIA. *See page* 103

From S. Sidney's *Book of the Horse*

Plate XXIII. SOCIABLE LANDAU. *See page* 106

reign) and, quite certainly, to the George IV phaeton. At least one reliable authority, A. E. T. Watson, gave the last-named vehicle the credit that appears its obvious due; he wrote in the 'eighties, 'In course of time this developed into the Victoria with a seat for the coachman, the vehicle which is at present as popular among open carriages as the brougham is among closed'.

The ownership of both a brougham and a victoria being accepted as the perfect arrangement, providing for all weathers and conditions, even when the establishment was modest enough and the mileage small enough for one horse to be a sufficient stud, it was still possible to carry economy a step further and make one carriage serve the purposes of two, if that one were the adaptable Landau. Here the double leather head, closing snugly over all the four-seated body converted in a minute an open carriage to a closed one. A contrivance of such obvious usefulness and good sense as this was too good a thing to remain a part only of important state and travelling carriages like the stately landaus mentioned in the previous chapter; though until the demand for simpler carriages became general in Queen Victoria's reign an everyday, un-elaborate landau that could be drawn by a single horse was a thing unheard of.

So great was the disparity between one kind of landau and the other that much trouble and confusion might have been saved if Victorian builders had given their new landaus a new name, one that was not shared by posting and dress vehicles that had been built and used in this country since the idea was first imported from the German town of Landau in mid-eighteenth century. These lesser, later landaus were as English as they were Victorian. They began, in 1838, when one Luke Hopkinson, a coachbuilder in Holborn, produced what he called a britszka-landau, distinguished by the first hood made to lie really flat and out of the way when the carriage was opened as in later landaus; this conquered an ungainliness noticeable in earlier heads, only folding incompletely like badly rolled umbrellas. Many improvements followed and contrivances of various kinds allowed of the hoods being raised or lowered from within the carriage, but not until the 'fifties were landaus built on light elliptic springs without perches; this being the period when smaller horses became generally used for private carriages. The whole tendency from then onward was toward lightness; blood harness-horses of from 15 to 16 hands were 'the thing' in the Park and West End, rather than the massive Yorkshire horses of earlier days; harness that was a mere featherweight compared to that used with such things as dress coaches was designed for the brougham and landau, and soon yet lighter for the victoria; if one horse could draw a brougham—and a fashionable brougham at that—so he could a landau, though the appearance of a landau never equalled that of either a brougham or victoria for single harness.

For that reason the landau for one-horse was a long time in making its début, and when it did so it appealed much more to the humbler users of carriages, concerned more with usefulness than grace, than it did to the world of fashion. The practical qualities that made it so popular with the former caused it to survive longer than most carriages in the dejected and ignominious ending of country 'fly,' the commonest of carriages used for hackney work in seaside towns and spas.

Hardly before the 'eighties did light landaus find their best forms, of which the principal were those of curved body, taking their name of Sefton landaus from the Earl of Sefton, who had the first one built, and Shelburne landaus of angular form called after the Earl of Shelburne for the same reason. Depth of coachwork varied much, from the shallow panelling of Canoe landaus to the comparatively deep well and correspondingly large doors of the angular kind, dropping to a lower level between the axles. In the Landaulet the seating was for two persons instead of the usual four. For smart pair-horse work in town Sociable-Landaus were fashionable; usually turned out with a footman seated beside the coachman and expensively horsed, they represented something of a dignified compromise between elaborate dress landaus and the simplest, as capacious as the former but following the latter in modern springing and inconspicuous finish. A low box was a distinguishing feature inherited from an old established relative, the Sociable, a low-hung angular carriage seating four but having only the hind part of the body protected by the folding head. Yet another form had been assumed by the Barouche-Sociable, its double body resembling two curved cabriolet bodies facing each other, with its box raised on curved iron supports.

If the coachman-driven carriages of the Victorian age lacked something of the impressive qualities and most of the romantic associations that belonged to vehicles employed before the railroad, they can never be accused of lacking variety. The almost endless types and sub-types of broughams, landaus and victorias differing one from the other in countless peculiarities and additions that had exerted the ingenuity of almost as many technically minded owners as coachbuilders, would make but dull reading now, supposing that anything like a complete list of them ever had been or could be made. No mere catalogue of such things could suggest the interest they had as moving and indispensable parts of everyday life, complete only with the horses, harness, appointments, liveried servants, passengers and surroundings that brought them to life, and perfected only by that meticulous attention to detail in turning out that was the pride of good stables.

Hyde Park in the 'eighties and 'nineties — and even later — was the Mecca of all that was best and neatest among carriages, those driven by their owners and those of the coachman's driving. In the London season every morning of early summer saw the Serpentine carriage road a continuous cavalcade of pairs, singles, and occasional teams driven to the variously formed but invariably brilliant products of Long Acre, the street of coachbuilders. Outside London an almost more diverse if smaller gathering of fashionable turnouts might be seen on summer's evenings at such places as Richmond, when the *Star and Garter* there held its place as a favorite rendezvous within easy driving distance of town; or in the autumn season on the front at Brighton, in days when every stable in or near that town was packed for a month or so each year with West End horses and on the front a daily stream of fashionable carriages, for the most part open-bodied ones, joined Hove and Kemp Town in an almost unbroken line of horses, harness and highly varnished vehicles.

Technically speaking, that is from the coachbuilders' point of view, these later Victorian carriages represented the peak of achievement. Neatness could hardly be carried further. The wealth of detail in structure, springing, accessories, contrivances for comfort and the like that have been so exhaustively dealt with in the writings of coachbuilders bear testimony to the advances made during the Queen's reign. Much less has been written about the painting and outward decoration of carriages, a point probably of greater interest now than it was then, the attainment of that lacquer-smooth finish and perfect gloss on carriage panels having become as much a thing of the past as have most patiently painstaking forms of craftsmanship. The long, unhurried process of building up paint and varnish to obtain this finish could be described briefly as a repeated succession of applications of both, each coat being rubbed or smoothed down before the next was put on and each allowed time in which to harden. To the original smoothed wood would be given some four coats of a first colour mixed with japan and turpentine, each succeeding coat containing a little less japan and a little more turpentine; next came as many coats of grounding, composed of powdered ochre, turpentine and japan, and the stopping of any minute crevices or marks in the panels with white lead and gold size. This surface, when hard, was rubbed down with pumice-stone and water to perfect smoothness in preparation for the priming, or preliminary painting in a colour suited to the shade of the eventual surface. Some three coats of priming were usual, each in turn when dry being smoothed off with sand paper. The body paint or ultimate colour was then put on in any number of coats — as many as were needed to produce a completely clear and unclouded surface — sandpaper being used between each. The next stage was the varnishing, at least six coats of fine copal being given, and all but the final one rubbed down with powdered pumice applied on a cloth; on roofs, backs and black panels, japan in several coats was used between painting and varnishing. First-rate London carriages were often delivered to their owners after the last varnishing, put into use for a month or so and then returned to the builders for the final process — polishing. This last process entailed rubbing down again, first with pumice and then rottenstone, followed by a prolonged massage with bare hands and, ultimately, polishing with flour and sweet oil.

Thereafter cold water, in the form of daily — often twice-daily — washing by a carriage-groom completed the hardening of a brilliant surface, nothing rougher than a sponge and wet leather ever being allowed to touch the panels. Particular artists employed by good coachbuilders were those who 'lined' spokes, fellies* and occasionally panels of many town and ladies' carriages with delicate, unbelievably thin strokes of paint demanding the steadiest possible hand and the use of a game-bird's feather rather than a brush; and those who, in paint and gold leaf, produced little works of art in armorial bearings on the panels. Large bold coats of arms such as took up half the surface of a carriage door were a part of some of the carriages of state, mainly of early days; on the quiet Victorian private carriage, a minute crest or intertwined monogram no larger than could be covered by a florin demanded the skill and precision of a miniature-painter. As a rule the colour of a brougham, victoria or small landau was a dark one and unobtrusive, and the liveries of accompanying servants were made to match it; yellows and loud colours were left to sporting vehicles and coaches, and in them generally confined to wheels and under-carriage, the body panels being dark in contrast. Discreet 'lining' in a brighter shade than the body might be used to relieve a too sombre effect; and not a few owners of park carriages revived what had been an occasional custom in the eighteenth century, and a most effective one, in accentuating the tone of dark panels by painting them with broad vertical stripes of a yet darker hue.

To ensure having carriages always kept perfect in order and appearance, many users, while keeping their own horses, had their vehicles on contract from a builder, preferring this arrangement to either owning their own or jobbing a complete turnout from a jobmaster. This providing and maintaining of carriages on a hire system was a speciality of some of the best known coachbuilding firms and a lucrative branch of their trade; some arranging to supply not only vehicles but the harness appropriate to them on annual or longer period terms that often were sufficiently complicated to need a legal document equivalent almost to a lease. Both the division of the responsibility between coachbuilder and client and the old establishment of

* Curved sections which together make up the rim of a wheel.

the system may be illustrated by an original manuscript dated as long ago as in 1787, and contracting for the provision of a town coach on perch, and the harness for it. Much is added to the interest of this agreement by the importance in driving history of this citizen in treaty with his coachbuilder for a carriage to use in London. He, John Palmer, having at the time filled the office of Controller-General of the Post Office for no more than a year, while his Royal Mail coaches, first established three years earlier, had inaugurated the new era of road travel.

'MEMORANDUM of an Agreement made this first day of April one thousand seven hundred and eighty seven between John Palmer Esqr. of Abchurch Lane in the City of London & Charles Biggar of St. Martin's Lane in the City of Westminster, Coach Maker. Whereas it is agreed that the said Charles Biggar do provide for the use of the said John Palmer Esqr. a new Coach with a Perch carriage & pair of Harness upon Terms & conditions as hereinafter mentioned that is to say for the full Term of four years from the above Date & the said Charles Biggar to keep the same in proper Repair during that term except as hereinafter mentioned & also to provide two new Hammercloths & to paint the Coach compleatly within the above term of four years and in consideration of the aforesaid agreement John Palmer Esqr. is to pay to Charles Biggar on his order the sum of thirty Six Guineas pr Annum & the first payment is to be made on this Day & to continue so to be paid on the first Day of April in every succeeding year during the said term of four years, it is also agreed that the said John Palmer Esqr. at his own proper Cost & charge is to provide new plate Glasses to the Coach whenever any are broke & new plated work to the Harness & every other accidental or wilful damage & everything to be left whole & delivered to the said Charles Biggar or Order at the Expiration of the above term . . . N.B.—The Difference of painting the Body with stripes the false lining the Expence of plated work to Body & Harness to be paid for by Jn Palmer Esqr'.

FOUR-IN-HAND COACHES

THE MOST dignified of moving objects, it has been said, are a full rigged sailing ship and a four-in-hand coach. Both the appearance and the importance of the Royal Mail and Stage coaches of the coaching age before railways earned them the name of the 'Kings of the Road.' Another distinction that can be claimed for them and for their descendants — the Drags and Road coaches of more recent times — is that of having been the most typically English of all vehicles; though they were in time much copied and adpated for use abroad they owed no part of their origin to other countries.

In form they changed less than most other vehicles that survived as long. Recent coaches were distinctively different from those of pre-railroad days in such things as height, weight, the number of outside seats, finish, refinement and important additions such as foot and hand brakes — unknown in the old days — but in structure and outline of body they followed the same plan. What practice had proved to be perfect in the coaches of necessity could be embellished in the coaches of pleasure but never fundamentally altered, and the dignity and grace of those depicted by so many of the old sporting artists in countless coaching scenes remained common to the recognized types of London-built coaches evolved later.

The best and greatest years of fast coaching, the eighteen twenties and thirties, saw the honours of the Road divided between the Royal Mail coaches — sponsored by the government, worked under official contract from the post office, and carrying both the mails and a limited number of passengers — and Stage coaches which carried the bulk of travellers and were run by proprietors many of whom were the owners of horses on an enormous scale and sometimes, also, contractors for the mails. Royal Mail coaches — known always in their day simply as 'Mails' — ran ceaselessly by night and day on all the principal roads, serving all towns of importance and observing an exacting and precise time table dictated by the post office authorities, and an extraordinary punctuality was their pride. As official vehicles they enjoyed certain privileges not shared by stage coaches — known simple as 'Coaches' — including those of paying no tolls, bearing no licence boards, running untaxed and claiming right of way before anything else on the road. Though not many stage coaches equalled the speed, efficiency and smartness attained by the mails, a few — particularly among the crack daytime coaches of the years immediately before railways — were so well horsed and driven as to bear comparison, though these had the great advantage of travelling the greater part of their distance by daylight and, with more help, making somewhat quicker changes of horses. Both types of coach, then, had advantages and disadvantages peculiar to them, sufficient to make comparisons in their speeds a difficult matter. In numbers stage coaches were naturally far greater than mails ;* in appearance they varied, but generally lacked that quiet superiority that made the latter so impressive, from their first building to the uniform regulation pattern and painting

Only for a little while after John Palmer, sometime manager of the Bath and Bristol Theatres, had prevailed against the reactionary forces of the civil service to give a trial to mail coaches (1784), were common coaches used for the purpose. With the complete success of the system, its revolutionary effect on business and the granting to Palmer of the post of Controller-General of the Post Office, came the regulation mail coach supplied on a contract basis, including maintenance, by the builder. In painting, mails varied only in the number on the sides of their hind boots and in the names of the termini in small letters on the door panels beneath the windows. From the beginning of the nineteenth century their standard form altered only with modifications in height and seating. In weight they were the lightest of all coaches carrying outside passengers,

* Reference to numbers and speeds of mails and stage coaches is made in the Introduction.

Author's Collection *Cooper Henderson*

Plate XXIV. ROYAL MAIL COACH, Leeds and London. *See page* 112

International Horse Show *Lynwood Palmer*

Plate XXV. DRAG OF PARK COACH. *See page* 123

scaling no more than 18 cwt. unloaded. Their distinctive painting in the same colours as those of Royal carriages proclaimed their official status; red wheels and undercarriage, maroon body panels bearing on each door the Royal arms in gold, the cipher of the ruling sovereign — G.R., W.R., or V.R. as the case might be; on the black-painted sides of the front boot, on each of the upper quarter panels (on either side of the windows) appeared one of the stars of the four great orders of knighthood of the United Kingdom — the Garter, Bath, Thistle and St. Patrick, while each mail bore its number on the hind boot and the words 'Royal Mail,' with the names of the two terminus cities on its road in unobtrusive gold letters on the door panels. Four passengers could be carried inside; only in the earliest mails was there room for six. Outside, one passenger sat beside the coachman — on the boxseat, always the place of honour on a coach — two, and eventually three, more could ride on the forward-facing roof-seat immediately behind the box. At the back, over the hind boot, were no passenger seats as in other coaches, only a little single round seat for the guard. The only access to this hind boot was by a trap-door or hinged flooring under the guard's feet, so that robbery of the mail-bags it contained became an impossibility while he was in his place. Opposite to him, attached to the coach roof, was his arms chest containing blunderbus, pistols and cutlas, and to his hand was a metal ring in the coach body in which rested his 'yard of tin,' the official three-foot-long mail horn with which he 'cleared the road' and announced the mail's approach to post office towns and villages and roused the toll pike keepers, and horsekeepers in charge of the changes of teams. Much of the equipment of a mail was peculiar to it; lamps of a long oblong shape and bars (swingletrees) with unusually long hooks for the attachment of the leaders' traces were among these; and spare bars as well as a single long bar that could be used to replace all three of the usual ones if they were broken were carried, together with a tool box and spare nuts, bolts, shackles, chain traces and the like, and a special small lamp for the guard's use when sorting his mail bags at night.

Captain Malet, one of the best informed writers on the mail system and author of *Annals of the Road*, was, like a score at least of his contemporaries, so full of enthusiasm for the subject that he devoted to it many chapters, all of them full of interest. One paragraph of his must be quoted as particularly informative:

'Early in the present century [nineteenth] it was deemed desirable that all the mail coaches should be both built and furnished on one plan. Hence the 'patent coaches' as they were then called. For many years the contract for building and repairing them was given to Mr. John Vidler, who had suggested many improvements in their construction. Although the post-office authorities arranged for the building of the coaches, the mail contractors were required to pay for them; the revenue bearing only the charges for cleaning, oiling, and greasing them, which amounted to about £2,200 a year. The official control of the coaches, mail guards, etc., was vested in the Superintendent of Mail Coaches, whose headquarters was at the General Post Office'.

It will be seen from this, among other things, how neatly the post office authorities avoided all the troubles and responsibilities of running the mails, yet retained the office of dictators, merely laying down the law to others as to the exacting speed and punctuality that must be observed without themselves owning a single coach, horse or side of harness or employing a single coachman. Only the guards were government employees, wearing scarlet coats in token of their position, while the coachmen were provided by the contractors, or sometimes were contractors themselves to the extent of providing a team or two working the stages they drove. On the guard of each mail rested the responsibility for the safe delivery of his mailbags and of seeing that the coachmen kept up to the precise time schedules arranged for the coaches. Timekeeping was the pride of mail coaching to the point of making the loss of a few minutes over a distance of many hundreds of miles a crime for which the guard was answerable. The outward mails from London left the General Post Office in St. Martins-le-Grand every night at eight o'clock, each guard on his departure being issued with an official timepiece, like a small chronometer, which was so secured in a locked case as to make any alteration of its time impossible. Carrying this in the leather satchel hung over his shoulder, the guard checked the arrival and departure time at every postal town and change of horses on his waybill, making a note of any reason for delay; so exact was the timekeeping that at every rural place on the road clocks and watches were set by the passing of the mail. On those rare occasions that made proceeding on its journey impossible for a mail it became the guard's duty to take on the bags by any means in his power, on horseback if necessary; and many instances have been chronicled of feats of great endurance and bravery on such occasions, notably in the great frost of December 1836, when coaches all over the country were snowed up on the road, some of them completely buried in drifts. Unlike coachmen, who generally drove a few stages one way on an 'up' coach and then worked the 'down' coach back over the same distance, the guards often went through on the whole of a long journey; winter and summer, exposure and hardship added to no little responsibility made their lot anything but a light one. For this a guard received an official salary of half a guinea a week — or was entitled to it, whether the post office paid it or not was another matter, as is shown by an original letter from a mail guard's widow to the 'Honourable Postmasters General,' written in the last decade of the eighteenth century, begging for payment of a year's salary earned some years before by her husband when acting as guard on one of the early Windsor mails. The tips and perquisites attached to the position no doubt accounted for the competition among applicants for it, though so much official work with the postbags left a guard but little time to be attentive to passengers, thereby earning the right to 'kick' them, which in Road language meant to solicit a tip. Coachmen, though never government servants, occasionally through long service on a mail were given the right to wear the official red coat like the guard, and those who drove in the annual London parade of mails that took place on the King's birthday were issued such coats; they are often so illustrated in the prints after Cooper Henderson and a few contemporary artists which provide a precise and vivid record of the pageantry of coaching.

These old pictures of the Road, show, too, the changes adopted in the structure of mails; their height being reduced when the perch — on which all coaches were built — ceased to be made straight, giving place to that of all more recent coaches and drags, bent in a downward curve to the coach body; and the eventual addition of seats at the rear of the roof in a few late mails running by day on short roads such as the Brighton and London. A feature common to all mails and eventually adopted in every coach worthy of the name (as well as in such sporting carriages as the mail phaeton) was the mail axle, with its boxes secured by bolts, making the loss of a wheel a virtual impossibility. In early vehicles only a primitive linch-pin kept the wheel in place and the resultant accidents were so frequent as to be considered an unavoidable part of road travel.

Though the mails represented but a small proportion of coaches on the road, theirs was the most important function and theirs the most distinguished history and appearance. In mail travel was the perfection of fast coaching, the inspiration of the majority of those countless writers, from authors of the first distinction to coachmen writing their reminiscences, who have left contemporary accounts of the 'Golden Age' of road travel and all that attended it — its discomforts as well as its glories, the accidents that sometimes were the penalty of speed, its horses, history and sporting flavour; most of all, perhaps, its characters, among whom those polished artists the coachmen were foremost. No greater admirer, among so many, had the mails than Thomas de Quincey, unfair to coaching only when he introduced stage coaches as objects of scorn compared to the mails that were to him beyond reproach.

Outside the first General Post Office, in Lombard Street,* at the nightly hour of departure of the mails, there was to be seen, he wrote:

'The absolute perfection of all the appointments about the carriages and harness, their strength, their brilliant cleanliness, their beautiful simplicity — but more than all, the royal magnificence of the horses — were what might first have fixed the attention. Every carriage, on every morning of the year, was taken down to an official inspector for examination — wheels, axles, linchpins, pole, glasses, lamps, were all critically probed and tested. Every part of every carriage had been cleaned, every

* Smirke's 'New General Post Office' in St. Martins-le-Grand was not opened until 1829.

horse had been groomed, with as much rigour as if they belonged to a private gentleman . . . Every moment are shouted aloud by the post-office servants, and summoned to draw up, the great ancestral names of cities known to history through a thousand years — Lincoln, Winchester, Portsmouth, Gloucester, Oxford, Bristol, Manchester, York, Newcastle, Edinburgh, Glasgow, Perth, Stirling, Aberdeen — expressing the grandeur of the empire by the antiquity of its towns, and the grandeur of the mail establishment by the diffusive radiation of its separate missions. Every moment you hear the thunder of the lids locked down upon the mail-bags. That sound to each individual mail is the signal for drawing off, which process is the finest part of the entire spectacle. Then come the horses into play. Horses! Can these be horses that bound off with the action and gestures of leopards? What stir! what sea-like ferment! — what a thundering of wheels! — what a trampling of hoofs! — what a sounding of trumpets! — what farewell cheers —'.

Now hear for a moment that appreciation of the mails turn to contempt — however unjust — of the stage coaches:

'Once I remember being on the box of the Holyhead mail, between Shrewsbury and Oswestry, when a tawdry thing from Birmingham, some "Tallyho" or "Highflyer," all flaunting with green and gold came up alongside of us. What a contrast to our royal simplicity of form and colour in this plebian wretch! The single ornament on our dark ground was the mighty shield of the imperial arms. Even this was displayed only on a single pannel, whispering, rather than proclaiming our relations to the mighty state; whilst the beast from Birmingham, our green and gold friend from false, fleeting, perjured Brummagem, had as much writing and painting on its sprawling flanks as would have puzzled a decipherer from the tombs of Luxor. For some time this Birmingham machine ran along by our side — a piece of familiarity that already of itself seemed to me sufficiently jacobinical . . .'

In point of fact that despised Birmingham *Tally-Ho* was, or became later, one of the crack stage coaches of the country in its speed and smartness. On it — or one of them, for there were three equally famous *Tally-Hos* on that road — Colonel Peter Hawker, "Father of Widfowling" and author of the shooting classic *Instructions to Young Sportsmen*, travelled home to London after a visit to Ireland in 1834, leaving an appreciative note in his diary: " July, 24th. Left Birmingham by the " Tally-ho " coach at seven this morning, and arrived at the coach office in Islington at half-past six in the evening — 108 miles ". Against this the Holyhead mail, timed one of the three fastest mails in England, used to cover its 261 miles from London in 26 hours and 55 minutes, including the time spent in changing horses 27 times and the 40 minutes allowed for meals.

Stage coaches, while varying tremendously in weight from the heavy, slow-travelling, night coaches to the crack fast coaches that weighed but little more than the mails, found room for six — sometimes eight — more passengers than a mail on two seats at the back of the coach roof. Half the number sat, with backs to the horses, on the roof seat commonly known as the " gammon board " ; the remainder faced them on the rearmost and forward-facing seat mounted above the hind boot, the guard, if the coach carried one at all, sitting on the nearside (left) corner seat. In front and inside the accommodation was usually similar to that of the mail, except in those of the heavy night coaches that, making no pretensions to speed, retained the old six-inside bodies. No mail-bags being carried, both the boots as well as the roof provided space for passengers' baggage; the roof having a railing to retain this and the hind-boot opening from the ground by a hinged door like that of a cupboard. Among the mass of laws that were introduced to govern the running of these public coaches were prohibitions of piling luggage on the roof to a greater height than two feet, or the carrying of an additional passenger in the luggage space. To some of the less rapid coaches was added a rack behind the rear seat, or even a tray slung beneath the body, to take more baggage, and hooks at the sides and on roof railings could be used for the hanging of parcels or game to be delivered on the road. Many designers produced vehicles of peculiar form designed for a greater number of passengers, such as double-bodied coaches, and there were no small number of ' patent safety ' vehicles of great ingenuity claiming that they could not be turned over, or providing spare wheels that came into action if the main ones came off. But in the main such freak coaches succeeded only in looking ungainly and offered no practical alternative to the graceful lines of the simple coach body set between two boots and in general use from the first years of the nineteenth century.

Plenty of quietly painted exceptions there were to the 'flash' turnouts so disliked by de Quincey, particularly when amateurs appeared on the Road in roles not only of professional Jehus but of stage coach proprietors; but on most public coaches a good deal of brilliance in decoration was usual. Most of the larger proprietors kept to a particular colour for all their vehicles. As for instance all Edward Sherman's coaches, running from his famous *Bull and Mouth* Inn at St. Martins-le-Grand, were yellow; among them being the celebrated Shrewsbury and London *Wonder*, the first and greatest of fast long-distance day coaches, with a regular speed of almost eleven miles an hour, and its counterpart the Manchester and London *Telegraph*. Nearly every stage coach had its name*, which would be painted up in large letters on the panel behind the back seat and often appeared elsewhere, as on the doors or quarter panels, in gold leaf letters. On the door panels, also, generally were painted reproductions of the sign of whatever terminus inn was the proprietors' headquarters. Above this would be the proprietor's name, and almost every available piece of space on panels, sides of both boots and box-seat supports, could be filled with the names of the towns of most importance on the road served, those of the two termini usually figuring on the door of the hind boot.

Beneath every coach — of whatever kind — hung its skid-pan, to be slipped under the near hind wheel in the descent of serious hills. The duty of putting on and removing this was the guard's, in which some were so skilled that they could perform both feats without getting down from their seats; a dangerous proceeding in which at least one guard lost his life through the pan flying off the tire. As a further resource in case of a skid chain breaking when going down hill, most coaches had a safety chain which looped like a shackle round the fellies and

* Unlike Royal Mail coaches, which bore numbers. One famous Mail, however, (The Devonport and London) was known always by the unofficial nickname of 'The Quicksilver.'

tire. Modern coaches, while generally carrying both skid and safety chain, seldom needed them except on very sharp hills with a heavy load, the pressure brake (hand lever or foot pedal for the coachman's use) generally being adequate. In old coaching days such brakes did not exist and a coach's safety down-hill depended, if the skid was not put on, entirely on the coachman's wrist and the holding powers of his wheel horses. Many of those accidents recorded in chronicles of the Road were directly due to the use of the skid pan having been neglected, usually on stage coaches carrying no guard, when it was expected of the coachman that he should pull up at the top and bottom of each steep hill, get down and himself put on and remove the skid, a proceeding that he avoided, quite naturally, whenever he thought it possible to drive down in safety without it. Numbers of the slower coaches, from motives of economy, were run thus without guards, but these were never otherwise than second-rate turnouts, run by proprietors who contended that a guard only occupied a seat that could otherwise be sold to a passenger, and driven by the more obscure coachman who accepted having no help in the thousand and one emergencies of the road as well as dealing with passengers' baggage rather than have another man to take his share of the tips. To a fast coach a guard was essential, a smart man adding as much as a mile an hour to its speed with his help at the changes of teams, dealing with passengers, parcels and road adjustments to harness and bitting, and keeping toll-keepers and other usual forms of hindrance warned of the coach's approach with his horn or key-bugle.

The latter instrument, though forbidden on the mails, was a great favourite with stage coach guards of a musical turn of mind; the forerunner of the cornet, with keys instead of valves, it was of a somewhat similar shape though much larger, made of copper, and brass-mounted. Its tone was mellow and well suited to the sentimental airs of the day, all, except the simplest of which were beyond the scope of a coach horn. Apart from recognized road calls, like the 'clear the road,' which had a definite meaning, the three foot straight horn of copper, brass or tin, when played by such experts as most of the old guards were, could produce with great effect such simple airs as 'Oh

F. Ambrose Clark Collection *James Pollard*

Plate XXVI. STAGE COACH, the *Tally-Ho*, Birmingham and London. *See pages* 112 *and* 117

F. *Ambrose Clark Collection* *Lynwood Palmer*

Plate XXVII. ROAD COACH. *See page* 122

dear! What can the matter be?' and 'Buy a broom' — both of them great coaching favourites; a fine bell-like tone belonged to these horns, a very different thing to the strident notes of a common bugle or what in the present day passes under the name of a post-horn. In shape they were made like extinguishers, gradually increasing in bore to a greatest width at the foot. In later years this type of 'yard of tin' became popular for use on sporting tandem carts, while with the guards of the road coaches of the 'revival' much longer horns of 52 inches and more came into use, made with a very narrow bore for the greater part of their length opening out into a 'bell' like that of a trumpet. Greater length gave coach horns greater scope, and to the best of the later ones belonged a peculiarly sweet and distinctive range of notes that some of the fine performers among the 'revival' guards could translate into calls and lullabies that were the perfect accompaniment to the rythm of a coach in motion — the composite sound of rattling bars, tapping traces, the clink of pole chains and bits and the trot of sixteen hoofs. Of one of the old stage guards it was said, so perfectly did he play, that in one town through which his coach ran it was customary to stop the church bells on Sunday evenings so that his music should be heard; of another that he was placed on the Cheltenham *Rival* when this coach was doing badly, with the result that it soon became a popular coach on account of the guard's musical talent. That such old stories are not merely legends overrating the beauty of coach horn music will readily be believed by those who have listened to such later guards as Arthur Bullock, Charles Minnett, and a few more who were still on the road within the last five-and-twenty years.

The few public passenger carrying coaches that, until so recently, kept stage coaching alive in England were the last survivors of the coaching revival having its beginnings in the eighteen-sixties. For years after the railways opened, stage coaching, as far as London was concerned, had been a thing entirely of the past, until gradually a few of the keenest of those amateur coachmen who had learnt their driving and their love of the Road in the 'Golden Age' tried the experiment of reviving some of their favourite roads, like the London and

Brighton. At first there were but one or two of such coaches running daily in the summer. Soon their number increased to an extent that saw in most years of the 'seventies ,'eighties, and 'nineties a score or more well appointed coaches leaving Hatchetts in Piccadilly each morning for as many popular places within some sixty miles of London, and similarly run coaches springing up in many provincial cities. A new generation of coaching men, with the old hands to teach them and inspire enthusiasm, came along in numbers, and a popular, thriving 'Coaching Revival' succeeded what had been thought at first a harmless amusement for a few elderly die-hards. Professional coachmen and guards, too, were the apt pupils — in some cases the sons—of those of the old days. Winter months as well as summer found some of the new coaches still running, with syndicates of proprietors or driving subscribers making up the difference, often a very wide one, between receipts from fares and cost of running. The best aspects of earlier coaching were reproduced in the new with the choice of the most suitable roads, good horsing, and smart — often lavish — turning out and appointing. Fresh achievements and records were added to coaching history with the running throughout the season of 1879 of the *Defiance* coach each day between Oxford and Cambridge, via London, a journey of 120 miles for which 120 horses were kept, and with James Selby's phenomenal driving of the *Old Times* coach from Piccadilly to Brighton and back in under eight hours, for a wager of £1,000 made in 1888.

The name of Road Coaches came to be given to these stage coaches run in the revival. The majority and the best of them were the products of two London firms, Shanks & Company, and Holland and Holland, and a few of them still survive to serve as examples of perfection attained in stage coaches. Outside seating was provided for fourteen, including coachman and guard, arranged in the same way as on the old stage coaches, the guard's seat at the back, to the near side, being raised to a slightly higher level than for the three passengers beside him. The two roof seats, each taking four people, were less high than in most of the pre-railway coaches, the lower body still providing four inside seats which in later days of pleasure coaching were seldom made use of. In most other particulars the road coaches followed the style of earlier stage coaches closely and it was generally the pride of those who ran them to reproduce the old way of doing things as far as possible, while combining with it often a neatness and polish in turning out and appointment equal to the smartest private stable. A thousand and one studied details about a well appointed road coach helped to impart a 'flavour' of the coaches that Cooper Henderson drew, from their similar naming, painting and 'writing' with the names of places, inns and coach in gold on panels and boots, to such finishing touches as a guard's coat of scarlet and the accompanying satchel containing a timepiece, inherited from the mails. All these distinctions of the road coach contrasted sharply with those of the Drag, its opposite number for private driving and the commonest surviving form of four-in-hand coach.

Four-horse driving, followed so enthusiastically as a sport from the Regency onward, had from the first led many of its devotees to set up private coaches and teams as an alternative to driving public coaches. Successive driving clubs helped to evolve the form such coaches should take and the recognised rules for their appointment, the most important and the last of the clubs being the Four-in-Hand Club and Coaching Club, the latter holding its regular meets in Hyde Park up to the season of 1939. These Park or Private coaches, as they were most properly called, reached their ultimate and most refined form in late Victorian times, commonly being given the name of Drags, at first a slang term used on the Road in pre-railway days to designate any smart and well built coach. The quiet neatness and unostentatious colouring befitting a private carriage were the hall-marks of the later park drag, which differed structurally from the coach of the road mainly in the matters of seating and finish and in being a little lighter. Comparisons between the two serve only to point out these essential differences in building. In the appointing, horsing and harnessing widely dis-similar rules governed the drag turning out for a 'fine weather' drive of a few miles behind a perfectly matched team of showy horses, and the road coach carrying public passengers day in and day out over a long road and in all weathers.

One characteristic of the drag was the form of its rear seat, made for two only and intended for the two grooms in livery (its invariable accompaniments) ; supported from the rear boot by branching irons, this seat usually had hung beneath it the folding ladder used by lady passengers for mounting the coach. On a road coach the corresponding seat carried four, and had beneath it the curved back panel on which the coach's name usually appeared, and two small side panels, the ladder hanging below the boot. The roof of a road coach was railed for luggage, unlike that of a drag; its cushions would be of bedford cord or heavy carpet material, those of the drag a cloth toning with the colour of the panels. The steel furniture of a road coach — the pole-hook, pole-chains and fittings of the swingle-bars — was finished in black, that of the park coach in bright burnished steel. 'Cottage' windows — those that divided a window into four small panes — were seen on many road coaches, and fittings like the large horn-basket, hung to the near-side at the back, helped to add to the stage coach character given by painting that might be brilliant in contrast to the quiet colours proper to a drag. The average weight of a road coach, unladen, would be a little over a ton, exceeding by a hundredweight or two that of most drags.

Not very many of the beautifully built Shanks or Holland road coaches of the revival survived so long as to be used in the last years of stage coaching in the present century. Drags, on the other hand, had been produced in such numbers in the 'eighties and 'nineties by builders all over the country, and often had had so little work, that it was always easy to find one in good condition. For this reason a good many drags were converted to fulfil the offices of road coaches in late years. With changes to panelling and roof-seats, given names and with appropriate painting, they answered the purpose well enough, though never quite reproducing the lines, character and substance of the real coaches of the road.

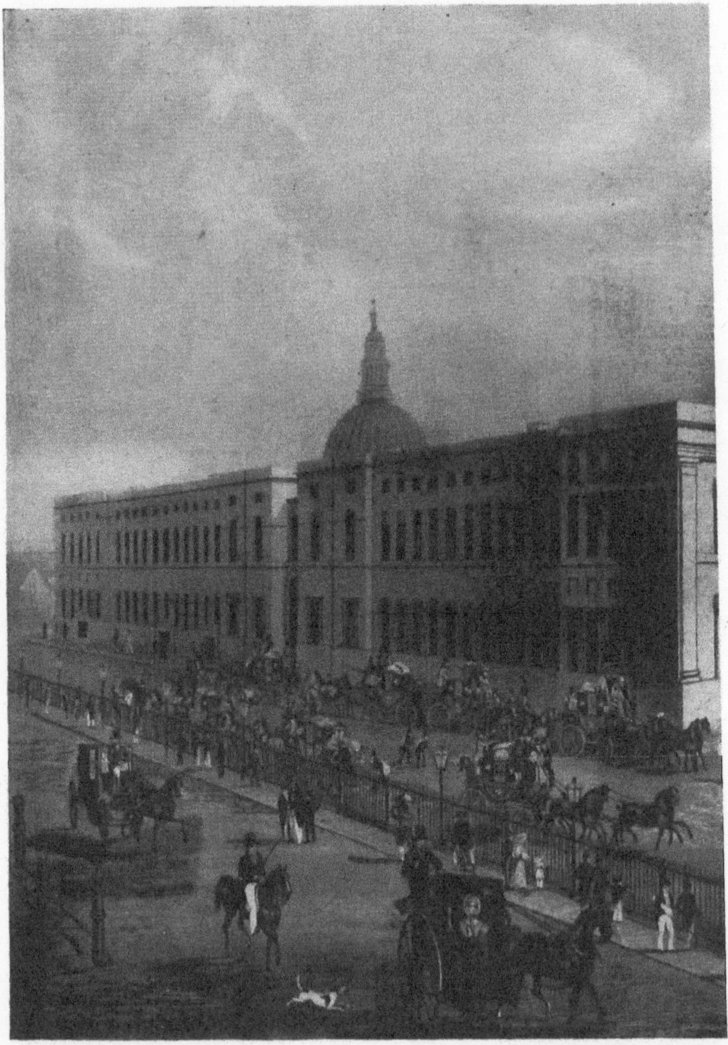

Authors' Collection

Plate XXVIII. ROYAL MAIL COACHES preparing to leave the General F
FOUR-WHEELED CAB, an early HANSOM CAB, two BOULNOIS

James Pollard

e, St. Martin's-le-Grand, showing in the foreground (*left to right*): Clarence
Door Cabs, and a Hackney Cabriolet. *See page* 134

LONDON CABS

FOR TWO centuries before London had its first single-horse hackney cab it had boasted public vehicles for hire which were drawn by a pair of horses and were known as Hackney Coaches. The name of hackney coach attended the first of such vehicles — a primitive springless box upon wheels which appeared on the streets in 1605 — and was used to describe its successors of the eighteenth and nineteenth centuries, regardless of period. The evolution of the hackney coach — considered as a vehicle — throughout its long history was identically the same as the evolution of the gentleman's coach of private ownership, for it was in fact nearly always the same thing. The handsome town coach when it became too shabby or infirm to present a decent appearance found its way to the hackney coach proprietor, and ended its days on a street rank as a discreditable old ruin with odd wheels of different colours and sizes, moth-eaten hammer-cloth, rattling doors still bearing the faded arms of a former owner, and a musty straw-filled interior; the usual accompaniments being a pair of broken-down 'screws' — in harness that had been much mended with rope — and an uncouth driver of questionable sobriety.

About the year 1790, when so much was afoot in carriage history, a certain number of coaches were built on purpose for hackney work in London. These were designed with small compact bodies for use in narrow streets, and represented a solitary attempt to produce a hackney coach as a distinct type of vehicle. The movement went no further because it was too easy and too cheap a proposition for the hackney coach proprietor to buy discarded town coaches that answered his purpose well enough, and the hackney coach of Dickens's earlier writings was as invariably the cast-off of a private stable as the hackney coach had been before 1790.

Of much that has been written about the hackney coaches of the first half of the nineteenth century little enough redounds to their credit. That they were in general sordid things, outwardly shabby and inwardly unsavoury, we know; though it is hard to believe that all of them have deserved such strictures as were levelled at them by a contributor to the *London Magazine* in 1825:

'A hackney coach — fogh! Who can be a gentleman and visit in a hackney coach? Who can, indeed? to predicate nothing of stinking wet straw and broken windows, and cushions on which the last dandy has cleaned his shoes, and of the last fever it has carried to Guy's, or the last load of convicts transported to the hulks'.

The hackney coach of a few years later became the subject of the young Charles Dickens's description, taking its place with other essential parts of London life in the *Sketches by Boz:*

'Our acquaintance with hackney-coach stands is of long standing. We are a walking book of fares, feeling ourselves half bound, as it were, to be always in the right on contested points. We know all the regular watermen* within three miles of Covent Garden by sight, and should be almost tempted to believe that all the hackney coach horses in that district knew us by sight too, if one-half of them were not blind. We take great interest in hackney coaches . . . There is a hackney-coach stand under the very window at which we are writing. There is only one coach on it now, but it is a fair specimen of the class of vehicles to which we have alluded — a great, lumbering, square concern, of a dingy yellow colour (like a bilious brunette), with very small glasses, but very large frames. The panels are ornamented with a faded coat-of-arms, in shape something like a dissected bat, the axletree is red, and the majority of the wheels are green. The box is partially covered by an old greatcoat, with a multiplicity of capes, and some extraordinary-looking clothes; and the straw with which the canvas cushion is stuffed is sticking up in several places, as if in rivalry with the hay which is peeping through the chinks in the boot. The horses, with drooping heads, and each with a mane and tail as scanty and straggling as those

* Attendants of coach ranks who watered horses.

of a worn-out rocking-horse, are standing patiently on some damp straw, occasionally wincing, and rattling the harness; and now and then one of them lifts his mouth to the ear of his companion, as if he were saying in a whisper that he would like to assassinate the coachman. The coachman himself is in the watering-house; and the waterman, with his hands forced into his pockets as far as they can possibly go, is dancing the 'double-shuffle' in front of the pump, to keep his feet warm.

'The servant-girl with the pink ribbons, at No. 5 opposite-suddenly opens the street door, and four small children forth, with rush out, and scream, 'Coach!' with all their might and main. The waterman darts from the pump, seizes the horses by their respective bridles, and drags them, and the coach too, round to the house, shouting all the time for the coachman at the very top, or rather very bottom of his voice, for it is a deep base growl. A response is heard from the tap-room; the coachman, in his wooden-soled shoes, makes the street echo again as he runs across it; and then there is such a struggling, and backing, and grating of the kennel, to get the coach opposite the house-door, that the children are in perfect ecstasies of delight. What a commotion! The old lady, who has been stopping there for the last month, is going back to the country. Out comes box after box, and one side of the vehicle is filled with luggage in no time . . . A cloak is handed in, and a little basket, which we could almost swear contains a small black bottle and a packet of sandwiches. Up go the steps, bang goes the door; "Golden Cross, Charing Cross, Tom," says the waterman; "Good-bye, grandma," cry the children; off jingles the coach at the rate of three miles an hour'.

That perfect picture of the hackney coach of the early eighteen-thirties belongs to a time when single-horse cabs had become established rivals. The supremacy of hackney coaches in the streets was on the wane, and their drivers and owners, who for so long had had things nearly all their own way, were fighting a losing battle with the cabmen, abusing them in much the same terms as those used long before by Thames wherry-men when the first hackney coaches were stealing their trade. River travel in hired wherries had been the only means of public transport in London before the hackney coach; after the latter, about the year 1635, the sedan chair, in which one person could be carried by two chairmen, put in its first appearance to flourish throughout the eighteenth century. Of horse-drawn rivals to the hackney coach there was none until the nineteenth century, unless a few chariots which differed from the coaches to the extent of seating two instead of four persons within are to be counted as separate vehicles. Hackney coach proprietors had gained so strong a hold, with the official right to be the only carriers of paying passengers in the London area, that they were able to put up a prolonged fight against the faster travelling single-horse cabs which seemed inevitable and overdue so many years before they became established. The battle between cab and coach went on for very many years before the last hackney coach owner either went out of business altogether or became instead a cab proprietor, and it was not until the late 'fifties — when severa types of cab had come and gone — that hackney coaches disappeared altogether from the London streets. Entering into the spirit of the hackney coachman's resentment of his rivals, Dickens was eloquent with, characteristically, his tongue in his cheek :

'Talk of cabs ! Cabs are all very well in cases of expedition, when it is a matter of neck or nothing, life or death, your temporary home or your long one. But, besides a cab's lacking that gravity of deportment which so peculiarly distinguishes a hackney coach, let it never be forgotten that a cab is a thing of yesterday, and that he never was anything better. A hackney-cab has always been a hackney-cab, from his first entry into public life ; whereas a hackney-coach is a remnant of past gentility, a victim of fashion, a hanger-on of an old English family, wearing their arms, and, in days of yore, escorted by men wearing their livery, stripped of his finery, and thrown upon the world, like a once smart footman when he is no longer sufficiently juvenile for his office, progressing lower and lower in the scale of four-wheeled degradation, until at last it comes to *a stand*'.

The fore-runners of London one-horse cabs were a few two-wheeled gig-like vehicles which appeared in 1805. There were not many of them ; like other gigs they seated only two, which meant that they could carry only one passenger sitting next to the driver ; and the amount of ground they could cover was very

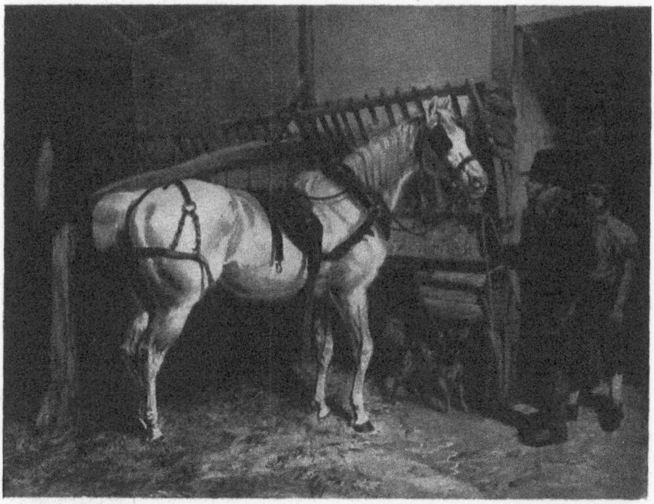

Author's Collection *J. F. Herring senior*

Plate XXIX. HACKNEY CABRIOLET HORSE and CABMAN. *See pages* 41 *and* 130

Plate XXX. A typical London HANSOM CAB of later years. *See page* 135

limited, the law having made most of central London an area sacred to the hackney coach. Not until 1823 did cabs take on a distinctive form and appear on the streets fully licensed to ply for hire. The first dozen of them began operations on April 23rd of that year — the King's birthday — from their headquarters in a Portland Street mews. Called Hackney Cabriolets, they followed to a certain extent the form of the private cabriolet, but without sharing its grace. Two passengers were carried, apart from the driver, side by side in a body resembling a crude cabriolet and protected by a hood made rigid at the back but unfolding to a 'half struck' or a fully extended covering. A stiff apron enclosed the lower part of the body, and curtains could be drawn across the upper half as a further protection to the occupants in wet weather. The two large wheels were set wide enough apart to allow room for a little seat for the driver level with the passengers' but outside the body — squeezed in, in fact, between the body and the offside wheel. This peculiar little driving box and its quaint position formed the most distinctive features of the hackney cabriolet. No luggage room was provided at the back of the cab, but it was possible to carry baggage in the limited space between the apron and a dashboard which curved outward over the horse's quarters. The height of the carriage from the ground was sufficient for two iron steps, affixed to the root of the nearside shaft, to be necessary.

'Cabs, with trunks and band-boxes between the driver's legs and outside the apron, rattle briskly up and down the streets on their way to the coach-offices or steam-packet wharfs', wrote Dickens in *Sketches by Boz*, alluding to hackney cabriolets in the early eighteen-thirties. A few years later he mentioned in *Pickwick Papers* that three people — Mrs. Cluppins and the two Raddles — 'squeezed into a hackney cabriolet, the driver sitting in his own particular little dickey at the side'. The second chapter of the same book contains the famous altercation between Mr. Pickwick and the driver of a hackney cabriolet after driving from St. Martins-le-Grand to the Golden Cross at Charing Cross — '"Only a bob's vorth, Tommy," cried the driver, sulkily, for the information of his friend the waterman' — which, but for Mr. Jingle's timely intervention, might have had such unfortunate outcome. Seymour, the gifted illustrator of London life who provided the plates accompanying the early chapters of *Pickwick*, introduced the hackney cabriolet in the background of his drawing of that occasion, showing clearly the arrangement of driving seat, hood and apron.

The rarity of authentic illustrations of early London cabs gives importance to any such drawings, however small, by artists as reliable as Seymour. His contemporary, George Cruikshank, who drew the illustrations for *Sketches by Boz*, included therein one of a variation of the hackney cabriolet that appeared on the streets about 1830. This type was distinguished by a body having a fixed panelled top, or permanent roof, instead of a folding hood, while otherwise conforming to the build of the original hackney cabriolet. The resemblance of these panelled cabs to coffins standing up-ended on two wheels was close enough to earn them almost immediately the nickname of 'Coffin Cabs.' Perhaps, also, something was contributed toward this sinister title by the dangers attending the services of the broken down horse and ruffianly driver associated with it, of which those shown in J. F. Herring's picture of the *Cab Horse, St. Giles'* can be considered typical and in no way exaggerated.

With their full name contracted — as it was in a very short while — to 'cabs,' hackney cabriolets introduced a new word of everyday use to the English language, ever since signifying a vehicle for hire. Hackney, too, became the accepted and official description of a licensed hire vehicle; though for this, hackney coaches — the first users of the word in that meaning — should be given the credit. If the fiction that Hackney, the place, first supplied hackney coaches with their name could be supported by reliable evidence it would give London all the honours in the matter; France, however, first supplied the word *haquenée* to designate a horse on hire for use on the roads, from which in time were derived both the hack — a horse for road-riding — and the hackney coach — a road hireling coach.

At about the same time as the coffin cab, or very soon after it, another two-wheeled cab of distinctive appearance made its *debut* on the streets. This was the Boulnois cab, designed and patented by one William Boulnois. Its permanently closed body resembled a small omnibus in shape and provided room for four passengers seated two on each side, as in an omnibus, with their backs to the wheels. Access was by a single door and step at the back; while the driver was perched very high, well above his horse, on a single seat on the front of the roof. Various nicknames were given to this vehicle, including 'Backdoor cab,' and the apt one of 'Slice-of-an-omnibus'; later the word Minibus was used sometimes to distinguish it from a larger version of the same design which came into use under the name of a Duobus.

Though practical and commodious from the public's point of view, cabs of this form did not have a long run of favour. Cabmen and proprietors were soon to learn that the design was a perfect one for the 'bilker,' who could slip out by the convenient back door before the end of his journey with the greatest ease, leaving the unconscious cabby on his remote front seat to whistle for his fare. H. C. Moore, the author of *Omnibuses and Cabs*, has related a story of a young nobleman who, as the result of a bet, set out to prove that pulling the leg of a Boulnois cabman was no very difficult matter;

'He hailed a cab outside his club and told the cabby to drive him to a certain address at Hammersmith. Just before he arrived at his destination he got out unobserved, and from a distance watched cabby's surprise and wrath on discovering his vehicle to be empty. After a time the cabman started back for town, and the youthful lord, seizing his opportunity, re-entered the cab, and shouted almost immediately, in well-assumed anger, 'Hi, you rascal! Where are you driving me? I told you to take me to Hammersmith.' The cabman, speechless with astonishment, turned round and made for Hammersmith once more, only however to discover on arriving there, that his "fare" had disappeared again. He became convinced that his cab was haunted, and this belief was strengthened as he drove back through Kensington, by discovering suddenly that his fare was sitting calmly in his vehicle as if nothing had happened. Cabby did not utter a word, for he was too frightened to address his "fare," but drove to the club, where he had picked him up, as quickly as possible. There the young peer alighted, and, without the slightest explanation, paid the cabman five times his fare'.

Four-wheeled cabs for one horse were not known in London before 1835. In the first place they were designed to hold only two inside passengers, and had a similar, if cruder, outline to the first brougham, of which in fact they were the models which suggested to Lord Brougham the idea of his private carriage. These Covered cabs, as they were called, were soon improved upon and built to seat four within, carrying also an outside passenger on the low box-seat beside the driver. Their later examples became the everyday 'Four-wheelers' or 'Growlers,' the standard London cabs of four-wheeled form which remained in use as long as horse-drawn cabs survived. Hung low, 'growlers' needed but a single step beneath the door on either side. Their roofs were provided with a low railing and chain to take luggage, and it was always something of a marvel that so great a weight as was represented by several heavy trunks on the roof, four passengers within, possibly a fifth on the box-seat and a portly cabman, was not only easily carried by the comparatively slight undercarriage and springs but easily drawn by one horse — often no more than a cob — over many miles of streets.

Clarence cab was the official name given to the London four-wheeled cab when it assumed the form, with four inside seats, in which it was to survive for so long, though few members of the public would have recognized the familiar growlers by this impressive title. Its patrons in Victorian times were mainly those who never quite got over the idea that it was more respectable to ride within a discreet, closed cab on four wheels than to travel faster in the dashing and much less sober hansom; hansoms, too, could accommodate only two passengers and had no luggage space, so that clarence cabs came in for all the 'family work' and most of the trade to and from railway stations. Much criticism came the way of the four-wheeler during its long innings, and much unfavorable comparison with its jaunty rival, the hansom, the critics of the 'growler' often overlooking its extreme usefulness in doing all the work for which a two-wheeled cab was unsuited. G. N. Hooper, however, compromised fairly between criticism of the failings of the four-wheeled cab and a compliment to its adaptability, when he wrote in the eighteen-eighties:

'These vehicles cannot be compared with the hansoms for style, comfort and finish. A large proportion of them are still coarse, noisy, odoriferous, and jumpy as regards the springs. When, however, it is considered to what uses they are put, some excuse may be offered for their shortcomings. For they take Jack and his mates on their arrival from Sheerness or Portsmouth; Tommy Atkins and his friends, perhaps fresh from camp life at Aldershot or Colchester; or Mary Jane and her boxes to her new place in a distant suburb; and as it is often cheaper to hire a cab than a cart to remove goods (other than personal luggage), it is hardly to be wondered at that the varnish is not as brilliant as on the duke's brougham or the countess's victoria'.

The first Hansom cab was an extraordinary looking vehicle, very little resembling the distinguished and distinctive two-wheeled cabs that later bore the name and eventually superseded all such vehicles as the coffin and Boulnois cabs. J. A. Hansom, an architect, and the builder of Birmingham's old Town Hall, designed and patented this original cab in 1834, having it built in Leicestershire and himself driving it from there to London. In appearance it was very like an enormous packing case, almost square, with a pair of shafts attached; two doors were placed in the front, on either side of the shafts; the driver's seat was perched high on the front of the roof, as in the Boulnois cabs; the two huge wheels, 7 ft. 6 ins. high, were as tall as the roof of the vehicle and revolved on two short lengths of axle protruding from the sides of the body. Much modified versions of this cab, with smaller wheels, were built and introduced for public work in London by a company who promised Hansom £10,000 for his design. The cabs were a failure and Hansom had to whistle for his money.

In 1836 appeared the first cabs made as the later hansoms all were, with the driver's seat placed behind instead of in front of the body; their wheels were carried on an axle bent downward beneath the whole body, but otherwise they had much the same appearance as the typical smart hansoms of later years. They were, in fact, the first recognizable 'hansoms,' although Hansom was not their designer. What had happened was that the secretary of a concern called the Safety Cabriolet and Two-wheeled Carriage Company, a certain John Chapman, had been enterprising enough to realise what was amiss with Hansom's design, and profiting by the latter's failure, to work out a fresh and infinitely superior cab of his own. It should, as H. C. Moore pointed out, have been called the Chapman cab rather than the Hansom; although it was the original Hansom company that bought Chapman's patent and put the first cabs of his design on the streets. A great welcome attended the launching of the first fleet of fifty of them, and their success was as unqualified as it was immediate. Countless imitations of their pattern soon appeared as rivals, proving a severe trial to the company who owned the patent rights of what was called officially Hansom's Patent Safety Cab, and it was a considerable while before the company realized that the continued prosecution of owners of 'pirate' cabs brought little satisfaction, while costing them many thousands of pounds. Eventually they accepted the unlimited competition of cabs indistinguishable from their own.

Once fairly established, the hansom superseded both hackney cabriolet and slice-of-an-omnibus altogether, and was not over-long in becoming the only two-wheeled type of cab in London, which, as long as the horse drawn cab survived, shared the work of the streets with the four-wheeled growler. For the first few years of Queen Victoria's reign a greater variety of cabs could be seen about town than at any other time; hackney cabriolets and Boulnois' back-door cabs, though growing rapidly fewer, were still competing with the new-come hansoms and four-wheeled clarence cabs, while the old hackney coach had by no means reached the end of its long life. A coaching print, after James Pollard, which was published at about this time* has a double interest in illustrating cabs as well as showing the Royal Mail coaches gathered in the great yard at the back of the General Post Office, St. Martins-le-Grand, just before the evening hour of their departure on their long journeys to most of the principal cities in the country. In this busy scene appear, in the foreground and outside the post office railings, a clarence cab and an early hansom, while to the right two of Boulnois'

* The print, an aquatint called *A North-East View of the New General Post Office*, was published first in 1832 in a form showing carts in the foreground. The plate was altered, and a second version of the print (undated) showing the cabs was published later.

back-door cabs (showing back and front of the vehicle) are prominent at the corner of what was then known as Lad Lane (later to be merged into Gresham Street), with behind them, approaching from Sherman's *Bull and Mouth* inn in St. Martins-le-Grand, a hackney cabriolet with its driver perched on the little outrigger seat inside the wheel.

Changes and improvements in the build of hansoms were constant and numerous from the first. The absurdly small side windows seen in the hansom in Pollard's print were soon replaced by bold plate-glass windows, furnished with blinds within, allowing the occupants a good view of both sides of the road. An early and obvious improvement was the replacement of the clumsy bent axle, passing under the whole of the body, by a straight one just below the seat level. An ever decreasing weight accompanied countless ideas that added to the passengers' comfort in succeeding vehicles, until, in the 'seventies, something near perfection was attained in the light, dapper Forder hansom, with its almost luxurious interior, jaunty appearance and easy motion. Forder, a Wolverhampton and London coachbuilder, produced cabs that typified all that was best in the hansom from the time that he carried off prizes, offered in 1873 and 1875 by the Society of Arts and a cab exhibition held at the Alexandra Palace, for improvements in London's street cabs. In the words of Hooper, Forder 'showed how the weight could be reduced by the use of better materials and more skilled workmanship. He mounted his vehicles on lighter wheels, reducing the weight of the undergear and making the body correspondingly lighter. His neater and more comfortable interior fittings suited the public taste in this country, and led to an export trade to other countries, where hansoms have since been adopted and copied'. Rubber tires, fitted to hansoms of the 'eighties and later, completed their comfort, and the London cab became, at its best, a very perfect thing indeed. Shabby cabs there were always, of course, but their failings served only to accentuate the brilliance of the many smart hansoms that graced the West End of the later years of the last century and the earlier ones of this. Sharp, blood horses drew them, neatly harnessed and turned out, and driven by cabmen who were often something approaching dandies in their personal get-up, and occasionally, even, were what were known on the cab ranks as 'broken-down toffs', who had seen better days. When sporting noblemen could be counted among the proprietors of London hansoms little was left undone that could add to the perfection of a public hire vehicle, and the result was such a cab as Athol Maudslay, writing in the late 'eighties, so well described:

'If we take one of the best hansoms, we will probably find it appointed as follows. To begin with the horse; between the shafts, you will observe, is a thoroughbred, drafted from some racing stable, not for any vice, but because he has not the requisite turn of speed; he has been sent up to Tattersall's or Aldridge's and has been purchased by some cab proprietor. The horse is a nice-looking beast, with a neat-looking head and neck, good shoulders and excellent limbs, and you probably remark that he is too good for a cab. He has on him a nice, light, well-made harness, the brass-work of which Mr. Cabby is continually polishing; the cabman himself is a smart-looking fellow and apparently takes a great pride in his horse and cab. The cab is built by Forder, the well-known coachbuilder of Upper St. Martin's Lane; the wheels have noiseless indiarubber tires, and in place of the old doors opening in the centre and falling back on either side, there is one large door like the apron of a carriage stretched out on a solid frame, which falls against the dash, leaving room for the fare to get in or out. As you enter the cab, the cabby, apparently conscious that you are wearing a good hat, lifts the reins out of the brass guide through which they pass, in order to avoid knocking it off. As you seat yourself inside the cab you observe the indiarubber mat at your feet, the two little looking-glasses, the place for your cigar ash and the box of lucifer-matches; in addition to these luxuries there is sometimes a pneumatic or electric bell. In one cab in which I rode, there was actually an apparatus for signalling the driver to stop, turn to the right or left, and so on; in addition to this there is a little silk blind to each side window; to this blind is frequently suspended an artificial flower similar to that which adorns the horse's head, just above his blinkers. If it be one of Lord Shrewsbury's cabs it will be marked S. & T. on the outside panel, and you will have the satisfaction of knowing that your cab-proprietor is Charles Henry Talbot, Earl of Shrewsbury and Talbot'.

Lord Shrewsbury went into business as a cab-proprietor in 1888, forming a company that combined with this trade the manufacture of the solid rubber tires with which all his cabs — built by Forder — were fitted. The late Lord Lonsdale, also, put a number of cabs on the streets of London, and himself saw to it that his hansoms were the last word in neatness and as well horsed and appointed as if they had been private carriages. Though anything but popular with the other cab owners, these aristocratic hansoms had a tonic effect on cabs in general, making it essential that every proprietor whose cabs were to stand a chance of equal competition should follow suit, fitting rubber instead of iron tires to his hansoms and smartening up their appearance. Another result of the hansom's making so smart a public showing, as well as offering greater comfort than any other two-wheeled vehicle had done, was a wider realisation of its merits as a private carriage, and many very beautifully finished hansoms were built for private ownership, to be used for town work as alternatives to the brougham or victoria.

Adapted and peculiar forms of the hansom were many. All kinds of variations of the standard type of body were thought out by those who could never be content to leave any vehicle alone, even so perfect a one as a Forder hansom, without trying to improve upon it. Some of these vehicles of hansom type dated from the early days of Chapman's cabs, many more were products of the 'eighties and 'nineties, and while a fair number of them were little better than freaks of quaint form and little practical merit, others succeeded to the extent of appearing on the streets as public cabs in use in limited numbers and, usually, for short periods. About 1840, a patent called a Tribus was given a brief and un-rewarding trial. It could be described as a cross between a hansom and a Boulnois cab, seating three passengers, who entered by a door at the back to the near-side, the driver's seat being moved to the off-side rear corner of the roof to allow for this. Rather like it was Parlour's hansom, which was introduced forty-seven years afterwards; this, while having the driving seat in the centre at the back, as in the standard hansom, provided two sliding back doors — on either side of the driver — and a little omnibus body like the Boulnois which carried four, seated two and two with their backs to the wheels. Floyd hansoms, produced in 1885, were fitted with a forward hood known as a calash, which, having front and side windows, fell in a curve from the front of the roof to the level of the dash board. This, while enclosing the passengers very snugly in bad weather, added much to the weight of the vehicle and gave it a cumbersome appearance. Very elaborately furnished with luxurious inside fittings, Floyd hansoms were designed for private ownership rather than hire work. Victoria hansoms had a folding hood in place of a permanent roof, but otherwise conformed to ordinary hansom lines. Hansom bodies mounted on four wheels were ungainly things, having, however, a limited success on the streets under the name of Court hansoms. Various attempts to combine brougham features with those of the hansom resulted only in failures, though upright doors from footboard to roof were used quite neatly, to replace the usual half-doors or apron, in a cab called the Arlington.

Several other forms, though ingenious enough, met with but a poor reception. None of them could be considered seriously as rivals to the familiar hansom, as graceful as it was practical and, though used in a hundred other cities, remaining to the end London's own cab — the 'Gondola of London.'

Printed in July 2021
by Rotomail Italia S.p.A., Vignate (MI) - Italy